Racial Fault Lines

Racial Fault Lines

The Historical Origins of
White Supremacy in California

Tomás Almaguer

UNIVERSITY OF CALIFORNIA PRESS
Berkeley · *Los Angeles* · *London*

Chapter 7 is reprinted in revised form by permission of *Labor History*. It orginally appeared as "Racial Domination and Class Conflict in Capitalist Agriculture: The Oxnard Sugar Beet Workers' Strike of 1903," *Labor History* 25, no. 3 (Summer 1984): 325–350.

University of California Press
Berkeley and Los Angeles, California

University of California Press, Ltd.
London, England
© 1994 by
The Regents of the University of California

Almaguer, Tomás.
   Racial fault lines : the historical origins of white supremacy in California / by Tomás Almaguer.
      p.   cm.
   Includes bibliographical references and index.
   ISBN 0-520-08947-2 (alk. paper)
   1. White supremacy movements—California—History.   2. Racism—California—History.   3. California—Race relations.   I. Title.
   F870.A1A46 1994
   305.8′009794—dc20   93-42513

Printed in the United States of America
9 8 7 6 5 4 3

In memory of my father,
with love, for my mother,
with pride, for David and Miguel,
and, with indebtedness, for Clementina.

Contents

PART THREE: RACIALIZED CLASS CONFLICT
AND ASIAN IMMIGRANTS IN ANGLO CALIFORNIA

Acknowledgments

This book initially began as a doctoral dissertation in the Department of Sociology at U.C. Berkeley. At that time, I was specifically interested in the historical origins of the relationship between Anglos and Mexicans in the southern California county in which I was born and raised. From the very beginning, this study has been informed by both academic concerns and a personal interest in locating my family history within California's racial and ethnic histories. In the early phase of research, however, I became intrigued by the interesting differences in the nineteenth-century historical experiences of the Mexican and the Indian, Chinese, and Japanese populations in this county. This early comparative interest took on major significance while I was investigating an important agricultural workers' strike led by both Mexican and Japanese farm workers in Oxnard, California, in 1903. In order to understand why organized white labor responded so differently to these workers, my initial interest in Chicano history was necessarily reframed into a comparative analysis of race relations in the entire state of California during the last half of the nineteenth century. Two chapters from this initial research that have autobiographical significance have ultimately made their way into the present study.

During the time between the completion of my doctoral dissertation and the completion of this book, I have had the opportunity to broaden my interests beyond the "race and class" issue that was so central to the earliest conceptualization of this project. The innovative literature that I have engaged since then has raised intellectual and political issues that have enormously influenced my thinking about racial and class stratification. Of particular importance was the powerful critique of Marxism developed in the burgeoning new literature on gender and sexuality and in racial theory. Under its influence, what began as a Marxist analysis of the impact of capitalist development on the multiracial working class in California was eventually transformed into a comparative analysis of racialization in which capitalism is viewed as part of the institutional apparatus structuring white supremacy in the state.

My first words of gratitude must go to the dissertation committee that helped shape my early thinking on racial matters and encouraged me to see this project to completion. Robert Blauner, Ronald Takaki, Albert Camarillo, and Michael Burawoy, in their own distinct ways, have been influential intellectual mentors who have inspired me through their own research to pursue the central issues that inform this comparative history. The debts that I owe to their pathbreaking scholarly research will be evident throughout the pages that follow. I extend to each of them my heartfelt appreciation for their ongoing support of my work and the humanity they have shown me.

Other colleagues and friends at U.C. Berkeley also influenced my thinking about the nettlesome relationship between race and class in the Southwest and the place of Chicano history within American history. Most important was the talented group of young faculty and graduate students that I worked with in the Chicano Political Economy Collective (ChPEC). Many of these individuals have gone on to make important scholarly contributions to Chicano and Chicana Studies as well as to their respective fields; it was my good fortune to have learned from them firsthand. David Montejano, Mario Barrera, Velia Garcia, Patricia Zavella, Felipe Gonzalez, Jorge Chapa, Lupe Frias, Andres Jimenez, Margarita Decierdo, Regino Chavez, Larry Trujillo, and Hisauro Garza were among the principals involved in this research collective and ongoing study group.

Special note must also be made of two other Chicano colleagues whose scholarly research has been enormously influential in shaping my thinking and who provided extensive assistance in the completion of this project. Without the unwavering support of Ramón A. Gutiérrez and David G. Gutiérrez this book would never have been completed. It will take me years to adequately repay the debt of gratitude that I owe them for their timely assistance at crucial junctures in its evolution.

Others at Berkeley who influenced my thinking on these issues and provided encouragement for this project were Michael Omi, David Plotke,

Michael Reich, the late Carol Hatch, and other members of *Socialist Review* editorial collective. In a different but equally central way, Troy Duster, David Matza, Steven Epstein, Jerome Karabel, Carol Stack, Kristin Luker, and Francisco Hernandez at U.C. Berkeley provided crucial support for this project at important points in its development. They too deserve much of the credit for seeing me through moments when I despaired at ever finishing this book. I am deeply indebted to all of them for their friendship and goodwill, but especially to Troy Duster and Francisco Hernandez, in ways that I cannot as yet adequately express.

In the course of preparing this study for publication, I have received generous support from a number of funding agencies and research institutions. Postdoctoral awards from the Institute for the Study of Social Change at U.C. Berkeley (directed by Troy Duster), from the Stanford Center for Chicano Research at Stanford University (directed by Albert Camarillo), and from the National Research Council provided me the opportunity to rethink my original analytical framework and complete the additional research. Continuing financial support from the Committee on Research at the University of California at Berkeley and the University of California at Santa Cruz allowed me to draw upon the valuable research assistance of Steven Epstein, Margarita Decierdo, Denise Segura, Judith Auerbach, Tina Shiffman, and Ellen Leonida. I thank them for their important contributions. Irene Moran, Peter Hanff, and the gracious staff of the Bancroft Library provided invaluable assistance during the research phase of this project. I thank them for their kindness and for providing the wonderful environment in which this book was nurtured.

During the final revisions of this manuscript I was especially appreciative of the goodwill shown by the fellows at Oakes College at the University of California, Santa Cruz, and by my new colleagues at the University of Michigan. I am particularly grateful for the friendship extended to me by Michael Cowan, José David Saldívar, and Angela Davis at UCSC. I also gratefully acknowledge the support that Susan L. Johnson of the University of Michigan has shown for this project. She provided important editorial recommendations that made their way into the manuscript before it went into production. A grant from the Office of the Vice Provost for Academic and Multicultural Affairs at the University of Michigan helped defray unanticipated publication expenses.

Finally, I want to acknowledge the crucial role of my immediate family and closest circle of friends; they never lost faith in this project. Clementina Duron, David Almaguer, Miguel Almaguer, and my family in southern

California have provided emotional grounding throughout the preparation of this study; I thank them for their patience, understanding, and affection. Velia Garcia, Patricia Zavella, Ramón Gutiérrez, and David Gutiérrez know only too well the hazards I negotiated in completing this project. They, above all, deserve special acknowledgment for seeing me through the adversities that befell this project before it finally made its way to press.

Introduction

California has experienced a distinct and unique history of race and ethnic relations, one whose fundamental pattern took shape during the last half of the nineteenth century. This pattern departs in many ways from the more familiar nineteenth-century one between European Americans and African and Native Americans in other regions of the country. The conquest of Western America through the U.S.-Mexico War of 1846–48 forged a new pattern of racialized relationships between conquerors, conquered, and the numerous immigrants that settled in the newly acquired territory. While longstanding race relations developed elsewhere were essentially binary in character, the United States' mid-nineteenth-century annexation of what is today the Southwest would incorporate three new cultural groups into existing racial patterns: the Mexican, Chinese, and Japanese populations. The structural position these ethnic groups would occupy was largely unscripted, unfettered by a historical legacy predetermining their "group position" in the new state.[1]

This history unfolded during a period of momentous political upheaval in the United States, one reverberating with intense sectional strife and the catastrophic effects of the Civil War. Moreover, it marked the moment in American history when the slave-based economic system in the southern United States was being successfully subordinated to the ascending capitalist social order of the more industrialized North. The ultimate triumph of modern capitalism was accompanied by a fierce struggle among various racial and ethnic groups for position within the emerging new class structure. Opportunities for individual and collective advancement were contested bitterly among the native-born and immigrant populations residing in every region of the country. The history of this competition between European-American immigrants and blacks in the northern and southern United States is well known and remains deeply rooted in the national consciousness.[2]

This contestation for group position at the national level was extended into the Far West with the United States' acquisition of over one-third of Mexico through the U.S.-Mexico War. The Gadsden Purchase of 1853 completed the United States' transcontinental expansion to the Pacific coast in the mid-nineteenth century. In the fifty-year period from 1803 to 1853 the United States increased its size tenfold through the acquisition of nearly 2.3 million square miles of land formerly claimed by France, Spain, England, and Mexico. In so doing, it laid the basis for the introduction of a new pattern of group relationships in the California territory during the next fifty years.

Our scholarly understanding of the historicity of "race" and racialized group relationships in the Far West, however, has developed largely in the shadow of the black/white encounter, and we continue to view racial matters in these paradigmatic terms. Further, academics have typically examined these racial patterns on the national level or have focused on parts of the country other than the American Southwest.[4] This has led to three related consequences: (1) we tend to see "race relations" as a binary and bipolar relationship, a perspective that offers little understanding of what happens when more than two racialized groups are competing; (2) we often view race and class hierarchies as neatly corresponding or symmetrical, as in the prototypical slaveowner/slave relationship; and (3) we generally assume that racializing discourses and practices are derived from or mask other, more fundamental underlying structures such as the class relationship between capital and labor.[5] California disproves these simplistic assumptions and provides unique opportunities to study both the evolution of racializing discourses and the hierarchical structuring of racial inequalities in a context where more than two racialized populations contest for group position within the social structure.

At its most fundamental level, this historical-sociological study traces the broad outlines of what Michael Omi and Howard Winant have termed "racial formation" in California during the last half of the nineteenth century. Omi and Winant define racial formation as "the process by which social, economic, and political forces determine the content and importance of racial categories, and by which they are in turned shaped by racial

meanings."[6] They introduce the term "*racialization* to specify the extension of racial meaning to a previously racially unclassified relationship,
social practice or group." In so doing, they underscore the fact that "racialization is an ideological process, an historically specific one."[7]

In this regard, Stuart Hall has astutely noted the formative role of the
ideological process in structuring hierarchical relations of group inequality. While acknowledging that historically specific "events, relations, [and]
structures do have conditions of existence and real effects, outside the
sphere of the discursive" he reminds us that "how things are represented
and the 'machineries' and regimes of representation in a culture do play a
constitutive, and not merely a reflexive, after-the-event, role. This gives
questions of culture and ideology, and the scenarios of representation—
subjectivity, identity, politics—a formative, not merely an expressive,
place in the constitution of social and political life."[8]

In outlining the contours of this racialization process, I argue that there
existed an "elective affinity" between the material interests of whites at
different class levels and the racial ideologies that simultaneously structured the new Anglo-dominated society in California. Neither the material
interests of class actors alone nor the ideological process pertaining to
racial formation ultimately determined the way hierarchies of group inequality were constructed. Rather, it was the simultaneous interaction of
both structural and ideological factors that ultimately shaped the trajectory of the historical experiences I explore.

Both the discursive dimensions of this racialization project in California
and the material structuring of racialized group relationships there are best
understood as unfolding within the context of the capitalist transformation
of the region and the ensuing competition between various ethnic populations for group position within the social structure. For various sectors of
the European-American population, located at different levels within the
emergent class structure, racializing discourses and practices served as
mechanisms to create, extend, or preserve their social position in the period
during which white supremacy was being systematically institutionalized.

The particular success of European-American men in securing a privileged social status was typically exacted through contentious, racialized
struggles with Mexicans, Native Americans, and Asian immigrants over
land ownership or labor-market position. These competitive struggles for
valued social resources, in turn, had direct consequences for the invidious
discourses that inscribed racial difference and provided popular ideological
support for California's white supremacist origins. The nineteenth-century
transformation of Mexican California, therefore, provides a unique oppor-

tunity for exploring the complex process whereby newly racialized relationships are forged and contested historically. Far from corresponding in any simple way, California's emergent hierarchies of racial and class inequality were mutually constitutive in ways that only historical analysis can explain.[9]

THE VARIETIES OF RACIALIZED EXPERIENCES

I came initially to my reading of racial and ethnic relations in California assuming that the experience of each cultural group would be similar to that of other minorities subjected to white supremacy. However, I was repeatedly struck by major differences. Why, for example, was the indigenous Indian population treated so differently from the indigenous Mexican population after California's annexation in 1848? The California Indians endured unrelenting vilification as "uncivilized savages" and were subjected to violent decimation or ruthless segregation at the extreme margins of European-American society. The Mexican population, on the other hand, was ambiguously deemed "half civilized" and ambivalently integrated into an intermediate status *within* the new society. Yet most Mexicans were dark complexioned *mestizos* with significant Indian ancestry. Why did they escape the harsh fate which befell their full-blooded counterparts?

The answer to these questions, I learned, stemmed from the different social evaluations that European Americans made of the racial status of these two cultural groups. Spanish colonization of the Southwest had conferred upon Mexicans a "white" racial status, Christian ancestry, a romance language, European somatic features, and a formidable ruling elite that contested "Yankee" depredations. Less cultural distance existed between European-American immigrants and "half civilized" Mexicans than between whites and other racialized, non-European ethnic groups. Mexicans, particularly the Californio elite, were as a result generally perceived as worthy of at least partial integration and assimilation into the new social order.

After U.S. annexation of California, the property-owning Mexican *ranchero* class mounted a losing battle against European-American immigrants for political and economic control of California. Mexicans gamely combated Anglo encroachment into California, effectively utilizing the legal rights that U.S. citizenship extended to them. Land was the major point of contention between the upper-class rancheros and white immigrants in the nineteenth century. The "decline of the Californios" and an increased immigration from Mexico at the turn of the century, however, would dramatically change the nature of Anglo-Mexican relations after 1900. Thereafter, this led to a reconfiguration of internal class divisions among Mexicans and altered the basis of group contention between Mexicans and European Americans from land to labor conflict. The nineteenth-century Mexican experience was in many ways unique and without parallel in the state.

No serious consideration, on the other hand, was ever given to integrating the California Indians into Anglo society, because of their "savage" culture and "heathen" traditions and rituals. Unlike Mexicans, they were categorically deemed nonwhite, politically disenfranchised, and ruthlessly segregated from European Americans in the state. Since they also occupied land that white settlers coveted, Indians in rural backwaters of the state were largely viewed as a troublesome obstacle in the path of Yankee progress and civilization. The California Indians became the metaphoric "devils of the forest" in the white mind, mere extensions of the wilderness Anglos needed to transform. As a consequence, the California state government launched a systematic policy of sanctioned decimation that resulted in the murder of as many as eight thousand Native Americans by white settlers and military units. Ultimately, Indians were either isolated on federal reservations in California's rural hinterland, succumbed to disease and malnutrition, or were violently eliminated through genocidal pogroms. Indians were consigned to marginal roles in the new political economy.

What was to become of the non-European immigrant population that made their way into California during this turbulent period? Would their fate parallel the experience of California's Mexican or Indian populations? Although other minorities migrating to California were also subordinated to European Americans, their histories differed significantly from the indigenous Mexican and Indian. The presence, or threatened presence, of blacks initially weighed heavily on Anglo-Americans after California's annexation. White immigrants intensely debated territorial issues such as slavery, free Negro migration, and the overall status of blacks. The black population was viewed largely as a symbolic threat to California's becoming a "free" state. Their arrival as slave laborers during the Gold Rush led segments within the white population, particularly miners, to virulently oppose their further immigration. Although these efforts ultimately were unsuccessful, blacks remained unwelcome because of their association with a slave system that was antithetical to the society being created in California. Consequently, blacks were relegated to the lower end of the new class society. They were largely segregated from whites or sought refuge in the creation of autonomous black towns.[10]

Chinese and Japanese male immigrants became yet another concern for European Americans during the late nineteenth century. These laborers were a principal source of cheap manpower that Anglo developers and capitalists required to successfully develop the state's mining, railroad, and agricultural industries. However, the "heathen Chinee," and later the Japanese "Yellow Peril," attracted intense opposition from segments of the white working class and self-employed, petit bourgeois commodity producers. White immigrants in these classes railed against the fundamental threat that these Asian immigrants posed to their rights and entitlements as "free white persons" in the new state.

As a consequence, the Chinese were initially subjected to widespread hostility from the European-American population. They too were categorically deemed nonwhite and therefore ineligible for the same rights held by white citizens. Moreover, anti-Chinese hysteria was punctuated by widespread antipathy to their "pagan idolatry," peculiar customs and attire, non-European features, and purported threat to white women. This virulent ethnocentrism and sexual hysteria over the large Chinese male population facilitated the rapid enactment of discriminatory legislation designed specifically to curb their symbolic or real competition with European Americans at various class levels. This opposition by skilled white workers competing with Chinese laborers in various urban industries culminated in the federal enactment of the Chinese Exclusion Act in 1882. The Chinese immigrant population that arrived in California during the 1860s bears the ignoble distinction of being the first immigrant group to be prohibited from immigration to the United States on the basis of racial status.

Both the dispossession of Indians and Mexicans and the economic restrictions imposed on black, Chinese, and Japanese immigrant workers contributed directly to the realization of European-American class aspirations in the state. Each ethnic group was racialized in unique ways and came to represent a different kind of class-specific obstacle to the life chances that the white population in the territory claimed for themselves. This arrogant sense of entitlement by the European-American population helped propel the racial stigmatization and structural subordination of California's minority populations. In succession, each group bore the stigma of being defined as an inferior race and accorded a subordinate structural position within the new white supremacist society.[11]

Why these cultural groups followed such divergent courses, however, requires more systematic sociological explanation. Why did these histories unfold in a context where race, rather than class, served as the key organizing principle of hierarchical relations of inequality? What were the specific symbolic and material factors that contributed to the economic mobility of certain groups and the disadvantaged status of others? What were the gendered dimensions of these class-specific, racialized histories? How, for instance, were relations between men and women of different cultural groups structurally mediated by the racialization process and the imposition of a new class system? What specific role did sexuality play in the structuring and imposition of racialized class relations among Californians during this period?

THE MASTER NARRATIVE OF "WHITE SUPREMACY"

The answer to these questions can be found in the way that race and the racialization process in California became the central organizing principle of group life during the state's formative period of development. Although California's ethnic populations were racialized in different ways, and the specific manifestations of racial and ethnic conflict were unique to California, at its most basic level it represented the extension of "white supremacy" into the new American Southwest. Historian George Fredrickson defines white supremacy as "the attitudes, ideologies, and politics associated with blatant forms of white or European dominance over 'non-white' populations."[12] The attempt to make race or color a basis for group position within the United States was defined initially during the colonial period when notions of "civility" and "savagery," as well as clear distinctions between "Christians" and "heathens," were used to inscribe racial difference and divide humankind into distinct categories of people. These notions provided the basis upon which European immigrants differentiated themselves from the diverse populations they encountered during their expansion into the Far West.

The cultural division of the world into different categories of humanity led white, European Americans in California to arrogantly privilege themselves as superior to non-European people of color. Although European Americans were situated unambiguously at the top of this social hierarchy, the racialized populations did not share a common structural position. Racialized relations in the state reverberated along a number of racial fault lines; they did not assume a simple binary form or erupt along one principal fault. The allocation of "group position" along these social strata was the outcome of both cultural and material considerations.

California Indians, for example, were singled out as the complete an-

tithesis of white Californians and were summarily relegated to the very
bottom of the racial hierarchy. White immigrants believed that the indigenous population was the lowest level of humankind imaginable. The California Indians wore little clothing, were perceived as horrendously ugly
and dirty, ate foods "Americans" deemed unpalatable, and practiced tribal
rituals and ceremonies that were anathema to European Christian practices. In short, they were cast as the extreme incarnation of all that was
both uncivilized and heathen.

Other cultural groups were judged less harshly and placed between the
extreme ends of the racial hierarchy. Mexicans, for instance, were perceived as much closer culturally to European-American immigrants than to
their Indian counterparts. The Mexicans' mixed European ancestry, romance language, Catholic religious practices, and familiar political-economic institutions elevated them above all other cultural groups in the
white man's eyes. Moreover, the continued political influence of the powerful Californio elite during the latter nineteenth century further attenuated more virulent expressions of anti-Mexican sentiment and allowed
Mexicans to challenge Anglo-domination for a time.

Black and Asian immigrants, finally, were culturally deemed to be
somewhere between the "half civilized" Mexican and "uncivilized" Indian
populations. Although antiblack animosity was widespread, blacks who
settled in California were at least Christian, spoke English, and had—after
years of enslavement—assimilated important European cultural patterns.
Most white immigrants grudgingly acknowledged this, a fact that contributed directly to blacks not becoming the major target of racist initiatives
in California that they were elsewhere in the country.

Americans perceived Asian immigrants, on the other hand, to have
fewer redeeming qualities and group attributes. While they too were unambiguously deemed nonwhite, these immigrants carried the extra burden of
being a "peculiar" people who spoke a completely unintelligible Eastern
language, had "abhorrent" culinary tastes, dressed "strangely," and practiced a form of "pagan idolatry" clearly at odds with Judeo-Christian
religious traditions. In cultural terms, Chinese and Japanese immigrants,
therefore, were perceived initially as more like the uncivilized and heathen
Indian population than any of the other cultural minorities in the state.

In sum, European-American immigrants in nineteenth-century California inherited and routinely relied on eurocentric cultural criteria to hierar-
chically evaluate and racialize the various cultural groups they contended
with in California. This process clearly privileged and elevated the status
of white immigrants in the social structure and placed below them, in

descending order, the Mexican, black, Asian, and Indian populations. This racialization process and conferral of group position in the state had important social consequences for the life chances of all racial and ethnic groups during the last half of the nineteenth century. It was not until the early decades of the twentieth century that this hierarchy of group position underwent major reconfiguration.

RACIALIZATION AND THE CONTESTATION OF RACIAL STATUS

It has become axiomatic in sociological research to view racial categories as sociohistorical constructs whose meanings vary widely over time and space. How people are defined as "white" or "nonwhite" is never a self-evident process. Because race is fundamentally a socially conferred status whose anthropological and biological underpinnings are dubious at best, how and where racial lines are drawn is an open question and the possibility for contestation always exists. Outcomes of struggles to define different ethnic groups in racial terms have been largely contingent on the collective power of the groups involved. Lacking any clear "objective" criteria other than phenotype and ancestry, conflict over the racial designation of groups in California devolved into questions over which group had enough power and influence to enact its interests. Consequently, the racial formation process that codified racial status in California was the result of political struggles contested at the state level.

One key aspect of the racial formation process in California was the differential racialization of the various cultural groups that settled within this geographical region. The very way in which racial lines were defined became an object of intense political struggle. Even before the granting of statehood in 1850, adjudicating the racial status of the indigenous Mexican and Indian population in the territory assumed crucial importance. California's State Constitutional Convention of 1849 fiercely debated how these racial lines were to be drawn and, consequently, who would and would not be extended the franchise and other important citizenship rights. In the final analysis, Mexicans were socially defined as "white" and extended citizenship while the California Indians, like Indians elsewhere, were deemed "nonwhite" and ineligible for citizenship. This question was crucial for groups on both sides of the racial divide, for the way these lines were construed structurally advantaged or disadvantaged collectivities competing for position in the state's new class structure.

The complexities of the racialization process in California between 1850 and 1900 are also vividly reflected in the case of Chinese immigrants. Unable to transcend the traditional binary racial categories utilized in the early nineteenth century, the 1854 case of *People v. Hall* decreed that the Chinese were generically "Indians" and, therefore, nonwhite. Despite this curious determination, there is evidence that some Chinese immigrants were mistakenly granted U.S. citizenship between 1850 and 1882. The naturalization court apparently mistook them for "free white persons."[13] The 1893 case of *Saito v. U.S.* ruled that Japanese immigrants were, like the Chinese, also nonwhite (the Japanese, however, were deemed "Mongolian" instead of "Indian") and, consequently, were equally ineligible for citizenship. There remained some ambiguity as to the status of some Japanese and it is estimated that at least 420 Japanese immigrants were granted citizenship before 1910. Federal restrictions placed on Japanese immigration after that date, plus the unequivocal ruling in *Ozawa v. U.S.* in 1932 legally confirmed the popular belief that the Japanese were, in fact, "aliens ineligible for citizenship."[14]

The social motivation of the political undertaking conferring racial status continued to be apparent in early-twentieth-century California in the case of immigrants from Armenia and India. In 1909, for example, federal authorities classified Armenians as "Asiatics" and consequently denied them naturalized citizenship. The *Halladjian* decision ruled shortly afterwards, however, that Armenian immigrants were indeed Caucasian due to their history, ancestry, and physical appearance.[15] This proved fortuitous for the Armenians as their racial status exempted them from the Alien Land Laws of 1913 and 1920 which prohibited the ownership and lease of California farm land by "aliens ineligible for citizenship," a euphemism for Japanese immigrants.

Another curious turn in American racial thinking occurred in the case of Asian Indians. In the 1910 *U.S. v. Balsara* and 1913 *Ajkoy Kumar Mazumdar* decisions, the federal courts held that Asian Indians were Caucasians and entitled to the same rights as "free white persons" to become naturalized citizens. A few years later, however, in the 1923 case of *U.S. v. Bhagat Singh Thind*, Asian Indians were suddenly denied the right to naturalized citizenship because they were not "white" according to the understanding of the common man and because they were not of northern or western European stock.[16] A year after the *Thind* decision, Congress enacted the 1924 Immigration Act, which effectively denied immigration quotas to people ineligible for citizenship, namely all nonwhites.

The racialization of various non-European groups during the last half of the nineteenth century also facilitated the construction of social boundaries around the white population. Michael Omi and Howard Winant have argued that the racial categorization of European Americans as "white" was forged at the national level during this period. Despite nativistic attempts to classify Southern Europeans, the Irish, and Jews as "nonwhite," these efforts were "effectively curbed by the institutionalization of a racial order that drew the color line *around* rather than *within*, Europe."[17]

The influx into California of a diverse European-American population, both foreign and native born, created a process in which ethnic differences among these groups was overshadowed by the construction of a collective racial designation as "white." European Americans drawn into competition and conflict with the nonwhite populations repeatedly referred to themselves in racial terms, as "white," rather than primarily defining themselves as Irish, French, English, German, or any other ethnicity. While these ethnic designations may have had importance among European Americans themselves, such identities were subsumed by the racialization process. White supremacist practices, in other words, forged a collective identity among European Americans in the state that crystallized around their racial status as a "white population."

In this regard, Omi and Winant have perceptively argued that

> by stopping short of racializing immigrants from Europe after the Civil War, and by subsequently allowing their assimilation, the American racial order was reconstituted in the wake of the tremendous challenge placed before it by the abolition of slavery. With the end of Reconstruction in 1877, an effective program for limiting the emergent class struggles of the later nineteenth century was forged: the definition of the working class in *racial terms*—as 'white.' This was not accomplished by any legislative decree or capitalist maneuvering to divide the working class, but rather by workers themselves. Many of them were recent immigrants, who organized on racial lines as much as on traditionally defined class lines. . . . Thus the very political organization of the working class was in important ways a racial project. The legacy of racial conflicts and arrangements shaped the definition of interests and in turn led to the consolidation of institutionalized patterns (e.g. segregated unions, dual labor markets, exclusionary legislation) which perpetuated the color line *within* the working class.[18]

Although class conflict within the white population had important consequences for the racial antagonism that flared in nineteenth-century California, it did not overshadow or functionally structure the way racial lines were drawn. The nineteenth-century transformation in local class structure was dependent upon the prior question of who was to be granted privileged access to the class structure. This, I will argue, was primarily a racial issue. Contrary to Karl Marx's expectation at the time, the salience of racial status did not diminish in the face of the expanded nineteenth-century proletarianization of the working class and polarization of class forces. Although class divisions and conflict were manifested openly, these lines were not the primary stratification dividing California's diverse population. The tremendous immigration of European and non-European immigrants into the state after annexation resulted in a hierarchy of group inequality in which race, not class, became the central stratifying variable. The primary racial division of Californians into white and nonwhite categories cut at right angles across the newly emergent class lines that divided capitalists, petit bourgeois commodity producers, and an increasingly segmented working class composed of free wage laborers and individuals held in precapitalist relations of production.

THE WHITE MAN'S BURDEN AND ENTITLEMENT IN CALIFORNIA

The imposition of a new racial order and attendant class structure in nineteenth-century California was greatly facilitated by popular ideologies that gave voice to the superordinate political and economic position of European Americans in the state. Two powerful ideas reflecting this white supremacist sentiment were fervently embraced by European-American men during the United States' westward expansion: "Manifest Destiny" and the "free labor ideology."

The United States' usurpation of Mexican territory laid the basis for rapidly transforming what would become the American Southwest along new sociocultural, political, and economic lines. This mission became the "white man's burden"—to extend their dominion over all obstacles placed in their path and to bring civilization and Christianity to the uncivilized heathens they encountered. During this period white Americans widely accepted the idea of populating all of the North American continent with a homogeneous white population. They believed it was their providential destiny to expand to the Pacific coast, bringing with them their superior political institutions, notions of progress and democracy, and their own economic system of production. Public support for extending national boundaries found fertile ground in this tumultuous period of expansion and reached its most explicit political expression in the notion of Manifest Destiny.

During the mid-nineteenth century, white supremacist practices also became intertwined inextricably with economic doctrines concerning the role of "free labor." As historian Eric Foner has shown, a free-labor ideology was widely embraced by European Americans at all class levels. White men in particular enthusiastically supported the vision of the social world this ideology promoted: an expanding capitalist society based on free wage labor. Those fervently advocating free-labor doctrines accepted the right to private property and economic individualism and fervently believed that free labor created all value. Moreover, they maintained that everyone could aspire to and achieve economic independence in a free society and that "today's laborer would be tomorrow's capitalist."[19]

The free labor ideology associated with the Republican Party during the mid-nineteenth century helped crystallize the beliefs of European-American men about their entitlement to privileged economic mobility in the new territories. It also specifically colored the way Anglo Californians initially assessed the various minority groups they competed with for position in the state's new class structure. Free-labor adherents believed that social mobility and economic independence were only achievable in a capitalist society unthreatened by nonwhite populations and the degrading labor systems associated with them. European Americans repeatedly associated nonwhite people with various unfree labor systems that ostensibly threatened their superordinate social standing and class prerogatives in California.

Like Manifest Destiny, the underlying tenets of the free-labor ideology squarely affirmed the superior position of European-American men and helped delineate the subordinate status that people of color would occupy in the Far West.[20] As a consequence, racial lines in California quickly became linked with class divisions in unexpected and complicated ways. Outward struggles over access and group position within the class system were given concrete form and substance by the underlying racialized struggle among its chief protagonists.

The powerful impact of white supremacist notions like Manifest Destiny and the free-labor ideology had important material consequences for these contesting groups. The competition for access to valued social resources did not result, however, in purely symmetrical hierarchies based on class and race. Far from simply paralleling each other, California's new class hierarchy and racial order were mutually constitutive and intersected in complex and shifting ways that were historically contingent.

How groups were accorded access to the ownership of productive property and proletarianized within the working class was not a random selection process impervious to popular perceptions of racial differences. Who gained access to land, owned businesses, became skilled workers, and, more generally, was subjectively placed in either a "free" wage-labor market or an "unfree" labor system was fundamentally determined on the basis of race. Access to every level of the capitalist system of production introduced in nineteenth-century California was largely determined by this status. Although this capitalist economy became a highly competitive system by the late nineteenth century, it remained an institution that limited social mobility to white, European-American men.

White Californians repeatedly claimed primary access to privileged positions within the system of production and effectively thwarted attempts by the nonwhite population to compete with them on an equal footing. Nineteenth-century legislation enacted in the interest and at the behest of European Americans cemented the placement of California's nonwhite minorities in various unfree labor situations (such as slavery, indentured servitude, contracted labor, etc.) or guaranteed their exclusion altogether from certain skilled occupations and self-employment opportunities. European Americans jealously sought to protect their privileged group position in California through the use of discriminatory social closures that impeded equal access to social mobility. Racial status clearly shaped each group's life chances and served as the primary basis for determining whether one was granted access to different strata within the new class structure.

The judicial decisions that formally conferred racial status in nineteenth-century California, therefore, had important consequences for the historical trajectories of each of these groups in California. As each of these "nonwhite" groups entered into competition with European Americans at different class levels after 1850, a series of protracted conflicts erupted along a number of racial fault lines. This was registered in white opposition to black, Chinese, and Sonoran miners in the 1850s; to Chinese workers in urban industries in the 1870s and 1880s; and to Japanese small farmers at the turn of the century. Racial enmity and bitter economic struggle with white competitors punctuated minority history in California during the nineteenth century. White antipathy crystallized most intensely in the case of Native Americans, Mexicans, Chinese, and, to a lesser extent, African-American and Japanese immigrants.

There emerged during this period a strong symbolic association between different minority groups, on the one hand, and various precapitalist economic formations on the other. White antipathy toward Mexicans, Native Americans, and Chinese and Japanese immigrants was typically couched within the rubric of this "free white labor"/"unfree nonwhite labor" dichotomy: Mexicans became inimically associated with the "unproductive," semi-feudal rancho economy that European Americans rapidly undermined after statehood; Indians with a "primitive" communal mode of existence that white settlers ruthlessly eradicated through violence and forced segregation; and Asian immigrants with a "degraded" unfree labor system unfairly competing with and fettering white labor. The class-specific nature of contention between these racialized groups and the European-American populations were all cast in terms of these symbolic associations.

White economic mobility and dominance in California required both the subordination of minority populations and the eradication of the precapitalist systems of production associated with them. Anglo entitlement to California's bounty could only be actualized when the symbolic and material threat these minority populations posed was effectively neutralized or overcome. The chapters that follow examine the major features of these historical contestations and specifically explore the sociological factors that shaped the divergent courses of the Mexican, Indian, and Asian immigrant experiences in nineteenth-century Anglo California.

Chapter 1 places the racial contestation in nineteenth-century California in historical-sociological perspective by situating it within the broader backdrop of racial and ethnic relations in the United States. It does so by foregrounding the centrality of "white supremacy" and illustrating how "Manifest Destiny" and "free labor" sentiments influenced the trajectory of racial and class conflict in California after U.S. annexation. These racializing ideologies provided the lens through which the new cultural groups European Americans encountered in California were racially stigmatized and structurally subordinated.

The central body of this study is composed of six historical-sociological essays that assess the major features of the Mexican, Native American, and Asian immigrant experiences. Part 1 focuses on the class-specific nature of the Mexican encounter with European Americans in the new state. Chapter 2 examines, on a statewide basis, the various factors that contributed to the divergent experiences of the Mexican ranchero and working classes. Chapter 3 provides a detailed case study of how this process unfolded in one particular Southern California county. It also provides a window into the complex interplay of class and racial forces that led to the differential placement of Mexicans, Native Americans, and Asians in the new social structure.

Part 2 is devoted to a broad-ranging analysis of the nineteenth-century experience of the California Indians. Chapter 4 assesses the cultural factors and racial discourses used to stigmatize Indians and justify their decimation through state-initiated pogroms. Chapter 5 analyzes factors that contributed to Indians playing a marginal role in the new capitalist economy introduced in California after 1848. It also chronicles the dismal failure of the federal government's policy of forcefully relocating thousands of California Indians onto segregated reservations.

Part 3 assesses the racialized class conflict between European-American working class and Chinese and Japanese immigrants in nineteenth-century California. Chapter 6 surveys the bitter, statewide clash between Chinese workers and European-American entrepreneurs and laborers. Chapter 7 provides a detailed, county-level analysis of the way anti-Chinese sentiment was displaced onto Japanese immigrants at the turn of the century. It does so through a careful examination of the class forces and racial issues that culminated in the first successful, minority-led strike against powerful agribusiness interests in California—the Oxnard Sugar Beet Workers' Strike of 1903.

The epilogue summarizes the major findings of this study and explores their implications for our broader understanding of the complex interplay between class, race, and ethnicity in the United States and for contemporary racial politics. It also briefly raises the autobiographical issues that were so central to the initial development of this comparative historical study.

CHAPTER ONE

"We Desire Only a White Population in California"

The Transformation of Mexican California in Historical-Sociological Perspective

In his comparative study *White Supremacy*, historian George Fredrickson astutely observes that "race relations are not so much a fixed pattern as a changing set of relationships that can only be understood within a broader historical context that is itself constantly evolving and thus altering the terms under which whites and nonwhites interact."[1] California's racial and ethnic patterns give ample support to this understanding of race relations in the United States, and so I want to begin by characterizing both the "historical context" within which California's racialization process evolved as well as the "terms under which white and nonwhite interact[ed]." This requires situating California's various racial histories within the broader history of race relations in the United States and clarifying the underlying social dynamics of the new state. In so doing, I want to argue that California's racial patterns were not monolithic but contained multiple racial histories that were unique in their own terms while also sharing elements with the racial formation process elsewhere in the United States.

For analytical clarity on these matters it is useful to turn to the important early work by sociologist Herbert Blumer. Writing in a period when sociological analysis focused attention on race prejudice as an irrational manifestation of individual pathologies, Blumer recognized that race relations were fundamentally organized at the group level, through a "collective process by which a racial group comes to define and redefine another racial group."[2] He suggested that an analysis of racial matters "should start with a clear recognition that it is an historical product. It is set

17

originally by conditions of initial contact. Prestige, power, possession of skill, numbers, original self-concepts, aims, designs and opportunities are a few factors that may fashion the original sense of group position. Subsequent experience in the relation of the two racial groups, especially in the area of claims, opportunities and advantages, may mold the sense of group position in diverse ways."[3]

Blumer appreciated the complex relationship between the stigmatization of social groups on the basis of physical characteristics and ancestry and the struggle for "group position" among racial and ethnic populations in this country. In fact, "the sense of social position emerging from this collective process . . . provides the basis of race prejudice" and crystallizes "four basic types of feelings" among the superordinate racial group: "(1) a feeling of superiority, (2) a feeling that the subordinate group is intrinsically different and alien, (3) a feeling of proprietary claim to certain areas of privilege and advantage, and (4) a fear and suspicion that the subordinate race harbors designs on the prerogatives of the dominant race."[4]

In drawing our attention to the relationship between racial ideology and social structure, Blumer made central "the sense of proprietary claim" of the dominant racial group in the structuring of racialized relationships among these ethnic populations. This sense of entitlement, according to Blumer, rested primarily on "either exclusive or prior rights in many important areas of life. The range of such exclusive or prior claims may be wide, covering the ownership of property such as choice lands and sites; the right to certain jobs, occupations, or professions; the claim to certain kinds of industry or lines of business; the claim to certain positions of control and decision-making as in government and law."[5]

Frank Parkin's insightful work in social stratification theory has also shown how these sentiments of superiority and entitlement to valued social rewards are structured historically. Working in the Weberian tradition, Parkin has argued that status monopolies, or "social closures," have historically served as institutional mechanisms that structure and reproduce racial and ethnic hierarchies in this country. According to Parkin, these closures refer to "the process whereby social collectivities seek to maximize rewards by restricting access to resources and opportunities to a limited circle of eligibles. . . . This monopolization is directed against competitors who share some positive or negative characteristic; its purpose is always the closure of social and economic opportunities to *outsiders*."[6] At their most basic sociological level, then, these closures represent attempts by one group of people to secure for themselves a privileged position in the social structure at the expense of stigmatized and subordinated social groups.

Since they typically entail the creation of a group of legally defined inferiors, such actions represent the use of power in a downward direction and "can be thought of as different means of mobilizing power for the purpose of engaging in a distributive struggle" over valued social rewards.[7]

These important sociological principles allow us to view the racialization process in nineteenth-century California, and the United States more generally, as a contestation over privileged access to either productive property (i.e., physical capital such as land or factories) or positions in a highly stratified labor market. Consequently, the broad historical context in which these racial lines were drawn and class-specific relationships constituted provides the main sociological framework informing this study.

RACIALIZATION AND WHITE SUPREMACY IN HISTORICAL PERSPECTIVE

I have suggested that the racialization process that evolved in nineteenth-century California was primarily an extension into the new territory of what Fredrickson has characterized as "white supremacy": the "attitudes, ideologies, and policies associated with the rise of blatant forms of white or European dominance over 'nonwhite' populations . . . making invidious distinctions of a socially crucial kind that are based primarily, if not exclusively, on physical characteristics and ancestry. In its fully developed form, white supremacy means 'color bars,' 'racial segregation,' and the restriction of meaningful citizenship rights to a privileged group characterized by its light pigmentation."[8]

Furthermore, Fredrickson argues that this systematic and self-conscious attempt to make race or color a basis for group position within American society was initially defined during the colonial period and the years following Independence.[9] He contends that such action reflects "a long and often violent struggle for territorial supremacy between white invaders and indigenous people" that was part and parcel of the global European colonial expansion inaugurated during the "Age of Discovery."[10] Starting with the small colonial settlements of the seventeenth century, Anglo-Saxon colonists established dominion over North America by successfully appropriating Indian communal land and transforming it into private property within an emergent capitalist economy. According to Fredrickson, "Land hunger and territorial ambition gave whites a practical incentive to differentiate between the basic rights and privileges they claimed for themselves and what they considered to be just treatment for the 'savages' who stood in their path, and in the end they mustered the power to impose their will."[11]

The white colonists contesting the native peoples of North America for control of coveted land brought with them well-developed assumptions about themselves and the people they encountered. As Fredrickson has shown, fundamental to these assumptions were the differentiations between *Christians* and *heathens* and between *civil* and *savage* peoples.[12] These eurocentric binary distinctions provided the cultural standard by which European settlers initially racialized the "nonwhite" black and Indian populations they confronted in America and were later used to differentiate the new cultural groups European Americans encountered during their mid-nineteenth-century expansion into the Southwest.

According to Fredrickson, the notion of "heathenism" initially "reflected the religious militancy nurtured by the long and bitter struggle for supremacy in the Mediterranean between Christian and Islamic civilizations. . . . In the fifteenth century, when Spain and Portugal were in the vanguard of Christian resistance to Islamic power, the Pope authorized the enslavement and seizures of lands and property of 'all saracens and pagans whatsoever, and all other enemies of Christ wheresoever placed.' This harsh and unrelenting attitude . . . was carried by the Spanish and Portuguese empire-builders of the sixteenth century to the New World and parts of Africa and Southeast Asia."[13] As a consequence, through the notion of heathenism religion became pivotal in socially differentiating the diverse populations that encountered one another in the course of European colonial expansion.

What typically differentiated "civilized" human beings from "savages" in the European mind was whether or not "they practiced sedentary agriculture, had political forms that Europeans recognized as regular governments, and lived to some extent in urban concentrations."[14] To these three factors we might add difference in the social organization of kinship, gender, and sexuality.[15] Fredrickson persuasively argues in *White Supremacy* that Europeans widely believed that civility was the original state of mankind and that "after the dispersal of the progeny of Noah after the flood some branches of the human race lost their awareness of God and degenerated into an uncivilized state. Sometimes this descent into barbarism and savagery was linked directly to the Biblical curse of Ham, which would later be used to justify African slavery."[16] Fredrickson further reminds us that Europeans drew upon classical thought when making their assessments of the newly encountered peoples. Although "Aristotle had maintained that even barbarians were social beings, Europeans had believed since the Middle Ages that some men were so wild and uncouth that they wandered in the forests and had no society of any kind. This category of ultra-barbarians or pure savages, who allegedly lived more like beasts than men, seemed to many Europeans of the sixteenth and seventeenth century appropriate for peoples like . . . the North American, Caribbean, and Brazilian Indians, who were commonly thought to be wilderness nomads utterly devoid of any religion or culture."[17]

These were the lines around which Europeans since the Renaissance and Reformation distinguished themselves from the diverse populations they encountered during the Age of Discovery. Notions of civility and savagery and clear distinctions between Christians and heathens provided the ideological basis for a social order that stigmatized the Indian population initially encountered in New England as well as the West Africans imported as slaves. Fredrickson argues, however, that these categories "were not yet racist in the nineteenth-century sense of the term because they were not based on an explicit doctrine of genetic or biological inferiority; but they could provide an equivalent basis for considering some categories of human beings inferior to others in ways that made it legitimate to treat them differently from Europeans."[18]

Beginning in the colonial period, America's English settlers drew upon these value-laden notions to craft a collective identity based upon the categories *English*, *Christian*, *free*, and, above all, *white*, and specifically defined in opposition to another, nonwhite category of people, initially Native Americans and Africans. According to Winthrop Jordan's study of this period, *White Over Black*:

> When referring to the Indians the English colonists either used the proper name or called them *savages*, a term which reflected primarily their view of Indians as uncivilized. . . . When they had reference to Indians the colonists occasionally spoke of themselves as *Christians*, but after the early years almost always as *English*.
>
> In significant contrast, the colonists referred to *Negroes* and in the eighteenth century to *blacks* and to *Africans*, but almost never to Negro *heathens* or *pagans* or *savages*. Most suggestive of all, there seems to have been something of a shift during the seventeenth century in the terminology Englishmen in the colonies applied to themselves. From the initially most common term *Christian*, at mid-century there was a marked drift toward *English* and *free*. After about 1680, taking the colonies as a whole, a new term appeared—*white*.[19]

In *Iron Cages*, his comparative study of race relations in the nineteenth century, historian Ronald Takaki has proposed that these opposing identities increasingly equated European Americans with the mind and nonwhites with the body. All that was rational, civilized, and spiritually pure was set off from that which was irrational, uncivilized, and tied to the body. Anglo-Saxon men became civilized republican men of virtue, devoting their lives to hard work, frugality, sobriety, and the mastery of both their passions and their lives. The nonwhite, in contrast, became the foil for the lofty self-image that white men accorded themselves. They were associated with qualities such as filth or dirtiness, impurity, vice, intoxication, and the lascivious indulgence of carnal "instincts." European Americans projected onto people of color all the qualities of depravity that they had difficulty repressing in themselves.[20]

ımericans also believed that they needed to control these evil
they were to prosper economically and achieve salvation. In this
)or assumed a spiritual dimension; belief in the dignity of labor
ive in colonial America and found its clearest expression in the
Ethic, which held that all persons had a divinely appointed
expressed their service to God on earth. It was also a way of
; whether they were among those predestined to enter heaven.
:conomic advancement in this world was regarded as a Chris-
) which all aspired. Success in one's calling necessitated strict
1e; to this end, the elect were guided by Christian virtues such
frugality, diligence, punctuality, sobriety, and prudence. There
was no Christian value in poverty; in fact, poverty was disdained as a sign of God's disfavor. It was seen as a product of individual shortcomings and vices such as laziness, drunkenness, or extravagance.[21]

The initial distinctions Europeans made between themselves and non-whites had significance for the social organization of the colonial economy. In addition to assuming a divinely appointed, spiritual dimension, individuals' economic positions generally reflected their racial status as well. Access to various economic opportunities was cast largely in racial terms. Questions of who owned property, became property, and entered "free" and "unfree" labor markets were answered in racial terms. These associations were not simply the product of irrational prejudices or ethnic chauvinisms: they had deep material moorings in the social organization of economic life.

The English colonial population, for instance, institutionalized labor status distinctions among themselves through the introduction of indentured servitude. As many as one-half to two-thirds of Anglo-Saxons who emigrated during the colonial period came as indentured servants. In return for passage to America they provided upward of seven years of unremunerated labor.[22] Indentured servants, however, were insufficient in number to meet labor needs and were expensive to retain; moreover, they often negotiated successfully for favorable terms and freely entered the wage labor force upon completion of contractual obligations. Because of these complications, chattel slavery ultimately proved more expedient and profitable than indentured servitude. Economic advantage intersected with racial prejudice to forge the equation associating whites with free and nonwhites with unfree labor. The temporary subordinate labor status of Anglo-Saxon indentured servants and the permanent, inheritable slave status of blacks put these differences into broad relief. Slavery economically subordinated this nation's black population to Anglo-Americans, and their second-class social and political status structurally ensured that blacks could not compete effectively with Anglo-Americans at any level of the social structure.

Unlike blacks, the Indians of North America generally were not seen as a useful laboring population worthy of even a subordinate place in the Anglo-Americans' economy. Although attempts were made during the colonial period to enslave Indians, they proved unsuccessful, because of Indian susceptibility to European-American diseases, their sparse population in the colonial region, their ability to effectively flee enslavement and exact reprisals, and their unwillingness to adapt to the system of production that white Americans had introduced.[23] As a result, in Anglo conceptions of progress, Indians were generally seen as obstacles to civilization. They became extensions of the untamed territory Europeans confronted in America. The traditional hunting and gathering of Indian subsistence, as well as their social-cultural world, were anathema to the society whites were creating in America. Indians remained "savages" and "heathens" in the eyes of the colonial population.

In *The Ethnic Myth*, sociologist Stephen Steinberg has noted that at its inception the United States was remarkably homogeneous both ethnically and religiously. He reminds us that by Independence the colonial population was overwhelmingly white, Anglo-Saxon, and Protestant and that in 1790 over three-quarters of the U.S. population had origins in the English-speaking states of the British Isles; 61 percent were of British descent and another 17 percent of Scotch and Irish extraction. A smaller number of Germans, Dutch, and Swedish settlers and a minute proportion of other nationalities accounted for the remaining population. Despite the initial presence of a few Jews and Catholics, nearly 99 percent of the colonial population was Protestant.[24]

According to one historian, by the late 1840s most Americans either thought of themselves as the descendants of English immigrants (bound together by a common culture and a common language) or as part of the superior, "American" race drawn from the very best stock of western and northern Europe.[25] The distinctive cultural values and world view of this population provided the normative standards by which other groups were later judged. The language and dominant customs of America were English, and all non-English groups immigrating to the United States were expected to conform fully to English culture.

Moreover, at a time when its population was still relatively homogeneous, the new nation decreed that only whites were eligible for U.S. citizenship and access to the opportunities generated by economic development. Neither African Americans nor Native Americans were accorded the legal rights and social status of free white men. The explicitness of this color line was captured clearly in one of the first congressional statutes enacted after Independence. Debates over naturalization led to enactment of the Naturalization Act of 1790, which stipulated that only "free white persons"

or citizenship and the rights held by white men in the
ugh this statute imposed restrictions on immigration, its
not want to discourage the immigration of white Euro-
regard, Steinberg observes that "long before the onset of
ion, there was a deeply rooted consciousness of the nation's
and Protestant origins. From the beginning, the nation's
utions, culture, and people all had an unmistakably English
ite denominational differences, Protestantism was the near-
d. The early stirring of nativism clearly signaled the fact that
h the nation might tolerate foreigners in its midst, it was
) protect its Anglo-Saxon and Protestant legacy."[26] The symbolic significance of this legislation cannot be overstated. Eligibility for citizenship was not meaningfully altered until one hundred and sixty-two years after this statute's enactment, when the Walter-McCarran Act of 1952 eliminated the racial basis for United States naturalization.[27]

The importance of racial status to the colonial and post-Independence economy laid the foundation for its continued centrality during the period of widespread immigration to the United States in the nineteenth century. Rapid economic development and industrialization during this period provided the structural foundations upon which further economic and social opportunities were systematically granted or denied on the basis of race. In this regard, Robert Blauner has argued in *Racial Oppression in America* that white European immigrants historically benefited from a labor market organized along racial and ethnic lines. In addition to advantages gained from voluntary immigration, white immigrants experienced more rapid

[handwritten margin notes: immigrants / whites married quickly / in social / cast]

social and economic mobility due to "the association of free labor with people of white European stock and the association of unfree labor with non-Western people of color."[28]

This overriding racial labor principle placed white immigrants in the free, wage-labor sector of the economy while relegating nonwhites to precapitalist labor systems. It had tremendous implications for the initial employment opportunities accorded immigrant groups and also for their collective movement up the occupational hierarchy. From the beginning, European immigrants had a foothold in the most dynamic centers of the economy and rose successfully to semiskilled and skilled positions. Racial minorities, on the other hand, were largely denied access to the industrial jobs that enabled millions of white immigrants to attain a modicum of social and economic mobility.[29]

Thus, the racialization process profoundly affected the social positions immigrants assumed upon entering this country. Beginning in the colonial period and continuing after Independence, race and ethnicity served as the basis upon which access to particular positions in the class structure was largely determined.[30] This was seen most clearly in the Southern slave economy but was also discernible in the capitalist sectors of the Northeast and West. The social organization of the economy mediated the broad allocation of groups into various class positions. This gave the nation's class structure in many regions a decidedly racial and ethnic form—European ethnic groups being disproportionately placed at the upper end of the class system and racial minorities at the bottom.

Historically, differential access to valued social rewards have shaped the course of ethnic and race relations in the United States. Their unequal extension to white and nonwhite groups via social closures led to divergent mobility routes and different "life chances" for these groups. Not every ethnic population that entered into competition with whites equally threatened their mobility aspirations, nor were they equally granted access to important institutional spheres. It is here that each group's collective attributes (such as their internal class stratification, gender composition, population demographics, literacy rates, occupational skills, employment background, physical differences from the white population, collective association with precapitalist labor systems, and explicit cultural factors such as values, religion, and ethnic traditions) were critically important. This complex of factors explicitly delineated these groups in racial terms and historically conditioned their mobility opportunities and potential conflict with the white population.

These collective attributes primarily served as benchmarks whereby the white population further differentiated itself from minorities. These perceived differences became the basis for group stigmatization that ultimately fueled racial antagonisms. They also were drawn upon to justify the enactment of discriminatory legislation designed to impede minority economic competition with European Americans. In sum, a complex matrix of attributes have at every historical moment shaped the broad contours of white competition and conflict with the racialized population in the United States. Let us now turn to how this drama unfolded in California after it passed from Mexican control to that of the United States in 1848.

THE PEOPLING OF ANGLO CALIFORNIA, 1848–1900

The United States' annexation of California and the momentous discovery of gold in 1848 sparked the rapid immigration of a diverse population into the newly acquired territory. It transformed California from a sparsely populated Mexican frontier department to a new state in which European-American immigrants quickly provided the mainstay of its population. Population demographers have noted that as late as 1848 the total non-Indian population in California was estimated at approximately fifteen thousand, or scarcely one person to every ten square miles. The majority of these individuals were Mexican Californians, followed by a few thousand European Americans, who had settled in the territory prior to U.S. annexation, and a smattering of individuals from other parts of the world. Although estimates vary considerably, California's Indian population in 1850 is generally thought to have numbered approximately 100,000 men, women, and children.[32]

Between 1848 and 1870, however, the state's population rose to well over half a million people.[33] The vast majority of the new inhabitants who settled in the state were young and male. According to historical demographer Doris Marion Wright, "In 1850, for example, 73 percent of the residents in the state were between the ages of 20 and 40, and 92 percent of them were males. . . . When the census was taken in 1860 the number of females was still less than 30 percent of the total population of the state, and ten years later it had increased to only 37 percent."[34] Aside from this stark gender imbalance, another important demographic feature of the new state's early population was the significant presence of a foreign-born stock. In 1850, the foreign-born population already comprised 24 percent of the state's total population. By 1860 the percentage rose to 39 percent and declined slightly ten years later to 37 percent.[35] Further, the principal source of the foreign-born population in California shifted dramatically during this early period. In 1850, for example, Mexico provided the single largest segment of the foreign-born population (6,454 of 22,358 foreign-born individuals enumerated on the census; as will be discussed in chapter 3, many of the foreign-born Mexican population were Sonoran miners who typically returned to Mexico after the gold rush). The Mexican-born population was followed by European immigrants from England (3,050), Germany (2,926), Ireland (2,452), and France (1,546). By 1860, China had become the source of the largest foreign-born population in the state (34,935 of 146,528 foreign-born individuals). Chinese immigrants were followed numerically by Irish (33,147), German (21,646), English (12,227), and Mexican-born (9,150) immigrants. Ten years later, Chinese immigrants remained the single largest foreign-born population in the state, followed by individuals from the British Isles, Germany, France, and Mexico.[36]

The class background of the European-born population was apparently not as diverse as one might have expected. The Irish immigrants who came to California, for example, had been displaced largely by the introduction of labor-saving devices in the spinning and weaving trades and by the fluctuations in Ireland's agriculture industry. According to Wright, they were "not of the poorest classes but were persons who could get together enough money to pay for their passage."[37] Speaking the same language and sharing the same cultural heritage as Anglo-Americans made Irish immigrants more assimilable than other European and non-European immigrants emigrating at the time.

California's German and French immigrants were also drawn from occupational strata in their native lands that in California were still in the nascent stages of development. Many German immigrants, for example, were from farming backgrounds and were more likely to venture into this industry than to seek their fortunes in the gold mines. They were described in one state report as "mostly all tillers of the soil, and invariably bring money with them to purchase lands."[38] Their occupational backgrounds facilitated their dominance in the grape industry and the grocery business, and their overrepresentation as mechanics and skilled laborers. Moreover, being northern European, these immigrants learned English quickly and more readily adapted to the pace of the new Anglo-dominated society.[39]

Similarly, the French immigrants who settled in the state were not generally impoverished or drawn from the peasant class. Instead, the "majority of those who arrived in California from France . . . were largely from the middle class; many of them were skilled mechanics, while others were drawn from the professions. Some came hoping to establish commercial houses, but most of them, especially during the extensive emigration of the early years, expected to dig for gold. . . . [T]hey came confident that the new life would be better than the old."[40] Unlike German or Irish immigrants, however, the French were not as rapidly assimilated into the Anglo-American population in California. According to one contemporary, the French were described as adhering "much to their own habits and society, and seem stoutly determined against acquiring the English tongue."[41]

The largest segment of California's new population in 1870, however, were native-born Americans: immigrants drawn from various regions of the country and persons born in the state. Unfortunately, Wright has little to say about the class background of this population. She does document, however, their regional origins and notes that they comprised 76 percent of the total state population in 1850, 61 percent in 1860, and 63 percent in 1870. According to Wright, most of the native-born, American immigrants in 1850

> were from the northern section of the United States, although the West was a close competitor. Over the next two decades the West was by far the largest contributor to California's population, while the percentage of residents born in the South grew successively smaller. Thus in 1860 the Southerners in the state numbered less than 29,000, whereas there were more than 74,000 persons from the northern section of the country. In 1870 the difference between the contribution of these two sections was even more marked; not quite 28,000 Southerners were reported in that year, while the number of those born in the North approximated 85,000.[42]

As we will see, the regional origins of the American immigrant population had tremendous implications for the type of society they sought to create in the state. California's Northern and Western immigrants, who carried with them antislavery and "free labor" sentiments, played a key role in the racial conflict that raged during the last half of the nineteenth century. Wright attests to the pivotal role these immigrants played in nineteenth-century California:

> Evidently during this period there was little doubt as to what sort of community California was destined to be. It was fairly obvious that Anglo-American civilization would predominate, and that, although there might be a number of Chinese or Mexicans or French in the region, the social and political and economic institutions were as clay in the hands of Americans from the United States. Foreigners who were not readily absorbed by the dominant society formed their own groups, but these did not seriously threaten the Anglo-American ascendancy. The northern Europeans were most readily assimilated, and in those instances in which a diversity of cultural heritages led to conflict, the newcomers usually accepted the customs of their adopted land.[43]

By 1900, California's population had skyrocketed to over one and a half million persons. Although the population was now largely European-American, other cultural minorities comprised a sizable segment of the state's total population. For example, the indigenous Mexican population remained relatively small, numbering 10,000 to 15,000 between 1848 and 1900. California Indians experienced a dramatic decline in their total population during this period. Most sources agree that the estimated 100,000 Indians in 1850 dropped precipitously to about 20,000 in 1870 and reached its nadir of approximately 17,500 in 1900.[44]

The number of other nonwhite immigrants in the state also fluctuated greatly during this period. The Chinese immigrant population, for instance, rose to its highest point in California at over 75,000 in 1880. It then declined slightly in 1890 (72,000) before settling at approximately 45,000 at the turn of the century. Japanese immigrants did not comprise a significant part of California's population until 1890 when just over 1,000 were enumerated on the state census. By 1900, the number of Japanese immigrants in the state rose sharply to over 10,000.[45] Blacks, on the other hand, remained a very small segment of the state's total population throughout the nineteenth century. Black immigrants numbered around 5,000 in 1860 and 1870 and climbed to just over 6,000 in 1880. The black population in the state would increase steadily after that date to over 11,000 at the turn of the century.[46]

THE CAPITALIST TRANSFORMATION OF MEXICAN CALIFORNIA

The diverse population that settled in California during the last half of the nineteenth century quickly entered into a competitive struggle over social resources and group position within the state's new class structure. Unequal access to the mobility opportunities engendered by capitalist development unleashed bitter conflict among the various ethnic populations: Native American, European, Mexican, African, Chinese, and Japanese. Western historian Patricia Limerick has succinctly assessed this racialized contention and social transformation in *Legacy of Conquest*: "Race relations [in the American Southwest] parallel the distribution of property, the application of labor and capital to make the property productive, and the allocation of profit. Western history has been an ongoing competition for legitimacy—the right to claim for oneself and sometimes for one's group the status of legitimate beneficiary of Western resources. This intersection of ethnic diversity with property allocation unifies Western history."[47]

The principal difference between the precapitalist economy of the Mexican period (1821–1848) and that which European Americans introduced after the United States-Mexico War was the predominance of a formal free-wage labor system: the coercive and paternalistic class relations of the Mexican period were quickly replaced by the instrumental and impersonal class relations of capitalism and its apparatus of legal enforcement. It was a period in California's history when once prominent Californios such as Mariano Vallejo, José del Carmen Lugo, Pio and Andres Pico, Pablo and Antonio De la Guerra, Manuel Dominguez, Ygnacio Del Valles, and Juan Bandini were displaced by nineteenth-century European American entrepreneurs and developers with names like Wells, Giannini, Huntington, Stanford, Hollister, Spreckles, Scott, Bard, Teague, and Oxnard.

Beginning quickly in the northern section of the state and expanding more slowly into southern California, white speculators and developers gained private control of land and created the basis for industrial development and the capitalist transformation of the state. Mining became the first major industry organized along a new system of production. The introduction of quartz and hydraulic mining techniques in the early 1850s rapidly transformed gold mining from an individual, labor-intensive undertaking to a corporate, capital-intensive venture. By 1860, there were over 7,000 firms engaged in gold-mining operations employing approximately 46,000 persons. For nearly two decades mining was both the single largest source of employment and the largest capital investment sector in the state.[48]

The mining industry's growth quickly led to the establishment of numerous small-scale businesses in the state. Gold-rush immigration resulted in the opening of merchandise stores, hotels, bank, restaurants, and saloons. Most of these concerns were family-run ventures that European Americans quickly monopolized. These small business ventures typically employed only a few wage workers. By 1860 there were also approximately 1,450 manufacturing firms in the state with a capital investment of $11 million. These firms were comprised of both small and large-scale employers who in 1860 paid wages estimated at $5.5 million.[49]

Mining's importance for the state's new economy waned after 1859. The annual gold yield reached $50 million in that year. Thereafter, the annual yield declined steadily until it stabilized at approximately $17 million in 1879, where it remained for the next thirty years. The decline in the importance of mining was accompanied by the rapid growth of extensive grain production and the further development of urban manufacturing. The most important new industry in this period, however, was the railroad industry, which dominated the expanding economy in the late 1860s and

1870s. It rapidly became the first "big business" in California and emerged as the largest employer of wage laborers for nearly twenty years.[50]

Agriculture succeeded the railroads as the center of economic development during the closing decades of the nineteenth century. The emergence of capitalist agriculture presupposed the resolution of a number of technological, climatic, and social obstacles. Adaptation to unfamiliar farm land, improvement in the state's transportation network and irrigation methods, and technological innovations such as the refrigerator car occurred during the late 1870s and 1880s. Expansion of the domestic market, the organization of growers' associations, and the avoidance of exorbitant commission fees extracted by "middlemen" helped agriculture become an extremely profitable venture.[51] In the process, California's farm labor force expanded dramatically, from 19,000 workers in 1870 to over 119,000 by 1900.[52]

Capitalist agriculture rapidly passed through two phases of development in California. The 1870s and 1880s were characterized by extensive farming on small-scale operations by a large class of self-employed or petit-bourgeois farmers. Grains such as wheat, barley, and corn became the main crops, and although the state market burgeoned, the principal markets for these products were the East Coast and England. By 1872 approximately two-thirds of the agricultural goods grown in California were destined for markets outside the state.[53] During the late 1880s and the 1890s, extensive farming gave way to intensive, as large-scale captitalist farmers became dominant in the industry. Under their leadership production shifted from grains to fruits and vegetables. In 1879 intensive crops accounted for only 3.9 percent of the value of all crops produced in California, but by 1899 their value had risen to 43.3 percent. During these twenty years, the annual value of intensive crops rose from $2.8 million to $52 million.[54]

By the turn of the century, California's new economy had passed through its formative stages. Most vestiges of the precapitalist, rancho economy of the Mexican period, which relied on Indian peonage and slavery, had vanished irretrievably by the end of the nineteenth century. By the early 1900s, California became a quintessential capitalist society based on free wage labor. [The vision of the early white settlers who immigrated to the state had been realized in less than fifty years, as capitalist replaced Californio and incoming European-American settlers replaced Indian villagers and Mexican small landholders and *pobladores* (town dwellers).

Three major groups composed the new class structure at the turn of the century. At the top were the European-American landholders and businessmen whose names are so prominent in California's history.] These entrepreneurial capitalists employed large numbers of wage workers and invested substantial sums of money in developing the mining, manufacturing, railroad, and agricultural industries. The next class comprised small-scale independent businessmen and small farmers who owned or leased land. This "middle class" was predominantly self-employed and occasionally hired a few workers. At the bottom of the new class hierarchy was the rapidly expanding laboring class. As the availability of farm land and opportunities for self-employment diminished, thousands of incoming white and minority immigrants were drawn into the capitalist labor market and became part of California's multiracial working class.

Access to the best skilled and semiskilled jobs, however, was largely reserved for the white population. European Americans rapidly monopolized the most coveted employment opportunities and gained virtual control of the middle and upper tiers of the new class structure.[55] It soon became apparent that avenues for social mobility and other fruits of unbridled capitalist development were to be reserved jealously for a single group: the white "producing class." Its members alone were seen as the "value carriers" of the new social order; only they would enjoy the enormous opportunities that rapid economic development made possible. Nonwhite populations, on the other hand, continued to be viewed as unwelcome obstacles to the economic mobility of European Americans.

"MANIFEST DESTINY" AND THE "FREE LABOR IDEOLOGY"

The rapid transformation of Mexican California into a white masculinist preserve for European-American men found popular support in racializing ideologies that rationalized the superordinate position of the white population. In the century after the American Revolution, as Reginald Horsman has argued, two powerful ideas reflecting this sentiment were ingrained in the Anglo-American psyche and drawn upon during the United States' westward expansion: Anglo-Americans believed "that the peoples of large parts of the world were incapable of creating efficient, democratic, and prosperous governments; and that American and world economic growth, the triumph of Western Christian civilization, and a stable world order could be achieved by American commercial penetration of supposedly backward areas."[56] European Americans saw it as their providential mission to settle the entire North American continent with a homogeneous white population, bringing with them their superior political institutions, notions of progress and democracy, and economic system. The United

States' incursion into sovereign Mexican territory in the war of 1846–48 was only the most explicit political expression of this notion of "manifest destiny."

In symbolic terms, the notion of manifest destiny implied the domination of civilization over nature, Christianity over heathenism, progress over backwardness, and, most importantly, of white Americans over the Mexican and Indian populations that stood in their path. United States' dominion over what was then Mexican territory laid the basis for rapidly developing the region along new socio-cultural, political, and economic lines.

Another important rationalization of white supremacy over the indigenous Mexican and Indian inhabitants of the new American Southwest grew out of the "free labor" ideology of the antebellum Republican Party.[57] Historian Eric Foner demonstrates that, during the mid-nineteenth century, white Americans of all classes—the European-American working class, petite bourgeoisie, and self-employed propertied class—accepted the social world this ideology promoted: an expanding capitalist society based on free labor, individualism, market relations, and private property.

The sanctity of free labor had a long history preceding the widespread immigration of European Americans into California during the mid-nineteenth century. Since the colonial period, white Americans had sought to establish a society unencumbered by the precapitalist feudal ties that had shackled peasants in Europe. They sought to build a society in which free labor was the source of all value as the embodiment of bourgeois ideals. An outgrowth of the Protestant ethic, this commitment found expression in numerous political doctrines, for example, the "producer ethic" of the Jacksonian period. Andrew Jackson viewed the "producing class" in society as all occupations involved directly in the honest production of goods, such as farmer, planter, skilled and unskilled laborer, mechanic, and even small businessmen and independent craftsmen. These productive workers—whether agricultural or industrial, self-employed or wage laborers—constituted the honorable and creative elements of society and included persons traditionally considered part of the middle class or petite bourgeoisie. They were viewed as having interests antagonistic to those of the wealthy, propertied class—slaveholders, big businessmen, industrialists, bankers, monopolists, and speculators—who were excluded from the "producing class" as profiting directly from the honest labor of others.[58]

A significantly different and more influential version of the free labor ideology, however, was formulated by the Radical Republicans in the decades preceding the Civil War. According to Foner, the Republican

Party's antislavery rhetoric represented much more than mere opposition to slavery. It also signified "an affirmation of the superiority of the social system of the North—a dynamic, expanding capitalist society whose achievements and destiny were almost wholly the result of the dignity and opportunities which it offered the laboring man."[59] Unlike the Jacksonian version, Republican ideology did not seek radically to subvert the United States' class structure. On the contrary, free labor thought was entirely consistent with the underlying tenets of competitive capitalism. Its advocates believed that free labor created all value but that "the interest of labor and capital were identical, because equality of opportunity in American society generated a social mobility which insured that today's laborer would be tomorrow's capitalist."[60] This vision deeply influenced the social, political, and above all, economic relations eventually forged between the majority and the minority populations in California.

THE "BANEFUL INFLUENCE" OF NONWHITE LABOR IN CALIFORNIA

The associations made by European Americans between nonwhite labor and unfree labor systems had tremendous import for the racial conflict that erupted in California after 1848. White Americans sought to create a society in which the presence of any labor system that threatened free white labor would be eradicated. Given the historical context in which the free labor ideology flourished, slavery was what initially preoccupied the white population immigrating to California. The introduction of black slavery, or the widespread use of other unfree laborers, threatened the creation of the capitalist society European Americans envisioned in the area. As a result, the status of blacks in California loomed as a question of more than symbolic significance to free labor advocates.

Because of widespread migration of persons from the Northeastern seaboard of the United States into California after 1846, sentiment on this issue crystallized around the entrance of California into the union as a free state. This commitment to a system of free labor was captured vividly in editorials of the first English-language newspapers published in California. On March 15, 1848, nearly two years before statehood was granted, editors of *The Californian* unequivocally argued against the territory becoming a haven for unfree labor:

> We desire only a White population in California; even the Indians among us, as far as we have seen, are more a nuisance than a benefit to the country, we would like to get rid of them. . . . [W]e dearly love the Union, but declare our

positive preference for an independent condition of California to the establish- [
ment of any degree of slavery, or even the importation of free blacks.⁶¹ [

Expression of this free labor sentiment was also echoed by the editor of
The California Star a few days later:

> We have both the power and the will to maintain California independent of
> Mexico, but we believe that though slavery could not be generally introduced,
> that its recognition could blast the prospects of the country. It would make it
> disreputable for the White man to labor for his bread, and it would thus drive
> off to other homes the only class of emigrants California wishes to see: the sober
> and industrious middle class of society.⁶²

White male opposition to the introduction of slavery in California was
widespread in these early years. Purveyors of the free labor ideology expressed the belief that slavery inevitably led to decadence, laziness, and
economic degeneration in the free white population. Their opposition to
slavery was not based on lofty abolitionist convictions, but rather on the
belief that slavery would inevitably degrade free white labor and undermine white workers' entitlement to economic development in the state.
Slavery would effectively discourage white migration and settlement by
stunting economic development, crippling society, and making white social
mobility virtually impossible. The presence of an exploitable slave labor
force would invariably drive enterprising white men from occupations
leading up the economic ladder and thus undermine their dreams of
becoming rising capitalists. It would lead to an economy headed by slaveholders and others who would profit from the exploitation of an unfree
labor force. Thus, from the free labor perspective the recreation of a
Southern society in California ran counter to the interests of the majority
of the state's earliest white immigrants.

These free labor sentiments were salient during the California State
Constitutional Convention debates on slavery and the immigration of free
Negroes. Convened in the fall of 1849, forty-eight delegates from districts
throughout California met at Monterey to draft the state constitution.
Submission of this document to Congress, after its ratification by the
people in the territory, was a necessary prerequisite to the admission of
California into the Union. The question of slavery was first raised on
September 10, 1849. While outlining articles for the proposed "Declaration
of Rights" of the new constitution, delegate W. M. Shannon of Sacramento, a lawyer originally from New York, moved to insert a section
specifically prohibiting slavery in the territory. Shannon's motion stipulated: "Neither slavery nor involuntary servitude, unless for the punish-

ment of crimes, shall ever be tolerated in this state." No objections were raised to Mr. Shannon's motion and the proposed section was adopted unanimously without debate.[63]

This opposition to the introduction of slavery in California was not a sign of an enlightened social attitude toward black people. It reflected a common belief that the presence of blacks or any nonwhite group associated with unfree labor posed a real or symbolic threat to the status of free white labor in the state. This was vividly demonstrated during the convention debates on whether or not to prohibit free Negro immigration into the state. Although the convention did not approve such an exclusion (largely from political considerations affecting California's rapid admission into the Union by Congress), debates on the matter illustrated the pervasiveness of free labor sentiment and the delegates' general antipathy toward the presence of nonwhites.

Perhaps the most explicit proponent of the free labor ideology was Delegate O. M. Wozencraft from San Joaquin. Wozencraft, formerly from Ohio and Louisiana, staunchly supported the prohibition of free Negro immigration:

If there is just reason why slavery should not exist in this land, there is just reason why that part of the family of man, who are so well adapted for servitude, should be excluded from amongst us. It would appear that the all-wise Creator had created the negro to serve the White race. We see evidence of this wherever they are brought in contact; we see the instinctive feeling of the negro is obedience to the White man, and, in all instances, he obeys him, and is ruled by him. If you wish that all mankind should be free, do not bring the two extremes in the scale of organization together; do not bring the lowest in contact with the highest, for be assured the one will rule and the other must serve.[64]

Wozencraft's position reflected a belief, shared with other Northern men, that blacks, whether free or slave, would unfairly compete with free white labor. Such competition already existed in the North and would surely flourish in California if blacks were allowed to emigrate freely. During debates on the prohibition of free Negro immigration, Wozencraft implored delegates to consider the evils that such immigration would inflict on the white workingman.

I wish to cast my vote against the admission of blacks into this country, in order that I may thereby protect the citizens of California in one of their most inestimable rights—the right to labor.... I wish, so far as my influence extends to make labor honorable; the laboring man is the *nobleman* in the truest acception of the word; and I would make him worthy of his high prerogative, and not degrade him by placing him upon a level with the lowest in the scale of the family of man. . . .

I desire to protect the people of California against all monopolies—to encourage labor and protect the laboring class. Can this be done by admitting the negro race? Surely not; for if they are permitted to come, they will do so—nay they will be brought here. Yes, Mr President, the capitalists will fill the land with these living laboring machines, with all their attendant evils. Their labor will go to enrich the few, and impoverish the many; it will drive the poor and honest laborer from the field, by degrading him to the level of the negro. . . .

The golden era is before us in all its glittering splendor; here civilization may attain its highest altitude . . . and the Caucasian may attain his highest state of perfectibility. . . . We must throw aside all the weights and clogs that have fettered society elsewhere. We must inculcate moral and industrial habits; we must exclude the low, vicious, and depraved.[65]

No better statement of the virtue of free labor, and the Northern Republican critique of the South, can be found in the debates that shaped the foundation of California's entrance into the union as a free state. But Wozencraft was not alone in using free labor arguments to oppose free Negro immigration. During the debates on this issue, Delegate H. A. Tefft, a Northerner representing San Luis Obispo, also argued against the "introduction into this country of negroes, peons of Mexico, or any class of that kind." Tefft claimed that such immigration would "degrade white labor" and make it impossible for Anglos "to compete with the bands of negroes who would be set to work under the direction of capitalists." San Francisco delegate W. M. Steuart, a lawyer formerly of Maryland, similarly opposed black immigration because of what he termed "its baneful influence." In his estimation it was "utterly impossible to unite free and slave labor" in one state. Even those who favored free Negro immigration often did so as a matter of expedience. Delegate Shannon, for example, favored free Negro immigration because "the necessities of the territory require them." Shannon believed that free Negroes were "required in every department of domestic life (in California)"; it did not matter to him if "they were baboons, or any other class of creatures."[66]

Shannon's belief in the degrading influence of "other class[es] of creatures" was shared by other convention delegates and by the white population in California more generally. These sentiments later provided the lens through which other racialized ethnic groups also were viewed as posing a threat to the white population immigrating into the new state at mid-century.

NEUTRALIZING THE PRESENCE OF
BLACKS IN ANGLO CALIFORNIA

Given these sentiments, it is not surprising that the same 1849 California State Constitutional Convention initially relegated blacks to second-class legal status. The first draft of the "Right to Suffrage" emphatically stated that only "white male citizens of the United States" would be entitled to vote.[67] No serious thought was given to enfranchising blacks who settled in California. To the contrary, one motion adopted by the Convention stated that "Africans, and descendants of Africans" were to be exempted from the right to suffrage.[68] Despite the later deletion of this explicit reference to blacks, there was no ambiguity in the minds of white Californians: blacks were nonwhite and, therefore, not eligible for the citizenship rights reserved exclusively for white men.

The subordinate political status of blacks in California carried tremendous implications for their "life chances" in the state. They were denied the rights to vote, to hold public office, to testify in court against white persons, to serve on juries, to attend public schools, or to homestead public land.[69] It was not until 1870, with the ratification of the Fourteenth Amendment, that blacks were granted the same legal rights as white citizens in California. Furthermore, it was not until 1880 that the segregated school system created for black (and Indian) children in the state was formally abolished.[70]

Widespread white antipathy toward blacks was also expressed in numerous attempts made to prohibit their immigration. An interdiction against free Negro immigration into California was formally approved at the 1849 Constitutional Convention. This section was deleted later when it became apparent to delegates that it might delay or even threaten congressional approval of statehood. Rather than hazard that possibility, the convention decided to leave the issue to the first state legislature.[71]

Subsequently, bills prohibiting free Negro immigration were introduced unsuccessfully in the California State Legislature in 1850, 1851, 1855, and 1857. A final attempt to bar blacks from entry into the state was made by Assemblyman J. B. Warfield in 1858.[72] The near passage of the Warfield Bill resulted in the large-scale exodus of many blacks in California to Victoria, British Columbia. An estimated four hundred to eight hundred blacks left for Canada in the spring of 1858, over 15 percent of their total population in the state. Life for the more than four thousand who remained was marred by continued discrimination and white hostility.[73]

Despite opposition to black emigration, hundreds of Northern free

Negroes came to California as independent miners during the Gold Rush. Others were brought into the state as slaves from the American South. According to historian Rudolph Lapp, "Coastal city free blacks, many from Massachusetts as well as New York, Pennsylvania and Maryland, came largely by the Panama route and some around the Horn. From the upper Mississippi valley states many earned their way as employees of the overland companies. From the slave states hundreds of blacks came with their gold-hunting masters, some with the promise of freedom in California if rewards of mining were great enough. By 1850 there were 962 Afro-Americans in California, mostly in the Mother Lode counties, probably half of them slaves."[74] The vast majority of these black immigrants settled in the six mining districts of northern California: Sacramento, Mariposa, El Dorado, Calaveras, Yuba, and Tuolumne.[75]

Despite the constitutional prohibition against slavery of 1849, from 1848 until 1856 slaveholders were granted continued legal possession of black slaves brought into the state. Slaves often were "hired out" to other parties by masters who found it more profitable to do so when returns from mining were scant. Through this arrangement a slaveholder received from $150 to $300 a month for the use of "rented" slaves who toiled as cooks, waiters, domestic servants, or mine workers for their temporary employers.[76] Their presence quickly raised the ire of a white population overwhelmingly committed to free labor sentiments; they did not want California to succumb to the "damning influence" of unfree black labor.[77] Nevertheless, the power of slaveowners was extended with the passage of the state's 1852 Fugitive Slave Law. Provisions of this bill affirmed the right of a slaveholder to obtain a warrant for the arrest and return of fugitive slaves or simply to seize such a slave himself. The 1852 law further permitted former slaves to satisfy outstanding claims their owners may have had to their labor by working off their debts in California. This provision notwithstanding, there are numerous instances during this period when fugitive slaves were openly sold in the state. In other cases, blacks brought into California under an agreement with their owners to work for their freedom were often forcibly seized after satisfying their obligations and reenslaved by masters.[78]

With the decline in mining opportunities in the mid–1850s, most free blacks left the mining region for urban centers such as San Francisco and Sacramento. By 1860, the largest black populations in the state resided in San Francisco (1,176 persons), followed by Sacramento (468 residents). Blacks in these northern California cities, as well as in towns like Stockton and Marysville, were racially segregated into separate communities or residential enclaves.[79] Blacks in San Francisco during the 1850s also were prohibited from using the city's three public libraries and relegated to sections reserved for "colored" people in other public facilities.[80]

Blacks in San Francisco, Sacramento, Stockton, and Marysville overwhelmingly were employed as unskilled day laborers. A few others toiled as bootblacks, porters, waiters, bell-ringers, laundrymen, cooks, stewards, and barbers, although a handful successfully established modest businesses such as furniture stores, clothing stores, boardinghouses, and saloons, and a very few even became doctors or engineers.[81]

The overrepresentation of blacks at the bottom of the new occupational structure largely reflected their subordinate legal-political status in the state. Smoldering competition and resentment between black immigrants and the large Irish population in California played a pivotal role in this subordination. According to Lapp, "Rivalry between the Afro-American and Irish working-class communities had arisen out of job competition at the lowest rung of the labor ladder in the early decades of the nineteenth century. This hostility in New England and New York then spread to the West Coast. The attitude of blacks toward unions is easy to understand since the emergence of unionism was so often associated with black exclusion from jobs."[82] Thus, the earlier competition between white and black labor elsewhere was partially reenacted in California during the 1860s and 1870s.

Despite the racial hostility they endured in the state, the black population in California grew steadily in the closing decades of the nineteenth century. Although blacks accounted for only one percent of the total state population at the time, the number of blacks in the state reached over 11,000 by 1890. Whereas during the gold rush period blacks were heavily concentrated in northern California, this new population settled largely in the southern part of the state. "The near doubling of the state's black population by 1890 is explained by the real estate and land boom in southern California, which produced a black population gain in Los Angeles County from 188 in 1880 to 1,817 in 1890, a tenfold increase. In the same general area similar sharp increases took place. In 1880 the Fresno County black population was 40 and by 1890 it was 457. Even Kern County went from 4 to 130 in that ten-year period."[83]

The successful completion of the transcontinental railroad also contributed to this population increase as many black railroad workers (especially sleeping car porters and "redcaps") settled or retired with their families in southern California. Also important in redirecting their settlement was the continued hostility by white trade unionists toward black labor in the northern part of the state. According to Lapp, "In the turn-of-the-century decades unionism made significant strides in San Francisco but was deterred in Los Angeles by powerful antiunion sentiment among employers led by Harrison Gray Otis, owner of the *Los Angeles Times*. . . . Blacks planning migration to California were often urged to avoid San Francisco and to go instead to Los Angeles, which was considered a 'good town for colored folks.' "[84]

The intense animosity toward blacks in San Francisco even caused many blacks to move across the bay to Alameda County and contribute to the significant increase of Oakland's black population. By 1900, there were over one thousand blacks in that community, an increase that occurred during a decade when the northern California black population either remained steady or numerically declined.[85]

Although antiblack sentiment was widespread, white Californians were never drawn into the same frenzied competition with blacks as they were with the thousands of Chinese immigrants who also immigrated into the state during the gold rush period. California's black population was never allowed to effectively compete with European-American immigrants in the state and, consequently, were never perceived as the same formidable threat that other racialized groups posed for white men. Repeated attempts to thwart black immigration, to deny blacks important human and civil rights, and to relegate them to the bottom of the new class structure militated against the eruption of widespread economic competition between black and white Californians.

The same, however, can not be said in the case of the indigenous Mexican and Native American populations. Their ruthless subordination was essential to the successful introduction of the new Anglo-American society in California. Its realization required the immediate dispossession of Mexicans and Indians from land needed for the development of the new political economy and class structure. Control of Mexican *ranchero* estates and Indian tribal lands was a fundamental prerequisite for this economic transformation. The Mexican ranchero class became the first formidable barrier to the realization of Anglo class aspiration in the state.

The next chapter chronicles the process by which Anglos struggled to undermine the superordinate position held by the rancheros during the Mexican period and successfully reorganize the underlying basis of production in the newly acquired territory.

PART ONE

Racial Ambiguities, Class Realities, and "Half Civilized" Mexicans in Anglo California

CHAPTER TWO

"The True Significance of the Word 'White' "

Given their free-labor sentiments and their profound belief in "Manifest Destiny," European Americans migrating into the new American Southwest could have been expected to despise completely the Mexican population they encountered in California. Although these prejudices undeniably affected their initial impressions of Mexican society, white immigrants actually assigned Mexicans an intermediate location in the new society they imposed in the region. Indeed, compared to the treatment ultimately afforded other racialized groups in California, the experience of Mexicans in the nineteenth century was without parallel.

For complex reasons, Mexicans occupied a qualitatively different "group position" from that of Indians, blacks, and Asian immigrants in the new racial hierarchy. Nineteenth-century relations between Mexicans and Anglos in California were powerfully determined by the class divisions within the two populations, divisions that led to divergent historical experiences for the Mexican working class and the ranchero elite. The introduction of a new, Anglo-dominated class structure led to bitter contention between powerful Mexican rancheros and European-American capitalists for control of the most arable land in the state. The strife that developed between the old Mexican ruling class and Anglo capitalists initially overshadowed the ethnic conflict that occurred at other class levels.

Unlike black, Chinese, and Japanese immigrants, for example, Mexican workers were not initially perceived as a formidable obstacle to white working-class aspirations, primarily because of such demographic factors as the relatively small size of the Mexican population, the low percentage of adult male laborers, and their concentration away from urban economic sectors employing white laborers. By 1900, however, these class lines had been blurred, if not obliterated, as the ranchero class irretrievably surrendered its earlier privileged position. These changes, plus widespread Mexican immigration during the 1910s and 1920s, set the stage for a twentieth-century experience qualitatively different from that of the nineteenth.

Another unique feature of Anglo-Mexican relations at the time was the ability of upper-class Mexicans to resist European-American encroachment and protect themselves from the intense racial animosity and virulent discrimination that Anglos inflicted on other groups during the nineteenth century. This was principally the result of important political rights Mexicans gained at the onset of American control of California, rights based on the guarantees extended by treaty and by the U.S. Constitution and largely denied Indians, blacks, and Chinese and Japanese immigrants. For example, the Treaty of Guadalupe Hidalgo enabled Mexicans to obtain U.S. citizenship rights in 1849. Citizenship carried with it suffrage, which empowered Mexican elites to politically challenge Anglo control in areas of Mexican concentration. The citizenship rights Mexicans came to enjoy, though often circumvented, nevertheless protected them from the more onerous discriminatory legislation enacted against other racialized groups.

The claimed European descent of the Mexican ranchero elite, the so-called *gente de razon* (literally, "people of reason"), also facilitated the assimilation of segments of the upper class into European American society. The cultural distance between these Mexicans and European Americans proved less extreme than that between white immigrants and the unambiguously "nonwhite" populations. One important measure of the perceived assimilability of upper-class Mexicans was clearly evident in the degree of intermarriage between old Californio families and prominent Anglo immigrants. In sharp contrast, the Mexican working class was generally viewed like other racialized groups. Their degraded class status, combined with their inability to claim "pure" European ancestry, contributed to Anglo perceptions that they were unassimilable and certainly unworthy of intermarrying. Unprotected by the status European ancestry afforded the *gente de razon*, they were much more vulnerable to having their political and legal rights violated with impunity.

This chapter examines the major features of the unique nineteenth-century Mexican experience in Anglo California, focusing specifically on the divergent fates of the Californio elite and the Mexican working class.

The class divisions of the Mexican period (1821–46) laid the basis for these class-specific experiences. Remnants of the old Mexican class structure persisted after 1848, coexisting briefly with the emerging capitalist sector as part of the new social formation. These old and new class divisions structurally placed the Mexican ranchero and working classes into divergent types of conflict with European Americans at different class levels. By way of background to this history, let us first turn to a brief assessment of the Mexican society that structured group relations among Californios prior to U.S. annexation of the territory.

THE CLASS STRUCTURE OF MEXICAN SOCIETY IN ALTA CALIFORNIA

Class and race relations in Mexican California were fundamentally structured by the land-tenure system introduced after Mexican independence from Spain in 1821, when the Mexican National Congress enacted a liberal policy of granting large tracts of unoccupied land to individuals and encouraged further territorial settlement through the Colonization Act of 1824. This act provided the legislative basis for the rapid development and expansion of private land grants. More than seven hundred such grants, each of up to eleven square leagues (approximately 49,000 acres), were issued by the Mexican government between 1833 and the American occupation in 1846.[1]

The land-tenure system led to the rapid crystallization of a class structure dominated by individual families monopolizing ownership of immense expanses of land known as *ranchos*. According to historian Leonard Pitt, in 1849 "an estimated two hundred Californio families owned 14 million acres of land in parcels of from 1 to 11 leagues (nearly 4,500 acres to the league)."[2] He also notes that a mere forty-six of these Californios dominated political as well as economic affairs in California during the Mexican period.[3] The de la Guerra family of Santa Barbara, for example, amassed fourteen separate land grants comprising over 488,000 acres. The Carrillo family of Los Angeles acquired over seventeen claims encompassing approximately 320,000 acres of land. Other Mexican grantees with multiple holdings included the Pico family with 700,000 acres, the Vallejo family with 294,000 acres, and the Yorba family with 218,000 acres.[4] These ranchos were semifeudal institutions similar to those found throughout New Spain and Mexico in the eighteenth and early nineteenth centuries.[5]

Below the ranchero class was an intermediate stratum composed largely of rancheros and farmers with smaller holdings, skilled rancho laborers and foremen, artisans in the Mexican pueblos, and a few territorial and local officials. This stratum consisted largely of mestizos (mixed racial ancestry) and was typically viewed as a "middle class" by travelers visiting California during the Mexican period. This nonranchero population, particularly the déclassé Mexican laborers in the pueblos, were contemptuously viewed as "greasers" by Anglos visiting Mexican California. For example, the historian Hubert Howe Bancroft described this stratum as "the baser stock of Hispano-Californians . . . [the] greasers."[6]

At the bottom of the Mexican class structure of Alta California were the subjugated Indian population and a few mestizos. Most of the Indians who worked the ranchos had formerly worked on the Spanish missions and were bound to their new employers in three principal ways. Some secularized Indians "voluntarily" attached themselves. These Indians were given a subsistence existence by landholders in exchange for their labor. A second group was bound through debt peonage. Before indebted Indians could leave an area they were required to prove they were free of outstanding debts to rancheros. Finally, when sufficient labor could not be secured by noncoercive means, rancheros resorted to kidnapping and directly enslaving Indians. An open traffic in Indian women and children for use as ranchero servants also flourished during the Mexican period. Although Mexican law formally abolished slavery in 1829, it proved impossible to enforce in the isolated northern frontier of Alta California. Moreover, this type of enslavement flourished and was typically rationalized by rancheros as necessary retaliation for Indian vandalism and thievery.[7]

Indians laboring on large ranchos generally were not remunerated through wages. The few laborers who received cash payment were usually skilled workers such as *vaqueros* (cowboys) or *mayordomos* (foremen). Vaqueros, for example, periodically received modest wages of twelve to fifteen dollars per month plus room and board, while mayordomos were paid approximately sixteen dollars per month. Unskilled Indian laborers occasionally received from three to ten dollars per month or were given grain or colored glass beads. As a rule, however, the Indian population on these large estates received only food, clothing, and shelter.[8]

The Indians attached to any individual rancho ranged from a mere handful to several hundred. The Yorba family of Los Angeles utilized twenty-six Indian servants to maintain their twenty-five room house. An additional one hundred laborers tended to the livestock on their 114,480-acre rancho. In northern California, Mariano Vallejo relied on an es-

[handwritten: Indians worded on Ranches]

timated six hundred Indian vaqueros and laborers to work his 66,000-acre Rancho Petaluma and 90,000-acre Rancho Suscol. John Sutter, one of the few Anglos given a land grant in Alta California by the Mexican government, held an estimated six to eight hundred Indian workers on his 160,000-acre rancho estate near Sacramento.[9]

Indian workers performed numerous tasks on these rancho estates. Many tended the livestock that provided the basis of the hide and tallow trade with foreign merchants who frequented the California coast by the late 1820s. These laborers also assisted in the annual *matanza* or slaughter that occurred in late summer. Others helped prepare the hides and tallow. A number of skilled workers labored as tanners, shoemakers, harnessmakers, carpenters, wine makers, plasterers, and dairymen, and a few also cultivated the small garden plots that provided fruit, vegetables, and grains for use on the ranchos.[10]

While Indian men generally toiled in field activities, a gendered division of labor assigned Indian women to serve principally as personal servants in the ranchero's home, where they ground corn, washed clothes, and spun and sewed cloth. A visitor to Mariano Vallejo's home in 1844 found Indian women performing these essential tasks. Doña Vallejo told her guest that:

> Each of my children, boys and girls has a servant who has no other duty than to care for him or her. I have two for my own personal service. Four or five grind corn for tortillas. . . . About six or seven are set apart for service in the kitchen. Five or six are continually occupied in washing the clothes in the house; and finally, nearly a dozen are charged to attend to the sewing and spinning; for you must know that, as a rule they are not much inclined to learn many things. . . . All these servants whom we have in the house are very much attached. They are not accustomed to ask for money, nor do they have any fixed wages. We give them all they need. When they are sick we care for them as though they belonged to the family. When their children are born, we act as godfathers and godmothers, and we take charge of the education of their children. When they want to go some great distance to see their relatives, we give them animals and guards for the journey. In a word, we treat the servants as friends rather than servants.[11]

Doña Vallejo's paternalism reflected a sentiment common among the ranchero class. This paternalism was similar to that which bound black slaves to white masters in the antebellum South.[12] It was not merely an expression of the rancheros' benevolence, as it helped morally justify their exploitative use of Indian labor. Indians were viewed as stepchildren of the ranchero class, as dependents bound by a series of mutual duties and responsibilities as well as binding *compadrazgo* (godparent) relationships.

The ranchero class tended to the daily needs of their Indian wards while Indians, in exchange, performed the labor needed to ensure the smooth operation of the rancho estate.

The paternalism that characterized ranchero-Indian relations was vividly captured in an interview with Salvador Vallejo in 1844. This prominent ranchero told one of Hubert Bancroft's associates collecting data for his *History of California* that:

> Many of the rich men of the country had twenty to sixty Indian servants whom they dressed and fed. . . . Our friendly Indians tilled our soil, pastured our cattle, sheared our sheep, cut our lumber, built our houses, paddled our boats, made tile for our homes, ground our grain, slaughtered our cattle, dressed our hides for market, and made our burnt bricks; while the Indian women made excellent servants, took good care of our children, made every one of our meals. . . . Those people we considered as members of our families. We loved them and they loved us; our intercourse was always pleasant.[13]

As many as four thousand Indians in California were pressed into service on these immense Mexican ranchos. In northern California many Pomo, Wappo, Patwin, Maidu, Plains Miwok, and Central Valley Yukots fell victim to this exploitative relationship. In the southern part of the state the Luiseno, Cupeno, and Serrano Indians suffered a similar fate while the Gabrieleno and Chumash Indians experienced the final stages of extinction.[14]

Many American visitors to California during the Mexican period openly attested to the exploitative treatment of these Indians. During his visit to the Vallejo estate at Sonoma in 1842, an American named George Simpson described the conditions of Vallejo's Indians in these terms:

> During the day we visited a village of General Vallejo's Indians, about 300 in number, who were the most miserable of the race that I ever saw, excepting always the slaves of the savages of the northwest coast. . . . They are badly clothed, badly lodged, and badly fed. . . . Though not so recognized by law, yet they are thralls in all but the name, borne to the earth by the toils of civilization superadded to the privations of savage life, they vegetate rather than live. . . . This picture which is a correct likeness not only of General Vallejo's Indians, but of all of the civilized (i.e. former mission Indians) aborigines of California. . . . [15]

A similar observation was offered by James Clyman, a trapper traveling through California in 1846 who described the handling of Indians held by John Sutter at his fort near Sacramento. "The Capt. [Sutter] keeps 600 to 800 Indians in a complete state of Slavery and I had the mortification of seeing them dine I may give a short description 10 to 15 Troughs 3 to 4 feet long ware brought out of the cook room and seated in the Boiling sun all the labourers grate and small ran to the trough like so many pigs and feed themselves with their hands as long as the troughs contained even a moisture."[16]

Despite their maltreatment, Indian laborers were crucial to the survival of Alta California. Their value was recognized by the Mexican and those few Anglo rancheros who dominated the regional economy. John Marsh, for example, extensively used Indian laborers on the rancho he acquired in 1837. The Indians, probably Bay Miwoks and Northern Valley Yokuts, manufactured the adobe bricks for his Rancho Los Medanos, ploughed and cultivated his fields, and set traps and collected furs. In return, Marsh fed them, clothed them, and attended to their medical needs. In a letter on the "Aborigines of California," Marsh candidly acknowledged that "throughout all California the Indians are the principal laborers; without them the business of the country could hardly be carried on."[17]

RACIALIZED IMAGES OF MEXICAN "GREASERS" AND THE "GENTE DE RAZON"

White immigrants venturing into California after 1848 were initially repulsed by the existence of an economic system based on servile labor. The Mexican cattle-raising economy did not require the direct cultivation of the territory's fertile land and thus was not a fully "civilized" society in European-American eyes. This seemingly "unproductive" use of such a precious resource kindled intense white antipathy toward the Californios and led to their portrayal as idle squanderers unworthy of the good fortune they possessed. In the view of one Anglo traveler visiting California in the early 1840s, "Nature doing everything, man doing nothing" was the essence of the Mexican economy.[18]

The sectional sentiments of northern white immigrants, particularly their antipathy to slave societies, clearly colored their attitudes toward the society and people they encountered in California. At first glance, white immigrants perceived little difference between the ranchero elite and the southern plantation slaveholders. Nothing offended Anglo speculators and developers more than contending with yet another "aristocratic" class whose continued prosperity impeded their own aspirations. Holding the Protestant Ethic and white Anglo-Saxon values as the criteria for evaluating Mexicans, Anglos believed that California's undeveloped state was simply the product of the Californios' cultural backwardness and lack of self-discipline. To overtake this class was no crime, for Anglo Americans were required to follow God's injunction to make the land fruitful, prosper economically, and attain their divinely appointed calling.

Given these sentiments, it is not surprising that European Americans believed Mexicans were an "indolent" people, whose backwardness reflected their having poor personal habits and collective deficiencies such as laziness or a penchant for extravagances. These disparaging evaluations were "class metaphors" fueled by class-specific perceptions of Californio society, especially of the ranchero elite.[19] The Anglo image of Mexicans as "lazy" was more than just a disparaging ethnic stereotype; the class-specific nature of these perceptions has not been fully appreciated.[20]

European-American evaluations of Mexicans were generally sensitive to the class-based differences among this population. Consider for the moment Richard Henry Dana's well-known travel account, *Two Years Before the Mast*. Therein he paints the Mexican rancheros as "thriftless, proud, and extravagant, and very much given to gaming."[21] While traveling in California in 1835, Dana disapprovingly lamented the absence of industry in the territory and made special note of the idleness of the Mexican elite. "The Californians," he wrote, "are idle, thriftless people, and can not make anything for themselves. The country abounds in grapes, yet they buy bad wine made in Boston and brought round by us, at an immense price. . . . Their hides too, which they value at two dollars in money, they give for something which costs seventy-five cents in Boston; and buy shoes (as like as not, made of their own hides, which have been carried twice round Cape Horn) at three and four dollars."[22] Dana was not the only European American who judged the Mexican ranchero class harshly for their lack of economic initiative and industriousness. Even Alfred Robinson, an Anglo merchant who married into the prominent de la Guerra family of Santa Barbara, shared this unflattering assessment. In his autobiographical *Life in California*, Robinson condescendingly described the Californio elite as "generally indolent, and addicted to many vices, caring little for the welfare of their children, who like themselves, grow up unworthy members of society."[23]

Some historians of the period have mistakenly attributed the rancheros' "indolence" and "thriftless" behavior to a dysfunctional value system stressing "an orientation toward the present." The Californios' penchant for making "pleasure the chief end of work" and reveling in the conspicuous consumption of food and drink at their innumerable *bailes* (dances), fandangos, and elaborate feasts ostensibly reflected this value system.[24]

There is little doubt that the Californios were fond of cultural-religious events that highlighted their superior status. The extravagance of Californio *bailes*, for instance, often involved the ostentatious display of precious silk and lace *rebozos* (shawls) and gowns, as well as elegant men's suits embossed with gold and silver. These displays, however, merely reaffirmed the status distinctions that were so central to semifeudal Mexican society. The Californios, after all, had only recently come into their wealth and status. Most rancheros had humble origins as Spanish soldiers or officials before being granted immense expanses of land. Conspicuously displaying their newly acquired wealth and social standing was merely a way of reaffirming the privileges this class enjoyed during the Mexican period. Unfortunately, the Californio's opulence and extravagant squandering (such as the merriment involving gold dust-filled *cascarones*, or hollowed-out eggs) held little value to most European Americans. Given the traditional Protestant value system which stressed hard work and frugality, it is not difficult to see why white newcomers witnessing these festivities would characterize them as flagrant examples of the spendthrift ways of an anachronistic gentry.

Most European-American travelers found little of value in assessing Mexican society. While they generally denigrated Mexican society in its entirety, some observers perceptively noted the class differences that internally stratified it. The readily apparent privileged station of the ranchero elite was described by Richard Henry Dana in 1840:

> There are but a few of these families in California; being mostly those in official stations, or who, on the expiration of their offices, have settled here upon property which they have acquired. . . . These form the aristocracy; intermarrying, and keeping up an exclusive system in every respect. They can be told by their complexions, dress, manner, and also by their speech; for, calling themselves Castilians, they are very ambitious of speaking the pure Castilian language, which is spoken in a somewhat corrupted dialect by the lower classes.[25]

Dana was particularly struck by the symmetry with which class divisions overlay differences in ancestry and skin color. He particularly noted that the Californio elite appeared to be composed largely of fair-complexioned individuals who proudly proclaimed their European ancestry. According to Dana, "From this upper class, they go down by regular shades, growing more and more dark and muddy, until you come to the pure Indian. . . . Generally speaking, each person's caste is decided by the quality of blood, which is itself, too plain to be concealed, at first sight. Yet the least drops of Spanish blood, if it be only a quatroon or octoon, is sufficient

to raise them from the rank of slaves, and entitle them to a suit of clothes
. . . and to call themselves Espanoles, and to hold property, if they can get
any."[26]

The claimed or real European ancestry of the Californio elite provided
an important basis upon which they differentiated themselves from the
more déclassé indigenous mestizo and Indian population in California.
European-American travelers, on the other hand, often viewed their purported European ancestry, and implicit claims to civility, with open deri-
sion. The Californios were neither truly "white" in the northern European
or Anglo-Saxon sense of the term, nor were they simply "uncivilized"
Indians. Terms such as "semicivilized" or "semibarbarian" best capture
the collective judgment European Americans made of Mexicans prior to
the U.S.–Mexico war. Although some Californios could in fact trace their
ancestry back to Spain, this did not lessen the contempt to which they were
initially subjected by European Americans. Still, although they were not
fully accepted as equals, their ostensible European ancestry and formidable
class position did insure that white immigrants could not dismiss them as
easily as the mixed or pure-blood indigenous populations.

THE PRIVILEGED POLITICAL STATUS OF MEXICANS
IN ANGLO CALIFORNIA

One important measure of the unique social position that Mexicans came
to occupy in the new Anglo society after annexation is clearly evident in
their legal-political status in California. It highlights their intermediate
"group position" as well as the modicum of deference and respect that
European Americans grudgingly accorded the "half civilized" Californios.
As noted previously, the Treaty of Guadalupe Hidalgo of 1848 guaranteed
"all the rights of citizens of the United States" to those Mexicans who
chose to remain in what is now the American Southwest one year after the
treaty's ratification. This international agreement virtually tied the hands
of white convention delegates when the issue of suffrage for Mexicans was
raised. The California State Constitutional Convention of 1849 formally
granted Mexicans the same citizenship rights as "free white persons" in
California.

The Mexicans' distinctive mixed-blood ancestry apparently played a
pivotal role in the extension of U.S. citizenship to them. Unlike other
minority groups in California, some Mexicans were arguably part of the
"white race." White immigrants generally made racial distinctions among

the Mexican population on the basis of the clearly perceptible class and somatic differences. Those whose class position and ostensible European ancestry placed them at the top of the hierarchy during the Mexican period, the "gente de razon," were reluctantly viewed as "white" by Anglo Americans. The dark complexioned, mestizo population (the "greasers" or *gente sin razon*—literally, "people without reason"), on the other hand, were viewed as "nonwhite" and not significantly different from pure-blood, Indian "savages" in the state.

Consequently, the designation of the Mexican population as "white" was not simply a matter of skin color or actual European ancestry but of the way European Americans came to define what they meant by race. Delegate Botts, for example, openly admitted that he "had no objection to color, except in so far as it indicated the inferior races of mankind." He was amenable to the extension of the suffrage clause to worthy Mexicans so long as it was denied "the African and Indian races."[27] During debates on suffrage for Mexicans one Anglo delegate, W. S. Sherwood of Sacramento, also openly stated that he did not wish to "debar the Spanish" from voting. Despite the fact that this population was "darker than the Anglo-Saxon race," he considered them "white men" and therefore entitled to vote.

Similarly, Delegate W. M. Gwin, who earlier had opposed the granting of the franchise to the "pure uncivilized Indians," ultimately (if reluctantly) conceded that "the descendants of Indians should not be excluded from the franchise." Delegate Kimball Dimmick of San Jose echoed this sentiment, commenting that "the mixed race, descended from the Indians and Spanish," should be permitted "to enjoy the right of suffrage as liberally as any American citizen." He had no objection to those who had a small amount of "Indian blood in their veins." In support of his view he noted that even "some of the most honorable and distinguished families in Virginia are descended from the Indian race."[28]

Don Pablo de la Guerra, a prominent ranchero and delegate from Santa Barbara, similarly argued that the term "white" was a reference to European ancestry and social standing, not merely to skin color. During the suffrage debate de la Guerra stated that "it should be perfectly understood in the first place, what is the true significance of the word 'White.' Many citizens of California have received from nature a very dark skin; nevertheless, there are among them men who have heretofore been allowed to vote, and not only that, but to fill the highest public offices. It would be very unjust to deprive them of the privilege of citizens merely because nature had not made them White."[29] Ironically, de la Guerra further noted that if the Anglo delegates used the word "white" only as a term intended to "exclude the African race" from the franchise, then he was in agreement with this usage.[30] The final approved version of the new article of the constitution formally disenfranchised both Indians and blacks in California. Those entitled to vote were "White male citizens of the United States and every White male citizen of Mexico, who shall have elected to become a citizen of the United States."[31]

This decision enabled the Californio elite to utilize their status as free white citizens to effectively challenge and resist the more onerous measures European Americans used to subordinate other racialized groups in California. Under ranchero leadership, Mexicans retained an important degree of political influence after statehood and even held political control of important communities in California for a number of years. For example, in his social history of Mexicans in southern California, Albert Camarillo found that the Californio elite retained political control of Santa Barbara as late as 1876. Despite being a numerical minority in that city after 1870, they remained a politically influential group until the early 1880s. Mexicans also enjoyed a modest degree of political success in Los Angeles and San Salvador, where the Mexican electorate constituted an important voting bloc well into the late 1860s.[32] The experience in San Diego, however, provided a sharp contrast. There, the Californio elite never contested the political domination of Anglo Americans; many had even supported the United States during the U.S.-Mexico War.[33]

From their stronghold in southern California, the Mexican population also helped elect a number of statewide representatives between 1850 and 1876. Prominent rancheros such as Pablo de la Guerra and José Maria Covarrubias (Santa Barbara), Andres Pico and Ygnacio del Valle (Los Angeles), Mariano Vallejo (Sonoma), and M. Pacheco (San Luis Obispo) served as senators and state assemblymen during the first legislative sessions. A Californio even occupied the governor's chair in 1875 when Romualdo Pacheco of Santa Barbara, who had been elected lieutenant governor in 1871, served out the final year of Newton Booth's term.[34] Governor Booth had vacated the position after his election to the U.S. Senate. By the time Pacheco assumed the governor's chair, however, Mexicans no longer had major statewide political influence. According to historian Leonard Pitt, the election of 1851 was a "turning point" for the Californios. Despite the election of Mexicans to a number of legislative offices after that year, the tremendous influx of Anglo voters into the state rendered the Mexicans' political influence marginal.[35]

The principal beneficiaries of the rights accorded Mexicans were the ranchero elite who remained politically influential in the state. They were primarily among those nominated and elected to public office during the period. Although technically entitled to these same rights, members of the Mexican working class were never viewed by Anglos as political equals of the old ranchero elite. Despite being eligible for citizenship rights, the Mexican working class was not afforded any better treatment than other racialized groups in the state. Some racially discriminatory legislation, in fact, was specifically enacted against this segment of the Mexican population during the period. One such law was the 1855 Vagrancy Act targeting "idle" Mexicans in the state. Popularly known as the "Greaser Act," this bill sanctioned the arrest and imprisonment of individuals guilty of vagrancy or levied fines against them, which they were forced to pay either in cash or through temporary labor service.[36]

Given perceptible class differences among Mexicans and their ambiguous racial status in the eyes of some European Americans, it is not surprising that their legal rights were not always respected. This is particularly true in the case of the working class. They were often denied their legal rights by being categorized as Indians. One notable instance reflects the ease with which anyone with a dark complexion could be so treated. Manuel Dominguez, who served as an elected delegate to the California State Constitutional Convention of 1849 and as a member of the Los Angeles County Board of Supervisors, traveled to northern California in April 1857 to enter testimony in a San Francisco courtroom. Before Dominguez could testify, however, the Anglo lawyer for the plaintiff objected to his taking the witness stand. The lawyer argued that Dominguez was an Indian and therefore ineligible to enter testimony. The judge upheld the objection and dismissed Dominguez.[37] Although Mexicans were legally accorded the same rights as free white persons, actual extension of these privileges to all segments of this population was quite another matter.

EUROPEAN-AMERICAN AMBIVALENCE
TOWARD MEXICAN ASSIMILATION

The class-specific treatment of Mexicans in the polity also had its parallel in European-American ambivalence about the assimilation of Mexicans into Anglo culture. Class-based status differences among Mexicans directly shaped views about their suitability for the new Anglo society. Nowhere was this perception more apparent than in attitudes toward intermarriage.

Unlike blacks, Indians, or Asian immigrants, Mexicans were the only ethnic population in California during the nineteenth century that Anglos deemed worthy to formally marry. The various antimiscegenation statutes that prohibited intermarriages between white Americans and other racialized groups were not enacted against Mexicans. This social tolerance toward Anglo/Mexican amalgamation was, nonetheless, rigidly circumscribed along predictable class lines. Only the daughters of the California elite were viewed as appropriate partners for European Americans, especially for white men of means. Occurring with less frequency were marriages between Californio men and middle-class Anglo women. Even more uncommon, and subject to greater social sanctions, were unions between Anglo men and women and lower-class Mexicans.[38]

Generally speaking, freely entered marital unions by men and women from both dominant and subordinate status groups can be taken as a measure of a host society's openness to amalgamation. The existence of de jure or de facto discrimination against such intermarriage (codified in antimiscegenation laws) clearly reflects a society's desire to maintain formal racial or ethnic boundaries and reinforce status distinctions.[39]

Historians continue to investigate the frequency of these Anglo-Mexican intermarriages. Richard Griswold del Castillo estimates that between 1850 and 1880 these endogamous marriages ranged from 12.2 percent (1850) to 8.7 percent (1880) of Mexican marriages in Los Angeles.[40] Unfortunately, Griswold del Castillo does not indicate if these marriages were predominantly between white men and upper-class Mexican women. In another study, historian Ronald Woolsey estimates that approximately 35 percent of Mexican marriages in Los Angeles between 1860 and 1870 were with Anglos.[41] Like Griswold del Castillo, Woolsey also does not indicate if these intermarriages were predominantly between Anglo men and Mexican women. (Methodological differences and use of different archival sources [manuscript census schedules or marriage certificates] account for the wide disparity in these figures.)

Given their privileged status during the Mexican period, it is not surprising that the Californio elite occasionally arranged marriages between their daughters and wealthy Anglos in an attempt to forestall their complete loss of influence. These Anglos had the financial resources and business acumen the new political economy required and which the rancheros sorely lacked. Indeed, Anglo sons-in-law provided some defense against the most egregious injustices that some European Americans inflicted upon rancheros. Negotiations with unscrupulous lawyers, merchants, and others who preyed on the ignorance of the Californios was but one important advantage that such intermarriages provided.

For their part, European Americans also were not oblivious to the advantages of marrying into wealthy ranchero families. With eligible white women being scarce in the territory, fair-complexioned, upper-class Mexican women were among the most valued marriage partners available. While white men derived a degree of status from marrying the Californio's daughters, more important were the tangible political and economic opportunities that such unions afforded. These marriages provided strategic access to land held by the old elite. Thousands of acres passed into the hands of Anglo men as part of the inheritances some Californio women brought to marriage. Moreover, Anglo sons-in-law were often the first ones given access to land sold by rancheros desperately needing cash.

Numerous marriages occurred during the nineteenth century between wealthy European-American settlers and upper-class Mexican women. No matter how sanctimoniously shrouded these marriages were in religious and romantic terms, these Californio women were arguably being "trafficked" between the old and the emerging ruling classes.[42] Such women may be viewed as the tribute offered by the pragmatic old ruling class to the new. They often became the exotic prize that many Anglo men arrogantly believed were part of the spoils of conquest.

Before statehood, well-known Anglo settlers such as Alfred Robinson, John R. Cooper, Abel Stearns, William G. Dana, and Thomas Larkin married daughters of the Mexican ruling elite. These "Mexicanized Anglos" played a key role in ameliorating animosity toward Mexicans in the postwar transition period. Although these Anglos were few in number, they were socially well-respected and often important figures in the economic affairs of the territory. Historian Leonard Pitt estimates that "two dozen of them owned one-third of southern California's developed land in estates as large as 60,000 acres."[43]

After statehood, prominent Californians such as Stephen Foster, Robert S. Baker, James Winston, and Henry V. Linsey also married into the Californio class. Important Californio families such as the Yorbas, Sepulvedas, Bandinis, Picos, and Dominguezes celebrated the marriage of their daughters to Anglo immigrants. According to Pitt, these marriages between the old Mexican ruling elite and prominent Anglos "made the Yankee conquest smoother than it might otherwise have been."[44]

Less common, because they violated white men's exclusive access to white American women, were marriages between the sons of elite Cali-

fornios and European-American women. Juan Sepulveda's son and Ra-
mualdo Pacheco, the former governor of the state, were among the few
Mexican men who successfully transgressed this norm and married middle
class Anglo women. So too did Platon Vallejo, son of Mariano Vallejo of
Sonoma, who married a young white woman he met while attending
medical school in Syracuse, New York.[45]

Many of the sons and daughters of the ranchero elite who married
Anglos were described by contemporary observers as being of "Caucasian
origin." If this observation is correct, it would seem to indicate that
intermarriage was selective and favored the more fair-complexioned members of elite families. There is little evidence that many marriages occurred
between Yankee men and mestizo women. But one such union did occur
between George Carson and Victoria Dominguez, daughter of the dark-
complexioned Manuel Dominguez of Los Angeles. Carson married Doña
Dominguez in 1857 and moved into his father-in-law's rancho in 1864 in
order to manage the elderly man's business affairs. After his death in 1882,
Don Manuel Dominguez's dwindling 24,000-acre estate was divided
among his six daughters and their spouses.[46]

THE CLASS AND GENDERED REPRESENTATIONS
OF MEXICANS IN ANGLO CALIFORNIA

This symbolic trafficking in upper class Californio women was accompanied by the emergence of a dichotomous image of Mexican women reflecting the salience of class lines among this population. One popular representation veiled her in positive terms: chaste, beautiful, and charming. Nearly
all nineteenth-century accounts by Anglo settlers and visitors in California
represented the rancheros' wives and daughters in these terms. For example, Alfred Robinson wrote in *Life in California* that "there are few places
in the world, where in proportion to the number of inhabitants, can be
found more chastity, industrious habits, and correct deportment, than
among the women of this place."[47] Similarly, in *Two Years before the
Mast*, Richard Henry Dana noted, with some surprise, the degree of chastity observed by these women. Although Dana questioned the virtue of
some of these women, he believed them to possess "a good deal of
beauty."[48]

Given their high estimations of themselves, white men generally believed that Mexican women welcomed their advances. This arrogant
sentiment was clearly reflected in a popular wartime folk song of the
period:

> Already the senoritas
> Speak English with finesse.
> "Kiss me!" say the Yankees,
> The girls all answer "Yes!"[49]

This white male attitude toward Mexican women was also expressed in a poem published in Boston in June 1846. Aptly entitled "They Wait for Us," it reflected the dominant racial stereotypes of Mexicans at the time— men being lazy and women being available. The poem's contribution to these popular representations lay in fusing an explicitly sexual theme to the Yankee's masculinist thrust into Mexico at midcentury:

> The Spanish maid, with eye of fire,
> At balmy evening turns her lyre
> And looking to the Eastern sky,
> Awaits our Yankee chivalry
> Whose purer blood and valiant arms,
> Are fit to clasp her budding charms.

> The man, her mate, is sunk in sloth—
> To love, his senseless heart is loth:
> The pipe and glass and tinkling lute,
> A sofa, and a dish of fruit;
> A nap, some dozen times a day;
> Sombre and sad, and never gay.[50]

A less poetic expression of European-American sexual bravado was baldly conveyed by a veteran Anglo miner in a letter to the *Stockton Times* on April 6, 1850. In the course of characterizing the animosity toward Mexicans born of wartime experiences, he stated flatly that most Anglos believed that "Mexicans have no business in this country. . . . The men were made to be shot at, and the women were made for *our* purposes."[51] Indeed, white men in California believed that their superior status entitled them to all of the bounty available in the new state. Mexican women, it appears, were often seen as mere spoils of war awaiting the amorous embrace of the white man's "valiant arms."

Unlike the elite Californio's daughters, however, lower-class Mexican women were rarely viewed and represented in positive terms. In fact, they were derisively portrayed in Anglo travel literature as sexually promiscuous women of ill-repute. This class-specific, dichotomous image of Mexican women in the Anglo mind simultaneously devalued lower-class Mexican women, who were deemed unworthy of marrying upstanding white men, while elevating the status of the elite women, who were openly courted. Although all Mexican women were viewed as available to white men, only the more fair-complexioned Californio women were loftily viewed as pure and chaste, an image they shared with middle-class European-American women. The unique status of elite Mexican women in Anglo society was a product of their privileged class position; it did not have a counterpart among other racialized women in California during the period.

These European-American perceptions of class-based differences among Mexican women also had a corollary in their representations of Mexican men. Lower-class Mexican men generally were seen as libidinally uncontrolled and sexually threatening. The Anglo mind conjured an image of them as "rapacious" and "hot-blooded" creatures who wantonly lusted after innocent white women. The inferior class position and mestizo ancestry of these men contributed directly to these negative sexual representations, which were clearly the product of the way class and racial stratification lines in California shaped popular perceptions.[52]

AT THE BORDERS OF HEATHENISM AND SAVAGERY

Religion was another factor contributing to potential assimilability. Despite widespread European-American hostility to Mexican society, Mexicans were much closer to white Americans in their religious beliefs and cultural sensibilities than were other racialized groups. Mexicans were, after all, a Christian people whose conversion under colonization by Spain had elevated them from the "heathenism" rampant in the territory. White immigrants were not, for instance, as alarmed by Mexican religious practices as they were by the more repulsive practices of California Indians or the Chinese "pagan idolators" who arrived after statehood. Although anti-Catholic sentiment among European Americans existed in the state, Mexican Catholics were at least a God-fearing people and therefore seen as more closely approximating European-American notions of civility.

During the postwar period many Californios were pleasantly surprised by the Bear Flaggers' deference to Church interests, protection of mission property, and respect of Catholic marriage traditions. Many Yankee Catholics who settled in racially segregated communities, such as Los Angeles, even attended ethnically mixed services. Historian Leonard Pitt has argued that tolerant Anglo attitudes toward Mexican Catholics in southern California helped mollify tensions during the turbulent period after U.S. annexation. He suggests that the strongest drive for religious conformity came from within the Catholic Church, which became the "prime mover for acculturation." Rather than confronting Protestant hostility from Yankee "blond-haired heretics," Mexican Catholics were coaxed into adopting American Catholic traditions and forms of worship.

Elements of the Catholic Church's "Americanization" program included changes in church personnel (typically Americans replacing Mexicans), diocesan reorganization, and the introduction of Baltimorean Church institutions such as bilingual parochial schools, orphanages, hospitals, and newspaper publications. These institutions functioned as acculturating mechanisms that drew religious boundaries and ethnic bonds among Mexicans and other Catholic populations in the area. As a consequence, Catholicism provided a stabilizing basis for Mexicans' ethnic identity and facilitated their structural integration into Anglo society in a period of intense political and economic upheaval.[53]

The presence of prominent "Mexicanized gringos" was also critical to the early stages of this selective assimilation. Individuals such as Abel Stearns, John R. Cooper, William G. Dana (Richard Henry Dana, Jr.'s uncle), and John Warner converted to Catholicism during the Mexican period, married into Californio elite families, and became economically influential. Their close relationship with the Californio elite led them to serve as mediators against the most virulent Yankee anti-Catholic sentiment. Others such as John Downey, Benjamin Hayes, and Stephen Foster generously helped finance the Church's reform efforts and also promoted ethnic harmony on religious terms.[54]

European-American attitudes toward Mexicans at the time were also shaped by other cultural considerations such as language. Unlike the completely alien tongues spoken by Asian immigrants or the California Indians, which were discordant to Anglos' ears, Mexican Spanish was at least a European romance language, which they had greater facility in comprehending. This shared linguistic tradition appears to have facilitated communication between both groups as Spanish-speaking Anglos and English-speaking Mexicans helped bridge cultural barriers before and after statehood. Because of the concessions agreed to after the U.S.-Mexico war, Anglos also acquiesced to the publication of all state laws in Spanish. In fact, such bilingual publication was specifically mandated in the 1848 California State Constitution. Although Anglos would not honor this commitment in later years, this proviso had no parallel in the experiences of other "nonwhite" groups or even foreign-born, white immigrants in the state.[55] The Mexicans' status as a conquered people who were nominally European, and at least partially "civilized" in the white man's eyes, positioned them to exact state-sanctioned concessions from Anglo society that other groups found impossible to secure.

Given European-American cultural assessments of Mexicans, it is not surprising that some Californios successfully made important inroads into the new social order. This partial integration largely befell the second generation, particularly the sons of the old ranchero elite. They gained access to Anglo public institutions and secured occupational niches that rapidly accelerated their structural assimilation. Throughout the period from 1850 to 1900, for instance, a small segment of the Mexican upper class attended state-financed public schools. Some of the sons of the ranchero elite even attended the University of California after its founding in 1869. Many later became professionals securely ensconced in privileged spheres of the class structure that were closed to other racialized groups.[56]

Romualdo Pacheco's colorful career best typifies the upper reaches of these second-generation Californio success stories. Born the son of a Santa Barbara army officer in 1831, the young Pacheco was educated in the Sandwich Islands and served as a supercargo on various trading vessels plying the California coast during the Mexican period. After U.S. annexation, Romualdo managed his family rancho in San Luis Obispo and parlayed his privileged status into a state assembly seat in 1862. He later served in the state senate and was successfully elected state treasurer in 1863. He relinquished this post four years later to his kinsman, Ramon Pacheco, and eventually became the Republican party's candidate for lieutenant governor in 1871. In February 1875 he served out the remaining year of Governor Booth's term when the state leader took an interim seat in the U.S. Senate. Upon leaving state office, Romualdo Pacheco also served as a northern California congressman before devoting his time to personal business ventures in San Francisco.

Another native-born Californio politico of this generation was Reginaldo del Valle, son of Ygnacio del Valle of Los Angeles. The young del Valle succeeded Antonio Coronel as "boss" of the "Spanish vote" in this region during the closing decades of the nineteenth century. Born in 1854, del Valle studied law and passed the bar in 1877. He was elected state assemblyman in 1880 (serving as president of the Assembly in 1881) and state senator in 1882. He later served as chairman of the 1888 state Democratic convention as well as on numerous government boards and civic communities before his death in 1938.[57]

Not every member of the second generation led such illustrious lives as these two. Many followed alternative paths that generally led them into the middle or lower end of the new class structure. Some took their turn at becoming agriculturalists in the emerging agribusiness industry, a fate most of their ranchero fathers were unprepared to successfully embark upon. Sons and grandsons of elite families such as the Ramirez, Pico, Castro, Coronel, and Olivera clans became farmers on small parcels of subdivided rancho land. Blas Lugo, for example, turned to farming a small family plot after he unsuccessfully tried his hand at law. A few of the young gentry found financial success in real estate. Relying on the sale of family land, the Sepulveda brothers from Los Angeles owned four thousand acres of San Pedro's best land, worth an estimated five hundred to two thousand dollars an acre in the 1880s. They parlayed their business success into a life in the finest residential area of San Pedro and membership in Anglo-dominated fraternal orders.[58]

Others made inroads into the sheep industry, which provided a transitional link between the old ranching economy of the Mexican period and the new agriculture industry of the American period. Given the limited opportunities within Anglo society, a few apparently gravitated to activities that labelled them as "thieves" or "bandits." Renowned local families such as the Castros, Sepulvedas, Vallejos, Amadors, and Lugos contributed to a breed of native-born "badmen" accused—often falsely—of preying upon European Americans and committing countless crimes such as highway robbery, stage holdups, and cattle rustling.[59]

The modest structural integration of segments of the ranchero class, however, was not paralleled by the Mexican working class. Sons and daughters of this class had little opportunity to attend public schools, to prosper economically, or to marry and mingle socially with upstanding European Americans. White Americans were acutely aware of the class differences within the Mexican population and viewed the largely mestizo working class as unassimilable. Their ambivalence toward the social integration of all Mexicans was clearly the product of the way class lines internally stratified this population both before and after U.S. annexation of California. These class-specific lines, and the gender-specific experiences therein, carried profound implications for the degree to which Mexicans would grudgingly be accorded an intermediate "group position" in the new Anglo society.

DISPLACING THE ANACHRONISTIC
MEXICAN RANCHERO CLASS

Although U.S. annexation of California may have led to the modest cultural assimilation of some Mexicans, this social accommodation did not also lead to their wholesale structural integration into the new capitalist economy. While some sons of the ranchero elite may have achieved some success in securing a niche in the new economy, the same cannot be said for the class as a whole. Statehood brought with it the rapid displacement of the Mexican ranchero class, as privately held land was transferred on a massive scale from Mexican hands into that of Anglo immigrants between 1848 and 1880.

This process was set in motion by the enactment of the Federal Land Law of 1851 which empowered a Board of Land Commissioners to verify Spanish and Mexican land grants in California. The right to retain ownership to these granted lands was initially conferred to Mexican citizens in the Southwest under provisions in the Treaty of Guadalupe Hidalgo. The Land Commission convened between January 1852 and March 1855, adjudicating 813 claims brought before them. The vast majority of these claims, over three-fourths, were adjudicated in favor of the claimants. Sixteen of the eighteen cases the government presented against Mexican rancheros before the U.S. Supreme Court were decided in favor of the original claimants. These cases involved the sixteen most strategically situated properties in Marin, Alameda, and Sonoma counties such as Mariano Vallejo's 44,380-acre Rancho Petaluma and Domingo Peralta's Rancho San Ramon.[60]

Nevertheless, in the process of defending their claims, the Californios' position was greatly weakened. While most Mexican claimants ultimately retained possession of their granted estates, they did so only after years of expensive litigation before the Land Commission, District Court of Appeals, California State Supreme Court, and, on occasion, the U.S. Supreme Court. The average time devoted to settling these disputed claims was seventeen years.[61]

This protracted and often bewildering litigation exacted a tremendous toll on the ranchero class. Legal fees to white lawyers were exorbitant, often forcing the Californios to sell portions of their holdings in order to meet their financial obligations. On some occasions, rancheros conveniently transferred ownership of portions of their newly certified titles to the lawyers who had represented them in U.S. courts. Overall, these white lawyers were unscrupulous in their dealings with the ranchero class, often scandalously defrauding them. One early European-American pioneer who befriended many of the Californios in southern California candidly characterized the demise of the ranchero class in the following way:

The Californians were very ignorant of business and this perhaps had been one of the greatest sources of their misfortunes. It has exposed them to the numberless traps that have been laid by designing and unprincipled foreigners to cheat them out of their property. The Land Commission, full of defects as it was, also contributed to defraud them when its object was to protect them in the rightful possession of their lands. Between the poor ignorant native and the lordly Land Commission, in too many cases the medium of communication was the lawyer, often crafty and dishonest, who in securing the approval of a title took half of the land as his fee, or even more when the pretext of appeals could be used to advantage. In countless other ways have their simplicity and ignorance been taken advantage of to the impoverishment of their estates.[62]

Individuals coveting the fourteen million acres of land formerly held by the Californio elite resorted to other questionable tactics to achieve this divestiture. Property transferred hands through outright sales, unlawful "squatting" on Mexican land, bankruptcy proceedings, and in payment for personal indebtedness resulting from extravagant expenditures, gambling, delinquent property taxes, and usurious interest rates to moneylenders and land speculators.[63]

This dispossession had a devastating effect on the old ruling families. According to one historian, of the forty-five "principal men" of the old regime, representing the twenty-five most prominent Californio families, the vast majority "went to their graves embittered. . . . [T]hey were a ruling class militarily conquered, bereft of national sovereignty and a constitutional framework, and alienated from their land, homes, civil rights, and honor. They had retained little else besides their religion and a thin residue of honorary political influence."[64]

From the European-American point of view, the demise of the ranchero elite was simply the product of their inability to adapt to the tempo of the new social order. They perceived this as an inevitability given the old elite's lack of business acumen and spendthrift proclivities; it was the necessary price that "progress" exacted. The Anglo's remorseless assessment of the ranchero's decline is vividly captured in Alfred Robinson's postscript to *Life in California*, where he attributes the Californios' fate to commonly-held sentiments about the role their "indolence" and "passivity" played in their deteriorating status: "The early Californians, having lived a life of indolence without any aspiration beyond the immediate requirement of the day, naturally fell behind their more energetic successors, and became impoverished and gradually dispossessed of their fortunes as they idly stood by, lookers-on upon the bustle and enterprise of the new world

before them, with its go-aheadativeness and push-on keep-moving celeb-
rity."[65] That the Californios' value system reflected the social organization
of the semifeudal society that this gentry class enjoyed throughout New
Spain cannot be denied. These traits were, from a European-American
point of view, "dysfunctional" in the new free-labor economy they introduced in the state.

However self-serving assessments such as Robinson's may now appear,
the actual fate of individual rancheros was a personal tragedy. Although
they were far from innocent victims of Anglo chicanery (their own widespread use of exploited Indian laborers makes such a defense impossible to
advance), their demise had devastating consequences. Ygnacio del Valle
provides us with a mild example of the fate that befell this elite. His
holdings during the Mexican period covered nearly 48,000 acres of land in
the mountains north of San Fernando Mission near present-day Newhall.
By 1861 he retreated to his beloved Rancho Camulos in order to cover
losses, resulting in a decline of his private property to a mere 1,500 acres.
He was forced to mortgage this estate in 1879 to the Newhall family for
$15,776. According to one source, the "gracious and charitable" Newhall
family never pressed the bill, which grew enormously due to the high
interest rate negotiated. Don del Valle went to his grave the following year
without having paid off the debt.[66]

Even more lamentable was the impact on Don Julio Verdugo, who
mortgaged his Rancho San Rafael (comprising present-day Glendale and
part of Burbank) in order to repair the deteriorating estate and meet
outstanding financial obligations. In 1861 he signed a $3,445.37 loan at 3
percent monthly interest (36 percent a year). By 1870 the mortgage had
ballooned into a debt of $58,750. This precipitated a foreclosure and
sheriff's sale at which his lawyers bought the 36,000-acre Rancho San
Rafael and forced the sale of his Rancho La Cañada. Thereupon, Don
Verdugo retreated to neighboring Rancho Los Felix. He eventually subdivided and sold large parcels of this estate in order to settle outstanding
debts and taxes. In 1871 an American court ordered the subdivision of the
6,600-acre Los Felix, ultimately leaving the former ranchero's children
with a meagre inheritance of 200 acres; a pittance in light of the ranchero's
former wealth.[67]

A similar fate befell Don Juan Bandini. Once one of the richest men in
southern California, Bandini gave up ownership of his Rancho Jurupa to
his son-in-law Abel Stearns in August 1859. The former baron died a
broken man three months later.[68]

THE PROLETARIANIZATION AND STRUCTURAL
SUBORDINATION OF THE MEXICAN WORKING CLASS

Unlike the bitter discord between the old and the emerging propertied classes, relatively little conflict flared between the European-American and Mexican working classes during the nineteenth century. The only notable instance of class-specific hostility between Mexicans and Anglos at this level erupted in the mining regions during the Gold Rush. Here Sonoran miners and independent white miners were pitted against each other in direct economic competition.

Approximately thirteen hundred native Californians entered the mining region in the early phase of the Gold Rush. Hostility toward them from "fist-swinging Oregon Yankees" was not moderated by their claim that the Treaty of Guadalupe Hidalgo guaranteed them the same rights to work the mines, and most quickly abandoned the mines.[69] Replacing them were thousands of Mexicans from Sonora, Peruvians, and Chileans. Anti-Mexican sentiment was principally directed at the highly successful Sonoran miners, who were categorically deemed "foreigners" at this time. These Sonorans were, according to one authority, "more visibly mestizo, less consciously Spanish than the Californians," and as a result, "seemed 'primitive' by local standards."[70] The negative image of Mexicans as "foreigners" was further darkened with the taint of unfree-labor systems by the arrival of Mexican *patrons* who brought bands of Indian and mestizo workers into the mining region, typically paying for their upkeep in return for half the gold they mined.

The success of the Sonorans, who were highly skilled miners, evoked the wrath of Anglo miners, who bitterly protested their "unfair competition." White miners typically came as independent, self-employed individuals seeking their fortune in an openly competitive environment. In this context, nothing infuriated them more than to compete with "bondsmen" tied to an "overlord" or *patron*. Anglos made little distinction between Sonoran independent miners and those Mexicans working in the mines as bondsmen for Mexican *patrones* and local rancheros. The success of both, but especially of the latter, was seen as, or at least rationalized as, cheapening and degrading the value of white labor.

The hostile treatment of Mexican nationals and Latin Americans in the mines was partially fueled by the specter of slavery that their presence evoked. According to historian Leonard Pitt, these Latin miners "came into California precisely when the Yankees felt most irritated on this score and could see most clearly the parallels between Negroes and their masters, on the one hand, and the peons and patrons, on the other. Yankee prospectors ejected from the mines with equal vigor any combination of bondsmen and masters. . . . The prospectors put into effect a local code prohibiting the mining operation of all master-servant teams, whatever their relationship."[71]

To compound matters, Anglos' resentment intensified when enterprising Sonorans managed to reap large profits from the sale of thousands of pack mules in the mining regions. This activity had unfortunate consequences when "Sonoran peddlers marched into the mines and sold 10,000 pack mules in three years, thereby depressing the price of mules (from $500 to $150 a head in a matter of weeks) and of freight rates (from $75 to $7 per hundredweight in two months)."[72] The Sonorans' business activities provoked the bitter ire of local Anglo entrepreneurs, who sought the mass expulsion of these business rivals. This competition between white miners and Latin Americans for economic position in the mining region led to the enactment of the Foreign Miners' Tax Law of 1850, a clear example of an attempt at social closure. The statute required a twenty-dollar mining permit from all "foreigners" in the mines. The bitter strife that followed the passage of this legislation led to thousands of Latin Americans fleeing the region and seeking their fortunes elsewhere. In due course, some relocated in bustling urban centers such as San Francisco and Stockton, a few fled to Southern California, while others simply returned en masse to Mexico or other parts of Latin America.[73]

Although anti-Mexican hostility flared throughout California, particularly in the southern section of the state, a unique aspect of the Mexican experience during this period was the relative absence of class-specific conflict between native-born, working-class Mexicans and white workers. This is accounted for by both demographic factors and the early pattern of Mexican working-class employment during the late nineteenth century. The Mexican population was relatively small; as noted above, from 1850 to 1900 the permanent Mexican population hovered around just thirteen thousand. The rapid increase in California's overall population after the Gold Rush quickly rendered Mexicans a minority. This occurred initially in northern California and by the early 1870s in southern California as well.[74]

California's population increased more than sixfold between 1848 and 1850, from approximately 15,000 to nearly 93,000 people. Even as early as 1850 Mexicans comprised only 11 percent of the state's total population.

Between 1860 and 1900 the total number of Californians rose from 380,000 to nearly 1.5 million. By 1900 Mexicans accounted for no more than 1 or 2 percent of the state population.[75] In that year, Mexicans were numerically surpassed by the Chinese and Native American populations and were about as numerous as black and Japanese immigrants. Moreover, the Mexican population in the state was principally concentrated in southern California, where they did not extensively compete with urban white workers. Furthermore, unlike the Chinese and Japanese population at the time, the Mexican population had a fairly equal sex ratio. As a result, fewer Mexican men were directly competing with white laborers, a fact that undoubtedly also mitigated against widespread working-class antagonism.

The slow integration of Mexican workers into the Anglo-controlled labor market also contributed to the surprisingly low level of racial conflict with European-American workers. Unlike racialized immigrant groups such as the Chinese, who were initially recruited as cheap laborers and rapidly integrated into the new economy, Mexican workers were a belated addition to the capitalist labor market. From 1850 to 1880, numerous Mexican workers in southern California, for instance, remained largely tied to occupations in the traditional Mexican economy. Many continued to work on Mexican ranchos in the seasonal rodeos (roundups) and matanzas (slaughters). Others retained employment as harness makers, saddlers, silversmiths, trasquiladores (sheepshearers), and vaqueros.[76] As a consequence, Mexican workers were not fully integrated into this labor market until the late 1870s and 1880s.[77]

The gradual decline of the Mexican pastoral economy during the 1870s and 1880s, however, forced Mexicans into the evolving capitalist labor market. The number of Mexican skilled workers employed on ranchos and in such Mexican pueblos as Los Angeles, Santa Barbara, and San Diego declined appreciably, because of the loss of rancho land to European Americans and its conversion from "unproductive" cattle raising to agriculture. In the pueblos, this shift also contributed to the inability of skilled Mexican craftsmen such as cigar makers, shoemakers, and hatmakers to compete successfully with white merchants selling Eastern manufactured goods.[78] Unskilled Mexican urban workers were also affected negatively. They were propelled into new forms of unskilled employment in the burgeoning urban economy where they were structurally integrated at the bottom end of the emerging labor market.

Mexican entrance into this market also coincided with the belated development of the employment sector in areas where Mexicans were most heavily concentrated. Employment opportunities in the new Anglo labor market did not fully emerge in southern California until the 1880s, two or three decades after it initially took root in the northern California mining and manufacturing industries. By 1880 approximately 85 percent of the male Mexican work force in Santa Barbara and San Diego and 65 percent in San Salvador (near San Bernardino) and Los Angeles labored as unskilled or semiskilled manual workers. They became construction laborers, street graders, pick and shovel workers, and teamsters, and toiled in numerous other menial jobs in the emerging cities of southern California.

At the same time, their limited access to employment opportunities compelled them to take jobs in new industries like agriculture where unskilled labor was in great demand. By the early 1900s, Mexicans had become the principal source of farm labor in the southern California counties of Los Angeles, San Bernardino, Tulare, and Ventura.[79] It was here, in the southern California farm labor market, that the first expressions of Mexican working-class opposition to agribusiness interests initially emerged. Successful unionization and strike activity among Mexicans first took place in the southern California community of Oxnard in 1903. (The issues and events leading to this successful effort are explored in detail in chapter 7.)

In sum, because Mexicans remained tied to the pastoral economy in southern California, a part of the economy most European Americans had no interest in entering, they did not pose a major threat to the white working class. Although some Mexicans and Indians were coercively incorporated into the Mexican rancho system, their unfree labor status did not ignite the same widespread white antipathy that the presence of blacks did. Their small numbers and initial concentration in the most undesirable sectors of the new economy effectively militated against white working-class antagonism.

Widespread labor-market conflict between Mexican laborers and the white working class did not occur until the early decades of the twentieth century. Not until the massive immigration of Mexicans during this period did organized white labor become alarmed by their presence in the state, and mounting white unemployment in the 1920s and 1930s eventually intensified animosity toward these Mexican immigrants. This hostility paralleled that faced by Chinese and Japanese immigrants decades earlier.[80] Moreover, the immigration of thousands of Mexican peasants to California after 1900 also led to a metaphorical "darkening" of the Mexican image in the white man's mind. The earlier moderating influence of the

Europeanized Californios had diminished as this elite was displaced and/or absorbed into Anglo society. The class and ethnic integration of the ranchero class, plus the rapid immigration of a largely mestizo Mexican peasantry, contributed to a major reinscription of the popular image and representation of Mexicans in the state.[81]

CONCLUSION

The Mexican experience in nineteenth-century Anglo California differed significantly from that of other racialized groups in the new state. The central conflict engendered between European Americans and Mexicans was a very class-specific struggle between Mexican rancheros and Anglo capitalists who bitterly contested control of the state's best farm lands. The white male businessmen and developers who ventured into California after 1848 sought their fortunes in a free state. The realization of their economic aspiration required the undermining of the Mexican economy and its reorganization along capitalist lines. White immigrants believed that only an economy structured this way held promise for the rapid development of the territory. Guided by Protestant values and a commitment to white supremacy, these free-labor advocates sought to rapidly undermine the society Mexicans had created in California. The dispossession of the rancheros who dominated the territory was an essential feature of this process.

This conflict notwithstanding, some segments of the Mexican population were structurally integrated into Anglo society more easily than other racialized groups. This was the result of their being deemed a "half civilized" population because of the Europeanized culture they had adapted through their initial colonization by Spain. As a consequence, there was less cultural distance between European Americans and Mexicans (principally the ranchero class) than with other racialized ethnic groups. Mexicans spoke a romance language, held Christian beliefs, and practiced traditions that placed them closer culturally to Anglo Americans than Indians or Asian immigrants.

Moreover, given their at least partial European ancestry, Mexicans were also legally defined as a "white" population in the state. The citizenship rights Mexicans were granted through the Treaty of Guadalupe Hidalgo included the right to vote, hold public office, offer testimony in U.S. courts, freely own and homestead land, and ostensibly enjoy the same privileged political status of European Americans. These rights momentarily empowered Mexicans, principally the ranchero elite, to contest white male domination and avoid the discriminatory legislation that structurally subordinated other racialized groups during this period. This rather anomalous historical circumstance would, of course, become subject to major reconfiguration with the demise of the ranchero class and widespread immigration from Mexico after the turn of the century. Thereafter, labor conflict replaced contention over land as the principal basis of group antagonisms between European Americans and Mexicans in the state.

CHAPTER THREE

"The Ravages of Time and the Intrusion of Modern American Civilization"

The broad, statewide pattern of Mexican-Anglo relations in nineteenth-century California had immediate consequences for both populations in various localities throughout the state. The contention between Mexican rancheros and European-American capitalists for control of land, for example, reached feverish proportions in southern California after 1860. This bitter strife was particularly pronounced in the "cow counties" of Santa Barbara, Los Angeles, and San Diego, the main Mexican population center and a region where the Mexican rancho system had reached its highest stage of development.

California historians such as Albert Camarillo, Leonard Pitt, Mario Garcia, and Richard Griswold del Castillo have skillfully documented the most important features of the region's transformation during the late nineteenth century.[1] One section of southern California that has not as yet been the subject of scholarly research in Chicano history or been brought into comparative analytical focus is Ventura County. This area was originally the township of San Buenaventura in the southeastern section of Santa Barbara county until 1873, when it secured separate county status. It was a region of the state in which a well-entrenched ranchero class was irretrievably undermined by the white supremacist transformation of California.

This chapter sharpens and refocuses our analysis of this transformation by carefully documenting its impact in this southern California county between 1860 and 1900. In so doing, it provides a window into the larger historical process explored in the previous chapter by elucidating the impo-sition of white supremacy in one specific county in the state. The displace-ment of the local ranchero elite and the proletarianization of both its Mexican population and other racialized groups in the area were crucial features of this historical process.

Far from being simply an anachronistic status designation or ideological construct, the racialization of ethnic groups in this locality illustrates the way race became the main organizing principle of group relations at the time. The privileged placement of white men in the upper tiers of the new class structure, and the relegation of racialized ethnic groups to the bot-tom, was part and parcel of the changing nature of racialized class relations in this area.

THE MEXICAN TOWNSHIP OF SAN BUENAVENTURA BEFORE 1860

As elsewhere in Mexican California, the social organization of group relations in what was to become Ventura Country were fundamentally shaped by the land-grant system that drew class lines among its residents. Twenty land grants were issued to individuals in Santa Barbara County's southeastern township of San Buenaventura during the Spanish and Mexi-can periods. These grants accounted for 415,959 acres of land and repre-sented 38.6 percent of the total land area in the county.[2] As in other sections of southern California during the Mexican period, cattle raising dominated the economic life of the region. One of the earliest English-language descriptions of life in the township appeared in 1872 in the county's first newspaper, the *Ventura Signal*.

> [U]p to 1864–5, its American population was but a handful, and stock-raising and trading the only occupations. Systematic farming and its kindred pursuits were not dreamed of, and its immense herds of cattle were chiefly slaughtered for their hides and tallow. Its innumerable bands of horses found a market in the northern part of the state at from twenty dollars per head, and the wool from its flocks of ill-bred sheep sold at ten and twelve cents per pound. . . . [T]he county was deemed a virtual paradise for stockmen and traders.[3]

The 1860 federal census schedules for the township of San Buenaventura document important features of the precapitalist economy of the era. As elsewhere in southern California at the time, the township of San Buena-ventura was stratified between two major classes and a small intermediate stratum. Large landholders, the so-called "gente de razon," represented the dominant class in the township; they dominated the local economy and exerted tremendous social and political influence over local affairs.

The agriculture schedule of the 1860 census captures essential features of the semi-feudal social world overseen by the rancheros. Of the thirty-four individuals enumerated as "farm operators" on this schedule, twenty-two were "pastoralists" owning from one thousand to seventy thousand acres of land. These larger estates were devoted primarily to raising sheep and cattle for the lucrative hide and tallow trade with northeastern merchants. The other class of farm operators in the town were primarily small-scale farmers with less than two hundred acres of land. These agriculturalists grew grains such as wheat, corn, and barley.

Most of the land in the township was used to pasture the livestock owned by the ranchero elite. Less than one percent of the ranch land in the San Buenaventura township was "improved" and given over to cultivation, a clear indication of the absence of "civilization" as European Americans defined it at the time. The relative importance of ranching in relation to small-scale farming in the area was apparent in the disparity in the cash value of each endeavor. In 1860, for example, the total value of agricultural products in the township amounted to less than $20,000. In sharp contrast, the value of livestock enumerated on the agriculture schedule surpassed $450,000.[4]

In 1860, Juan Camarillo, Isabel Yorba, José Arnaz, Juan Sanchez, and the de la Guerra brothers were among the most important rancheros in the area. Camarillo, for example, owned sixteen thousand acres of unimproved land on which he raised four thousand head of cattle and four thousand sheep valued at $100,000. The major landholder at the time, however, was Thomas W. More, an Anglo-American who purchased Rancho Sespe from the Camarillo family prior to 1860. As was often the case with the few Anglo rancheros in the state, More actively participated in the pre-capitalist rancho economy. In 1860 he owned seventy thousand acres of unimproved ranch land on which he grazed ten thousand head of cattle and two thousand sheep valued at $135,000.

An examination of the 1860 population schedule for the township reinforces the picture revealed by the agricultural census schedule for that year. It portrays a pre-capitalist world still dominated by the local Mexican population. For example, twenty-two of the twenty-nine ranchers or pastoralists had Spanish surnames, as did six of the ten farmers reported. The remainder were principally European-American immigrants and a few Indians.

Only a small segment of the township's male population were proprietors or professionals; these included a few Mexican and Anglo merchants, a Mexican hotel keeper, and a Chilean apothecary. Only three individuals engaged in skilled occupations: an Anglo baker and a painter, and a

Mexican cigar maker. No white-collar occupations were reported in the township.

In sharp contrast to this small middle stratum, over 70 percent of the adult male population held unskilled laboring jobs, with approximately one-half of adult men working as servants. As elsewhere in southern California, the majority of the servants in the township were Indians laboring on local ranchos and farms. Sixty-one out of seventy-three "day laborers" were Mexican; the others enumerated in the census were a few local Indians and a handful of European-American immigrants.

William W. Hollister, the prominent agriculturalist and sheep raiser from nearby Santa Barbara, was in a unique position to comment on the state of the local population and ranch economy in the San Buenaventura township. Having arrived in California in 1852 and settled in Santa Barbara County before Ventura County was created, Colonel Hollister was among the few European Americans that settled in this region during the late 1860s, and he exerted tremendous influence over the local economy. Reminiscing about life in California from 1852 to 1860, Hollister described greater Santa Barbara County as "devoted mostly to raising cattle and horses, and the chief exports of the country were hides and tallow;—a very primitive sort of life, and it did not amount to much. Until the plough came to be common in California, the country was devoted to grazing, and this whole life was what we called pastoral. A man wishing to begin agriculture had to commence it in the midst of cattle ranges. We had to fight these cattlemen; it was the civilized against the half civilized."[5]

European-American immigrants like Hollister who settled in the Ventura County area during the 1860s were particularly dismayed by the "half civilized" Mexican population they encountered there. They were as bewildered by the "backward" nature of the rancho economy as they were by the traditional, Catholic culture of the Mexican elite. One of the more benign characterizations of the local Mexican population was offered by the *Ventura Signal*'s editor in 1872. Writing in response to an inquiry about the local population from an Illinois resident, he described many of the local Mexican ranchers as "wealthy and educated and though not possessed of the 'get up' of the Anglo-Saxon, they are sober, quiet, hospitable and well disposed citizens."[6]

A less charitable impression of the Mexican population was offered by Thomas R. Bard, a northern entrepreneur who arrived in Ventura County in 1865 representing the business interests of Thomas A. Scott. Unconcerned with the need to convey a positive impression to prospective out-of-state immigrants, Bard candidly recounted his initial impression of the township's European-American and Mexican population in a letter of April 1865 to his mother: "That [first] evening we made the acquaintance of all the 'Americanos' of the place which number . . . 10 or 12 and out of these are about 5 who are respectable, the balance of the population consisting of greazers and Digger Indians. . . . These Greazers are the laziest cusses you ever saw. . . . They are idle and thriftless. The women are fond of dress and spend the last cent they have for gew-gaws."[7] Bard was well aware of the class lines that differentiated the Mexican population in the area and indicated that "only one respectable Spanish family" resided in the entire township: the Camarillo family that owned Rancho Ojai. Bard approvingly noted that the Camarillos were an upstanding family that did not associate with "the low Americanos or Greazers" in the area. Moreover, he made special mention of the grace and beauty of Don Camarillo's daughters, whose complexions he described as ranging from dark to "nearly white." Aside from the Camarillo family, however, Bard believed the remainder of the Californio elite in the county, as well as the other local Mexicans, to be a "queer people" with peculiar social customs and a backward local economy.[8]

THE DISPLACEMENT OF THE MEXICAN RANCHERO CLASS IN VENTURA COUNTY

The surrender of the Mexican forces in California on July 12, 1847 formally marked the territory's passage into U.S. military control. Although little was written about the early effects of this momentous change in Ventura County, one firsthand account by a local ranchero has survived and is particularly noteworthy. In his 1878 recollection of life in California, José Arnaz recounted to one of H. H. Bancroft's associates (who was collecting data for Bancroft's *History of California*) the devastating impact of Anglo-American military conquest on the township. Recalling his experience with U.S. military forces headed by Colonel Stevenson, Arnaz lamented that "making use of an armed force, Stevenson took possession of the Mission San Buenaventura and all of the property that was in that establishment and at other points, such as the rancho of San Pedro, that of Miguel Dominquez, the Piru Rancho and others. He even despoiled me of my orchards and vineyards at Los Angeles, which he occupied with his soldiers, who burned the house and the still, with whatever was there. In their excitement they even took away my saddle horse, leaving me with my family buried in poverty."[9]

Since Mexicans were assured protection of important legal rights through the Treaty of Guadalupe Hidalgo, this form of outright land seizure was not, however, allowed to continue unchallenged. Shortly after California became a state, Congress enacted legislation creating a Board of Land Commissioners responsible for adjudicating Mexican land claims protected by the treaty.

Ownership of twelve of the twenty original Spanish and Mexican land grants conferred in Ventura County was eventually upheld by either the new Land Commission or the District Court of Appeals. These rancho estates remained the property of the original grantees or their legal heirs. Of the remaining eight grants brought before U.S. authorities, one was rejected, five passed into the hands of other ranchero families, and two became the property of Anglo-Americans. The claim by Pedro Carrillo to Rancho Camulos, for instance, was ultimately rejected by both the Land Commission and the district court. Three of the five grants that passed into the hands of other rancheros later became the property of José de la Guerra. (These included Rancho El Conejo, Rancho Las Posas, and the immense Rancho Simi.) Rancho Ex-Mission, originally granted to José Arnaz, was subsequently sold to and patented by Manuel Antonio Rodriquez de Poli. Rancho Temescal, originally granted to Francisco Lopez and José Arellanes, was later transferred into the hands of Ramon de la Cuesta and Francisco Gonzales Cimino. Rancho San Pedro, originally granted to José Chapman, would legally become part of Rancho Rio de Santa Clara o La Colonia and become the property of that claim's original grantees. The Mexican ranchos that passed into European-American hands before legal title was finally determined were Rancho Sespe and Rancho Santa Paula y Saticoy. The former was patented by Thomas W. More in 1872 and the latter by five Anglo speculators in the same years.[10]

Proving legal title before the Land Commissioners and the U.S. courts was only one of the many battles that local rancheros in the area confronted after California became a state. As noted in the previous chapter, while many rancheros successfully retained legal title to disputed grants, a number of other factors contributed to the eventual demise of the ranchero elite. Among these were the unlawful "squatting" on Mexican land by Anglo settlers; the sale of Mexican land to secure payment of exorbitant interest rates on mortgages and delinquent property taxes; through protracted bankruptcy proceedings; and personal indebtedness resulting from gambling and other extravagances. In Ventura County, four additional factors played an important role in the dispossession of land: the payment of exorbitant legal fees to Anglo lawyers, the loss of land to local merchants, the coerced sale of land to Anglo speculators, and the sale of land in order to meet debts resulting from the ruinous drought of the 1860s.

The payment of legal fees incurred in proving title to rancho claims was a particularly crucial factor. Ygnacio del Valle, for example, paid A. P. Chittenden $1,000 in legal fees to defend his claim to Rancho San Francisco. Half of Chittenden's fee was paid in advance, with the remainder paid once the claim was approved by the Land Commissioners. Del Valle was also responsible for paying all the expenses of the witnesses called to testify on his behalf. These expenditures included money for food, lodging, and transportation to and from San Francisco. Aside from Chittenden's fee and these related expenses, del Valle also paid another lawyer, Joseph Brent, $400 for additional legal services and $400 for copies of documents needed to present his case before the district court.[11]

In order to meet these unexpected expenses del Valle was forced to borrow money from Anglo creditors at very high interest rates. In 1855, for example, he borrowed $3,000 from Louis Crothal of Santa Barbara at a rate of 3 percent interest per month.[12] Before del Valle was able to meet his obligation on this loan, hundreds of dollars in interest accumulated. Del Valle ultimately compounded his embattled situation and succeeded in delaying only momentarily the eventual sale of most of his property to Thomas A. Scott in the late 1860s. According to one source, "only the land immediately surrounding the adobe was spared the del Valles. Land which today encompasses the towns of Newhall and Saugus and most of the best Newhall Ranch . . . changed hands for $53,330."[13] By the early years of the twentieth century, the economic situation of the del Valles deteriorated to the point where they were forced to sell their remaining holdings in order to forestall complete bankruptcy.[14]

A good deal of Ventura County rancho land was lost through indebtedness to local merchants, who often preyed on the rancheros' extravagance and fiscal ineptitude. The Californio elite were notoriously prone to making lavish purchases on credit and later finding themselves unable to meet their debts to local merchants. As a result, large portions of rancho estates were either sold to these merchants or taken in payment for outstanding debts. One Anglo-American resident of Ventura County who arrived in 1876 described the plight of the local ranchero class in these terms:

> The Californians handled very little money and needed little until Americans came in and established stores and American business methods. Perhaps because of these conditions they were considered very unbusinesslike, from our point of view. The land-owning and cattle-owning class received quite large sums when ships came in for hides, wool, etc. When this was gone, largely because of lavish entertainment, they ran store accounts until the next sale was made. They felt

that their cattle and land holding were sufficient to guarantee store obligations, so why worry. But the merchants took quite a different view of the matter. They wanted money, not cattle or even land.[15]

While some European-American merchants undoubtedly preferred cash to land, others were quite willing to take land as payment. Antonio Schiappa Pietra, an Italian immigrant who became one of the first merchants in the county, secured possession of nearly all of Rancho Santa Clara del Norte from the Sanchez family as a result of such indebtedness. By 1883 Schiappa Pietra had gained control of 12,000 of the original 13,989-acre Sanchez grant in order to satisfy the Sanchez family's indebtedness to his business.[16]

While Schiappa Pietra's acquisition of Rancho Santa Clara del Norte was legal, attempts to defraud the local ranchero elite of their holdings were not unheard of. One such attempt was recounted by William Streeter, an Anglo pioneer in the region, who exposed one unsuccessful scheme involving a local Catholic priest from Mission San Buenaventura. Streeter recalled that in September 1850 Father Brachi proposed to him that they jointly establish a merchandise store in the township in order to attract the patronage of the local ranchero class. According to Streeter, Father Brachi stated that by "letting the Californios run up accounts with us we could, by taking advantage of their carelessness in business matters, soon possess ourselves of their land and cattle."[17]

In undertaking this business venture, however, Father Brachi insisted that his involvement in the project could not be made public. While he chose to remain a hidden partner, Brachi informed Streeter that he would support their endeavor "in every possible manner." Despite the likelihood that such a venture would be successful, Streeter refused to participate. He readily acknowledged, however, that other local Anglo-Americans actively entered into such schemes. Streeter admitted that similar schemes were used "time and time again" in the early decades of the American period to divest the local ranchero class of their immense holdings.[18]

Many of the Anglo-American speculators and developers who came to Ventura County in the late 1860s were also extremely successful in using legal intimidation to coerce the landed elite to part with large portions of their estates. One of the major figures involved in this method of land acquisition was Thomas A. Scott. Prior to his aggressive speculation in Ventura County land, Scott served as Acting Assistant Secretary of War under the Lincoln administration and Vice President and Manager of the Pennsylvania Railroad. Scott's principal interest in Ventura County was to buy county land in order to develop its oil production potential. Under

Scott's leadership, a retinue of highly persuasive lawyers and a skillful personal agent (the aforementioned Thomas R. Bard) successfully purchased large parcels of the best land in Ventura County during the mid 1860s and 1870s. By 1868, Scott's Philadelphia and California Petroleum Company became the largest single landholder in the Ventura County area. By 1874, Thomas Scott owned one-third of Rancho Ojai; nearly one-half of Rancho Simi; all of Rancho Las Posas and Rancho San Francisco; five-sevenths of Rancho La Colonia, Rancho San Pedro, Rancho Calleguas, and Rancho Conejo; and all of Rancho Cañada Larga. Moreover, Scott secured title to four hundred acres of land in Los Angeles County, twelve thousand acres in Humbolt County, and held the lease to at least five other rancho estates in various parts of the state.[19]

By 1875, Scott held title to the three major ranchos in Ventura County: Rancho Cañada Larga (6,600 acres), Rancho Las Posas (26,623 acres), and Rancho Ojai (17,717 acres). He later increased his ownership of Rancho San Francisco and Rancho Simi from nearly 50 percent to over 85 percent. Scott eventually owned over 230,000 acres of the best farm land in Ventura County.[20] This represented over 55 percent of all the land granted in the county during the Spanish and Mexican periods.

Scott's lawyers used ruthless methods to secure title to much of this rancho land. They frequently bought a share in an estate and then pressed for the estate's partition as a way of forcing Mexican rancheros to sell their land. The legal proceedings of such partition suits were extremely expensive and often forced Mexican co-owners to sell their share of the estate rather than face further debilitating legal expenses. One of Scott's lawyers, for instance, described his negotiations with Joaquin Ormat over his principal share of Rancho El Rio de Santa Clara o La Colonia as a particularly difficult case. In a letter to another of Scott's lawyers in San Francisco, Charles Huse candidly wrote of the necessity to utilize the threat of legal proceedings to force Ormat to sell his land. According to Huse, "Ormat was ugly, and I had to labor with him quite earnestly in order to effect an arrangement. . . . The remaining interests in the Colony [Rancho La Colonia] must be acquired, either by purchase or by a suit of partition and sale."[21]

After successfully completing his purchase of Ormat's five-seventh share of La Colonia, Huse negotiated with the Gonzales family for the remaining two-sevenths. Huse made it clear that he was determined to secure this portion by whatever means necessary. The callousness of his approach was vividly captured in a letter written to his co-counsel in December 1864: "I am trying to induce the Gonzaleses, who own the remaining two-sevenths of the Colonia, to sell out on some reasonable terms. If they are obstinant, their share can be secured by a sale in a partition suit. As they now have no cattle and no money, it will be most for [sic] their interest to sell."[22] Despite Huse's best effort, however, the Gonzaleses refused to sell, and Scott had to remain content with owning only five-sevenths of La Colonia. In later years, the Gonzaleses eventually sold their interest in La Colonia to the Camarillo family, who also refused to sell this land to the Scott interests.[23]

Negotiations between Thomas Scott's attorneys and the de la Guerra family, once the principal landholders in the county, were also difficult and fraught with enmity. Levi Parsons, another of Scott's numerous lawyers, encountered great resistance from this family when attempting to secure payment on a mortgage note to their interest in Rancho Simi and Rancho Las Posas. Parsons wrote of this difficulty to a colleague in 1867, stating that "the family dislikes very much to give up the property, having it so long. . . . I employed [Joseph B.] Felton yesterday and filed papers here in our District Court for an ejection suit against the whole tribe. I will pile the litigation on them until I make them sick."[24]

Although Scott's attorneys met with great resistance from the de la Guerra family, they were later able to gain control of both Rancho Simi and Rancho Las Posas. The acquisition of this land by Scott enabled him to replace José de la Guerra as the principal landholder in Ventura County by 1880.

Thomas Scott was not the only Anglo-American who successfully wrested control of the immense ranchero holdings. Thomas W. More acquired a great deal of rancho land through outright purchase. Shortly after the death of Josefa Carrillo, heir to Rancho Sespe, More and his two brothers secured most of this rancho for $17,500.[25] Less than a year later they bought the remaining portion for another $1,000, bringing the total purchase price of the 8,800 acre rancho to approximately two dollars per acre. Thomas More was the principle figure in this joint partnership and later purchased additional parcels of former rancho land. With money derived from his participation in the cattle business, the Mores "bought one great ranch after another, until their holding extended thirty-five miles in an unbroken line down the valley of the Santa Clara [River], from the Rancho Camulos to the sea." The Mores also later acquired the 65,000-acre offshore island of Santa Rosa as well as the approximately 50,000-acre Rancho Lompoc in Santa Barbara County.[26]

The ruinous floods and severe drought of the 1860s were yet another crushing blow to the Californio elite's retention of land in Ventura County.

The flood of 1862 had a particularly devastating effect on the ranchos in the San Buenaventura township. Hundreds of the ranchero's cattle drowned and a major portion of the community was leveled. On February 1, 1862, the *Los Angeles Star* reported that a "torrent rushed through the town with such force, as to wash away the street to a depth of fifteen feet, carrying several houses with it. The town was abandoned, the people taking refuge in the church and other elevated places. In the valley, the grass, timber, and lands have been destroyed, and eight or ten houses knocked to smash."[27]

The flood was followed by two years of drought. Historians have estimated that a quarter of the state's wealth, including as much as 40 percent of the state's livestock, was lost between 1862 and 1864. This devastation was greatest in the "cow counties" of southern California. In Los Angeles County alone, for example, as much as 70 percent of the livestock perished in the drought. In Santa Barbara County, the nearly two hundred thousand head of cattle owned by local rancheros in 1862 were leveled to a mere five thousand.[28]

Approximately two-thirds of all the cattle in the San Buenaventura township perished as a result of the calamitous drought. The del Valle family at Rancho San Francisco lost nearly all the livestock on their estate. Over three hundred head of cattle died on their rancho in one week alone.[29] The Sanchez family of nearby Rancho Rio de Santa Clara del Norte was also severely devastated. Only a mere two thousand of the sixty thousand head of cattle they owned in 1862 survived the two-year drought.[30]

A similar fate befell the Camarillo family, whose situation had deteriorated by 1875 to the point that they liquidated their holdings in Santa Barbara and Ventura counties in order to maintain Rancho Calleguas. In that year Juan Camarillo was forced to sell his 17,716-acre Rancho Ojai to Thomas R. Bard for $17,000. The Camarillos' financial situation continued to decline, however, and they were eventually compelled to sell portions of their cherished Rancho Calleguas. By 1883, the Camarillo family retained less than 4,000 acres of this 9,993-acre rancho.[31]

Compounding this rapid loss of rancho land was the accompanying drop in the value of land in southern California due to the drought. In Los Angeles County, for example, the assessed value of county land fell nearly 50 percent, while land in the San Buenaventura area assessed at twenty-five cents an acre in 1863 dropped in value to ten cents an acre by 1865.[32]

The havoc that befell the ranchero elite in the San Buenaventura township between 1860 and 1870 was summarily described by the *Ventura Signal* in 1872: "The drought of 1864 killed over sixty thousand head of cattle and forced the slaughter of many more. . . . No provisions had been made by the princes of these rich domains in the years of their prosperity, and they were nearly all irretrievably ruined at one fell swoop. Their great landed estates fell bodily into the hands of speculators, or were cut up and sold out piece meal; or, worse, mortgaged, and finally lost."[33]

While a few rancheros momentarily delayed their eventual impoverishment, most families witnessed their fortunes fatefully disappear in the 1860s and 1870s. What U.S. courts, newly assessed taxes, mortgages, personal indebtedness, and the efforts of conniving lawyers and merchants were unsuccessful in accomplishing, nature finally helped along. In the wake of floods and droughts, developers increased the widespread purchase of county land and prepared the way for the capitalist transformation of the area. The rancheros' ill fortunes due to this natural disaster proved a boon to European-American capitalists investing in the county.

By the late 1860s the Mexican ranchero class was no longer the dominant economic force in the county. In 1868, for example, the principal owners of the three largest tracts of land in San Buenaventura were Thomas A. Scott's Philadelphia and California Petroleum Company, the Anglo-run San Buenaventura Mining Company, and local entrepreneur Thomas R. Bard. Of the forty-eight owners of tracts of land larger than five hundred acres, only six were Spanish surnamed. Of the ten major property owners in the county, only one was Mexican: Ygnacio del Valle of Rancho San Francisco. He was listed as the eighth-largest property owner in the county, still controlling 10,390 acres of land. Other local rancheros further down the list included R. G. de la Riva (twelfth), Ramon Olivas (thirteenth), José Arnaz (fourteenth), and Juan Camarillo (seventeenth).[34]

By 1880 only a few of these prominent ranchero families retained any semblance of their original affluence and local influence. An examination of the agricultural schedules of the 1880 Census, for example, documents that only Ygnacio del Valle and Juan Camarillo were among the ten wealthiest property owners in the county. (Both men, however, had considerably less wealth than in earlier years.) This fact plainly illustrates that from 1860 to 1880 European-American speculators successfully became the most prosperous individuals in the area. In 1860 only one Anglo-American, Thomas More of Rancho Sespe, was among the county's most affluent persons. The remaining nine major landholders were Spanish or Mexican rancheros. By 1880 there were seven Anglo-Americans and one Italian immigrant (Antonio Schiappa Pietra) in this elite group. The Mexican ranchero class that formerly held uncontested control over economic affairs in the San Buenaventura township during the Mexican period were effectively dispossessed of their land within a decade after county status was secured.

UNDERMINING THE POLITICAL INFLUENCE
OF THE RANCHERO CLASS IN VENTURA COUNTY

This economic decline was also accompanied by the rapid erosion of the ranchero's social influence and political power in the area. Although the ranchero class in San Buenaventura was still able to retain some political influence through the late 1860s, by 1873 (the year county status was attained) they were no longer a significant political force in the county. The crucial turning point in the political fortunes of the Mexican population in Ventura County occurred in 1867 and 1868, when European-American male settlers finally outnumbered Mexican voters.

Although a few white immigrant trappers, mountaineers, and sailors found their way into the township after statehood, there was no significant European-American settlement in the area until nearly two decades after U.S. annexation. In the 1860s, for instance, there were only twenty Anglos living in San Buenaventura. Anglos comprised less than 4 percent of the total population in that year and only nine were registered voters.[35] By the mid-1860s there were still no more than six Anglo-American families and perhaps a dozen single men in the entire township.[36]

By 1870 a dramatic demographic change had occurred in the township's population; Anglos now comprised 70 percent and Mexicans less than 30 percent of the total population. This significant increase in the European-American population led directly to an alteration in the balance of political power. In July 1867, the Great Register for Santa Barbara County contained only 71 registered Spanish-surnamed voters and 51 Anglo-American voters in San Buenaventura. From July 30, 1867, to October 31, 1868, 106 new Anglo-American voters and only 12 Spanish-surnamed voters were added to this register.[37] This brought the total of Spanish-surnamed voters to 83 and European-American voters to 157.

By the time that Ventura County was officially formed on January 1, 1873, the proportion of Spanish-surnamed voters in the county had dropped to only 16 percent of the total electorate. Throughout the period from 1873 to 1894, the Mexican population remained between 14 and 16 percent of the voting population.[38]

Before the Mexican population became a voting minority in Ventura County, the local "gente de razon" retained undisputed control of the political process. At the time of San Buenaventura's incorporation as an official township in Santa Barbara County in 1866, four of the five elected Board of Town Trustees were prominent Mexican landholders. On the first board were Angel Escandon, Juan Camarillo, Victor Ustesaustegui, Fernando Tico, and Walter S. Chaffee. The first town clerk, Tadeo Sanchez, was also a wealthy Mexican landholder. Moreover, the first five supervisors elected to represent the San Buenaventura township on the Santa Barbara County Board of Supervisors were also Mexican rancheros: Fernando Tico, Ysidro Obiols, José Arnaz, Juan Camarillo, and Juan Rodriguez.[39]

Control of local politics by the Mexican ranchero elite was not meaningfully challenged until Anglo voters overwhelmed the Mexican electorate. In 1867, Thomas R. Bard, a Republican candidate, was elected to represent the San Buenaventura township on the Board of Supervisors by a seventy-one to sixty-seven vote. He joined Antonio Maria de la Guerra, from Santa Barbara township, and Thomas W. More, from Santa Ynez township, as representatives on the Board.[40] Bard's election marked the first time that an Anglo-American represented the San Buenaventura township in this important capacity and also signalled the first Anglo-American majority on the Santa Barbara County Board of Supervisors. At this point the balance of political power in the area began to shift to the European-American population and, in particular, into the hands of wealthy capitalist developers.

The election of Bard over Tadeo Sanchez, the Democratic candidate for supervisor in 1867, was particularly important because Mexican voters still comprised nearly 60 percent of the registered voters in the township. Bard's success in this election was only possible because of divisions among the Mexican electorate. One significant expression of this division was Bard's success at drawing support from the Camarillo family. The daughters of Juan Camarillo reportedly persuaded numerous male relatives and friends to vote for Bard in the election.[41]

In recounting his election victory to Thomas Scott, Bard acknowledged both the ascension of Anglos to political power in the area and the creation of a favorable climate for capitalist development. In a letter to Scott dated September 6, 1867, Bard wrote, "In the election which came off on the 4th . . . I was elected county supervisor, and I can assure you that hereafter, you can rely on equitable assessments and equalization of taxes, so far as your properties are concerned. I am told the [de la Guerra] family, who are the worst enemies to American interests, spent a large sum of money to defeat me and other American candidates. The issue in this county is [the] Spanish element against Americans—and has resulted favorably to us."[42]

Representation of the ranchero elite in county offices continued to diminish once county status was secured in 1873. In the first special election held after county status was conferred, not one candidate nominated for office was of Mexican descent. The only visible presence by the Mexican population in this election was the role they played as election officials.[43]

During the first regular election held in the fall of 1873, only two Mexican Democratic candidates sought office: Angel G. Escandon for State Assembly representative and A. del Campo for County Treasurer. Both men were soundly defeated. Their defeat was part of the overall poor showing of the Democratic party in this election.[44] The defeat of Escandon, del Campo, and all the other Democratic candidates was at least partially attributable to the defection of Mexican support for the Democratic party.

Evidence suggests that many Mexican Democrats in the township actually voted for Anglo Republican candidates. The stunning defeat of the Democratic party, which had a larger number of registered voters in the township, was once again due largely to Thomas Bard's success at "influencing" Mexican voters to support Republican candidates. Bard was very candid about his methods. In a letter to colleague J. P. Green on the eve of the election, Bard admitted buying the support of Mexican voters: "Our old allies the Spanish element were at first inclined to go back upon us but the contribution of a fat cow at my expense for a jolly time on the day before the election promised to give us 1/2 their vote."[45]

In later years, Bard and the special interests that he represented continued to court the Mexican population. Bard made extensive use of one of his Mexican employees from Rancho Las Posas, José Lopez, to convince Mexican voters in the county to support his candidates. During the general election of 1879, for example, Lopez persuaded a number of Mexicans in the area to once again support the Republican ticket. On August 28, 1879, Lopez informed Bard of his success by stating, "This goes to tell you that I have got 15 votes for your candidate. Those go to Santa Barbara and vote there. They are safe and five more will remain here and vote for the same man. They are willing to vote for your man or men and I think they'll be faithful to you."[46] In return for Lopez's efforts, Bard gave him a small amount of money for campaign "travel expenses" and sponsored a dance for the Mexican population after the election.[47]

Only a few Spanish-surnamed candidates ran for public office in the years after the Mexican population became a minority in Ventura County. In 1882 the venerable Angel G. Escandon was again elected to the Ventura Town Council and became the only Mexican candidate elected to an important county office during the period from 1874 to 1900. His presence on the council, however, was hardly a sign of any resurgence of Mexican political strength in the county. By the time of Escandon's election, the Mexican population had been rendered politically powerless.

The political and economic marginalization of the Californio ranchero class in Ventura County was seen by the local European-American population as the inevitable consequence of a superior race overtaking an inferior one. Because of their often dubious claims to European ancestry, Mexicans were only seen as a "half civilized" people whose social-cultural world greatly dismayed most Anglo immigrants. This sentiment was captured in a number of newspaper articles appearing during the 1870s. An article published in the November 9, 1879, issue of the *Ventura Signal* described the economic decline of the ranchero elite in the county, and more generally in southern California, in the following terms: "The Spanish race is in its decadence here. . . . It is the history of the world repeated; the progressing forces crowding out the passive element, and although we obtained this land by conquest, it would seem to be a good thing to secure it with all its possibilities from a people that have shown so little appreciation of its worth."[48]

European Americans' arrogant belief in their cultural superiority and their destiny to spread "modern American civilization" also colored their views of the ranchero class. This sentiment contributed to the old landed Mexican elite being viewed as an obstruction to Yankee "progress." Such a view was conveyed in an editorial that appeared in the *Signal* on October 4, 1873, where the editor boasted that "Yankee genius and enterprise has done more for this country than four hundred years under the reign of the lazy greaser, stunted in growth and benighted in the intellect, by the religious enslavement of both mind and body, the effect of which are still visible in the ancient adobe structures which disfigure the town, but which, thanks to the ravages of time and the intrusion of modern American civilization, are fastly crumbling away."[49]

THE CLOSING OF ONE ERA AND
THE DAWNING OF A NEW

The transformation of the Mexican economy in Ventura County passed through three principal phases: (1) the rapid dispossession of the local Mexican rancheros between 1860 and 1870; (2) a brief transition period during the 1870s and early 1880s in which small-scale extensive grain farming and remnants of the Mexican pastoral economy predominated; and (3) the rapid emergence of intensive agriculture and the widespread proletarianization of the local population during the late 1880s.

Beginning in the late 1860s, the Mexican estates acquired by Anglo speculators and developers were subdivided into small plots and resold to new white immigrants. One of the first of the new Anglo-American land-holders to subdivide was George S. Briggs. In 1862 Briggs purchased the 17,773-acre Rancho Santa Paula y Saticoy from Manuel Jimeno for $40,000. After unsuccessfully experimenting with citrus fruit production on his land, Briggs subdivided the rancho in 1867 and sold small parcels to farmers who planted wheat and barley. By 1915 Briggs' Rancho Santa Paula y Saticoy had been subdivided into 410 separate holdings, most of which were parcels less of than 250 acres.[50]

Thomas A. Scott's 1867 subdivision of San Buenaventura rancho land after failing to quickly develop oil production was the most extensive. This enabled him to defray the costs of developing the property he re-tained while also decreasing his property tax obligations. Furthermore, Scott was convinced that the rapid settlement of the county would have a positive impact on the overall development of his interests in the re-gion.[51]

Under the able guidance of Thomas R. Bard, Scott's holdings were subdivided and sold to prospective Anglo farmers entering the county with entrepreneurial aspirations. Bard believed there to be several classes of prospective buyers: speculators interested in securing large tracts; cattle and sheep raisers, vintners, and farmers interested in tracts of 300 to 1,000 acres; and farmers and vintagers interested in 160 acres or less. Bard was quite certain that the various ranchos owned by Scott could easily accom-modate all these groups.[52]

Bard personally oversaw the initial subdivision and sale of Scott's prop-erty in Ventura County. In 1867 Rancho La Colonia was initially subdi-vided into forty-seven separate plots, most consisting of parcels of less than 500 acres. By 1915 the original 44,883-acre rancho had been subdivided into 332 separate holdings, all but eleven of which were less than 500 acres. In 1888 Rancho Simi was also subdivided in a similar way and portions sold to incoming settlers. By 1915 this immense 113,009-acre rancho con-tained 223 separate holdings, approximately 75 percent of which were under 250 acres.[53]

The land subdivided by Thomas Scott was also leased and share-cropped. On Rancho La Colonia, for example, land was leased in the late 1870s from $1.50 to $3.00 per acre per year.[54] Sharecropping on nearby Rancho Las Posas was carried out on different terms. In 1877 a two-hundred-acre parcel of this land was leased to farmers at $500 per year or offered in return for one-fifth of the crop produced on the land. This sharecropping arrangement also entitled the lessor to the stubble remaining on the land after the harvest season. The stubble, in turn, was sold to sheep raisers at approximately fifty cents per acre.[55]

Nearly every major landholder in Ventura County subdivided their holdings during the period from 1860 to 1900. The actual number of separate farms and ranches rose from 34 to 1,249. By 1915 Rancho Santa Clara del Norte had been divided into 75 separate holdings, of which 60 were less than two hundred fifty acres. Similarly, Rancho El Conejo now consisted of 43 separate plots, 27 of which were holdings of less than two hundred fifty acres. Rancho Ex-Mission, once owned by José Arnaz, was cordoned into 90 different parcels of land by 1915, with 71 less than one hundred acres.[56]

The subdivision and sale of rancho land acquired by Anglo speculators and developers in Ventura County was not without problems. A sizable portion of the newly acquired land became the center of bitter struggle between this new Anglo landholding class and the white squatter population that immigrated into the area after the Civil War. The squatter movement in the county both drew on the right of individuals to settle public land through the Pre-Emption Law and the Homestead Law and took advantage of the ongoing legal disputes over ownership of rancho land. These opportunistic squatters posed a variety of legal and political problems for major Anglo landowners and speculators like Scott and Bard. As one landholder from nearby Santa Barbara described the problem,

> The squatter would squat anywhere, he didn't care where, and he did all that he could to damage the land claims in California. He came in to fight, to contest the claims of actual settlers. He would set up the most unheard of claims to retard the settlement of land grants, and would fabricate all sorts of spurious testimony in support of them. The real *bona fide* settlers suffered a great deal from the squatters. . . . The squatters just simply fought for the sake of blackmailing, without any just claim whatever. This has been a great injury to the state.[57]

Lawyers working on behalf of Thomas Scott referred to these squatters as a "pestilential class" or as persons of "desperate character." Their leaders were described as "low sneaking dogs." Thomas Bard referred to squatters in the Ventura area as a "beggardly, unconscienceless, and ungreatful [sic] lot."[58]

Squatter settlement in Ventura County proved to be quite extensive. By the late 1870s over three hundred persons had illegally settled on approximately 17,000 acres of land on Rancho La Colonia.[59] Their settlement there, resting on their belief that this land was public domain, was fiercely contested by Thomas Scott and Thomas Bard for a number of years.[60] By

1880 legal ownership of La Colonia was finally adjudicated in favor of Scott, and although the squatters' claim to this land was not upheld by the courts, neither Scott nor Bard resorted to forcibly evicting the large settlement on the rancho. Most of the land settled by the squatters was either sold or leased to them at a fair market price. In a letter to an associate of Scott's, T. R. Bard described his resolution of the squatter problem at Rancho La Colonia: "I go to every man on the property, ascertain what he wants to do, what he had got, and if possible convince him that I have 'malice toward none,' and we get along well enough I suppose. I have leased to the best of them and arrange with all in some way or another."[61]

Despite these contentious moments, the number of farmers in the township multiplied dramatically between 1860 and 1870. The actual number of individuals engaging in farming rose from only 10 to 375 during this period. This represented an increase from 5.5 percent of the local population engaged in farming to 45.9 percent. As was also now the case for the rancher stratum, European Americans accounted for 90 percent of the farming population. In fact, over one-half of the male white population in the township (55.5 percent) owned or leased farms in 1870.

THE DEVELOPMENT OF INTENSIVE AGRICULTURE AND THE TRANSITIONAL ROLE OF THE SHEEP INDUSTRY

The subdivision of rancho lands and eventual resolution of the squatter problem led to the rapid development of extensive grain production in Ventura County. Grain production in the area was first undertaken successfully as early as 1783, in the Spanish period, when wheat, barley, corn, and beans were raised on Mission San Buenaventura. At the height of the Mission's prosperity during the early 1800s, an average of nearly 9,000 bushels of these grains was harvested annually. The production of grain crops on nearly three hundred acres of mission land continued until the secularization of Mission San Buenaventura in 1834.[62]

After California gained statehood, grain production diminished in importance to the economy of Ventura County. In 1860 only 5,200 bushels of wheat, 4,000 bushels of barley, and 2,900 bushels of oats were harvested in San Buenaventura.[63] This was not significantly larger than grain production had been decades earlier during the Spanish period.

The first significant increase occurred in the late 1860s. According to the *Ventura Signal*, it was not until this point that "a general system of agriculture was begun . . . by a handful of immigrants of small means."[64] The overall profits from agricultural goods produced in the county first rose significantly in 1870, when profits from the production of barley and wheat more than quadrupled those of the previous year.[65]

During the 1870s, the volume of grain production increased as county land was further subdivided and placed under cultivation by small farmers. In 1873 nearly 160,000 sacks of barley and 10,000 sacks of wheat were shipped from the county wharves at Ventura (formerly San Buenaventura) and the new township of Hueneme. Two years later the county deputy assessor estimated that county grain farmers shipped over 700,000 sacks of barley, 20,000 sacks of wheat, and 50,000 sacks of corn from these county wharves. Most of this grain was shipped by steamer to San Francisco, where it was then sent back east or shipped to England.[66]

The swift introduction of extensive agriculture in Ventura County was accompanied by a brief resuscitation of one important facet of the Mexican economy. Sheep raising continued to play an important role in the local economy for at least a decade after the destruction of the cattle industry in the mid 1860s. It appears that sheep were more drought-resistant than cattle, a fact that certainly contributed to the revived interest in sheep raising at the time. Moreover, this industry allowed many new Anglo landholders to make enough money to pay local property taxes and also utilize their land until more profitable ventures could be developed.

The magnitude of importance of the sheep industry in the area during this transitional period is clearly documented in data drawn from the agricultural schedules of the federal manuscript census. In 1860, for instance, there were only 30,710 sheep in the San Buenaventura township. In the decade after the ruinous drought of the mid-1860s, however, the number of sheep in the county rose to an estimated 74,000, while cattle numbered only 6,000. By 1875 sheep in the county had increased to approximately 250,000.[67]

The omnipresent Thomas R. Bard also played a prominent role in developing this industry. In 1875 Bard joined in partnership with Logan Kennedy and John Erringer in raising over 11,000 sheep on a section of Rancho Las Posas. In later years, Bard and his associates grazed an additional 11,000 sheep on Rancho Simi.[68] Despite the backing of these prominent businessmen, however, the sheep industry was short-lived in Ventura County. The profitability of sheep raising was undermined by a second serious drought which ravaged southern California in 1876–77. By 1878 there were only 50,000 sheep left in the county, the destruction being so great that Bard and his associates dissolved their partnership in 1880.[69]

By 1870 a marked decline in the importance of ranching underscored the major structural changes that occurred in the local economy of Ventura county. The percentage of individuals engaged in ranching declined from

18 percent in 1860 to less than 4 percent a decade later. By 1870 the majority of pastoralists were now European Americans, eleven of the sixteen stock raisers and eleven of the fifteen sheep raisers being white American immigrants. The changing composition of the rancher stratum reflected the overall displacement of Mexican rancheros by Anglos and the erosion of the traditional rancho economy.

Another measure of the declining importance of ranching is evidenced in the number of farm operators in the county. The number of farmers rose from 49 to 577 between 1860 and 1880. Most of these farmers were European-American immigrants who purchased or leased small parcels of land on which they initially developed the small-scale production of grain. According to the 1880 agriculture census, nearly 85 percent of the county's farmers operated modest farms of 199 to 500 acres.[70] These individuals contributed significantly to the prodigious increase of extensive agriculture in the area and also played an important role in the eventual development of intensive agricultural production (the large-scale farming of vegetable, fruit, and orchard crops). As a measure of this explosive growth, the total cash value of farm products produced in the county shot from $22,800 in 1860 to over $600,000 in 1880. Significantly, the eight largest county landholders were Anglo farmers who accounted for nearly ten percent of this prodigious production.[71]

AGRIBUSINESS ELITES AND THE DEVELOPMENT OF INTENSIVE AGRICULTURE

During the closing decades of the 19th century, two intensive agricultural crops—citrus fruits and sugar beets—became the mainstay of Ventura's new economy, which was characterized by the predominance of large-scale agribusiness concerns. These local growers became the major employers of the expanding farm-labor class and the most influential men in the county's economy.

The development of citrus fruit was guided by a small group of agribusiness families such as those which founded the Limoneira Company in Santa Paula. In 1893, W. L. Hardison—a principal owner of Union Oil of California—organized the Limoneira Company with Nathan W. Blanchard. Originally only a 400-acre citrus firm known as the Limoneira ranch, the company rapidly blossomed into a 3,000-acre ranch and one of the largest lemon producing farms in the world. The tremendous volume produced on the Limoneira Ranch helped make Ventura County the leading lemon-producing county in the state at that time.[72]

In 1895 a grandnephew of Hardison, Charles Teague, was appointed to succeed the retiring Blanchard as manager of the Limoneira Company. Under Teague's leadership the citrus industry in the county continued to flourish and eventually became one of the most profitable businesses in all of southern California. Agribusiness families in the industry such as the Teagues, Blanchards, and Hardisons joined early financial developers like Thomas R. Bard and Thomas Scott as the principal economic moguls and powerbrokers in the county.

In addition to controlling privately owned farms such as Limoneira, these families controlled the major banking firms in the northeastern portion of Ventura County. As well as managing the Limoneira Company, Charles Teague became president of two local banks, the First National Bank of Santa Paula and the Santa Paula Savings Bank. Other prominent agribusinessmen in the industry like A. C. Hardison and Nathan W. Blanchard, Jr. served on the board of the First National Bank, with Blanchard also serving as a director of the Savings Bank. Through these positions, these agribusiness families were able to exercise tremendous influence over the funding of local business operations.[73]

Their influence also extended to the control of local water resources. In 1893, for example, the founders of the Limoneira company also organized the Thermal Belt Water Company to supply water for their ranch. This new company rapidly monopolized control over local water through an adjunct company, the Santa Paula Water Works, which became a major supplier of water for local residents and farmers in the area.[74]

These agribusiness families also had tremendous influence on city politics. Their stature as leading local businessmen enabled them to gain direct or indirect control of the mayor's office, the city council, the chamber of commerce, and even the local high school board. Their support was indispensable to a successful campaign. In discussing the influence of the Limoneira company families over the Santa Paula City Council and Chamber of Commerce, one local historian notes that "they were able to participate as members of both bodies, because the big citrus ranch maintained offices in town. Indeed, the board of trade, a predecessor of the chamber, held its meetings in the Limoneira office, and its president was C. C. Teague."[75]

Another method utilized to exert control of the local economy was the development of growers' associations. Beginning in the late 1890s, a number of these "cooperatives" were organized throughout the state. Among the first in Ventura County were the local branches of the Southern California Fruit Growers' Exchange, the Southern California Walnut Association, and the California Lima Bean Growers' Association. Members of the

Limoneira Company were among the prominent figures involved in their formation. Charles Teague, for example, helped organize all three and served as president of both the Southern California Walnut Association and the California Fruit Growers' Association.[76]

These associations enabled local growers to gain control over the marketing and distribution of their crops, which previously had been largely under the direction of crop speculators. Once the cooperatives were formed, local farmers eliminated these middlemen and oversaw a marketing network that eased the underlying tension between small- and large-scale growers in the country.

The associations proved to be a crucial factor in the development of California agriculture into a multi-million dollar industry during the early twentieth century.[77] They enabled local growers to influence consumer demand through collective advertising, reduce the cost of sale and distribution of their products, and establish better ties with public universities, which helped increase crop yield and aid in pest control. They also enabled growers to gain control of subsidiary businesses (such as the by-products industries) and secure control of resources and materials needed for production (such as irrigation water and shipping containers). Other practical help included acquiring cheap transportation rates from the railroad and shipping companies, ensuring the availability of a labor force paid at industry-controlled wages, successfully lobbying for passage of legislation favorable to their particular industry (such as the California State Agricultural Prorate Act of 1933, which stabilized the citrus market), and finally, gaining passage of protective national tariffs through such grower lobbies as the Agricultural Council of California and the National Council of Farmers' Cooperatives.[78] The passage of the Dingley Tariff Act in 1897, for instance, stimulated widespread capital investment in the sugar beet industry in Ventura County. By imposing a heavy duty on imported sugar, the Dingley Tariff contributed directly to the introduction of the sugar beet industry in the Santa Clara Valley section of the county and to the founding of Oxnard in 1898.

Henry, James, and Robert Oxnard, prominent sugar refiners in New York, were major figures in developing the sugar beet industry in Ventura County. Before investing in the county, the Oxnard brothers founded six sugar beet refineries in Nebraska and Colorado, and the Chino Sugar Company in Chino, California. In 1897 they opened their second plant in the state in the section of Ventura County that later became the city of Oxnard. The construction of the Oxnard sugar beet factory was initially undertaken under the auspices of the Pacific Beet Sugar Company. When the factory began operation in 1898, the company was reorganized as the American Beet Sugar Company, which served as the controlling body for the six beet factories owned by the Oxnard brothers. Henry T. and James G. Oxnard served as president and vice president, respectively, of the newly formed corporation.[79]

These entrepreneurs also invested in related facets of the area's economy during the early years of their operation in Ventura County. Like the families involved in the Limoneira Company, the Oxnard brothers also appreciated the advantages of gaining control over local banking institutions. In 1899 Henry and James Oxnard became the principal founders of the Bank of Oxnard, which loaned capital to local sugar beet farmers. Moreover, in 1901 Robert Oxnard also entered into the production end of the new industry when he became president of the nearly 6,000-acre Patterson Ranch. This ranch quickly became the major producer of sugar beets in the county and among the most profitable in the entire state.[80]

The sugar beet industry in southern California quickly became a multi-million dollar business in which the Oxnard brothers were leading figures. The Oxnard refinery rapidly became one of the major processing centers for the sugar beet industry in the world. During the factory's second year of operation, it processed over 63,000 tons of beets. In 1901 the volume climbed to over 160,000 tons, which represented approximately two tons of sugar beets processed daily during the harvest season. In 1902, Henry T. Oxnard boasted, "The sugar beet investment in southern California amounts to upwards of $6,000,000, and we pay out for labor, beets, lime rock and freight, all of which dispenses in this part of the state about $4,000,000 annually."[81]

By 1903 the factory employed nearly seven hundred people during its peak period and processed almost 200,000 tons of sugar beets. At the end of its first decade of operation, the sugar beet industry in Ventura County accounted for $2,380,000 in annual sales in the state.[82]

The development of the sugar beet industry in the Santa Clara Valley had important repercussions on the economic and social life of Ventura County. Prior to the construction of the sugar beet factory in 1897, most of the economic activity in Ventura County was centered in the port city of Hueneme. When the factory began full operation the following year, a dramatic shift in the fortunes of this community occurred. Employment opportunities generated by the factory led to the relocation of local residents and new settlers to the area around the Oxnard refinery. According to the *Oxnard Courier*, "the citizens of Hueneme began to flock to the new townsite . . . and their once flourishing town was gradually depopulated during the years 1898–1903 until it became but a shadow of its former self." Almost overnight, a full-fledged community developed around the refinery that later took "Oxnard" as the official town name.[83]

The emergence of Oxnard as the center of economic activity in Ventura County reflected the underlying changes occurring in southern California's economy. The wharf constructed at the port of Hueneme was once the focal point of commercial activity for grain farmers in the county. Nearly all of the county's trade with Los Angeles and San Francisco was originally carried out by steamers which docked at the Huemene Wharf. Once the Southern Pacific Railroad entered Ventura County in 1887, however, Hueneme's fortunes as a shipping center precipitously declined. The development of the Oxnard sugar beet industry and the Santa Paula citrus industry, both of which utilized the railroad for marketing, also contributed directly to the demise of Hueneme.[84]

RACIAL STATUS AND CLASS POSITION IN THE LOCAL ECONOMY

The development of intensive agriculture in Ventura County stimulated a rapid increase in the county's population. In 1870 the federal census enumerated only 2,491 individuals living in the portion of Santa Barbara County that became Ventura County three years later. Sixty-nine percent of the population in the township were Anglo-Americans, while Mexicans made up approximately 27 percent and the Native American and Chinese populations together less than 4 percent of the total (3.1 and .4 percent, respectively).[85]

The population in the county more than doubled to 5,074 in 1880 and nearly tripled again to 14,367 by 1890. The vast majority were again Anglo-Americans, who now made up approximately 75 to 80 percent of the county's population between 1880 and 1900. Mexicans continued to be the largest minority group in the county, representing approximately 15–20 percent of the total population during this period. The Chinese population remained small at nearly 3 percent, while the Japanese and Native American residents accounted for less than 2 percent.[86]

By 1900 there were seven communities in the county: Ventura, Hueneme, Santa Paula, Saticoy, Ojai, Simi, and Piru. Although founded in 1898, Oxnard was not formally recognized as a separate community on the 1900 census. Many of the names given to communities, such as Hueneme and Piru, were local Chumash names for former Indian villages or rancherías around which these new communities were built.

Most of the new communities in Ventura County were closely tied to the expanding agribusiness economy. Hueneme remained the important grain port in the county and a center for the cultivation of lima beans, wheat, and barley. Simi also became a center for grain production and the grazing of cattle and sheep. Santa Paula emerged as the center of the county's citrus fruit industry and the nascent oil industry in the county. The major industry in the town of Oxnard, of course, was sugar beets. Finally, Ventura became the nucleus for local retail businesses in the county. By 1885 there were nineteen dry goods and grocery stores, two hardware and tinning businesses, three furniture establishments, and a number of other small businesses. The area surrounding the town of Ventura was also the site of extensive oil operations.[87]

The widespread capitalist development of the area did not result, however, in equitable employment opportunities for the nonwhite populations. As elsewhere in the state, racial status continued to play an important role in shaping the economic opportunities for the European, Mexican, and Native Americans and the Chinese and Japanese. European Americans enjoyed overrepresentation at the upper end of the local class structure throughout the period from 1860 to 1900. Their ability to secure a privileged class position in the county was clearly reflected in their monopolizing of self-employment opportunities and their concentration in certain occupations within the working class.

Anglo immigrants virtually monopolized the farming, proprietorial, professional, low white-collar, and skilled labor strata. The county's decennial censuses between 1860 and 1900 report that all the hotel keepers, saloon keepers, lumber dealers, and dry-goods merchants in the proprietor stratum, and physicians, druggists, and jurists in the professional stratum, were white men. They also monopolized all white-collar jobs (such as real estate agent, bank teller, constable, and clerk), skilled jobs (such as blacksmith, butcher, baker, and carpenter), and a wide range of artisan occupations (wagon maker, tinsmith, cabinetmaker, shoemaker, carriage and harness maker, brick maker, brewer, and gunsmith). White male laborers also monopolized the best jobs in the unskilled stratum, where they accounted for all the teamsters (which was a partly skilled occupation) and livery stablers in the county.

The trajectory of these overall patterns was clearly evident by 1880, the point by which capitalist relations of production structured the local economy. The 1880 census reveals that European-American men enjoyed distinct advantages in both the self-employed as well as the wage-labor segment of the new economy. They accounted for 90 percent of all individuals in the farmer stratum and for 90.6 percent of all men in the proprietor stratum (saloonkeepers, grocers, hotel keepers, and restaurateurs). They also totally monopolized the professional stratum (principally doctors, lawyers, clergymen, and pharmacists) and accounted for 95 percent of individuals in the skilled occupations (blacksmiths, cabinetmakers, brick masons, and printers). White male laborers working in these skilled occupations received the highest wages in the county, approximately three to five dollars per day during the 1870s and 1880s.[88]

Overall, approximately 60 to 70 percent of the Anglo male population in the county could be classified as self-employed in 1880. Within the paid labor force, Anglo men monopolized new white-collar occupations, such as bank cashier, postmaster, telegraph operator, deputy assessor, and real estate agent. In 1880 only 22.7 percent of the white male population labored as unskilled workers and farm laborers. Moreover, as in 1870, those in such occupations often held the better jobs in this economic sector (such as teamsters).

Between 1870 and 1900 the percentage of Anglo men engaged in farming dropped from 55.5 percent to 28.1 percent. Increased costs in farm production (intensive agricultural practices necessitated high capital investment) and competition from large-scale farming operations both contributed to this decline. As a direct consequence, the number of Anglo men absorbed into the capitalist labor market between 1880 and 1900 rose dramatically. The rapid development of capitalist agriculture, for example, accounted for a threefold increase in the number of white farm laborers (as opposed to farm operators) employed locally.[89] The percentage of Anglos employed as farm laborers doubled between 1880 and 1900 (8.9 percent to 18 percent). The overall incorporation of these individuals into the farm labor market eventually led to an increase in the number of Anglos located at the bottom end of the new class structure. By 1900 nearly one-third of all adult Anglo males in the local economy held either unskilled or farm labor jobs.

The type of work relegated to racialized ethnic groups, on the other hand, revealingly captures the importance of "race" in the allocation of group position within the new relations of production in Ventura county. As early as 1870, for example, the overwhelming majority of Mexican, Native American, and Chinese men were employed in the unskilled stratum of the working class. In a year when only 17.6 percent of the white men worked as unskilled laborers, 60.2 percent of Mexican, 90.5 percent of Indian, and 100 percent of Chinese males labored in unskilled, menial jobs.

Nearly all the Mexican unskilled workers noted on the 1870 census were "day laborers" performing various unskilled jobs in the township, while others worked as shepherds and *transquiladores* (sheep shearers) on Anglo-owned ranchos. These Mexican shepherds and shearers were among the first Mexicanos integrated into the new capitalist economy. Unlike during the Mexican period, when these workers labored without monetary remuneration, in 1870 those employed by Anglo ranchers received wages for their labor. One major sheep raiser, for instance, paid his shepherd an average of $20 per month. The average wage received by trasquiladores hired seasonally ranged from $1.50 per day or four cents per fleece sheared.[90] Other skilled workers utilized on the few remaining ranchos in the area also underwent proletarianization. These included a handful of Mexican vaqueros and skilled tradesmen.

In 1880, the majority of Mexicans working in Ventura County (57.4 percent) held unskilled jobs, while another 10.9 percent were enumerated in the census as farm laborers. In total, more than two-thirds of Mexicans remained concentrated at the bottom end of the capitalist-dominated class structure. The only exception to this pattern were the numerous Mexican farmers and ranchers in the county (nearly 24 percent of the Mexican population) who were principally small-scale farmers owning less than two hundred acres of land.[91] The existence of this property-holding class clearly distinguished Mexicans from other minority groups in the county, but this advantage was short-lived and generally reflected their ability to only momentarily delay their widespread proletarianization in later years.

By 1900 the Mexican male population was securely positioned at the bottom of the county's occupational structure. Between 1870 and 1900, for example, the percentage of Mexicans employed as farm workers rose from 2 percent to an astounding 47.6 percent. With an additional 29.7 percent in the unskilled labor stratum, the total proportion of Mexican workers at the lowest levels of the working class reached 77.3 percent in 1900.

Unlike Mexicans, nearly all of the local Native American males enumerated in the 1870 census worked as day laborers or servants. The few employed outside of the unskilled labor stratum worked as vaqueros and saddlemakers (both skilled occupations), undoubtedly retaining some connection with the few remaining ranchos in the area. The restriction of opportunities available to Indians during the late 1860s was vividly illustrated in the case of those employed by the aforementioned Thomas W. More. The six Indian men under his charge performed a variety of tasks on More's Rancho Sespe (such as laboring in the asphaltum mine) and on his offshore property on Santa Rosa Island (primarily tending sheep).[92]

All the Chinese males enumerated on the 1870 census were also unskilled laborers working as day laborers, cooks, laundrymen, and servants.

The Chinese population in the area at the time encountered more racial enmity from European Americans than either Mexicans or Indians and, consequently, endured highly restricted employment opportunities. In 1872, for example, an article in the *Ventura Signal* reported that the "few Chinese" in the township were "only employed as house servants or day laborers."[93] During the early 1870s Chinese day laborers secured employment as unskilled mine workers or in miscellaneous construction and road work.[94]

The vast majority of Chinese men working in the county in 1880 continued as unskilled laborers. Over 85 percent worked as "day laborers" or held other unskilled jobs such as laundrymen, servants, and cooks in county oil operations, railroad camps, and large farms.[95] Another 8.1 percent worked as farm laborers. During the late 1870s and throughout the 1880s, they were also hired as seasonal workers in the weeding and harvesting of lima beans, mustard, and other crops.[96] Only a few Chinese males remained outside of the unskilled and farm labor strata. These included a few labor contractors and merchants who catered to the county's Chinese population.

The percentage of Chinese employed as farm laborers increased significantly from 8.1 percent in 1880 to 47.7 percent in 1900. The burgeoning lima bean and sugar beet industries extensively drew upon these workers as an important source of cheap labor.[97] Elsewhere they again remained a primary source of unskilled labor, working as cooks, laundrymen, gardeners, and day laborers.

Only a handful of Chinese successfully secured employment outside of these two strata. The number of Chinese farmers, proprietors, or professionals in Ventura County was negligible in 1900. These included a few small-scale vegetable growers, merchants, restaurateurs, boardinghouse keepers, and labor contractors. Those in these occupations faced a variety of discriminatory measures designed to curtail competition with their European-American counterparts. During the late 1870s and 1880s, for example, Chinese laundry proprietors were forced to pay a fifteen-dollar license fee and endured popularly supported boycotts of their establishments.[98] These discriminatory measures were local manifestations of the virulent anti-Chinese movement that gripped the state at the time.[99]

Federal enactment of the Chinese Exclusion Act in 1882 led to the decline of this population and their importance as a labor force in Ventura County. Between 1890 and 1900, for example, the Chinese population declined from 4.5 percent to 2.8 percent of the county's total population. This situation caused the *Ventura Free Press* to comment approvingly in

1903 that "the Chinese population is smaller now than it ever has been."[100] Their decline led Anglo farmers to turn to Japanese, as well as Mexicans, as an alternative source of cheap agricultural labor.

The Japanese immigrants who first settled in Ventura County in the mid-1890s arrived as single men who secured local employment through local farm labor contractors. By the turn of the century, the vast majority of these new immigrants labored in the burgeoning sugar beet, lima bean, and citrus industries. More than two-thirds (68.2 percent) of Japanese males worked as farm laborers in 1900. The scant number not employed in agricultural fields worked as unskilled day laborers, cooks, and section hands for the railroads. Only a mere handful of Japanese immigrants successfully became proprietors or white-collar workers. Like Mexicans and Chinese, they were largely excluded from the middle levels of the new class structure. The experience of the Japanese once again highlighted the importance of racial status as the central organizing principle of the new economy.

CONCLUSION

This chapter has documented through various archival sources the momentous change in class structure that occurred in Ventura County between 1860 and 1900. Beginning in 1870 and intensifying dramatically in the 1880s, an economy based on wage labor eclipsed that based on the unfree labor system of the Mexican period. Once unleashed, this proletarianization absorbed both the indigenous Mexican population and the numerous white and nonwhite immigrant groups that settled in the area.

This case study demonstrates that the central role of racial status in shaping group relations at the state level was clearly reflected in the placement of local white and nonwhite populations in this emerging class structure. Far from being merely an ideological construct or an anachronistic status designation, race became the key organizing principle structuring white supremacist economic, as well as political, institutions that were introduced in California. White male immigrants became farmers, proprietors, professionals, and white-collar employees, while the Mexican, Japanese, Chinese, and Indian male populations were securely ensconced at the bottom end of the class structure as unskilled manual workers. European Americans also jealously retained important advantages over the racialized populations in certain occupations within the unskilled labor stratum of the working class, giving further evidence of the racialized nature of class relations that accompanied the imposition of white supremacy in the state.

PART TWO

White Civilization's Crusade against the "Devils of the Forest"

CHAPTER FOUR

"Before the March of Civilization He Must Give Way"

Although capable of an equivocal accommodation of Mexicans, European Americans never gave serious consideration to integrating Indians into the new society they introduced into California after 1850. While Mexicans were viewed as "half civilized" at best, Indians were seen as the complete embodiment of both heathenism and savagery. Moreover, by straightforwardly defining the indigenous Indian population as "nonwhite," European Americans in a stroke denied Indians the citizenship that they had grudgingly extended to the "white" Mexican population.[1] Whereas the relations between Anglo and Mexican "citizens" were institutionally mediated, white and Indian societies confronted one another in the frontier wilderness of the state, not in courtrooms, voting booths, town meetings, the labor market, or juridical contestations over land.

It should come as no surprise that European Americans never viewed the California Indians as being as assimilable as the Mexican population; they possessed none of the latter's redeeming qualities. The cultural gulf between Indians and Anglos was simply more insurmountable than that separating Anglos and Mexicans. Unlike Mexicans, with their class-coded, Europeanized attire, Indians sported tattooed bodies and scarred faces and wore little more than animal skins and grass shirts. Indians also ate insects, rodents, and reptiles, dug for roots, relied on acorns and pine nuts, and foraged in the wilds for berries and grass seeds. These dietary practices were beyond the pale of traditional culinary customs in both Mexican and Anglo societies. Moreover, European Americans were also repulsed that

Indians had no sense of "hard work" and had not even matched the ranchero elite's feeble attempt to develop the territory. The Indians' traditional hunting and gathering economy and their system of gender and sexual meanings proved to Anglos that they were not only uncivilized but heathen as well.

Being deemed "nonwhite," uncivilized, and unchristian placed the California Indians totally at odds with European-American racial, religious, and cultural norms. Moreover, Indians occupied the land that these settlers wanted and which they believed to be their entitlement. Thus, from the initial period of Anglo settlement, they became both the real and symbolic antithesis of the European-American population. Rather than being integrated into Anglo society at a subordinate level, Indians were ruthlessly segregated onto reservations, marginalized in the new Anglo economy, and subjected to violent pogroms no other racialized ethnic group experienced.

"Civilized" Anglo and "savage" Indian society symbolically clashed in areas such as Mendocino, Humboldt, Del Norte, Trinity, and Siskiyou counties in northwestern California and sections of the immense central valley of California. It was in the rural hinterlands of the state that Indians became the symbolic enemy in the white man's mind—the "devils of the forest," as an Oroville newspaper article characterized them in 1863.[2] Like other game in the wilds, Indians became the object of brute domination or even potential annihilation if they threatened the white population's personal safety or property.

These bloody conflicts reached unparalleled ferocity in the early decades after statehood and demonstrated that few Anglos ever recognized Indians as human beings. California's white population retained the most barbaric claim one person can hold over another: the right to murder with impunity. Even the horrors of slavery—where one man retained another as personal chattel—pale in comparison to the wanton, state-sanctioned destruction of a people and their culture. By 1880, an estimated eight thousand Native American men, women, and children had died violently at the hands of white Americans.

This chapter explores the violent conflict that flared in the state between Indians and European-American settlers seeking economic advancement in California's rural frontier. It was the troublesome persistence of the native people's traditional way of life on coveted land that convinced Anglos that Indians had no meaningful place in Anglo California. In exploring this historical process, I give special attention to unraveling the racializing ideology used by European Americans to both racially demonize the Indians and justify their decimation.

SOCIAL ORGANIZATION OF PRE-CONQUEST
INDIAN SOCIETY

At the time of Spanish arrival in 1769 an estimated 300,000 Indians inhabited the region of Alta California, living in relatively small tribal groupings of fifty to five hundred persons. This represented a higher pre-conquest Indian population density per square mile than in any other region in North America.[3] In the eighteenth century, the Indian population of California was internally divided into six major language families.[4] According to historian George Harwood Phillips, in southern California

> the majority of the Indians belonged to the Uto-Aztecan language family, especially the Shoshonean subfamily. These Indians were further separated into numerous language divisions, including Cahuilla, Luiseno, Cupeno, Serrano, Chemehuevi, Gabrieleno, Fernandino, and Juaneno. Located to the south and east of the Shoshonean-speakers were Indians who spoke the languages of the Hokan-Siouian family of which Yuman was the subfamily. They were also separated into several language divisions, including the Quechan (Yuma), Halchidhoma, Cocopa, Mohave, Kamia, and Diegueno.[5]

Phillips notes that by the time of Spanish movement into the territory, the California Indians "had developed a highly specialized hunting and food-gathering economy . . . [and] were divided into autonomous, localized patrilineages." While all lineages were similarly structured, "there were basic differences in demography and modes of lineage interaction. Cupeno lineages were limited to a small area and were distributed between two main villages, producing a good deal of social and political integration. Cahuilla lineages were quite dispersed and were grouped into several clans. The Luiseno apparently lacked clans, and their lineages remained isolated from and often hostile to one another."[6]

One anthropologist characterizes the Indian societies in the territory at the time as "quite sedentary hunter-gatherers."[7] The Ohlone Indians of the San Francisco–Monterey Bay area provide a good example of the California Indians' hunting and gathering existence prior to 1769. A part of the Penutian linguistic family, the Ohlones represented forty or so Indian tribal groupings, each with its own territory, distinct language structure, and unique adaption to the local environment. The average size of these Indian groupings was only about 250 people, and they were distributed within the wide geographical expanse from Big Sur just south of Monterey to the greater San Francisco Bay area.[8]

Like all other California Indians, the Ohlones used no metal, had no cultivated agriculture (in the Western sense of the term), wove no cloth, and did not utilize pottery.[9] According to Malcom Margolin, "Their arrows were tipped with flint or obsidian, their mortars and pestles were of stone, and other tools were made of bone, shell, or wood. . . . They lived entirely by hunting and gathering."[10] The abundance of live oaks throughout the region also provided a principal food source for the Ohlones. Indian women hulled the acorns from the oaks and ground them into a thick mush or processed them into bread. "Unlike wheat, corn, barley, or rice, acorns required no tilling of the soil, no digging of irrigation ditches, nor any other form of farming. Thus, while the preparation of acorn flour might have been a lengthy and tedious process, the total labor involved was probably much less than for a cereal crop. Yet the level of nutrients in acorns was extremely high—comparable in fact with wheat and barley." Moreover, "the extraordinary virtues of the acorn help explain why the Ohlones and other Central California Indians never adopted the agricultural practices of other North American groups who raised squash, corn, and other crops. Lack of agriculture was not the result of isolation, conservatism, laziness, or backwardness. . . . The truth is far simpler: Central California Indians did not adopt traditional agricultural methods because they didn't have to. Acorns, along with an extremely generous environment, provided them with a more-than-adequate diet."[11]

Like other hunter-gatherer Indians, the Ohlones supplemented their basic diet by eating various insects, reptiles, and rodents as well as both large and small game animals. Only a few animals were considered inedible for religious reasons. When viewed cross-culturally and in broad historical terms, there was nothing particularly unusual about the Ohlone diet. According to Margolin, "only in recent times . . . have people narrowed their preferences to a few major species, such as cows, pigs, goats, sheep, and chickens." Before the recent widespread dependence on domesticated animals, "human societies everywhere lived on insects, reptiles, and rodents as well as larger game animals. So it was with the Ohlone."[12]

Though food was plentiful, the seasonal availability of the Ohlone's foodstuffs required constant migration. "There were trips to the seashore for shellfish, to the rivers for salmon, to the marshes for ducks and geese, to the oak groves for acorns, and to the hills and meadows for seeds, roots, and other greens. There were also trips to quarries where the men collected minerals and stones, and still other trips for milkweed fiber, hemp, basket materials, tobacco, and medicine."[13] This wandering existence set the Ohlone apart from other Indians of the Southwest, such as the Pueblos, who built cities and lived settled lives cultivating various crops.[14]

Instead of living in permanent structures made of wood or adobe, the

Ohlones lived in skillfully made tule homes that were well adapted to the moderate climate. In their temporary nature, these homes held the advantage of requiring just a few hours for construction and could later be deserted when the Ohlone seasonally migrated to secure other foodstuff.[15]

Living arrangements in these tule huts typically consisted of multiple family dwellings, single-family units, families where wealthier men had two wives, the village chief's home (where he lived with three wives), and an occasional unit comprised of two men (one of whom typically assumed a female gender role). These same-sex couplings were an institutionalized feature of Ohlone Indian society.[16] (The social organization of gender and systems of sexual meaning among the California Indians would later provide an important basis upon which European Americans would deem them "savages.")

THE RACIAL DEMONIZATION OF THE CALIFORNIA INDIANS

One key aspect of the bitter hostility that Indians initially confronted during the last half of the nineteenth century was their unambiguous representation as subhuman beings. There were a number of crucial features of the European American's racialization of the California Indians. Some Anglos simply believed that the Indians were remarkably dirty, ugly, and very dark complexioned. Others inscribed racial difference because of the alleged "animal-like" nature of the native peoples' existence.

Historian James Rawls has argued insightfully that Anglo contempt and revulsion toward the California Indians was intimately bound to the Anglos' image of them as an unusually dirty people. What captured the imagination of Anglo-Americans was the belief that the Indians were unspeakably filthy. Rawls notes that the longstanding Anglo-American tradition of viewing cleanliness as a virtue—i.e. "cleanliness being next to godliness"—provided a critical basis for Indians being seen as an ugly, primitive people.

Rawls argues that the very term "digger," which was a commonly used racial epithet, evolved "from the Indians' alleged burrowing under the ground or from their digging and eating roots."[17] Similarly, anthropologist Robert Heizer has argued that the term "digger" was "originally coined as a term of opprobrium and was intended to reflect the inferior status of natives who did not farm but hunted and collected seeds, or even dug up edible roots, to sustain themselves."[18] It is likely, he suggests, that the term "digger" was a shortened version of the label "root digger" which appeared widely in various newspapers and travel journals during the 1840s. The term clearly had a pejorative connotation that reflected the utter contempt that California's white population had for the traditional Indian way of life.[19] Consequently, the derisive appellation "digger" captured Anglo-American attitudes of Indians being "dirty," "dull and ignorant," animal-like creatures who grubbed for roots and lived in primitive dwellings that Europeans considered unfit for human habitation.

Hinton Rowan Helper's characterization of life in California in his *The Land of Gold: Reality versus Fiction* (1855) provides a good example of the Anglo view of Indians as a "filthy and abominable" people. "A worse set of vagabonds cannot be found bearing the human form. Their chief characteristics are indolence and gluttony. Partially wrapped in filthy rags, with their persons unwashed, hair uncombed and swarming with vermin, they may be seen loitering about the kitchens and slaughter-houses waiting to seize upon and devour like hungry wolves such offal or garbage as may be thrown to them."[20]

A related aspect of the racialized imagery that crystallized in the white man's mind was the belief that the California Indians were also exceedingly ugly. European Americans frequently made special mention of the dreadful appearance of the Indian population, whose physical appearance they deemed the antithesis of their own ideals of beauty. The Indians' basic somatic features (complexion, hair, physique, and physiognomy) were all invoked as proof that they made up a completely different category of people. This perception was reinforced by the fact that some Indian women tattooed their bodies, wore very scant clothing made of tule reed and deer skins, and pierced their noses and ears, while the men were either naked or wore short capes of woven rabbit skins and occasionally daubed themselves with mud to keep warm on cold days. George Payson, in his *Golden Dreams and Leaden Realities* (1853), contemptuously and colorfully wrote that the Indians' "monstrous heads, covered with a thick thatch of long black hair, and mounted on dwarfish bodies and distorted limbs, gave them a peculiarly inhuman and impish aspect."[21]

Skin color provided another important means of racialization. Numerous characterizations of the Indian as "chocolate brown," "dark mahogany," or simply as "very dark" or "black" was common throughout the period after statehood. Unlike "the tawny red color usually associated with North American Indians, the Californians were described as dark brown or black. Their color was such a salient feature that it bound together the other associations of primitiveness, dirtiness, and ugliness in the whites' minds."[22] As with other groups, however, "the dark complexion of the

California Indian" served as the most readily observable "badge of inferiority," clearly setting them off from the superior white population.[23]

White immigrants also felt that Indians were a "beastly," "brutish," "subhuman" species. According to Rawls, "the Indians were considered so primitive (or 'degraded' or 'wretched') that some whites regarded them very nearly as beasts. California whites used animal metaphors to suggest the status of the Indians and to register their own sense of extreme distance or difference from the people that they described."[24] This dehumanization was linked to Anglo perceptions of Indians as subsisting in an almost instinctive, animal-like fashion. If Anglos were the embodiment of all that was rational, civilized, and "spiritual," Indians were the incarnation of the irrational, the uncivilized, and all that was associated with instinct, the body, or animal life.

We recall that Hinton Helper described the Indians he encountered as eating like "hungry wolves." Other characterizations of the traditional mode of Indian subsistence centered on their "grazing" like cattle, eating like "little pigs," "like dogs," or simply "like beasts." Similarly, the Indians' traditional housing was seen as quite crude and inferior even to the beaver's or muskrat's. Anglos referred to these dwellings as places where Indians hibernated like bears or "coiled" together like snakes. Finally, this subhuman status led to Indians being associated with simians. Like blacks before them, the dark-skinned California Indians were likened to the "baboon," "orang-outang," "gorilla," or the common "monkey."[25] This, of course, led to speculation that the California Indian was the "connecting link" which bound the human race with the lower forms of animal life.[26]

While traveling through the Sacramento Valley, Jedediah Smith made special mention in his diary that the local Indians he encountered were so depraved that he believed them to be more animal-like than human. He disdainfully observed that "a great many of the Indians appear to be the lowest intermediate link between man and the Brute creation. In the construction of houses they are either from indolence or from a deficiency of genius inferior to the Beaver and many of them live without anything in the shape of a house and rise from their bed of earth in the morning like the animals around them and rove about in search of food."[27]

UPROOTING THE TRADITIONAL INDIAN MODE OF SUBSISTENCE

As suggested above, these images of the California Indian were closely associated with the Indian's traditional subsistence economy. Anglos believed that, unlike "half civilized" Mexicans, Indians resided at the very lowest levels of the hierarchy of humankind. Not only were California Indians filthy, ugly, dark, and animal-like, but they were also "uncivilized" in their mode of economic livelihood.

The California Indians' traditional way of life was totally different from the Western European system of economic production the Anglos sought to develop in the state. This cleavage became a key basis of anti-Indian sentiment and is vividly captured in the numerous references to Indians' "laziness" and primitive subsistence livelihood. More important, few Anglos believed the Indians capable of *ever* breaking out of their old patterns and entering the American economy. The conflict between Anglo and Indian societies, therefore, represented the clash of two divergent ways of life; as one Anglo pioneer put it in 1852, "the two extremes of American civilization and Indian barbarism."[28]

By Western European standards, California Indians such as the Ohlone were a pathetically backward, uncivilized people who lived in grass hovels, made boats and tools from unacceptable material, and even preferred baskets to pottery. Furthermore, the Indian's cultural values and traditions were completely at odds with those of European Americans. The Ohlones, for instance, developed a deeply spiritual sense of the world that contributed to their balanced relationship with the environment and a communal economic system based on sharing and mutual cooperation; as a result, they had no need for a strong, state-based governmental system recognizable to Europeans. According to Malcolm Margolin, "Rather than valuing possessions, the Ohlones valued generosity. Instead of having inheritance, which is a way of perpetuating wealth within a family, the Ohlones generally destroyed a person's goods after his or her death. . . . Thus a wealthy man was expected to contribute generously to the group's many feasts and festivals and he was expected to throw his most precious gift baskets and other offerings onto the funeral pyre of a deceased friend or relative. To be wealthy was not to have; to be wealthy was to give."[29]

European Americans also viewed Indians such as the Ohlone as a "lazy" people whose hunting and gathering form of livelihood was a great failing. Hard work for the Ohlones came infrequently, and it was typically followed by periods in which they enjoyed the bounty they seasonally procured.

> Deer hunting, for example, was an arduous pursuit that demanded fasting, abstinence, great physical strength, and single-mindedness of purpose. The acorn harvest, the seed harvest, and the salmon harvest also involved considerable work for short periods of time. But when the work was over, there was little

else to do. Unlike agricultural people, the Ohlones had no fields to plow, seeds to plant, crops to cultivate, weeds to pull, domestic animals to care for, or irrigation ditches to dig or maintain. So at the end of a harvest they often gave themselves over to 'entire indolence,' as one visitor described it—a habit that infuriated the Europeans who assumed that laziness was sinful and that hard work was not just a virtue but a God-given condition of human life.[30]

Continuation of the Indians' subsistence livelihood impeded the creation of the new system of production Anglos sought to introduce in the state, a view widespread during the early years after United States annexation of California. An editorial in the January 13, 1859 edition of the *San Francisco Weekly National* posed the problem in this way:

> The California Indian is perhaps the most inferior of all the North American races. Reared in our salubrious climate—procuring abundant food in the shape of acorns, roots, game and fish, *without labor*—inured, in fact, to no hardship—he has become a weak, degenerate creature, both physically and mentally. He is a child in moral restraint and mental capacity, with the animal passions, propensity and appetites. . . . He, therefore, needs a master, and one too who can *compel* him to obey. Leave it all optional with him, and he will labor not, neither will he spin. There must be employed a sufficient white force to work the fields with him, and if necessary, inflict occasional chastisement. [Emphasis in original.] [31]

A similar assessment was offered by Special Agent G. Bailey in his November 4, 1858, report to the Commissioner of Indian Affairs in Washington, D.C. Bailey stressed the difficulty of attempting to "civilize" the California Indians to a Western way of life. According to Bailey, the key to making Indians self-sufficient was to convince them of the value of labor and the necessity of giving up their traditional way of life:

> By the term civilization, then, as applied to the Indians, I understand, not the mere teaching him to ape the dress and habits of the white man, or even the instructing him of the rudiments of mechanical and agricultural knowledge, but the planting in his mind the germ of some idea which shall be self-developing, and which in its development shall lift him out the slough where he now wallows. It implies the teaching him, practically, the 'immense superiority of a fixed over a roving life,' and the dignity of labor and this is not so much by ministering to his physical appetites as a reward for labor done, as by enabling him to apprehend how labor, properly applied, will procure for him the objects of his desire. . . . Some few of them, it is true, are taught to plough, to sow, to reap, to handle an axe, and the like, but they are not taught the use of this knowledge. They learn the thing but not the reason for it, and therefore it makes not permanent impression and leads to nothing. The Indian performs his task because he is told to do it. He does it mechanically and is not more improved by it than the ox he drives. They are both (the Indian and the ox) educated by

the same method, to about the same degree, and with very nearly the same results; and even this education is confined to a very small number. . . . The great mass of the Indians live exactly as their ancestors did: an occasional blanket is doled out here, or a quart of beans there, to eke out the scanty subsistence nature furnishes them; but with these exceptions their condition is precisely the same as before they were brought upon the reserve.[32]

In the same annual report, Vincent Geiger, the Indian Agent at the Nome Lackee Reservation, also acknowledged the great difficulty in getting the Indians to appreciate the value of labor. In July 1858, Geiger lamented that despite some success in teaching Indians the value of labor, fundamental problems remained: "To make their labor remunerative, however, requires the constant attention and supervision of experienced and practical white men. The Indians left entirely to themselves would do little towards growing and providing the necessary food for their subsistence. Deprive them of the governing power and protecting care of the white man, but a short time would elapse before they would fall back into their former condition of destitution, misery and want."[33]

European-American attitudes such as these persisted for decades and were at the heart of conflict between Anglo settlers and the California Indian in the frontier hinterlands of the new state. Despite some benevolent intentions, Anglo-American attempts to improve the condition of the Indian were heavily laden with ethnocentric assumptions about the superiority of the Protestant work ethic and of Western ways of relating to the environment. Time and again Anglos noted the great difficulty of getting the Indian population to accept Anglo-American values and traditions. Although efforts were repeatedly made by some Anglos to bring the Indians "into contact with the arts and tastes of civilized life," they preferred to "hold tenaciously to their old primitive character of 'Digger'."[34]

As late as the 1880s Anglos continued to bemoan the difficulty of civilizing the California Indian. In August 1883, for example, Indian Agent Charles Porter wrote of his dismay over getting the Indian population to "reach a certain grade of civilization" beyond that attained before the arrival of the European American. Agent Porter's report intoned the unquestionable superiority of the Protestant work ethic to traditional Indian values and mode of subsistence:

Many of them are still indolent, immoral, and unsteady, feeble in their domestic and family attachments, untruthful, and extremely superstitious. Their present condition is one of self-complacent lethargy and moral and mental stagnation. They evince no desire to acquire knowledge, to learn useful trades, to gain possession of and cultivate lands of their own, or to better their condition in any respect, when the doing so necessitates exertion, application, self-denial. Plodding industry, constant application, and steady work are their especial abhorrences. Only the pressure of some actual necessity or of some extra inducements will induce them to work. Even when hired by citizens for good wages they work merely long enough to "raise a stake," which is almost invariably wasted in idleness, frivolity, and dissipation.[35]

All these characterizations made it easier to justify the often inhumane treatment that European Americans inflicted upon the California Indians after 1848. The reduction of the indigenous population to the level of "wild beasts" was a necessary precondition to their brutal decimation and the expropriation of their land during the early decades of Anglo control of the state.[36] Historian James Rawls has cogently summarized the role these eurocentric images played in the Indian experience during the early American period: "The California Indians evoked expression of contempt and repulsion. They seemed so primitive and degraded that they were more like animals than men. This radical loss of humanity made the prospects of Indian extermination and extinction palatable and even highly desirable, as if with their extermination California would be purified and cleansed of a set of degraded and repulsive creatures."[37]

THE WHITE MASCULINIST ASSAULT
ON THE CALIFORNIA INDIANS

The decimation of the California Indians between 1848 and 1870 reflected the symbolic clash between Anglo "civilization" and Indian "savagery." This confrontation crystallized in violent encounters between rural European-American settlers and the "wild tribes" of California. It is important to note that the white men reportedly involved in these bloody skirmishes were typically singled out as the fringe of the new Anglo society. They were portrayed as a vanguard of single male settlers, frontiersmen, slave traders, fugitives, and so-called "trash" of white society who were to dominate Gold Rush California society. What distinguished these individuals was the precarious position they held in the newly emerging capitalist class structure. Contemporaries viewing the conflict between these white settlers and Indians in the rural frontiers of the state repeatedly described the Anglos involved as belonging to the "lowest class of the white population." They were clearly differentiated from the more "upstanding" urban semiskilled and skilled Anglo working class and urban-based small businessmen and professionals. Nor were they representative of the class of Anglo family farmers developing in the recently subdivided rancho land along the rich coastal range. Instead, those white men most directly implicated in the violent decimation of the native peoples were drawn from the margins of the new Anglo society. They were among those who had most to lose from the presence of Indians in regions where they settled. The persistence of the Indian's traditional subsistence way of life and potential Indian vandalization of their property all posed immediate obstacles to their economic well-being. Moreover, in the view of these men, Indians represented a direct symbolic threat to the racial and class prerogatives that "manifest destiny" and the "free labor ideology" held out to all white men in California. It was this underclass that most actively participated in wanton attacks on Indian men, women, and children in northeastern and central California.

By the early 1850s a clear pattern of conflict between Indians and these marginalized men was readily apparent to most observers in California. In an 1853 report to the Commissioner of Indian Affairs, an Anglo Indian agent in the state observed that "if ever the secret history of the late disturbances is written, we have no doubt but nineteen out of every twenty will be found to have had their origin in the direct aggression on the part of unprincipled white men, or failure on their part to supply the Indians with beef and flour, as the promised reward of their labor."[38]

The character of the actors involved in these "disturbances" was even more apparent by the mid-1860s. In 1866, for example, Superintendent of Indian Affairs Charles Maltby offered the following candid assessment of the role these white men played in the bloody confrontations with Indians:

> The Indians . . . reside in various sections of the State, in small communities; in some localities their presence is obnoxious to the citizens; in others they are tolerated on account of the labor they perform for whites; their condition is deplorable and pitiable in the extreme; they are demoralized both physically and morally. This condition, lamentable as it is, is the result of their intercourse and contact with the lowest class of the white population, and they more readily embrace the vices of civilization because it is only with its vices they come in contact. . . . With no land, no treaties, no annuities, no power or means of extricating themselves from the influences with which they are surrounded, and which are rapidly and surely working their destruction and extermination . . . the case of the poor Indian is hopeless, and before the march of civilization he must give way; and instead of civilization reaching out a helping hand to elevate and redeem, it is used to hasten his destruction and effect his entire demoralization and degradation.[39]

Indian Agent J. Ross Browne, however, noted that this class of "renegade whites" was unrepresentative of the European-American population at large. According to Agent Browne, it was "a particular class of white settlers, whose misconduct towards the Indians has always been a prolific source of trouble. This class exists in all frontier countries. It is not practicable to get rid of them by written complaints. They will be found on the outskirts of civilization wherever it goes."[40]

As more and more Anglo settlers extended their "march of civilization" into the California Indians' traditional hunting and gathering grounds, a steady increase in the incidence of violence against Indians and Indian retaliation against white Americans ensued. For the Indians' part, attacks made on white settlers were usually reprisals for the brutal murders of Indian men and women, and the wholesale kidnapping of Indian children. The rapid migration of European Americans into northern California also had devastating consequences for the Indians' traditional mode of economic subsistence. The flood of gold seekers and, in their wake, farmers who preempted traditional Indian land, drastically reduced or eliminated the California Indian's local food supply. Hungry Indians were forced to steal food or kill a cow in order to avoid total starvation. From the Indians' point of view these acts represented both a necessary and a logical retaliation for the depredation of their food supply by encroaching settlers.

One of the first documented accounts of the impact of Anglo society on the California Indians involved the aforementioned Ohlones. Indian Agent Adam Johnston's 1853 report to the Commissioner of Indian Affairs contains one of the very few firsthand Indian accounts of the lamentable situation they confronted after 1848. Johnston discusses the condition of the Ohlone, also known as the *Costanoes*, at Mission Dolores in San Francisco as follows:

> Within the short period of time since the occupancy of this country by the whites, the red man has been fast fading away. Many have died with disease, and others have fled to the mountains to enjoy, for a brief period of time, their primeval sports of hunting and fishing. Almost the entire tribe of *Costanoes*, or Coast Indians, have passed away. Of the numerous tribes which but a few years ago inhabited the country bordering on the bay of San Francisco, scarcely an individual is left. The pale-faces have taken possession of their country and trample upon the graves of their forefathers. In an interview with a very aged Indian near the mission Dolores, he said, "I am very old; my people were once around me like the sands of the shore—many, many. They have all passed away—they have died like the grass. They have gone to the mountains—I do not complain; the antelope falls with the arrow. I had a son—I loved him. When the pale-faces came, he went away; I know not where he is. I am a Christian Indian; I am all that is left of my people—I am alone." His age, his earnestness, and decrepit condition, gave full force to his language. . . .[41]

A similar process unfolded elsewhere in northern and central California. In the nearby Sacramento area, for instance, the *Sacramento Union* posed the problem in September, 1856 in this way: "From recent information the s will suffer more than usual during the coming months of the year. little streams and springs are dried up, so they will not be able to est their customary crop of corn, nor pumpkins, and beans. Necessity will drive them to prey upon the cattle of neighboring ranches. In truth, starvation, or robbery for the sake of food, is the only alternative left for the Indian."[42]

European Americans steadfastly believed that the California Indians were an obstacle to white civilization and their providentially ordained economic development of the state. As long as Indians remained in the area, progress in mining, agriculture, and other entrepreneurial ventures would be hopelessly impeded by the threat of Indian "depredations" on white property. Only the total elimination of the Indian population would ensure Anglo settlement, security, and economic prosperity.[43]

Another source of the cycle of Indian/Anglo conflict was the flagrant abuse of Indian women by white men. Although Anglos found that some Mexican women had redeeming qualities, they almost uniformly viewed Indian women with complete disdain. Unmediated by the class cleavages that segmented Mexican society and helped to moderate Anglo views of upper-class Mexican women, Anglo views of Indian women typically objectified them as mere "squaws." Their complete devaluation in the white man's eyes reduced them to mere property or sexual commodities. White men believed that they could freely have their way with Indian women, even if the latter were married.

In the early 1850s, Indian women were routinely captured and either held as concubines by their kidnappers or sold to other white men for their personal use.[44] One Anglo pioneer in Trinity County reported that traffickers of Indian women had even devised a system which classified them into "fair, middling, inferior, [and] refuse" categories of merchandise.[45]

Not unexpectedly, this situation often led Indian spouses and other male relatives to retaliate against Anglos for their degradation of Indian women. Such abuse led one Indian official in Mendocino County to acknowledge that "a very large majority of white unmarried men" there during the 1850s and 1860s would "constantly excite the Indians to jealousy and revenge by taking their squaws from them."[46] Skirmishes due to this practice were also acknowledged by another Anglo citizen in the Klamath region of northern California in July 1858. "Nearly all the difficulties that have occurred in this district during the past year have had their origin in, and can be traced to the filthy alliance of men, calling themselves white, with squaws. How far degraded a man may become by pandering to the corrupt and unrestrained propensities of his animal instinct . . . is best illustrated in that class of individuals who, forgetting their origins, cut themselves loose from their fellows, and bow at the shrine of Digger prostitution."[47]

This objectionable practice was also attested to in *The California Farmer*, which reported in October 1860 that "hundreds of white men" were living with Indian women "whom they have taken from their Indian companions" in Trinity County.[48] This sexual abuse was so widespread in Eureka that a mass public meeting was organized by outraged local citizens in June 1862. The local citizenry at this meeting vented its hostility at the numerous "white men who live with Indian squaws" in the area.[49]

But rather than compel white men to end this abusive treatment of Indian women, state authorities targeted Indians as the source of this intolerable situation. In order to neutralize the threat of Indian reprisals against the continued misuse of Indian women and pillage of their hunting and gathering grounds, the California state government initiated an aggressive military counteroffensive. This policy was advocated forcefully by California's first Anglo governor, a Southerner named Peter H. Burnett. In his annual message to the state legislature in January 1851, Governor Burnett assured the body that "a war of extermination will continue to be waged between the two races until the Indian race becomes extinct . . . while we cannot anticipate this result with but painful regret, the inevitable destiny of the [white] race is beyond the power and wisdom of man to avert.[50]

The oratorical invective of one Horace Bell provides further evidence of this growing sentiment among different classes within the white population. In his *Reminiscences of a Ranger*, Bell justified the decimation of the California Indians as the inevitable and necessary price required for attaining European-American dominion over the state. "We will let those rascally redskins know that they have no longer to deal with the Spaniards or the Mexicans, but with the invincible race of American backwoodsmen, which has driven the savages from Plymouth Rock to the Rocky Mountains and has headed him off here on the western shore of the continent, and will drive him back to meet his kindred fleeing westward, all to be drowned in the great Salt Lake."[51]

Shortly after the granting of statehood in 1850, the new California government formally implemented a military policy designed to eliminate Indian depredations against its Anglo citizenry. The state directly subsidized "private military forays" against the California Indians. Almost any white man could raise a volunteer company, outfit it with guns, ammunition, horses, and supplies and have these expenses defrayed by the state government. The state legislature passed acts in 1851 and 1852 authorizing payment of over $1.1 million for the suppression of Indian hostilities. In 1857 the legislature again issued bonds amounting to $410,000 for the same purposes. The U.S. Congress would eventually reimburse the state for nearly all the expenses these military forays incurred in achieving their ignoble mission.[52]

For the next twenty years the state government waged an unrelenting campaign to exterminate the "wild Indian tribes" of California. Repeated attacks were made on Indian villages throughout the state, especially in central and northwestern California, by volunteer military companies and regular U.S. army units.[53] These assaults were ostensibly reprisals for Indian thievery and attacks on white settlers. While some of the attacks on the Indian population resulted in only a few deaths, there were instances when entire villages were wiped out.

One of the first of these state-sponsored expeditions occurred in 1849 and resulted in the massacre of a village of Pomo Indians at Clear Lake by seventy-five volunteers. A firsthand account was reported in the *San Francisco Alta California* on May 28, 1850:

> The troops arrived in the vicinity of the lake, and came unexpectedly upon a body of Indians numbering between two and three hundred. . . . They immediately surrounded them and as the Indians raised a shout of defiance and attempted to escape, poured in a destructive fire indiscriminately upon men, women, and children. They fell, says our informant, as grass before the sweep of the scythe. Little or no resistance was encountered, and the work of butchering was of short duration. The shrieks of the slaughtered victims died away, the roar of muskets ceased, and stretched lifeless upon the sod of their native valley were the bleeding bodies of these Indians—nor sex, nor age was spared; it was the order of *extermination* fearfully obeyed. The troops returned to the stations, and quiet is for the present restored. [Emphasis in original][54]

One of the most heartbreaking descriptions of this attack on the village at Clear Lake was recounted in later years by William Benson, a Pomo Indian known for his integrity and honesty. Benson's father was a white settler who followed the practice of some early "squaw men" by abandoning white life entirely and residing permanently in the Pomo village. Benson's father died while his son was still a child. The young Indian spoke only Pomo as a child and obtained knowledge of English from later contacts with the Anglo population. Although Benson was without formal schooling, he taught himself to read as well as write English, with only a phonetic spelling of the language. William Benson, whose Pomo name was Ralganal, was later used as an informant and interpreter for many Anglo-American anthropologists such as A. L. Kroeber, who conducted field work in Lake County.

In 1932 Benson recounted his recollection of the "massacre" at Clear Lake. His narrative of the events painfully describes the unconscionable treatment of the Indians living in the region. It appeared that the interracial conflict had its origins in the practices of two Anglo settlers, Andrew Kelsey and Charles Stone, who ruthlessly exploited local Pomo Indians as virtual slaves on their farm. Some of Stone and Kelsey's associates were also reportedly involved in exploiting Indian labor in the local mining region. Driven to the mines by Kelsey's brother Benjamin, the Indians were treated like slaves, receiving woefully inadequate supplies of food and water and no wages.[55] Two collaborative Indian accounts of the situation leading to the military attack on the Pomo indicate that only a handful of the 100 to 150 Indian men taken to the mines by Stone and Kelsey's associates returned from the ordeal. The ruthless treatment of these Indians contributed to the hostile feelings the Pomo had for both Andrew Kelsey and Charles Stone.[56]

Of the various abuses inflicted by the two on them, Benson writes that one of the most common consisted of

> whipping and tieing their hands togather with rope. the rope then—thrown over a limb of a tree and then drawn up untell the indians toes barly touchs the ground and let them hand there for hours. this was common punishment. when a father or mother of young girl was asked to bring girl to his house. by stone or kelsey. if this order not obeyed. he or she would be whipped or hung by the hands. such punishment occured two or three times a week. and many of the old man and women died from fear and starvation.
>
> these two white men had the indians to build a high fence around thir villages. and the head riders were to see that no indians went out side of this fence after dark. if any one was caught out side of the fence after dark was taken to stones and kelseys house and there was tied both hands and feet and placed in a room and kept there all night. the next day was taken to a tree and was tied down. then the strongs man was chosen to whippe the prisoner.[57]

It was this reprehensible mistreatment, plus the urgency of impending starvation, that eventually led the local Pomo Indians to raid Stone and Kelsey's livestock and storage bins. With the assistance of some Indian servants who smuggled all of Stone and Kelsey's weapons out of their homes the evening before the fateful expedition, two of their farm hands led the attack that resulted in Stone and Kelsey's death. The *coup de grace* for Kelsey was actually delivered by an Indian woman who stabbed him in the heart in retaliation for killing her son, a young boy murdered for taking wheat to her starving family.

Once word of Stone and Kelsey's death reached the local white population, a volunteer military party was sent to revenge their murder. The attack of this military unit on the Pomo village situated on the island near the white men's home was described by Benson:

> the next morning the white warriors [the volunteer unit] went across in the long dugouts. the indians said they would met them in peace. so when the whites landed the indians went to wellcom the. but the white man was determined to kill them. Ge-Wi-Lih said he threw up his hands and said no harm me good man. but the white man fired and shoot him in the arm and another shoot come and hit a man staning along side of him and was killed. so they all had to run and fight back; as they ran back in the tules and hid under the water; four or five of them gave a little battle and another man was shoot in the shoulder . . . many women and children were killed on around the island. one old lady a (indian) told about what she saw while hiding under abank, in under cover hanging tuleys. she said she saw two white men coming with their guns up in the air and on their guns hung a little girl. they brought it to the crek and threw it in the water. and alittle while later, two more men came in the same manner. this time they had alittle boy on the end of their guns and also threw it in the water. alittle ways from her she, said laid a women shoot through the shoulder, she held her little baby in her arms. two white men came running torge the woman and baby, they stabed the woman and the baby and, threw both of them over the bank in to the water. she said she heared the woman say, O my baby; she said when they gathered the dead, they found all the little ones were killed by being stabed, and many of the women were also killed stabing. she said it took them four or five days to gather up the dead. and the dead were all burnt on the east side the creek.[58]

The following day the volunteer unit continued their attack on the Indian population in the area. Of these further attacks Benson writes that

> one old man said that he was a boy at the time, he said the solders shoot his mother, she fell to the ground with her baby in her arms, he said his mother told him to climb high up in the tree, so he did and from there he said he could see the solders runing about the campe and shooting the men and woman and stabing boys and girls. he said mother was not yet dead and was telling him to keep quit, two of the solders heard her talking and ran up to her and stabed her and child. and a little ways from her mother, he said laid a man dieing, holding his boy in his arms the solders also stabed him.[59]

The Clear Lake massacre was not unique. Another early instance of the settlers' lethal enmity toward the California Indians occurred in 1850 at Wolf Creek near the Yuba River. The incident began when a group of ten white men reportedly killed at least two Indians belonging to a tribe in the area considered friendly to the local Anglo population. The Anglo attack was precipitated by the belief that these Indians were responsible for the theft of some of their missing cattle. The day after the attack on the Indian village, the lost cattle were found unmolested. Outraged by this unwarranted violence the Indians retaliated against the local white population, killing one man, seriously wounding another, and destroying a cabin and sawmill.

In response, local authorities set after the Indians involved in the attack. After failing to locate them, they arrested and charged the only Indian they encountered. He was held for "loitering near the scene of the depredation," and suspected of being a look-out for the "war-like party" involved.[60]

Yet another tragic Anglo military expedition against the California Indians occurred in the northwesternmost section of California against the Tolowa Indians. In *Genocide in Northwestern California*, Indian historian Jack Norton recounts the massacre of the Tolowas in 1853, using information from an interview with a Tolowan man who recounted the events as handed down among the tribe. Norton indicates that the attack occurred in the midst of a Tolowan sacred ceremony. After harvesting and storing their food for the coming winter, the Tolowas met at Yontoket, their holy shrine along the Smith River, to give thanks for their bountiful harvest and pray that prosperity would come to all mankind. In the middle of one of their ceremonial prayers, the Tolowa were attacked by a volunteer company of Anglo citizens from nearby Crescent City. According to Norton's informant:

> The whites attacked and bullets were everywhere. Over four hundred and fifty of our people were murdered or lay dying on the ground. Then the white men built a huge fire and threw in our sacred ceremonial dresses, the regalia, and our feathers, and the flames grew higher. They then threw in the babies, many of them were still alive. Some tied weights around the necks of the dead and threw them into the nearby water.
>
> Two men escaped, they had been in the Sacred Sweathouse and crept down to the water's edge and hid under the Lily Pads, breathing through the reeds. The next morning they found the water red with blood of their people.[61]

Some of the most intense conflict involving European Americans settling in northeastern California occurred in the vicinity of Mendocino. The underlying basis of this bitter enmity was once again the cyclical pattern of Anglo settlers encroaching on the local Indians' traditional hunting and gathering sites and Indian retaliations to this depredation. This cycle of conflict finally exploded in 1858, culminating in the so-called "Mendocino War."

The 1860 report of the Special Joint Committee of the California legislature on the confrontation clearly outlined the prevailing sentiments of European Americans in the area toward the local Indian population. It attested to the inevitable confrontation between "white civilization" and the California Indians in this part of the state. According to the report:

> The march of civilization deprives the Indian of his hunting grounds and other means of subsistence that nature has so bountifully provided for him. He naturally looks at this as an encroachment on his rights, and, either from motives of revenge, or what is more likely in California, from the imperious and pressing demands of hunger kills the stock of the settlers as a means of subsistence, and in consequence thereof, a war is waged against the Indian, with its incidents of cruelty, inhuman revenge, rapine, and murder, which we are sorry, from the evidence before us, to be compelled to acknowledge, have in some instances, been perpetuated by some few of our citizens.
>
> History teaches us that the inevitable destiny of the red man is total extermination or isolation from the deadly and corrupting influences of civilization. There is no longer a wilderness west of us that can be assigned them, and our interest, as well as our duty and the promptings of humanity, dictate to us the necessity of making some disposition of the Indian tribes within our borders that will ameliorate their sad condition, and also secure the frontier citizen from their depredations.[62]

The situation in the Long Valley section of the county deteriorated to the point where a standing armed unit of forty men had been formed "for the purpose of hunting Indians whenever they are satisfied that any stock has been slaughtered . . . and without ascertaining the guilty parties, shoot them down indiscriminately, and afterwards seek for the evidence of guilt."[63]

After concluding their investigation, the majority report of the Joint Committee investigating the Mendocino War documented that numerous Indian women and children had "fallen in the indiscriminate attacks on the Indian rancherias" in Mendocino County. The Joint Committee's report noted that this situation was not an isolated incident, for throughout the county "accounts are daily coming in . . . of sickening atrocities and wholesale slaughters of great numbers of defenseless Indians in that region of county." The deteriorating situation in the county reached the point that within "the last four months, more Indians have been killed by our own people than during the century of Spanish and Mexican domination."[64]

Although this was certainly an exaggeration, the testimony of local farmers before the joint California legislative committee upheld their final conclusion. The testimony of a local Anglo farmer before the committee, John W. Burgess, corroborated that the source of this tension rested squarely on the local Anglo population whose disruption of the Indians' subsistence way of life forced the indigenous population to resort to theft in order to avoid starvation. According to Burgess:

Owing to the settling up of the valley by farmers, they [local Indians] have been deprived of the fruitful source of subsistence, such as roots, acorns, and clover; the hogs eat the acorns and roots, and the cattle take the clover, and, therefore, they kill stock to subsist upon; were it not for this, from my knowledge of the character of the Indians, I think they would have stopped killing stock, for I believe that <u>for every beef that has been killed by them ten or fifteen Indians have been killed</u>.[65]

In testimony before the Joint Committee on the Mendocino Indian War of 1860, an Anglo settler named William Frazier testified that he and a group of white men visited an Indian *rancheria* (village) in Mendocino county "for the purpose of chastising the Indians" for the ostensible theft of three head of cattle. Hearing that Indians in one particular rancheria had some beef, they descended on the village and "when all fled but one . . . we shot his head off."[66]

Sometime later, Frazier, as a member of a forty man company of local citizens, ventured on an expedition after some Yuca Indians believed to be responsible for "depredations" in Mendocino County's Long Valley. According to Frazier, who was elected lieutenant of the volunteer company, "We left Long Valley in the evening and traveled in the night until we saw the fire of an Indian rancheria, which rancheria we surrounded when day was breaking, and waited until near sun up before we attacked and killed twenty, consisting of bucks, squaws and children . . . we found in this rancheria no signs of any depredations having been committed by these Indians."[67]

About a week later this company set out on another expedition in the same locality and "on the first night we found and surrounded a rancheria in which we found two wounded Indians and one old squaw, all of which we killed; on our return home we found another rancheria . . . and killed thirteen bucks and two squaws.[68]

Frazier testified further that these attacks were necessary despite the fact that "there has been no white men killed in Long Valley, that I know of, and no buildings burnt." At the time his deposition was taken the company was still in a state of "readiness to act when necessity requires it" and was prepared to see to the "protection of the lives and property of the . . . white population in that Valley."[69]

In order to secure the welfare of the white population they sought to protect, another local farmer and stockraiser, one William J. Scott, testified before the committee about another nefarious practice utilized to eliminate threatening Indians. Scott acknowledged that in addition to killing Indians encountered in the vicinity, it was the common practice of one local citizen to also "put strychnine in their baskets of soup, or what they had to eat" after attacking and driving local Indians from their rancherias. Scott added that he personally had "never lost any stock because of Indian thievery" or "felt in danger" in the valley where he resided.[70]

The attacks on the Indians in Mendocino county contributed to the loss of hundreds of Indian lives during 1859 and 1860. In March 1859, for instance, a volunteer party of European American settlers set off against Indians near the Round Valley area in retaliation for the killing of a prized gray stallion belonging to a local white resident. In the two week period following the incident approximately 240 Indians were murdered by the armed expedition for the death of the horse.[71] One particularly ruthless Indian fighter named Captain Walter Jarboe led a company of Anglo volunteers against the local Indian population in late 1859. Jarboe reported that by January 1860, his company had directly encountered Indians on twenty-three different occasions and killed 283 Indians, wounded an unknown number, and took another 292 prisoners who were sent to the Mendocino Indian Reservation.[72]

Commenting on the "causes and nature of most of the Indian 'wars' in the state," the *Marysville Daily Appeal* laid the source of this conflict squarely on the shoulders of Anglo immigrants. In the February 15, 1860 edition of the newspaper, a reporter for the *Daily Appeal* concluded that the extreme reaction of white settlers precipitated the bloodbaths that raged in northern California in the 1850s and 1860s. According to this commentary:

> A white man loses a hog or some other animal, or thinks he does, and, incontinently seized with the idea he is a victim of Indian dishonesty and depredations, he calls a party of his neighbors together, magnifies his losses and exalts them to an immediate hunt for Indians. The first party of which is found, is generally annihilated before search is made among them and their effects for the missing property . . . Of course these attacks have driven the Indians into the mountains, and caused many of them to desert the reservation. While they are out in the bleak, barren mountains, they steal and slay what straying stock they can find, preferring to take the risk of being shot, therefore to starvation. The Indian has not only to answer for his own sins, and those imagined against he, but he is held to answer for the acts of thieving white men as well.[73]

A similar view was expressed by one California correspondent writing for *Harper's Monthly Magazine* in 1861. He posed the situation of Indians in the state at the time as follows:

> It was found convenient to take possession of their country without recompense, rob them of their wives and children, kill them in every cowardly and

barbarous manner that could be devised, and when that was impracticable, drive them as far as possible out of the way. Such treatment was not consistent with their rude ideas of justice. At best they were an ignorant race of Diggers, wholly unacquainted with our enlightened institutions. They could not understand why they should be murdered, robbed, and hunted down in this way, without any other pretense or provocation than the color of their skin and the habits of life to which they had always been accustomed.[74]

CONCLUSION

Both Anglo-American and Indian historians have decried this policy of sanctioned decimation. John Caughey has characterized the campaign against the Indians as "one of the most disgraceful chapters in the entire history of the state. Armed bands took the field against the Indians on an almost completely indiscriminate basis. A whole series of Indian "wars" ensued . . . they featured wholesale butchery and seemed to aim at complete liquidation of the Indians."[75] Likewise, Indian historian Jack Norton has characterized these military excursions as ultimately the responsibility of the local [Anglo-American] citizenry, who, for fourteen long years, had committed every human atrocity upon the original people of this land."[76]

The magnitude of the destruction these campaigns wrought on the California Indians is, unquestionably, the most egregious chapter of the white supremacist transformation of the state. Rationale and resolve for pursuing such a devastating policy rapidly emerged after statehood. Expressions of these sentiments were widespread throughout the state and conveyed a common theme: Indian "savagery" obstructing Anglo progress.

Even as sympathetic a commentator as O. M. Wozencraft, an original member of the California State Constitutional Convention, could not help but reflect upon the conflict that raged during the 1850s and 1860s as an inevitable clash between two antagonistic social worlds. He believed that it was "not in the nature of things that two races, whose habits, manners, customs, and religion are so different, could live amicable together" in the state.[77]

Historian James Rawls has argued persuasively that the threat the California Indians posed to white settlers in the rural hinterlands of the state was effectively overcome by the early 1870s. According to Rawls, "They presented some minor irritations later, but for the most part their days as 'obstacles' were over."[78] The victimization of the California Indians by state-sanctioned military expeditions, however, contributed significantly to the dramatic decline in the overall Indian population in the decades after statehood. The policy of extermination proved the most effective method used by European Americans to solve their "Indian problem."

The Indian population declined dramatically during the early decades of Anglo control of California. Some historians and anthropologists have estimated that the Indian population numbered approximately 150,000 individuals in 1845, others place their numbers at 100,000 in 1850. By 1870, the Indian population declined precipitously to only 30,000 and by 1880 to a mere 16,000 individuals.[79] In his comprehensive study of the decline of the California Indians, anthropologist Sherburne Cook has attributed these losses to three major factors. The single largest reason for the decline was disease, with approximately 60 percent of the Indian population dying from syphilis, smallpox, measles, and tuberculosis. Not surprisingly, given what has been chronicled above, another 30 percent died from malnutrition and starvation. Finally, the remaining 10 percent of the Indian losses resulted from physical assaults at the hands of European Americans. These included formal military campaigns, informal expeditions by volunteers, and various other forms of homicide.[80] In the process, sixty-three percent of the original California Indian tribes became extinct, or nearly so, by 1910.[81]

If one accepts Cook's assessment, this meant that approximately 8,000 Indian men, women, and children lost their lives due to direct physical violence at the hands of Anglos. This is certainly one of the most deplorable chapters in the history of racialized ethnic groups in California, but an understandable one in light of the material interests of white settlers and their racialization of Indians at the time.

Not all Indians, however, were victimized in this way. Others found their way into a marginal status in Anglo society, relegated to a second class status as non-citizens and effectively denied the rights and entitlements of the white population. Thousands more were forcefully segregated onto reservations where, by all accounts, they lived out a miserable existence. Others found their way into the most subordinate levels of the new Anglo economy, working as servants, or farm laborers, while others less fortunate were temporarily placed into slavery. It is these encounters and experiences in the interstices of Anglo society that are taken up in the next chapter.

CHAPTER FIVE

"Unfit and Incapable of Being Associated with Whites on Any Terms of Equality"

The Indians of California who escaped the state government's policy of sanctioned decimation contended with European Americans at the margins of society. The Indian's ostensible "heathenism" and "savagery" resulted in their being placed at the extreme end of the new racial hierarchy. Their unambiguously nonwhite racial status and alien cultural practices made them a population unworthy of assimilation into Anglo society on any terms. There was simply no place for the Indian population in the social world that European Americans successfully introduced in the new state.

The Indian's degraded "group position" was structurally reinforced through two legislative pronouncements, bills sanctioning their use as unfree laborers and calling for their segregation onto federal reservations. The ongoing use of Indians as an unfree laboring class after statehood represented a temporary concession by European Americans to the still powerful Mexican ranchero class. State legislation enacted at the behest of the Californio elite in 1850 placed as many as ten thousand Indians into "apprenticeships" and also permitted their use as servile laborers through "vagrancy" statutes. These repressive measures were also accompanied by the flagrant kidnapping and ongoing sale of four thousand Indian men, women, and children into virtual slavery after 1848. Although such practices were at odds with "free labor" sentiments in the state, the demand for unfree Indian labor by both Mexicans and some white settlers persisted for decades. This chapter examines the degradation of Indian labor through these various state-sanctioned measures and briefly looks at the federal government's futile attempt at making them a "useful class" on isolated reservations.

THE SUBORDINATE POLITICAL STATUS OF INDIANS IN ANGLO CALIFORNIA

The initial political status of Indians in Anglo California was formally adjudicated by delegates at the 1849 California State Constitutional Convention. During convention debates on suffrage, delegates agreed that Indians would not be eligible for citizenship in the state and therefore not entitled to the same civil rights granted Mexicans and European Americans.[1] Most convention delegates believed that the Indians' nonwhite racial status provided sufficient grounds for their disenfranchisement and relegation to a second-class status before the law.

Other delegates, however, also expressed more pragmatic concerns over the explosive political implications of granting the "wild" Indians suffrage. Delegate L. W. Hastings argued that giving Indians this right would precipitate serious political problems for European Americans, chief among which being the potential control and manipulation of Indian votes by the Mexican ranchero elite. Delegate Hastings cautioned that a number of rancheros were "very popular among the wild Indians" and that they could potentially "march hundreds of them up to the polls."[2] Delegate J. D. Hoppe of San Jose expressed similar fears. Hoppe argued against granting Indians the franchise because of the inordinate influence that these rancheros had over them. In supporting this contention, Hoppe noted that in California "there was not a rancho where you would not find fifty or a hundred buck Indians, and the owner could run these freemen up to the polls, and carry any measure he might desire. . . . There were ranchos in certain districts where the California proprietors could control at least two hundred votes in favor of any particular candidate; and these votes could be purchased for a few dollars, for the Indians knew no better."[3]

Although some consideration was given to a motion that would have allowed "civilized" Indians who owned property and paid taxes to vote, this proposal was soundly defeated.[4] Ultimately, the convention delegates unequivocally agreed that all full-blooded Indians, whether "civilized" taxpayers or those from "uncivilized tribes," were unworthy of citizenship.

The subordinate political status accorded the California Indians profoundly impacted their history during this period. It provided ample justification for the enactment of numerous legislative statutes that further discriminated against them. Some of the most odious examples of these measures were the draconian Indenture Act and Vagrancy Act of 1850; an 1851 law prohibiting Indians from serving as witnesses in any legal proceeding involving a white person; bills enacted in 1863 and 1864 denying Indians admission to public schools; an 1870 "separate but equal" education act segregating Indian children in California public schools; and legislation that, from 1854 to at least 1913, made it illegal to furnish firearms or ammunition to Indians.[5]

In addition to these patently discriminatory measures, the 1886 case of *Thompson v. Doaksum* preempted any legal claim that Indians had to land they formerly held by right of occupancy. The California State Supreme Court ruled that land previously occupied by Indians during the Mexican period but not claimed under the Land Law of 1851 was part of the public domain. In the 1889 case of *Botiller v. Dominguez*, the U.S. Supreme Court further decreed that all Indian claims to land, whether by title or occupancy, were invalid if they had not been previously presented for legal confirmation.[6]

Not until 1872 were the California Indians granted even the most basic legal rights in the state. In that year the prohibition against Indians entering testimony in legal cases involving white people was formally rescinded and a section of the California Statutes denying Indians the right to testify was repealed. In 1879 the state legislature granted Indians the right to vote in all elections. (The U.S. Congress finally conferred citizenship to all previously non-citizen Indians born in the U.S in 1924. This federal declaration of citizenship extended to all Indians the right to vote and testify in states where they were still prohibited from doing so.)[7]

The subordinate political status of Indians in California was initially based on their being defined categorically as nonwhite. Unlike in the case of the indigenous Mexican population, no serious consideration was given to integrating Indians on equal terms into the body politic of Anglo society. A careful examination of the racially discriminatory legislation enacted against Indians—legislation that placed them at the margins of white society—illustrates this quite clearly.

THE IGNOMINIOUS VAGRANCY LAW
AND INDENTURE ACT OF 1850

Two legal measures helped reinscribe the unfree labor status to which the California Indians were relegated after 1850. The first session of the California legislature enacted a vagrancy law that legally sanctioned the temporary use of Indians as bonded servants, authorizing Indians arrested for vagrancy to be sold into the service of the individual paying their legal fines. Once discharged to prospective employers, convicted Indians were required to work for upward to four months. Indians received no monetary compensation for their labor; they were merely guaranteed a subsistence livelihood.[8]

In that same year the Los Angeles City Council also enacted a law to incarcerate local Indians for public drunkenness and vagrancy. This ordinance, too, required arrested Indians to work for local employers who paid their fines. The procurement of Indian labor through this law followed a predictable pattern. At sundown on Sunday the town marshall and an Indian deputy would routinely round up intoxicated Indians found on Los Angeles streets—especially in so-called "Nigger Alley." These Indians were usually found intoxicated on *aguardiente*, a native brandy that local vineyardists often paid Indians in lieu of wages. The arrested Indians were sobered up and placed at auction on the Monday morning "slave market." Anglo vineyardists or others needing casual laborers typically paid an average of from one to three dollars per person to retain these Indians. One-third of this sum went to the Indian at the end of the week—often in the form of *aguardiente*—and two-thirds to the City of Los Angeles. This process was repeated weekly and proved a convenient way of procuring cheap labor and solving local labor shortages for many employers.[9]

Although Indians bound through these vagrancy statutes never became a major source of labor in the state's new economy, they continued to prove valuable to Mexican rancheros and many European Americans in the rural backwaters of the state. As early as January 1848, for example, white settlers in northern California publicly voiced support for establishing an apprenticeship system that would put an end to the "drunken, roving vagabond life" of the Indians in the territory. A letter published in the *California Star* by a correspondent named "Pacific" from Sonoma called for the establishment of an apprenticeship system that would utilize passes to regulate Indian travel in the state and ensure that they not flee employers. While Pacific acknowledged that such a system was "severe and anti-democratic," it was necessary, he wrote, for the protection of both the white population and the Indians. He rationalized their continued use as an unfree labor force on the basis of their being an "inferior" race,

> unfit and incapable of being associated with whites on any terms of equality, or of being governed by the same laws; and if retained among us, must necessarily have a code and treatment applicable to their particular character and condition.
> Were it possible to have all masters just, mild, and good, I would—I say it

for the benefit of the Indians themselves—make slaves of them. But since this cannot be so . . . I would suggest the propriety of some sort of an apprentice system being established, and Indians prohibited from passing through the inhabited parts of the country without passes.[10]

The Sonoma correspondent noted that provisions could be made that would protect employers against others enticing Indians out of their service with higher wages. Such a practice, he argued, was an "impolitic and pernicious course pursued by some" that inevitably contributed to Indians becoming "more idle, roving, and dissolute" and adopting "a much worse character than they would otherwise acquire."[11]

Another early expression in support of such an apprenticeship system that would ostensibly teach Indians the value of labor under Anglo guidance appeared in the *Marysville Herald* in November, 1856. Commenting on the "miserable condition" of the Indians in nearby Yuba City, the newspaper's editor argued that "there is something so utterly abhorrent in the thought they must waste away life like that in inactivity. . . . Could not those who live among us by some law be required to bind their children to farmers and others, for a given period, so as to make them useful, and thus induct them to habits of cleanliness and industry?"[12]

A similar view was voiced by the California Legislature's Special Joint Committee on the Mendocino War, which was initially appointed to investigate the facts surrounding Indian-Anglo conflict in the Mendocino area of Northern California. This committee's minority report argued that a system of peonage would help facilitate the "management" of Indians in the state. The minority report's concluding recommendation stipulated that

> the state should . . . adopt a general system of peonage, or apprenticeship, for the proper disposition and distribution of the Indians by families among responsible citizens. General laws should be passed regulating the relations between master and servants, and providing for the punishment of any meddlesome interference on the part of third parties. In this manner the whites might be provided with profitable and convenient servants, and the Indians with the best protection and all the necessities of life in permanent and comfortable homes.[13]

Sentiments such as these led to the legislative enactment of the "Act for the Government and Protection of Indians" in April, 1850. Historian James Rawls has argued convincingly that this statute reflected the continuing concerns of ranchero interests, and of white settlers as well, to perpetuate the subordinate labor status of Indians.[14]

The Indenture Act of 1850 provided the legal means whereby citizens in the state were able to take legal custody of Indian minors and transform them into virtual slaves. Indian children from the age of seven to twelve were initially bound through this "apprenticeship" law to white "guardians" until they reached the age of eighteen.[15]

Popular support increased after 1850 for a more comprehensive statute that would liberalize the acquisition of the Indian "apprentices" and lengthen the time that they could be bound to Anglo guardians. One such call was echoed in an editorial in the *Sacramento Standard* in March 1860, which argued that Christian charity dictated the expansion of this apprenticeship system in light of the deteriorating condition of the local Indian population in the vicinity. The *Standard*'s editor held that: "The most humane disposition that could be made of them, is, probably to reduce them to a mild system of servitude. Call them slaves, coolies, or apprentices—it is all the same; supply them with Christian masters and make them Christian servants."[16]

Sentiments such as this led to the revision of the Indenture Act in 1860. James Rawls has described the main provisions of the new act: "The old law, of course, had provided only for the apprenticeship of minors. The new law considerably lengthened the terms of service and also included adults. Under the 1860 amendment Indian men apprenticed under fourteen could be held until they reached twenty-five; those obtained between fourteen and twenty could be held until they were thirty. Indian women could be held until they were twenty-one and twenty-five years old. The terms for adult Indians were limited to ten years at the discretion of the judge."[17]

The 1850 law, and its amended version in 1860, had devastating consequences for the conscripted Indians. According to Rawls, "It was popularly understood, when the law of 1860 was passed, that it legalized a system of involuntary servitude in California. . . . All that a white person had to do, if he or she wanted some Indian apprentices, was to take a list of their names to a judge and have him sign it. In practice, the judge made no effort to determine the consent or condition of the Indians or to ensure that the prospective masters would clothe, feed, or protect them."[18] The total number of Indians directly affected by this legislation has been estimated by one authority as ranging upward to ten thousand Indian men, women, and children.[19] This represented approximately 10 percent of the total Indian population in the state. The number of Indians actually apprenticed to any one individual varied from only one person to more than fifty. In one case, a former Indian agent in the state, V. E. Geiger, reportedly had eighty Indians legally indentured to his care.[20]

Indians apprenticed through this system were held in a state that some scholars have equated with slavery in the American South. In their study of *The Other Californians*, anthropologists Robert Heizer and Alan Almquist argue that this apprenticeship system represented "a legalized form of slavery of California Indians. . . . No other possible construction can be made of the facts."[21] A similar conclusion is reached by Rawls, who argues that this legislation "revealed a continuing concern with subordinating the Indian and facilitating white access to their labor."[22] Moreover, the law of 1850 and "related acts of the legislature were an attempt by the state government to legalize the peonage system that had existed during the Mexican period. . . . Whatever the precise arrangement—whether Indians were sold at the state's public auctions to the highest bidder, bailed out of jail by whites seeking their services, or held as 'apprentices'—the relationship established under the law was essentially that of master and serf."[23]

This legislation represented the still-powerful rancheros' successful use of the state apparatus to promote their economic interests despite the decline of the old rancho economy. The principal author of the Indenture Act, for instance, was John Bidwell, one the most prominent Anglo Californios of the pre-conquest era. Bidwell had owned a rancho in the territory during the Mexican period and continued to make extensive use of Indian labor through the mid-1860s. Two others involved in drafting the Indenture Act were Mariano Vallejo and David F. Douglas. Vallejo, one of the most prominent Mexican rancheros in the state, relied extensively upon Indian labor on his Rancho Sonoma, and the Vallejo family was also well known for its active involvement in the kidnapping and sale of Indians during the 1830s and 1840s.[24] David Douglas had arrived in California in 1848 as a volunteer in the U.S.-Mexico War from the antebellum South, whose system of slavery he admired. The odious similarities between the southern "black codes" and the basic features of the 1850 law have not escaped the attention of historians, who have suggested that this reflected Douglas's contribution to this legislation.[25] (As the black codes did to southern blacks, the Indenture Act legally sanctioned the binding of Indians to labor contracts and the flogging of Indians convicted of stealing horses, cattle, or any other valuable item.)[26] The final key figure behind this bill was Elam Brown, a member of the California Assembly who had arrived in the territory prior to annexation and acquired Rancho Acalanes; like the other authors, he made extensive use of servile Indian laborers. As Rawls observed, "It was thus no mystery that the 1850 law represents a continuity with the Hispanic tradition of Indian labor exploitation; its authors had dedicated their efforts to the achievement of precisely that continuity."[27]

THE BRIEF REPRISE OF INDIAN KIDNAPPING AND SUBJUGATION INTO SLAVERY

One major factor differentiated the widespread use of coerced Indian labor on ranchos during the Mexican period from their use after 1846. According to Rawls, "The important change after 1846 was that Anglo-Americans, rather than simply seizing Indians for their own use as the rancheros had done, came to realize that profit could be made in securing Indian 'apprentices' for other whites and so began traffic in Indian slaves. This traffic was a grotesque extrapolation of the traditional image of the Indian as a useful class."[28]

In addition to being formally bound to guardians through the apprenticeship system, therefore, Indians experienced continued kidnapping and virtual enslavement during the early American period. During the Mexican period, Indian *rancherias* (villages) were routinely raided in order to secure the Indian labor needed by the Mexican ranchero class. This widespread practice occurred with increased frequency between 1845 and 1850. Both Anglo Americans and some Mexicans participated in the sale of Indians into bondage during the American period because of its profitability; personal use by kidnappers was a secondary consideration. A newspaper item in the *Humboldt Times* in May 1855, for example, reported that Indian slave traders in the area were selling Indian children at $50 to $250 each. By the early 1860s Indian children in the vicinity were still being sold at $37.50 to $100 each.[29] One authority estimates that three to four thousand Indian children were stolen and sold as servants from 1852 to 1867 by these slave traders.[30]

The prevalence of such trafficking was further attested to in numerous newspaper articles during this period. One such article, appearing in the *Alta California* on October 2, 1854, openly acknowledged that "abducting Indians' children has become quite a common practice. Nearly all the children belonging to some of the Indian tribes in the northern part of the state have been stolen. They are taken to the southern part of the state and there sold."[31] A more detailed account appeared in 1861 in the *Marysville Appeal*, whose editor observed that

> it is from these mountain tribes that white settlers draw their supplies of kidnapped children, educated as servants, and women for the purposes of labor

and of lust. . . . It is notorious that there are parties in the northern counties of this state, whose sole occupation has been to steal young children and squaws from the poor Diggers, who inhabit the mountains and dispose of them at handsome prices to the settlers, who, being in a majority of cases unmarried but . . . willingly pay fifty or sixty dollars for a young Digger to cook and wait upon them, or a hundred dollars for a likely young girl. Recent developments in this vicinity are sufficient proof of this.[32]

Other acknowledgments of this disgraceful practice also appeared in the *Butte Record*, *Sacramento Union*, *San Francisco Bulletin*, and *Petaluma Journal* during the 1850s and 1860s.[33] Most of the Indians victimized by this enslavement were from the northern part of the state, particularly the Mendocino and Humboldt areas.[34]

A candid description of this process was given by Indian agent George Hansen in his 1861 report to the Committee on Indian Affairs:

In the frontier portions of Humboldt and Mendocino counties a band of desperate men have carried on a system of kidnapping for two years past. Indian children were seized and carried into the lower counties and sold into virtual slavery. These crimes against humanity so excited the Indians that they began to retaliate by killing the cattle of whites. At once an order was issued to chastise the guilty. Under this indefinite order, a company of United States troops, attended by a considerable volunteer force, has been pursuing the poor creatures from one retreat to another. The kidnappers follow at the heels of the soldiers to seize the children when their parents are murdered and sell them to the best advantage.[35]

Evidence suggests that not all of these traffickers were unconscionable European-American men; many were also Mexicans. One Indian agent reported during the mid-1850s that this "traffic was conducted by Mexicans desperate in character and difficult to arrest. They reside at remote points in the vicinity of the Indians, and were strongly banded together by the prospects of gains in this inhuman trade." Moreover, this agent claimed these Mexicans had stolen and sold "hundred of Indians," and, in some instances, "entire tribes were taken *en masse*." In many cases these traders were believed to have killed parents who resisted the kidnapping of their children.[36] Indians captured by these Mexicans were reportedly taken to a convenient hiding place where those most likely to be sold, usually healthy women and children, were prepared for sale. The old and infirm were routinely left to starve or make their way back to their tribal homelands.

Such activity by Mexican traffickers was reported in the upper Sacramento valley and elsewhere in northern California during the mid-

1850s.[37] This activity also captured the attention of Thomas J. Henley, Superintendent of Indian Affairs in California. Responding to a call by Henley to investigate the condition of Indians along the Berryessa Valley, Indian Agent William McDaniel wrote in 1854 that

> at the Bariessa [Berryessa] Valley on the Peuta [Putah] Creek we found something like one hundred and fifty Indians whose condition is that of slavery. We made inquiry in regard to the kidnapping referred to in your letter of instruction and found the Bariessa family in possession of numerous gang of Indians at work on their ranch of different tribes, all of whom had been driven from the valley and mountains of Stone [Stony] Creek by violence, and they and certain Sonora Mexicans living with them are constantly in the practice of selling the young Indians, both male and female to whomsoever will purchase them.[38]

Historical evidence documents that not all Indians sold to either Mexican rancheros or Anglo settlers were victims of outright kidnapping. One of the most poignant accounts of the slavelike condition to which California Indians were subjected is captured in a rare autobiography by a Diegueno Indian, one Delfina Cuero. This woman recounted the impoverished circumstances in which she and her family were placed after the accidental death of her husband. In order to fend off impending starvation, Delfina Cuero relied on the help of her twelve-year-old son Aurelio to provide for her five other children. According to Mrs. Cuero,

> Things got pretty bad. I went out on my own and gathered food. I had been taught all these things about how to gather and prepare wild food. I went out and hunted for wild greens and honey. I took Aurelio and we hunted with his bow and arrow and his rabbit stick. Sometimes we found things. Lots of times we did not and we went hungry. I had to beg for food from neighboring Indians and ranchers. Some neighbors helped me sometimes. I went hungry and my children were hungry. Sometimes for two or three days we found nothing. I didn't have anybody to help me anymore, I just went here and there looking for food.
> I finally had to sell Aurelio to a Mexican to get food. He and his wife said they wanted a son because they had no children.[39]

Unfortunately, her hopes that Aurelio would be well cared for by this Mexican family proved ill-founded. According to Delfina Cuero, her son became a virtual slave:

> They didn't treat him like a son. They were mean and made him work like a man all the time and even beat him. The food they gave us to pay for him lasted a month. Aurelio stayed with that man and his wife for three or four years, working like a man for him. He finally ran away because he wasn't going to be beaten again. Aurelio couldn't stay with us then because that man came looking

for him and would take him back and beat him some more. Aurelio worked here and there on various ranches and sometimes hunted. He brought me a little food for the smaller children whenever he could. While he was a boy, he was never paid in money for any work, just food.[40]

Widespread abuses of the apprenticeship system as in cases like Aurelio Cuero's eventually led to its repeal in 1863. The section of the act sanctioning Indian servitude was rescinded and the remaining sections of the bill finally repealed in 1937.[41] Proponents of the repeal argued that the law had directly contributed to escalations in the kidnapping and conscription of Indian children. Although popularly supported when enacted in 1850 and extended in 1860, the act and the resulting enslavement of Indians ultimately met with disapproval by most Californians. The kidnapping of Indian children was seen both as morally reprehensible and as contributing to the accelerated cycle of Indian-Anglo conflict throughout the state. Although the kidnapping and sale of Indian children was not allowed under the law, prosecution for this offense could not be assured (in part because Indians were not allowed to enter testimony in cases involving Anglos); the repeal of the law provided a way of reducing these abuses. Few Indian kidnappers were ever brought to trial, however, and fewer still ever convicted of this crime. Since local authorities in the state were largely uninterested in pursing this matter, those cases that were prosecuted were pressed forward at the behest of federal Indian agents.[42]

THE DEMISE OF INDIANS AS A "USEFUL CLASS" IN CALIFORNIA

It was primarily European-American frontiersmen, single small farmers, and independent white working-class men without families who made the most extensive use of Indians victimized by the vagrancy and indenture statutes. It was apparently the rancho interests, both Mexicans and European Americans, that relied most heavily upon the Indians who were kidnapped and sold into slavery. By the time of the vagrancy law's repeal, however, the Indian population was only infrequently a source of labor in California. Three factors help explain why, unlike the Mexicans, the Chinese, and later the Japanese, the California Indians never become a principal source of labor in the expanding capitalist sector of the state's urban economy.

First, the demand for cheap labor became so great in California after 1860 that Indian labor alone could not adequately provide for the expanding needs of agriculture and industry. The once-large Indian population in

California, which numbered approximately 100,000 in 1850, declined precipitously after statehood. Their dwindling numbers and rapidly deteriorating social condition made European-American employers skeptical of the role they could play in the new capitalist economy.[43]

Second, Indian labor could not be utilized profitably on the small subsistence agricultural farms that initially replaced the great ranchos of the Mexican period. In the early decades after annexation, agricultural production was primarily a small, family-farm undertaking. The need for a large agricultural labor force did not exist until the introduction of irrigation and intensive agricultural production in the 1880s. It is doubtful that many small family farmers had the resources, or the desire, to maintain permanent Indian populations on their subsistence operations; it was simply easier and more profitable to hire seasonal laborers when they were needed. Using the same system of unfree labor that existed on the immense ranchos, even if doing so had been legal, would have been tremendously expensive for small landholders. Furthermore, Indians were not particularly adept or willing to work as agricultural laborers. As we saw, their primary use on the Mexican ranchos was in cattle-related occupations or as personal servants.[44]

Finally, the marginal role of Indians in the new economy was due also to the much greater availability of Chinese contracted laborers and, to a lesser extent, Mexican and white laborers.[45] These groups provided most of the labor needed by the expanding capitalist agricultural economy; all were seen as more reliable and efficient than Indians.

Some California Indians nevertheless found employment at the edges of the new economy or in the vestiges of the declining rancho economy. Although less in demand, Indians were still being used in southern California after 1850 as vaqueros, farm and ranch workers, and sheep shearers. They were also found in the mining districts of northern California as both hired and independent miners, as well as in transportation-related areas as muleteers, packers, deckhands, and longshoremen.[46]

Historian George Phillips notes that during the 1850s some Indians in Los Angeles found steady employment earning upward to one dollar per day. Most Indians, however, worked periodically for nearby rancheros and vintners who paid them from eight to ten dollars per month. More often than not, as we have seen, these winegrowers paid their Indian laborers with *aguardiente*.[47]

In addition to such employment at the fringes of the new Anglo labor market, the California Indians continued to perform tasks that were part of their traditional way of life before the arrival of Europeans. In order to survive outside the new economy, Indians sold fish, game, wild crops, animal pelts, and basketry and native dry goods. Still others found their only means of survival in begging and performing miscellaneous odd jobs in the rapidly growing new Anglo towns.[48]

One important consequence of the negligible role of Indian labor was the absence of direct economic competition with European Americans in the working and middle classes. There did not exist the widespread Anglo agitation against Indian laborers that was directed at blacks and Asians. The inferior position of Indians within the capitalist labor market, their declining population, their continued use on the ranchos, and their ability to resort to traditional ways of subsistence worked against the emergence of such class-based conflict. Although once the principal source of cheap labor during both the Spanish and Mexican periods, Indians were never strategically integrated into the new Anglo economy. After 1850 there was a perceptible decline in Indians being viewed as a "useful class" in Anglo California.

INDIAN REMOVAL AND SEGREGATION ONTO FEDERAL RESERVATIONS

Although many Indians were structurally situated at the margins of Anglo society, a significant number of the "wild tribes" in California were also subjected to a federal policy designed to "civilize" them under the benevolent tutelage of white Indian agents. Since 1820 the federal government had undertaken a policy of forcibly removing Indians away from white society as a way of addressing the "Indian problem," and this policy was continued in California. Shortly after statehood, the Department of the Interior divided California into three regions—northern, middle, and southern—and sent three federal Indian commissioners with specific instructions to negotiate the relocation of Indian tribes not already decimated by military pogroms or slavery.[49]

In January 1851, the newly appointed agents—Redick McKee, O. M. Wozencraft, and George Barbour—publicly expressed the paternalistic federal policy of Indian "domestication":

> The Indians of this country are represented as extremely ignorant, lazy, and degraded, at the same time generally, harmless and peaceable in their habits, indisposed to controversy or war with whites, until actually goaded to seek revenge for injuries inflicted upon them. Their very imbecility, poverty, and degradation should, with enlightened and liberal white men, entitle them to commiseration and long forbearance.

> The Indians were the original owners of California. Indian removal is out of the question because there is no further west to which they can be removed. There are two alternatives: extermination or domestication. Domestication means civilization and a cheap labor force; domestication is the one which we deem the part of wisdom to adopt, and if possible, to consummate.[50]

Beginning in February 1851, Commissioners Wozencraft, Barbour, and McKee successfully negotiated eighteen treaties involving approximately 25,000 California Indians from 135 different tribal groupings. One source estimates that these treaties involved from one-quarter to one-half of California's Indian population at the time.[51] All eighteen treaties required that the Indians agree to place themselves under the jurisdiction and authority of the U.S. federal government; live in peace and friendship with both citizens of the U.S. and all neighboring Indian tribes; relinquish all further claims to land in the state; allow federal and local civil authorities within the state to adjudicate all grievances; and abide by all stipulations in the treaty upon its ratification by the Senate. All treaties called for the establishment of reservations for their permanent occupancy. The California treaties contained two features that distinguished them from federal treaties made with Indians elsewhere: (1) the California Indians were to settle within state boundaries, instead of being "removed" out of state, and (2) there were no stipulations for perpetual annuities other than the original provisions, cattle, blankets, and other supplies agreed upon.[52] The commissioners requested that the Indians leave their mountain homes and relocate on lands in adjacent valleys. After the Indians took counsel among themselves and agreed to the terms, a delegation of Indians and the commissioners examined the lands selected for relocation.[53]

It was estimated that the initially proposed reservations totaled approximately 7,488,000 acres, or one-fourteenth of the state.[54] Although this area appears quite large, it was not considered at the time to be valuable. According to historian John Caughey, "With insignificant exceptions the lands involved had no white occupants or claimants and were regarded by the commissioners as relatively worthless. Most of the tracts were on the floor of the Central Valley, before long to prove fabulously productive."[55]

The commissioners' efforts aroused great public controversy. If ratified by Congress, the total cost to the federal government was estimated at nearly three-quarters of a million dollars ($716,394.49).[56] Eventually all eighteen treaties submitted to the U.S. Senate were summarily rejected in a secret session. Evidence suggests that the Senate's decision was a direct response to being deluged with protests from California citizens and state legislators who opposed the treaties.[57]

The California State Senate, for instance, encouraged the state's two senators in Congress to "oppose the confirmation of any and all treaties with the Indians in the State of California, granting to Indians an exclusive right to occupy public lands in the state." The resolution also called upon the federal government to bodily remove the California Indians from the state.[58]

The editor of the *Los Angeles Star* also expressed the prevailing point of view of many white citizens when on March 13, 1852 he vehemently opposed the treaties' ratification:

> To place upon our most fertile soil the most degraded race of aborigines upon the North American continent, to invest them with the rights of sovereignty, and to teach them that they are to be treated as powerful and independent nations, is planting the seeds of future disaster and ruin. . . . We hope that the federal government will let us alone—that it will neither undertake to feed, settle, or remove the Indians . . . and that they will leave everything just as it now exists, except affording us the protection which two or three cavalry companies would give.[59]

In response to public sentiments such as these, California senators Gwin and Weller petitioned Congress for funds to increase the military forces needed to rebuff any Indian retaliations against the treaties' rejection. They succeeded in obtaining these funds and an appropriation of $100,000 to purchase supplies and gifts for the appeasement of the California Indians.

Once the U.S. Senate rejected these treaties, the federal government proceeded to survey the lands that the Indians had surrendered claim to and prepare it for white immigrants to homestead. The immense reservations initially proposed in the ill-fated treaties became part of the public domain and subsequently were also opened to Anglo settlement.[60] As these lands were gradually occupied by European Americans, the former Indian occupants either scattered from their path or were driven into the hills, where they often met the carnage discussed in the previous chapter.

As had been anticipated, the California Indians were incensed by the U.S. Senate's rejection of the treaties they had agreed to in good faith. In February 1852, Indians in southern California reacted violently to these broken promises and to their having been altogether excluded from the treaty-making process. The Cauhillas in San Diego, for instance, were particularly angered by Indian Agent Barbour's failure to even meet with them, and they retaliated by attacking white settlers in the area.[61]

Another Indian revolt against Anglo citizens occurred in the San Diego area in 1851. Know as the "Garra uprising," this rebellion was precipitated by attempts by local officials to impose a new tax on the few "Christianized

Indians" owning small ranches in San Diego County. In response to the new tax and to ongoing Anglo hostility toward them, Indians led by Antonio Garra attacked the local white population in Agua Caliente near San Diego. Garra and other Cupeno Indians joined forces with some Yuma Indians and stole a large herd of sheep grazing west of the Colorado River. Five of the six Americans tending this herd were killed and their bodies reportedly mutilated in the attack. The Cupenos involved in the hostility lost ten men. Antonio Garra was subsequently captured for his participation in this uprising, convicted of murder, and shot on January 10, 1850, in Old Town San Diego. Five of Garra's accomplices were caught later, tried separately, and also killed for their participation in the uprising.[62]

As a response to Indian hostilities over the broken treaties, the federal government enacted legislation in 1853 to establish a more modest reservation system for the impoverished "wild" Indian population in California. These reserves were modeled after the infamous mission system of the Spanish period and were ostensibly designed to protect the California Indians from the state government's military policy of extermination.[63] According to one California historian, "the Indian reservation boundaries formed a frontier line that amounted to a racial barrier, which whites and Indians could cross only with federal permission."[64]

In 1853 this federal program to establish the first Indian reservation system in the nation went into effect in California under the leadership of Edward F. Beale, the new Superintendent of Indian Affairs in the state. The federal government funded the establishment of five reservations located at Tejon (in the Tehachapi foothills), Nome Lacke (in Colusa County), Mendocino (on the Pacific Coast), Klamath (along the lower Klamath River), and Fresno (in the Central Valley). In 1856 a number of smaller Indian "farms" were also established at King River, Tule River, Round Valley, and Fresno.[65]

Important differences among the California Indians at the time led federal authorities to coordinate their resettlement with some forethought. In an early report to the Commissioner of Indian Affairs, Special Agent G. Bailey described the existence of "three classes" of California Indians, each requiring special coaxing and treatment. The first class comprised the "wild tribes, occupying the Coastal Range north and east of Mendocino and the slopes of the Sierra." Agent Bailey described them as "a timid and inoffensive race, rarely wandering beyond the limits of the mountain valleys, where they and their ancestors have lived from time immemorial." Indicating that nothing could be done to induce this group to resettle upon the reservations, Bailey concluded that "years will elapse before the wave of civilization invades their hereditary domain. Nothing is required to be done for these Indians at present, except to embrace all proper opportunities of establishing friendly relations with them and gain their confidence."[66] As we have seen, Bailey's optimism proved ill-founded. It is precisely these Indians who were targeted by the military policy that the California state government deployed in the early decades after statehood.

The second class of Indians were those residing in San Bernardino, Santa Barbara, and San Diego Counties, as well as a few tribal groups at various points in the state such as Tejon and Owen's Lake. According to Bailey, these Indians were largely "devoid of intelligence, and retain a certain rude civilization, the fast fading traces, perhaps, of the old Mission system." The special agent advocated supplying these Indians with seeds, agricultural implements, and clothing, and rendering them assistance that would ensure their "self reliance" and thus avoid becoming further "degraded to the level of the mere 'Digger' " he had described earlier.[67]

The third class of Indians consisted of those at the periphery of Anglo society who might be coaxed into relocating onto reservations. These included Indians formerly occupying the Sacramento, San Joaquin, and other valleys of the state. These Indians were reportedly living in "a pitiable condition" and could be found loitering about mining towns "where they drag out a miserable existence" and posed "a nuisance" to the white communities in the area. The only salvation for these Indians was their relocation to a nearby Indian reservation where they could potentially be "made to labor for their support."[68]

The federal government's reservation system in California was by all accounts a lamentable failure, rife with financial corruption, malfeasance, mismanagement, patronage, abuse, and widespread labor exploitation. Moreover, only a fraction of the total Indian population in the state was relocated onto these reservations and farms. Even the most inflated estimate of the number of Indians who "voluntarily" settled there never exceeded more than one-sixth of the total population. In 1856, one government report claimed that 10,000 of the 61,600 Indians in the state were residing on the reservations. A more reliable estimate, however, places the figure much closer to only one-tenth of their total population.[69]

The conditions on these reservations was invariably described as utterly deplorable. The Nome Lacke reservation in 1857 provides a good example. A report by Lt. M. R. Morgan in that year documented that the Indians in Yuba County were greatly displeased with their situation there. According to Morgan,

They every now and then run away in squads. Some are caught and brought back; others escape to their old homes. The reason for the discontent is plain.

... They had an abundance of fish and other things that they have not here. On
the Reservation at the present time they are furnished with flour and clothes—
nothing more. If they want anything besides bread to eat they must go out and
hunt for it as they did years ago. There is no water here and they are for this
reason deprived of their most necessary recreation. Some work hard and live,
others keep out of the way and they live, too. There is no inducement for them
to work.[70]

The impoverished condition of the Indians on these reserves and reports
of widespread corruption eventually led to an internal investigation of the
entire system in 1858, when J. Ross Browne inspected the reservation
system in California and subsequently offered his views in an article published in *Harper's Magazine* in 1861. He tersely concluded that the reservations he visited were nothing more than places "where a very large amount
of money was annually expended in feeding white men and starving Indians."[71] A similar assessment was offered in the same year by Indian Agent
J. L. Capp, who described the Tule River reservations as being "very badly
managed." Capp observed that "two thirds of the time the Indians have
been starved and forced to steal. Only those who worked on the [reserva-
tion] building were fed. The rest were left to shift for themselves, and no
attention was paid them."[72]

A classic example of the depths to which this corruption sunk can be
seen in the case of Indian Agent V. E. Geiger of the Nome Lacke Reservation. Agent Geiger was charged with absconding portions of the wheat,
barley, and hay produced on the reservation and selling it for his personal
profit. These crops had been planted at public expense and grown with
Indian labor for Indian use on the reservation. Furthermore, citizens of
Tehama County were so infuriated by Geiger's mismanagement of Nome
Lacke that they also wrote the Secretary of the Interior to inform him that
the reserve had become an unbearable "disgrace and nuisance" to the local
white population. They made special mention of Geiger offending the
moral sensibilities of the white settlers "by habitually living in a state of
open adultery with a white prostitute." In addition, his "worthless horde"
of Anglo employees were also "compelling the squaws" on the reservation
to "submit to their lecherous and beastly desires"—even in the presence of
their husbands. The "disgraceful conduct" of the agent and his associates
had become such a public scandal that the reservation was commonly
referred to by local citizens as "the Government Whore House."[73]

By the early 1860s the situation of the California Indians relocated on
these federal reserves was deteriorating rapidly. In 1862, Commissioner for
Indian Affairs William F. Dole acknowledged in his report to the Secretary

of the Interior that the plight of Indians in the state was the product of the numerous depredations inflicted upon them by Anglo settlers.

> All, or nearly so, of the fertile valleys were seized; the mountain gulches and ravines were filled with miners; and without the slightest recognition of the Indian's rights, they were dispossessed of their homes, their hunting grounds, their fisheries, and, to a great extent, of the productions of the earth. . . . They are not even unmolested upon the scanty reservations we set apart for their use. Upon one pretext or another, even these are invaded by the whites, and it is literally true that there is no place where the Indian can experience that feeling of security which is the effect of just and wholesome laws.[74]

By the time Ulysses S. Grant became president in 1869, the federal government had virtually abandoned the reservation system in California. All the reservations and farms, except those at Hoopa Valley in Humboldt County, Round Valley in Mendocino, and Tule River in Tulare County, had been abandoned or sold.[75] In that year only an estimated 1,700 Indians were left on the three remaining reservations. This figure reflected a precipitous twelve-year decline from a high point of approximately 10,000 in 1857.[76] By 1872 the reservation system had become so ineffective that the Superintendent of Indian Affairs in California at the time, B. C. Whiting, informed superiors in Washington that "it is no longer a mooted question whether bad white men, willful trespassers, liquor-dealers, murderers, thieves, and outlaws shall be kept off and away from the reservation, but rather shall the reservations be permitted or kept up at all."[77] Although some reservations were reestablished after 1872 under the guidance of religious organizations, the overall federal policy of Indian segregation had ultimately proved totally ineffective in solving the "Indian problem" in California.

CONCLUSION

Although the federal government's policy of "domestication" failed miserably, it nonetheless proved less directly lethal than the state government's policy of sanctioned decimation. As was documented in the previous chapter, an estimated eight thousand California Indians were killed by the state's military pogrom in the period from 1848 to approximately 1870. Thousands of others remained in the grasp of the Mexican rancho system where they labored in a state of debt peonage and virtual slavery. Indians were also continually victimized by both Mexican and Anglo slave traffickers, who kidnapped and sold upwards of four thousand Indian children to Mexican rancheros and Anglo settlers between 1852 and 1867.

Those not devastated by this decimation or exploitation by the rancho economy were forced to contend with Anglos at the periphery of their new society. After 1850, the California Indians were routinely subjected to discriminatory legislation that sanctioned their use as conscripted laborers through "vagrancy" statutes or the "apprenticeship" system. I have suggested that the exploitation of these Indian laborers in Anglo California was the product of early political concessions made to the Mexican ranchero class. Only the downfall of the rancho system and the rapid settlement of California's rural frontier contributed to the demise of Indians as a "useful class."

By the early 1870s the California Indians were no longer perceived as obstacles to Anglo civilization or to the rapid reorganization of the state's economy along capitalist lines. Their rapid demise due to military annihilation, malnutrition, and disease effectively marginalized Indians to the periphery of Anglo society. In later years they eked out a meagre existence on segregated federal reservations where many languished through the rest of the century.

The social marginalization and flagrant exploitation of Indians in Anglo California was fundamentally rooted in the European-American vision of Indians as culturally unassimilable and unambiguously non-white. Being regarded as uncivilized and heathen placed the California Indians at total odds with European Americans in racial, religious, and cultural terms. Thus, from the initial period of white settlement in the state they became both the real and symbolic antithesis of the European-American population. Rather than being integrated into Anglo society at a subordinate level as the Mexicans were, the Indians were ruthlessly segregated onto reservations, became a marginal element in the new Anglo economy, and were subjected to violent pogroms no other racialized ethnic group experienced in the state.

PART THREE

Racialized Class Conflict and Asian Immigrants in Anglo California

"They Can Be Hired in Masses; They Can Be Managed and Controlled like Unthinking Slaves"

The consignment of Indians and Mexicans to different "group positions" in the social structure of Anglo California vividly illustrates how the racialization process helped structure the imposition of white supremacy in the state. Although each ethnic group was racialized differently, neither was ever seen as the equal of white Americans; neither ever posed a serious threat to the superordinate racial status or privileged class position of white male immigrants. Indians became a marginal part of the new society while Mexicans were subordinated at the lowest levels of the working class, where they did not pose a serious problem for European Americans. Moreover, both groups remained tied to the precapitalist ranching or hunting and gathering economies of the Mexican period for decades after statehood and did not contend with European-American men who were rapidly being integrated into the capitalist labor market.

White Californians, however, grew rapidly alarmed by the presence of other racialized, non-European groups in the state: African-American, Chinese, and Japanese immigrants. As discussed earlier, the arrival of black slaves during the Gold Rush heightened anxiety among European Americans that slavery might compromise California's prospect of becoming a haven for free white labor. When Chinese immigrants followed blacks into the mining region, whites drew close analogies between black slaves and Chinese "coolies." This relationship was further reinforced by the unfortunate timing of the arrival of the Chinese; they came to California in the midst of mounting sectional conflict over slavery. The replacement, to all intents and purposes, of the African slave trade by the traffic in Chinese "coolies" only reinforced the image of the Chinese as a threat to the status of free white labor.[1]

It is against the backdrop of this class-based controversy among white Americans over the presence of unfree labor in the state, and the displacement of antiblack sentiment onto Asian workers, that the Chinese experience in nineteenth-century California initially unfolds. These concerns, plus widespread anxiety over the Chinese immigrant's ostensible "heathenism" and "savagery," rapidly ignited virulent anti-Chinese sentiment throughout California during the last half of the century.

This chapter examines the major features of this anti-Chinese sentiment, situating it specifically within the context of the emerging class antagonisms and conflicting interests between white capitalists and white workers. Racialized hostility against the Chinese is best understood in light of the way class-based interests among European Americans were defined in relation to this immigrant population. American capitalists sought to utilize Chinese labor whenever possible and profited handsomely from doing so. White workers, on the other hand, railed against the Chinese because of the threat they ostensibly posed to their status as a "free" laboring class. They believed that the Chinese were mere pawns of capitalist interests and other monopolistic forces that relied upon unfree labor. Consequently, white male laborers believed that Chinese workers threatened both their precarious class position and the underlying racial entitlements that white supremacy held out to them and to the white immigrants who followed them into the new class structure.

THE UNWELCOME ARRIVAL OF "JOHN CHINAMAN"

The Chinese immigrants who first arrived in California during the 1850s came from the agricultural district of Kwangtung province in southeastern China. These immigrants were largely an agricultural peasantry drawn to California by either the lure of the Gold Rush or by promises of lucrative employment opportunities made by overseas shipping companies. Within China, overpopulation, floods and other natural catastrophes, and the social dislocation wrought by the Opium Wars and the Taiping Rebellion also stimulated Chinese emigration.[2] Although these immigrants initially were seen as "coolies," they were not actual victims of the coolie trade that enslaved many Chinese nationals at the time.

The vast majority of Chinese who came to California arrived as indentured immigrants through the "credit-ticket system." They were a semifree population who secured passage to America by entering into contract labor arrangements whereby they were bound for a period of time to labor "bosses" in order to repay their debt.[3] They were typically bonded for passage by Chinese merchants in California who then rented them out in gangs of fifty to one hundred men. Alexander Saxton succinctly summarizes the major features of this debt bondage system:

> In effect [the worker] was at the mercy of the American employer, and of the Chinese merchant associations, agents, or contractors, who had arranged his passage from Canton, who hired him out, received his wages, provided his food and protection, and determined when, if ever, he would return home again. To complete this circle, an extra-legal but firm understanding between Chinese merchants associations and the Pacific ship operators hindered any Chinese from booking return passage until he had been cleared by the merchant association. It was a tight system, not exactly the same as slavery, but not altogether different.[4]

Although indentured Chinese workers were typically advanced approximately seventy dollars (fifty for passage and twenty for expenses), they were routinely required to repay upward to two hundred dollars.

While most came to the United States as indentured servants, some Chinese immigrants managed to secure the necessary funds for the trip from informal rotating credit associations in south China or from family resources.[5] A few of the first Chinese immigrants were merchants and shopkeepers who later became part the Chinese community's small middle class. This merchant class became a localized ruling elite within San Francisco's Chinatown between 1847 and 1858. According to Stanford Lyman, "Because commercial success was so closely tied to social acceptance and moral probity in America, this elite enjoyed good relations with public officials. Chinatown merchants controlled immigrant associations, dispensed jobs and opportunities, settled disputes, and acted as advocates for Chinese sojourners before white society."[6]

Historian Sucheng Chan also notes that the largest merchants owned import-export businesses and often established political organizations on the basis of homeland ties. According to Chan, "as almost all the imported goods were sold to Chinese—who favored food, clothing, and utensils from China—it was in the interests of these merchants and directors of community associations to help their customers and clients maintain strong ties to China. After all, provisioning their fellow countrymen was the chief source of the merchants' profit, and helping to retain an orientation to the homeland was the main basis of the association leaders' power."[7]

Furthermore, Chan estimates that between 1870 and 1900 approximately 40 percent of the Chinese residing in San Francisco and Sacramento were entrepreneurs and 5 to 12 percent professionals and artisans, while the working-class population comprised less than 50 percent of the urban Chinese. In sharp contrast, 80 percent of the Chinese rural population were farm laborers and service workers, 1 to 3 percent professionals and artisans, and only about 15 percent farmers, labor contractors, and merchants—the "rural elite."[8]

While only a few hundred Chinese immigrants arrived in California during the initial phase of the Gold Rush, by 1851 that number had swelled to 2,716 and by 1852 reached over 20,000. By 1870, approximately three-quarters of the 63,000 Chinese in the United States resided in California, where they comprised 9 percent of the total population.[9] Most of these Chinese immigrants initially settled in rural areas as well as the northern mining region of the state. Only one-quarter of the Chinese population resided in San Francisco by 1870, with other urban centers such as Sacramento, Stockton, and Marysville also having significant Chinese populations. In 1900, however, 45 percent of all Chinese in the state resided in the San Francisco Bay area alone; over two-thirds were already urban dwellers by this date.[10]

A crucial demographic feature of Chinese immigration was that it was overwhelmingly male from the outset. In 1860, for example, only 1,784 of the more than 34,000 Chinese residing in the United States were women—a ratio of one to eighteen. This ratio increased to a high of one to twenty-six in 1890 before settling once again at the 1860 figure in 1900. Even as late as that, there were only 4,522 Chinese women enumerated on the federal census of that year.[11] This accounts for the common reference to the early immigrant population as a "bachelor society."

According to historian Ronald Takaki, Chinese immigrants brought with them three main social organizations that structured their lives in California: the *huiguan* (district associations), the *tongs* (secret societies), and the *fongs* (clans) which were comprised of close family and village members or larger village associations. The latter two organizations were devoted primarily to the provision of illegal goods and services (such as the *tong*'s opium trade, gambling, and prostitution) and to mutual aid activities (such as the *fong*'s maintenance of clubhouses and temples, its transmission of letters to China, and its shipping home of the remains of deceased Chinese).[12]

Takaki maintains that the most important of these organizations was the *huiguan* or district associations from regions such as Toishan, Tan-

ping, or Namhoi in southern China. These associations received immigrants, provided initial housing, secured employment, and administered
the "credit-ticket" system.[13] The main district associations in San Francisco during the 1850s were the Sze Yup, Ning Yeung, Sam Yup, Yeong
Wo, Hop Wo, and Yan Wo. These organizations came to be known as the
Chinese Consolidated Benevolent Association (CCBA) or, more popularly,
as the Chinese Six Companies. The CCBA settled interdistrict conflicts and
provided important educational and health services to the community.[14]
They also played a major role as spokespersons for the Chinese immigrant
community. They often hired prominent white attorneys to represent their
commercial trade as well as the general interests of the Chinese community.[15] Lacking any meaningful recourse to state and local government, the
Chinese Six Companies frequently functioned as a quasi-government for
the Chinese community. Indeed as one scholar maintains, the Chinese
community was "more like a colonial dependency than an immigrant
settlement in an open society."[16]

Sucheng Chan maintains that three fundamental differences between the
Chinese-American communities established in the U.S. and the original
communities in China profoundly shaped the Chinese immigrant experience in California.

> First, Chinese immigrant communities, though semiautonomous enclaves, were
> profoundly shaped by forces emanating from the larger society around them.
> Not only did the Chinese quickly adapt to the functioning of a capitalist
> economy, they persisted despite legal exclusion and anti-Chinese violence. Sec-
> ond, since few members of gentry families emigrated . . . merchants who had
> a low status in China became the elite in Chinese-American communities by
> virtue of their ability to deal with whites and to provide for the needs of other
> Chinese. Finally, as few women emigrated to the United States, Chinese Amer-
> ica was virtually a womanless world, especially in rural areas. Consequently,
> Chinese-American communities were socially incomplete.[17]

THE "DAMNING INFLUENCE" OF
THE "HEATHEN CHINEE"

European Americans found much about Chinese immigrants distasteful—
physical appearance, language, manner of dress, food, religion, and social
customs. If being Christian and civilized were the principal cultural criteria
by which white Californians evaluated new groups they encountered in the
state, then the Chinese fell short in both areas: they were "heathen" as well
as "uncivilized." Their clothing, for example, was radically at odds with
European-American conceptions of proper attire. The Chinese immigrants

wore broad trousers, blue cotton blouselike shirts, wide-brimmed straw hats, and closely cropped hair with a long black queue down their backs.[18]

"The first impulse of an American, when he see for the first time a Chinese, is to laugh at him," wrote an American trader in 1830. "His dress, if judged by our standards, is ridiculous. . . . His trousers are a couple of meal bags . . . , his shoes are huge machines, turned up at the toe, his cap is fantastic and his head is shaven except on the crown, when there hangs down a tuft of hair as long as a spaniel's tail."[19] The invidious comparison between the queue and a dog's tail symbolically reflected the inferior status the Chinese held in this trader's mind. The Chinese, like Indians in the state, were routinely likened to animals and unequivocally deemed "uncivilized."

Stuart Creighton Miller's exhaustive study of white Americans' perceptions of Chinese immigrants in the nineteenth century perceptively documents the demeaning racialized representations that crystallized in the popular white imagination. According to Miller, the Chinese were viewed as "ridiculously clad, superstitious ridden, dishonest, crafty, cruel, and marginal members of the human race who lacked the courage, intelligence, skill, and will to do anything about the oppressive despotism under which they lived or the stagnating social conditions that surrounded them."[20] Miller concludes that the Chinese were seen as a "peculiar" people having "bizarre tastes and habits" that included making medicines from rhinoceros horns and soup from bird's nests, and for allegedly eating dogs, cats, and rats.[21] "Virtually every aspect of Chinese life was used to illustrate and lampoon the Chinese propensity for doing everything backwards: wearing white for mourning, purchasing a coffin while still alive, dressing women in pants and men in skirts, shaking hands with oneself in greeting a friend, writing up and down the page, eating sweets first and soup last, etc."[22]

These early images of the Chinese found fertile soil in the United States, where they were further expanded upon by other racializing American commentators. Ronald Takaki argues, for instance, that Bret Harte's popular poem the "Heathen Chinee" greatly influenced public perception of the Chinese in America as "mice-eaters," "pagans," "dark," "impish," "superstitious," "yellow," and as "heathens" with a "peculiar odor" that reeked of ginger and opium.[23]

As noted earlier, white Californians' derisive stereotypes of blacks apparently shaped their initial perceptions of Chinese immigrants as well. As competition between white and Chinese laborers increased in later years, a number of the negative stereotypes associated with black slaves were displaced onto the Chinese. Both groups were seen as being docile, humble, irresponsible, lying, thieving, and lazy.[24]

Like blacks, the "China boys" were infantilized and summarily relegated to a subordinate status in relations to "white men."[25] While white
immigrants arrogantly viewed themselves as rational, virtuous, civilized,
libidinally controlled, and Christian, the Chinese were perceived as irrational, morally inferior, savage, lustful, and heathen. The most noxious representation of the Chinese portrayed them as a cross between a bloodsucking
vampire, with slanted eyes and a pigtail, and a "nagur" with dark skin and
thick lips.[26] One author has referred to this racial stigmatization as the
"negroization" of the Chinese stereotype.[27]

Religious differences provided a major basis of the broad cultural chasm
that socially differentiated the Chinese and white populations in the state.
Most Chinese immigrants practiced a folk religion that combined the
beliefs of Confucianism, Taoism, and Buddhism. They built altars to
honor deities such as Kwang Kung, god of literature and war; Bak Ti, god
of the north; Hou Yin, the monkey god; and Kwan Yin, goddess of
mercy.[28] Nothing, of course, offended the Christian sensibilities of European Americans more than having a heathen group of "pagan idolaters"
in their midst. Horace Greeley, for example, in an 1854 editorial in the
New York Tribune lashed out against the religious practices of Chinese
immigrants, arguing that only the "Christian races" or "white races"
should be allowed to settle and "assimilate with Americans."[29]

Reverend S. V. Blakeslee, editor of *The Pacific*, the oldest religious
paper on the West Coast, echoed a similar view in his 1877 address before
the General Association of Congregational Churches of California. Reverend Blakeslee warned that the presence of the Chinese in California posed
a greater threat to the state's Christian population than blacks had to the
South's:

> Slavery compelled the heathen to give up idolatry, and they did it. The Chinese
> have no such compulsion and they do not do it. . . . Slavery compelled the
> adoption of Christian forms of worship, resulting in universal Christianization.
> The Chinese have no such influence tending to their conversion, and rarely—
> one or two in a thousand—become Christian. . . . Slavery took the heathens and
> by force made them Americans in feeling, tastes, habits, language, sympathy,
> religion and spirit; *first* fitting them for citizenship, and then giving them the
> vote. The Chinese feel no such force, but remaining in character and life the
> same as they were in old China, unprepared for citizenship, and adverse in spirit
> to our institutions.[30]

White intolerance and racial animosity toward the Chinese were further
exacerbated by inflammatory characterizations of social life in California's
"Chinatowns." Everywhere the Chinese lived, their detractors argued, one
found crowded living conditions, gambling, opium smoking, prostitution,

and a number of other despicable vices. Chinatown was "simply a miniature section of Canton transported bodily," proclaimed one anti-Chinese spokesperson.[31] Indeed, such perceptions later led to the enactment of San Francisco's infamous "Cubic Air" ordinance of 1870, which required lodging houses in Chinatown, the only place where the ordinance was enforced, to provide "at least five hundred cubic feet" of clean air "for each adult person dwelling or sleeping therein." Violation of this ordinance resulted in a fine of ten to five hundred dollars, imprisonment from five days to three months, or both.[32]

GENDERED AND SEXUALIZED REPRESENTATIONS OF CHINESE IMMIGRANTS

The perceived menace that the few Chinese immigrant women in the state posed to white men was yet another aspect of anti-Chinese sentiment at the time. Like lower-class Mexican women and Indian women in general, Chinese women were portrayed as hypersexual and readily available to white men. In his annual address to Congress in 1874, for example, President Ulysses S. Grant openly addressed the issue:

> The great proportion of the Chinese immigrants who come to our shores do not come voluntarily. . . . In a worse form does this apply to Chinese women. Hardly a perceptible percentage of them perform any honorable labor, but they are brought for shameful purposes, to the disgrace of communities where they settled and to the great demoralization of the youth of these localities. If this evil practice can be legislated against, it will be my pleasure as well as duty to enforce any regulation to secure so desirable an end.[33]

Horace Greeley echoed a similar view in an 1854 *New York Tribune* editorial. The arrival of Chinese women in the United States had to be prohibited because they were "uncivilized, unclean and filthy beyond all conception, without any of the higher domestic or social relations; lustful and sensual in their disposition; every female is a prostitute of the barest order."[34]

Like Chinese women, Chinese men also were perceived as a threat to the moral well-being of the white population, and most especially to white women. As an overwhelmingly male immigrant population, Chinese men were initially seen as menacing sexual "perverts" that preyed upon innocent white women. This view first gained currency on the East Coast, where newspapers sensationalized accounts of Chinese men luring and debauching young white girls in opium dens and laundries. An 1873 *New York Times* article, for instance, reported the presence of "a handsome but squalidly dressed young white girl" in an opium den in that city's China-town. When the Chinese owner of the den was asked about the girl, he was reported to have "replied with a horrible leer, 'Oh, hard time in New York. Young girl hungry. Plenty come here. Chinaman always have something to eat, and he like young white girl, He! He!.'" The *Times* later reported that Chinese men were so depraved that they often attended Christian Sunday schools only to solicit sexual favors from the white female instructors. As proof they cited the case of one Sunday school teacher who apparently married one of her Chinese students. The girl's father publicly insisted that she had been drugged into marrying the man. "No matter how good a Chinaman may be, ladies never leave their children with them, especially little girls," warned another 1876 article in *Scribner's*.[35]

Expressions of public concern for the virtue of white women were more than mere moral posturing, for they often led to direct violence against Chinese men. In one incident in 1889 an angry mob of two thousand people demolished a Chinese laundry in Milwaukee after its two owners were accused of ravaging more than twenty young white girls in the back room. In 1883 in Waynesboro, Georgia, townsmen chased the "rat-eaters" out of town and burned their business to the ground, fearing that white girls would be "caught in the toils of Chinese duplicity."[36]

Fears and suspicions similar to these led to the enactment of an antimis-cegenation statute in California in 1880 that prohibited the issuance of a marriage licence between white persons and "a Negro, mulatto, or Mongo-lian."[37] Consequently, there are only a few cases in California of Chinese men marrying white women in the state. Those who did were most often drawn from the Chinese immigrant middle class: urban merchants, entre-preneurs, or agriculturalists in rural areas.[38] As in the case of Mexicans, class position apparently moderated the otherwise rabid antimiscegenation sentiment directed at the Chinese in the state.

There is evidence that some Americans were sympathetic toward the first Chinese immigrants, especially those of the merchant class, and per-haps—as long as their numbers were small—even welcomed them. This reception quickly changed, however, as the Chinese increasingly ruffled the cultural sensibilities and sexual anxieties of the white population.[39] Most public expressions of anti-Chinese hostility centered on their cultural dif-ferences and on the fact that the Chinese were unambiguously nonwhite. Pointed testimony to this effect is captured in the minority report to the 1877 Joint Special Committee of Congress on Chinese immigration. Therein, Senator Oliver P. Morton of Indiana, chair of the committee, summarily acknowledges that "if the Chinese in California were white people, being all other respects what they are, I do not believe that the complaints and warfare made against them would have existed to any considerable extent. Their difference in color, dress, manners, and religion have, in my judgment, more to do with this hostility than their alleged vices or any actual injury to the white people of California."[40]

THE SUBORDINATE POLITICAL STATUS OF THE CHINESE IN ANGLO CALIFORNIA

From the standpoint of popular opinion, the Chinese were clearly perceived as nonwhite, a fact that was reinforced by their close association in European-American consciousness with blacks. The official political status of Chinese immigrants in California was formally adjudicated in 1854, when the case of *People v. Hall* legally restricted the Chinese to the same second-class status of blacks and Indians; they too were officially deemed nonwhite and, therefore, ineligible for citizenship rights.

This case turned on the question of whether or not three Chinese witnesses would be allowed to testify against three white men (one of whom was George W. Hall) accused of murdering a Chinese man named Ling Sing. The California Supreme Court overturned Hall's murder conviction, ruling that the testimony of Chinese witnesses was inadmissible because state law stipulated that "no black or mulatto person, or Indian, shall be permitted to give evidence in favor of, or against, any white person."

Writing for the majority, Justice Charles J. Murray stated that "the words, Indian, Negro, Black and White," were generic racial terms that embraced all nonwhites and as such prohibited Chinese immigrants "from being witnesses against whites." In support of the decision, Justice Murray argued that the legislative prohibition against blacks and Indians entering testimony had "adopted the most comprehensive terms to embrace every known class or shade of color, as the apparent design was to protect the white person from the influence of all testimony other than that of persons of the same caste. The use of these terms must, by every sound rule of construction, exclude every one who is not of white blood."[41] Thus, this case juridically decreed that the Chinese were unambiguously nonwhite and therefore not entitled to testify against white citizens in the state.[42]

The court's decision was made on the basis of some curious anthropological reasoning. In his majority decision, Justice Murray argued that the Chinese should be prohibited from entering testimony because they were ancestrally related to the California Indians. Murray made special note that "the name Indian, from the time of Columbus to the present day, has been used to designate, not alone the North American, but the whole of the Mongolian race, and that the name, though first applied probably through mistake, was afterwards continued as appropriate on account of the supposed common origin."[43] Moreover, "The similarity of the skull and pelvis, and the general configuration of the two races; the remarkable resemblance in eyes, beard, hair, and other peculiarities, together, with the contiguity of the two Continents, might well have led to the belief that this country was first peopled by the Asiatics, and that the difference between the different tribes and the parent stock was such as would necessarily arise from the circumstances of climate, pursuits, and other physical causes."[44]

People v. Hall had far-reaching implications. Murray's closing arguments show that the court was fully aware of its impact:

> We have carefully considered all the consequences resulting from a different construction and are satisfied that, even in a doubtful case, we would be impelled to this decision on grounds of public policy.
>
> The same rule that would admit them to testify, would admit them to all the equal rights of citizenship, and we might soon see them at the polls, in the jury box, upon the bench and in our legislative halls.
>
> This is not a speculation which exists in the excited and overheated imagination of the patriot and statesman, but it is an actual and present danger . . . [45]

The effects of the *People v. Hall* decision were catastrophic for the Chinese. After the case, they were subjected to numerous legislative initiatives that specifically targeted them on a racial basis. In 1863 and 1864, for example, the California State Legislature included the Chinese in a law prohibiting the entry of "non-whites" into public schools. Reorganization of the state's educational laws in 1870, which formally institutionalized a policy of segregating white and nonwhite students into separate schools, also mandated the segregation of the Chinese. This law remained in effect for the Chinese until 1929, when the revised School Code repealed the sections that had racially segregated both Chinese and Japanese children.[46] This was eight years after such segregation was rescinded for Indians and thirty-one years after blacks were no longer required to attend segregated public schools.

It was not until 1872 that the 1854 *People v. Hall* case was rescinded with the passage of the Federal Civil Rights Act.[47] In the period during which it was legally in effect, Chinese immigrants were frequently targeted by discriminatory legislation and by unprincipled white men who committed crimes against them with impunity. Denied the basic right to have recourse to the state apparatus on their own behalf, Chinese immigrants in California were relegated to a second-class status.

THE CLASS BASIS OF ANTI-CHINESE SENTIMENT IN CALIFORNIA

Despite the animosity and political marginalization that the Chinese experienced in California, they nonetheless made valiant efforts to survive and prosper in the face of daunting odds. In so doing, they managed to secure a modest foothold in the self-employment sector of the new economy, where their entry was greeted with widespread hostility from whites of this class.

Although anti-Chinese sentiment was widespread in California, it was powerfully mediated by short- and long-term class interests of the white population. Although privately many capitalists held the Chinese in contempt, they were not oblivious to the advantages of their use as a tractable and cheap labor force. Such material interests often outweighed or counterbalanced the private racism that these entrepreneurs harbored.

White workers who were drawn into competition with the Chinese, however, had little reason to mitigate their racial and cultural antipathies. Instead, they routinely attempted to create, extend, or preserve their social position against the perceived threat that the Chinese posed to their superordinate status in the state. White supremacist sentiments were readily inflamed and provided ample justification for driving the Chinese out of sectors of the economy where they competed with skilled white workers. (The racial animosity exhibited by the white working class has been well documented by numerous scholars of the anti-Chinese movement and will be discussed briefly below.)[48] Small-scale, independent businessmen (petit commodity producers) such as self-employed laundrymen and independent miners were also drawn into competition with the Chinese and responded similarly, seeking to drive the Chinese from areas of the economy in which they were making inroads and to undermine the competitive threat they posed through the use of racially discriminatory legislation.[49]

During the initial period of their settlement in California, mining served as the principal sector of the economy in which the Chinese secured a livelihood. Initially arriving in small numbers during the Gold Rush, by 1855 two-thirds of the 24,000 Chinese in the United States, having fulfilled the terms of their indenture, worked placer mining claims as independent prospectors or in small group partnerships.[50] The Chinese population engaged in mining climbed rapidly to nearly 35,000 in 1860, when over 70 percent of all gainfully employed Chinese male adults were placer miners.[51]

Opportunities in mining, however, were finite, and success or failure of the Chinese in this endeavor structured other employment opportunities. According to Sucheng Chan, the presence or absence of mining in a particular area affected what other occupations the Chinese successfully entered. She has shown that there was an inverse relationship between the percentage of the Chinese population in the mining industry and the percentage earning a more menial living. "When mining was available, a few became laborers and providers of personal services, but as mining waned from the 1860s onward, an increasing number of Chinese became laundrymen, laborers, servants, and cooks. When mining was not available, the first Chinese to enter those areas had to take menial jobs from the beginning."[52] Consequently, as the Chinese turned away from mining, "the more enterprising ones became manufacturers or merchants in the urban areas and truck gardeners in the rural and suburban areas, while the less fortunate everywhere became laborers, cooks, and servants."[53]

Opposition to Chinese immigrants in California, however, developed as soon as they came into direct economic competition with the white population. The first expressions of such anti-Chinese sentiment came from independent white miners in the mining districts of northern California, who quickly concluded, despite evidence to the contrary, that Chinese miners were primarily gang laborers unfairly competing with the white "producing class." European-American miners claimed that the Chinese drained wealth from the country by sending part of their earnings to China, encouraged "monopolies" in the state, posed a serious moral threat to the entire white population, and, finally, threatened the tranquility of the mining districts.[54]

This early opposition to the Chinese was spearheaded by self-employed, independent white miners. It was largely through their efforts that many Chinese placer miners eventually were driven from the mines.[55] In addition to committing brutal acts of violence against the Chinese, these miners successfully lobbied for the passage of "foreign miners" tax in 1852. This legislation required non-citizens to secure a license in order to mine in California. While these laws also affected "foreign miners" from Mexico, Peru, Chile, Australia, and the Pacific Islands, the Chinese were the primary targets of this social closure.

In May 1852, the California State legislature enacted the first foreign miners' tax which required a monthly payment of three dollars from every foreign miner who did not desire to become a citizen. (Since the Chinese were deemed nonwhite, they were ineligible for citizenship.) This blatant discrimination remained in effect until it was overturned by the federal Civil Rights Act of 1870.[56] While it was in effect, however, it garnered the state over $100,000 in annual fees and through the 1860s accounted for a large segment of the state's revenues.[57]

Clearly delineated class lines emerged around the "Chinese question" in the mining district. Anglo slaveholders, monopolists, and "foreign task masters" (such as Mexican patrons and rancheros who profited from the use of unfree labor in the mines) were drawn into competition with white independent miners in the region, who, as we have seen, considered themselves the embodiment of Andrew Jackson's "producer class." The class nature of this racial antagonism is clearly captured in the various resolutions put forth by the white miners who opposed both the Chinese and the white "monopolist" interests aligned with them. One such pronouncement stated: "It is the duty of miners to take the matter into their own hands [and] erect such barriers as shall be sufficient to check this Asiatic inundation. . . . The Capitalists . . . who are encouraging or engaged in the importation of these burlesques on humanity would crown their ships with the long tailed, horned and cloven-hoofed inhabitants of the infernal regions [if they could make a profit on it]."[58]

Widespread hostility along with diminished opportunities in placer mining effectively drove many of these Chinese immigrants from the mining districts and into the new capitalist labor market. The railroad industry, in desperate need of labor at the time, immediately benefitted from the sudden availability of "surplus" Chinese labor. From 1866 to 1869 the Central Pacific Railroad became the employer of over ten thousand Chinese, who dug the Sierra tunnel and extended the railroad across the deserts of Nevada and Utah.[59]

There were at least three advantages that large-scale employers like the Central Pacific saw to using Chinese laborers. First, they were readily available. The prohibition against slavery, the relatively small free Negro, Indian, and Mexican populations in the state, and the opportunities for self-employment of white immigrants made labor a scarce commodity in California. From the viewpoint of American capitalists, the Chinese were ideal in that they could be employed for a short period and then conveniently sent back to China.

Second, the Chinese were also a source of *cheap* labor. Alexander Saxton has estimated that the Central Pacific Railroad hired unskilled Chinese laborers at approximately two-thirds the cost of unskilled white laborers. Although both white and Chinese workers received the same monthly wage of thirty dollars in 1865, the railroad had to provide room and board for its white employees, whereas Chinese laborers were housed and fed by their contractors.[60]

Third, American employers found the Chinese more reliable and tractable than other laborers. The contract labor system made them extremely exploitable and compliant, and employers of Chinese labor in California readily attested to the system's advantages. In testimony before the Joint Senate Committee on Chinese Immigration in 1876, for example, Charles Crocker of the Central Pacific Railroad acknowledged that he preferred Chinese labor to white because of their "greater reliability." He also admired the Chinese laborers' "steadiness, and their aptitude and capacity for hard work." Moreover, Crocker argued:

> I think that the presence of Chinese as laborers among us goes very far toward the material interest of the country. . . . I believe that the effects of Chinese labor upon the white labor has an elevating instead of degrading tendency. . . . I believe, today, if the Chinese labor was driven out of this State . . . there are 75,000 white laborers who would have to come down from the elevated classes of laborers they are now engaged in and take the place of these Chinamen, and therefore it would degrade white labor instead of elevating it.[61]

Farmers struggling to develop capitalist agriculture at the time also appreciated the role that a cheap and tractable labor force afforded them. William Hollister, the aforementioned agriculturalist from Santa Barbara, stated in 1876 that there was "common sentiment and feeling in favor of the Chinamen" among agriculturalists in the state. "They are our last resort," Hollister told the committee, "They are the only thing that the farmer can rely upon at all."

At a meeting of the California Fruit Growers' Association at the turn of the century, one farmer argued that Chinese labor was indispensable to California agriculture because the Chinese were so "well adapted to that particular form of labor to which so many white men object. They are patient, plodding and uncomplaining in the performance of the most menial service." Another member of the association added that one distinct advantage to the use of "the short-legged, short-backed Asiatic" was his ability to tolerate even the most adverse working conditions. "He works in every sun and clime, and as far as the Chinese are concerned they faithfully perform their contract and keep their promise, whether the eye of the employer is on them or not." According to this agriculturalist, the need for Chinese labor in California was not merely "a question of cheap labor, but of reliable labor."[62]

THE CLASS NATURE OF ANTI-CHINESE SENTIMENT
IN RURAL CALIFORNIA

After the decline in mining and the completion of the transcontinental railroad in 1869, Chinese laborers began to enter the nascent truck and fruit farm industry in California as seasonal laborers. By 1870 they accounted for one-tenth of all agricultural laborers, and by 1880 they had become the backbone of the industry, one-third of the total farm-labor force in California. They also were used throughout the state in land reclamation and irrigation projects.[63]

By 1880, a few Chinese immigrants had successfully begun small farming ventures as owner-operators and tenants. Sucheng Chan's splendid study of the Chinese in California agriculture comprehensively documents the extent to which the Chinese entered this sector of the new economy. In areas where white farmers had not already preceded them, Chinese truck gardeners were able to capture the Chinese market as early as the 1860s and, in the northern mining region, even part of the non-Chinese market.[64]

Despite these modest advances and occasional success stories, only limited opportunities existed for Chinese farmers in the state's agricultural districts. In the Sacramento–San Joaquin delta, for example, most Chinese farmers were cash tenants who grew potatoes in the backswamps. Only a few Chinese sharecropped. In contrast, white farmers were overwhelmingly owner-operators who farmed grain, hay, vegetables, fruit, beans, and livestock. Chan has shown that most of the white farmers originally from New England and the Middle Atlantic states were owner-operators who eventually dominated grain farming; other white owner-operators, such as Northern European immigrants, grew grain but also engaged in diversified farming.[65]

Assessing the nature of the class forces that structured the lives of the Chinese in rural California, Chan stresses that they differed significantly from those in urban centers such as San Francisco. In rural California, the Chinese "ruling elite" were often agents for urban-based firms who helped distribute imported goods to Chinese clients. More importantly, they primarily served as intermediaries, or as Chan refers to them, as "compradors," who facilitated the interaction between Chinese and white employers and Chinese laborers in farming and construction projects. They occupied a contradictory class location in that they were both benefactors and exploiters of the Chinese workers bound to them through the contract labor system. "Since it was difficult for Chinese workers to survive without the knowledge and contacts that the tenant farmers, rural merchants, and labor contractors possessed, the latter were in a position to exploit as well as aid the former. At the same time, since white landowners found their services so convenient, these members of the rural Chinese elite were also in a position to strike relatively good bargains in land leasing and other business transactions."[66]

In this context, it would be a mistake to see the Chinese intermediary class of tenant farmers, labor contractors, and merchants as merely exploiters of less fortunate Chinese laborers. As a class of "middlemen," they also served as the first line of defense for their compatriots against the abuses of American employers. This was particularly true in instances where bargaining favorably on behalf of the laborers, as labor contractors often did, also benefited these intermediaries monetarily. As Chan has perceptively noted, in their leadership they tended to "facilitate rather than dominate agricultural production," and consequently they cannot assume the full blame for the mistreatment that befell many Chinese laborers in that sector of the economy.[67]

In this regard, Chan argues that, although

> there seemed to be no rigid class barriers among different groups in the Chinese population in rural California—movement in and out of various occupations being quite fluid—such divisions become more apparent by the turn of the century as upward mobility became more difficult to achieve. On the other hand, it is important to realize that whatever class divisions that might have existed were mitigated by mutual dependence, kinship and village ties, and ethnic solidarity in the face of hostility from society at large.[68]

Given these differences in regional class actors, hostility toward the Chinese in rural California crystallized along different class lines than in urban centers such as San Francisco where white, working-class men swelled the ranks of anti-Chinese groups. According to Chan, hostility to the Chinese in rural California was "led either by men espousing white supremacist values or by hoodlums out to enjoy themselves by tormenting 'Chinamen.'"[69] Moreover, the main rural class—white farmers—with the potential to rally forcefully against the Chinese saw them as tools of "land monopolists" and turned their hostility toward the latter rather than scapegoating the Chinese. White farm workers, the other important class protagonist in rural California, were often characterized as tramps, drunkards, and shiftless individuals and thus generally perceived by Californians as not particularly organizable.[70]

In the absence of concerted class opposition by the rural white population, anti-Chinese sentiment was spearheaded by white supremacist organizations such as the Order of Caucasians (also known as the Caucasian League), who agitated against the Chinese in Truckee, Red Bluff, and Marysville in 1876.[71] Opposition to the Chinese also occurred in Chico and in Sacramento, where in 1877 one group threatened local farmers with the following letter: "Notice is heare given to all men who owns lands on the Sacramento River is heare ordered to dispense with Chinese labour or suffer sutch consiquinces as may follow within tenn days. We have heaved and puked over Chinese imposition long a nuff. Good-by John Long Taile."[72]

In April 1882 another organization, carrying the name "American and European Labor Association," formed in Colusa County in reaction to Chinese workers demanding wages equal to those paid white Americans. The new organization sought to replace these Chinese workers with young women imported from Europe and the East Coast and also called upon the local white population to patronize only businesses that employed white labor.[73] It was common practice at the time to pay white farm laborers one-and-a-half times the wages paid Chinese laborers.[74]

Anti-Chinese sentiment in rural California developed, as it did elsewhere in the state, against the backdrop of an emergent class conflict within the white population between white capitalist interests and white immigrants, who were increasingly being proletarianized and placed into competition with nonwhite labor. One anti-Chinese proponent writing in the *Pacific Rural Press* in April 1886 vividly expressed the popular belief among white farmers that the Chinese were the hapless pawns of capitalist and other monopolists attempting to degrade the status of white labor. He railed against both the Chinese and their employers in these terms:

> A class supporting and degrading civilization in China has chained with the shackles of a relentless superstition and unresisting subservency an inbred race of miserable slaves, who are satisfied with a miserable fare the merest pittance can procure. What more natural than that the services of such a race is desirable by men disposed to regard labor as a mere article or commodity to be purchased low that the proceeds resulting, may, in competition with his fellows, bring him greater profit? . . .
>
> The Chinese slave invasion of our State has been imposed upon us against our constant expostulation as a people. It has been encouraged only by scheming companies and equally selfish individuals. . . . This slave system must not only stop its invasion, but it must leave our shores.[75]

In short, the racialization of the Chinese in rural California often reflected the way class lines were being forged and contested among the white population in these regions of the state. The antimonopolist sentiments of white small farmers provided an important basis of their bitter opposition to Chinese laborers and their opposition to the commercial interests utilizing them.

RACIALIZED CLASS RELATIONS
IN URBAN MANUFACTURING

After 1867 the Chinese found work in a number of the newly opened manufacturing industries in the urban centers of northern California. San Francisco already had about two hundred manufacturing firms employing approximately fifteen hundred workers in 1860. By 1870 the number of laborers employed in local industries in the city had skyrocketed to over twelve thousand, making San Francisco the ninth-leading manufacturing city in the United States.[76]

Paul Ong's study of Chinese labor in early San Francisco provides us an extraordinary glimpse into the structure of the urban economy and the class relations that bound the Chinese and white populations in that city. He has shown that relatively few Chinese were available for wage work during the 1860s. Most who initially settled in San Francisco developed an ethnic economy that catered to their compatriots' demands for Chinese goods and services. Chinatown became the core of this economy, serving as the major retailing, service, vice, and entertainment center for Chinese in the entire state. As late as 1860, only 10 to 15 percent of the Chinese in San Francisco earned a living as laundrymen and laborers in the city's Anglo-dominated labor market. But this ethnic economy could not absorb the continuing influx of immigrants, and so, according to Ong, "by 1870, over half, and perhaps as much as three-quarters of the Chinese were a part of the larger urban economy. In the labor market, they constituted up to one-fifth of the potential wage workers."[77]

This proletarianization process reflected the racial division of labor that became an integral component of the white supremacist transformation of urban California. The Chinese primarily labored in lower-paying industries and firms, with those unable to secure jobs in manufacturing usually forced to take service jobs, such as domestic and laundry work.[78] According to Ong, there were several facets to the placement of Chinese laborers in this racially segmented labor market. First, the Chinese were concentrated in low-wage industries such as those that produced cigars, woolen goods, and boots and shoes. Second, the Chinese often worked for lower wages within certain industries. Shoe firms, for example, paid Chinese laborers an average annual wage of $311, while similar firms employing white laborers paid $901. Third, employers hiring a racially mixed labor force assigned the less desirable jobs to the Chinese while whites held the skilled and better-paying jobs. Whites also generally served as foremen in these plants even when the crew was overwhelmingly Chinese.[79]

As a result of this racialized division of labor, Chinese became the principal work force in San Francisco's woolen mills, cigar factories, and boot, shoe, and textile industries during the 1870s, accounting for 46 percent of the total labor force. As in other segments of the urban labor market in which they were employed, these workers either were heavily concentrated as the principal work force in the low-wage industries or held the most menial jobs in racially mixed firms where they were routinely paid less than white workers performing the same task.[80]

Other Chinese immigrants dominated the local fishing industry, which provided employment for 15 percent of the Chinese population at the time.[81] In addition, many Chinese secured employment as cooks, laundry workers, and personal servants.[82] A significant number also became artisans working independently or with a small number of partners and assistants as shoemakers, cigar makers, tailors, and seamstresses. It is difficult to determine, however, how many of these individuals were independent producers and how many were actually wage laborers in these industries.[83]

The degree to which the Chinese successfully entered sectors of urban manufacturing varied according to the status of the firm and the way white employers defined their class interests in relation to the Chinese. According to Ong, the "role of Chinese labor within an industry depended on the relative power of white capital and white labor and the strength of these two groups was influenced by the degree of competition in the product market and the prevailing production process. It was only in industries where competition was high and labor was in a weak bargaining position that the Chinese were used."[84]

White labor in the competitive sector of small manufacturing (of such things as cigars or shoes) was in a tenuous position vis-à-vis white capital, having to contend both with owners who had great incentives to use cheap labor and with a host of newly established businesses that made it difficult for workers to organize.[85] Capitalists in these competitive industries routinely sought the Chinese as a cheap labor force whenever it was profitable to do so without arousing the opposition of white laborers.

Capitalists in noncompetitive industries based on large factories, on the other hand, could not successfully employ Chinese because of the powerful position that skilled white laborers held in the production process, and thus such sectors of the urban economy as the metal, machinery, and sugar industries did not hire large numbers of Chinese. Owners of these firms often catered to the racial prejudices of the white craftsmen who participated actively in anti-Chinese organizations in San Francisco.[86] Only a few large-scale enterprises such as the cigar box, cordage, and woolen-goods industries were able to hire Chinese workers, because the white laborers in these industries needed fewer skills and thus had less direct control over the production process. Employers in these industries successfully manipulated the racial composition of their work force in order to dampen efforts by labor to organize against them, creating a racially mixed labor force in which Chinese held the most menial jobs and the lowest of the semiskilled occupations.[87]

The opposition of the white working class to the Chinese in urban manufacturing centered on a number of related factors. One was the threat that the Chinese ostensibly posed as strikebreakers. During the period when the Chinese entered the urban manufacturing centers of California, they were successfully used as strikebreakers on the East Coast. For example, in September 1870, seventy-five Chinese laborers were transported from San Francisco to North Adams, Massachusetts, to break a strike by white workers in a local shoe factory. During this same period, Chinese laborers were also used as strikebreakers in Beaver Falls, Pennsylvania, and Belleville, New Jersey.[88] Their use as strikebreakers in California first occurred in 1869, when a large number of Chinese laborers were brought in to break a strike in the San Francisco boot-and-shoe industry.[89] These strikebreaking activities were bitterly resented by the white working class and fueled their virulent opposition to the Chinese.

A second area of contention concerned wages. As we have seen, employers were able to hire the Chinese at wages lower than those paid white workers. The vast majority of Chinese in California were single male laborers who had their basic necessities provided by labor contractors. Arriving in California with hopes of improving their families' standard of living, white workingmen were unable and unwilling to live as cheaply as the Chinese workers. The 1878 report by the California State Senate Committee on Chinese Immigration stated explicitly that white labor

> cannot compete with Chinese labor, and are now suffering because of this inability. This inability does not arise out of any deficiency of skill or will, but out of a mode of life heretofore considered essential to our American civilization.
> Our laborers have families, a condition considered of vast importance to our

civilization, while the Chinese have not, or if they have families they need but little to support them in their native land. . . . The cost of sustenance to the whites is four-fold greater than that of the Chinese, and the wages of the whites must of necessity be greater than the wages required by the Chinese. The Chinese are, therefore, able to underbid the whites in every kind of labor. They can be hired in masses; they can be managed and controlled like unthinking slaves. But our laborer has an individual life, cannot be controlled as a slave by brutal masters, and this individuality has been required by the genius of our institutions, and upon these elements of character the State depends for defense and growth.[90]

This passage suggests one final basis of working-class anti-Chinese agitation: the ostensible threat that the Chinese posed to the overall status of free white labor in the state. Because of their early use as strikebreakers and as cheap labor, the Chinese were viewed as having a degrading influence on the white population. As noted earlier, this perception was also largely shaped by white labor's previous attitude toward blacks and the institution of slavery.

Some anti-Chinese even argued that the Chinese contract labor system in California was more degrading to the white Californians than was Southern slavery. When comparisons were made, black slavery was typically seen as more desirable. The California State Senate Special Committee on Chinese Immigration in 1878, for instance, argued that the use of Chinese contracted laborers in California lacked any semblance of the "beneficial influence" associated with chattel slavery. While "the slaves of the south were, as a race, kind and faithful," the Chinese were characterized as being "cruel and treacherous." In weighing both systems, the report summarily concluded that "all the advantage was with Southern slavery."[91]

THE STATUS OF CHINESE WOMEN IN URBAN CALIFORNIA

The final sector of the urban economy in which the Chinese successfully carved a niche and evoked the ire of European Americans was the vice industry. By 1860 over 10 percent of the Chinese employed in San Francisco were males working in gambling, the sale of opium, or prostitution. Another 23.4 percent of the city's Chinese, all of whom were female, worked as prostitutes. "Thus, fully one-third of the gainfully employed Chinese in the city were engaged in providing recreational vice—an unfortunate fact which gave rise to strong negative images of the Chinese."[92]

Sociologist Lucie Cheng Hirata's important research on Chinese immigrant women in nineteenth-century California provides us with the most detailed and sympathetic analysis of their experience to date. Hirata situates Chinese female prostitution within the context of the patriarchal gender relations of Confucian China and the "semifeudal" system that was carried over into the Chinese immigrant experience in California. As other scholars have also noted, the relegation of Chinese women into prostitution was facilitated by their utterly subordinate status in patriarchal Chinese society. A Chinese woman was obligated to serve her father during childhood, her husband during adulthood, and her sons during widowhood. Her marriage was arranged by parents and clan elders and the betrothed typically met for the first time on their wedding day. The wife subsequently moved into her husband's family home, where she was, in turn, obliged to serve her mother-in-law. Not surprisingly, Chinese women's labor was less valued than men's; her primary contribution was the bearing of children, especially male children.[93]

In this context, female prostitution was an important and acceptable recourse to a family facing impoverishment.[94] According to Hirata, prostitution relieved the family of having to "provide for the girl's upkeep, and her sale or part of her earnings could help support the family."[95] Consequently, "the family, not the girl, arranged for sale. Girls often accepted their sale, however reluctantly, out of filial loyalty, and most of them were not in a position to oppose their families' decision. In addition, the sheltered and secluded lives that women were forced to live made them particularly vulnerable to manipulation, and many were tricked or lured into prostitution."[96]

Some of the first Chinese women who came to California in the gold rush period were self-employed, "free-agent" prostitutes who through various means had attained some individual agency. (One such woman, one Ah-Choi, arrived in late 1848 or early 1849 and within two years had accumulated enough money in prostitution to own a brothel. Most of her customers were reportedly non-Chinese men).[97] The majority of Chinese prostitutes, however, were pressed into service by the Chinese secret societies, or tongs, that organized this lucrative operation in the state. Hip-Yee Tong appears to have been the main importer of Chinese women for prostitution during the last half of the nineteenth century. One source estimates that this tong alone imported six thousand Chinese women between 1852 and 1873 and netted an estimated $200,000.[98] Their operation afforded a lucrative profit for Chinese men who acted as procurers,

importers, brothel owners, and highbinders, and also proved profitable for
white policemen who accepted money for keeping them from being arrested and white property owners in Chinatown who leased the buildings
where these businesses operated.[99]

The highly organized nature of this operation, plus the lack of alternative employment opportunities, facilitated the widespread relegation of
most Chinese immigrant women into prostitution. In 1852 there were only
seven women out of a total of 11,794 Chinese immigrants in California.
Two of these women were independent prostitutes and two others were
thought to be working for Ah-Choi in San Francisco.[100] Hirata has documented that by 1860 there were 654 Chinese prostitutes enumerated on the
San Francisco census: this represented 85 percent of the total Chinese
female population. The other women listed on the census were employed
as laundresses, gardeners, laborers, shopkeepers, fisherwomen, or clerks.
Ten years later, the number of Chinese women in that city working as
prostitutes had doubled, to 1,426, but had dropped proportionally to 71
percent of the total employed female population. Finally, in 1880 the total
number of Chinese prostitutes had declined to only 435 and represented
only 21 percent of Chinese women in the city. These figures indicate that
the "heyday of Chinese prostitution in San Francisco was around 1870, and
its precipitous decline occurred just before 1880."[101]

Chinese female prostitutes were procured in three ways: deception and
kidnapping, contractual agreements, and sale. The following account is a
poignant example of how Chinese women could be lured into prostitution
through false promises:

> I was nineteen when this man came to my mother and said that in America there
> was a great deal of gold. Even if I just peeled potatoes there, he told my mother
> I would earn seven or eight dollars a day, and if I was willing to do any work
> at all I would earns lots of money . . . so my mother was glad to have me go
> with him as his wife. . . . When we first landed in San Francisco, we lived in a
> hotel in Chinatown, a nice place, but one day, after I had been there for about
> two weeks, a woman came to see me. She was young, very pretty, and all dressed
> in silk. She told me that I was not really Hucy Yow's wife, but that she had
> asked him to buy her a slave, that I belonged to her, and must go with her, but
> she would treat me well, and I could buy back my freedom, if I was willing to
> please. . . . I did not believe her. . . . So when Hucy Yow came I asked him why
> that woman had come and what she meant by all that lying. But he said that
> it was true; that he was not my husband, he did not care about me, and that this
> was something that happened all the time. Everybody did this, he said, and why
> be so shocked that I was to be a prostitute instead of a married woman.[102]

In the case of contractual agreements, women typically were offered free passage to America and an advance of over $400 in return for a promise of four and a half years of service. Each woman was required to work a minimum of 320 days a year and faced an extension of up to one additional year if she failed to meet this obligation.[103]

An example of the process whereby Chinese women were sold into prostitution is found in an 1870s account from San Francisco, which came to light when the slave girl's owner was arrested for striking her.

> I have been in this country about nine years. I was brought here from China by an old woman. . . . She bought me in China for something over $20. I stayed with her for about a month. . . . I was bought by Dr. Li-Po-Tai for something from $20 to $40. . . . I lived with the Doctor for a short time only, his wife saying I was of no account. Li-Po-Tai owed a man named Loo Fook some money, and I was given to Loo Fook in part payment of that debt. . . . I was afterward transferred to one Lee Choy, who said he intended to make a courtesan of me. I was then between eleven and twelve years old. One night I went with Lee Choy, and we met a man who say I was young, and said I was good looking, and he wanted to know if I was for sale. . . . I was finally sold to him for about $100. . . . I lived with him about three or four years, and he sold me to Lee Chein Kay for $160. I lived with him both as servant and wife. . . . I have lived at different wash-houses during the last four months, acting as servant for the men there. . . . I have received no pay for my labor in the wash-houses, and, worse than that, have been whipped a number of time . . . [104]

Other Chinese women were also routinely abused and beaten; in addition, they were susceptible to syphilis and gonorrhea and always in danger of being killed by their customers or owners. They often anesthetized themselves from their daily abuse and degradation by smoking opium; some committed suicide by taking an overdose of drugs or drowning themselves.[105] Adding insult to injury, the remains of these women were rarely sent back to China for burial (as was the common practice for Chinese men who died in the United States). According to Hirata, "few cared about the remains of these women. The [San Francisco] *Alta* reported in 1870 that the bodies of Chinese women were discarded and left in the streets of Chinatown."[106]

Those who survived these physical abuses were also subjected to legal harassment from white authorities. Despite the bribes and other extralegal measures used to protect this operation, Chinese female prostitutes were specifically targeted with legislation designed to curtail public "vice." Between 1866 and 1905 at least eight California laws were passed designed to restrict the importation of Chinese women for prostitution or to suppress the Chinese brothel business. "Although white prostitution was equally if not more prevalent, these were additional and specific laws directed only against the Chinese. Chinese prostitutes, if caught, were sentenced to a fine of $25 to $50 and a jail term of at least five days."[107] It appears that Chinese women in this industry were perceived as constituting a more "damning influence" on white men than were white female prostitutes.

Such sentiment also led the California state legislature in March 1870 to enact an "anti-prostitution" measure that required any Chinese or Japanese woman entering the United States to present satisfactory evidence that she had "voluntarily" immigrated and was "a person of correct habits and good moral character." Proof to this effect was necessary to obtain a permit authorizing immigration from the Commissioner of Immigration.[108]

One cannot avoid concluding that these women were taken advantage of by both Chinese and white men as well as by a few Chinese women who managed brothels and served as intermediaries in the procurement process. Chinese male entrepreneurs, who may have been merchants or associated with various tongs, profited handsomely from this lucrative operation. Most of the prostitutes procured through contracts, calling for an initial $530 capital outlay, earned an estimated $850 a year, or $3,404 for the four years of servitude. (This is based on earning an average of 38 cents per customer and seven customers per day.) Since their upkeep was less than $100 per year (which included two or three meals per day and a place to sleep), profits from this type of prostitution were very high.[109]

Those who came voluntarily or were lured into prostitution proved even more profitable. In a case discussed by Hirata, one female procurer obtained the consent of the mother of one women to take her to America for a mere $98. Upon arrival, the woman was immediately sold for $1,950. After working two years for her new owner and reportedly earning no less than $290 per month, she was resold for $2,100. The gross income that this brothel owner received from her labor during these two years was in excess of $5,500. This does not include the profit from the sewing and other forms of work that this woman was assigned to do in the brothel during the day.[110]

WHITE WORKING-CLASS CLAIMS
TO RACIAL ENTITLEMENT

Although the plight of Chinese female prostitutes evoked a sympathetic response from some white women, only a few strata within the European-

American population looked favorably upon the presence of Chinese men in the state.[111] Sentiment favoring the use of Chinese male labor generally was limited to such economic interests as large-scale agriculturalists, railroad operators, manufacturers, and merchants interested in trade with the Far East. Continued Chinese immigration was also supported by some Protestant clergymen who saw proselytizing possibilities.[112]

Opposition to the Chinese, in contrast, was widespread among other segments of the white population elsewhere in the class structure. Once the Chinese were driven from the mines and resettled in urban manufacturing centers, it was the white working class which took up the anti-Chinese banner. The urban anti-Chinese movement of the late 1860s was, from the very beginning, dominated by skilled crafts workers who rallied against both the Chinese and the capitalists who employed them.

This widespread antipathy of the white working class toward the Chinese in California during the last half of the nineteenth century served a number of purposes. First, anti-Chinese sentiment among the white population brought together various white ethnic groups in a common cause, helping to bridge even the most diverse cultural, religious, and linguistic differences among white immigrants. Secondly, this antipathy was used by politicians to mobilize support of these settlers for the Democratic and, to a lesser extent, the Republican parties.[113]

Above all, the anti-Chinese sentiment of the period served as a major unifying force for the organization of white skilled labor in California. Rather than viewing the Chinese as a particularly vulnerable and unorganized sector of the working class, craft union leaders used racial antipathy as a tool to further the organization of an exclusively white skilled labor movement. It was precisely this sector of the white working class, which ironically had the least to fear in terms of direct economic competition with the Chinese, that spearheaded the anti-Chinese movement in California. There is agreement among historians that the leaders of the white craft union movement used the anti-Chinese agitation as a means of unifying and strengthening their political influence in the state. Such agitation also served as a means whereby these leaders diverted the attention of unskilled workers and the unemployed from the privileged position that unionized, skilled occupations were developing at the time.[114]

Largely through the efforts of leaders of the craft union movement and anti-Chinese agitators, a number of legislative bills were enacted benefiting this segment of the white population. Most of these bills were designed to curtail the threat that the Chinese posed to the white working class and functioned as a form of social closure. In 1852, for example, white workers played a key role in the legislative defeat of a bill which would have sanctioned the importation of Chinese contracted laborers into the state. The so-called Tingley "coolie bill" proposed that contracts made between Chinese laborers and Anglo employers in California, who paid their passage to the United States, be legally binding and would have required Chinese contracted laborers to serve employers for a period of ten years or less at a fixed wage, further institutionalizing the subordination of the Chinese population to capitalist interests.[115]

In addition to this legislative victory, white labor was able to manipulate the state apparatus into a number of measures targeting Chinese labor. In 1860 the state legislature passed a $4 monthly tax on Chinese fishermen. In April 1862, the legislature enacted the "Chinese Police Tax" whose stated purpose was to "Protect Free White Labor against Competition with Chinese Coolie Labor and to Discourage the Immigration of Chinese into the State of California." In 1876 the San Francisco Board of Supervisors passed an ordinance which levied a quarterly tax of $2 on horse-drawn laundry deliverymen (who were mostly white) and a $15 tax on those who delivered their laundry without a vehicle (mostly Chinese). Finally, in 1879 a provision was included in the new California State Constitution which specifically prohibited the employment of Chinese laborers on any public works projects.[116]

Perhaps the most important victory of the white working class in California and the West against Chinese labor was the passage of federal legislation that ultimately prohibited their further immigration. The 1882 Chinese Exclusion Act barred the immigration of Chinese laborers into the United States for a ten-year period and expressly excluded the Chinese from naturalization. In 1892 the Geary Act extended the Chinese Exclusion Act for another ten-year period, at the end of which the 1902 Immigration Act permanently prohibited further Chinese immigration. It was not until 1943 that the Chinese Exclusion Act was repealed by Congress.[117]

CONCLUSION

Who ultimately orchestrated and benefited from the calamity that befell Chinese immigrants in nineteenth-century California? What was the relative role of white capital and white labor in structuring the placement of the Chinese in the urban economy and promoting the racialization of the Chinese in California? Did capitalists divide the working class along racial lines to maximize profits and thwart class opposition? Or did segments of the white working class define their class interests along narrow racial lines so as to exclude and vilify their Chinese counterparts?

In the final analysis, the answers to these questions lie partly in the tenuous balance of power between white capital and labor in the state—one which shifted with fluctuations in the business cycle, growing competition, and the mechanization of industry. The ability of these class actors to realize their narrowly defined interests helped structure the integration or exclusion of the Chinese in the urban labor market. Privileged white workers clearly turned their hostility toward the Chinese underclass rather than joining with them in a common struggle against capitalism or its agents. As Paul Ong has perceptively concluded, "While capitalists such as those in the woolen industry attempted to 'divide and conquer' workers, the economy provided few such opportunities. The most active agents in dividing labor were the workers themselves . . . [who] often succeeded in protecting a desirable niche of the labor market from outsiders, creating monopolies which maintained high wages. Racism, along with trade unions and nativism, became the bases for organizing such a group—in this case white labor."[118]

At its most fundamental level, this process of exclusion represents the utilization of social closures by white workers who attempted to limit Chinese access to privileged sectors of the new capitalist labor market. Their racial animosity toward the Chinese reflected both the general acceptance of white supremacist sentiments among white Californians and also reflected the emerging class tensions within white society.

However, at the moment when capitalism created a common labor market and the basis for collective class organization, the white working class responded by narrowly defining their interests solely as *white* workers—rather than in more inclusive class terms. Although Chinese and white workers may have shared some underlying class interests, these interests never crystallized in common opposition to capitalist interests. Instead, white craftsmen and other skilled workers consistently sought to maintain their privileged racial status over the Chinese and, in the process, reaffirmed the centrality of race as the primary organizing principle of nineteenth-century Anglo California. In sum, only a historical analysis of the Chinese immigrant experience that explores the complex way white supremacy racialized class as well as gender relations illuminates the broad contours of their nineteenth century experience in the state.

The next chapter extends this analysis and examines how anti-Chinese sentiment was displaced onto the Japanese who immigrated into the state in the aftermath of the Chinese Exclusion Act of 1882. It does so through an analysis of the Japanese-Mexican Labor Association's successful agricultural strike in Oxnard, California in 1903. The issues raised by this organization of Japanese and Mexican farm workers highlight the complex ways that racial status and class position structured social relations between white Californians and racialized ethnic groups at the turn of the century.

"In the Hands of People Whose Experience Has Been Only to Obey a Master Rather than Think and Manage for Themselves"

The successful agitation by the white working class for the Chinese Exclusion Act in 1882 represented a momentous victory by European-American workers over both capitalist interests and Chinese laborers in California, successfully thwarting encroachment into sectors of the labor market that skilled white workers sought to arrogate exclusively to themselves. By the mid-1880s, however, a new threat to white racial entitlement emerged in California: Japanese immigrants. At the end of the nineteenth century, Japanese farm laborers, labor contractors, and small farmers became the next formidable challenge to the class opportunities that white Californians sought to retain for themselves. This chapter explores, through a case study, one particularly bitter episode in the ongoing class-specific confrontation between European Americans and racialized ethnic groups in California. The unionization drive by Japanese and Mexican farm workers in the southern California town of Oxnard in 1903 also provides a window into the changing nature of racial and class hierarchies and the differences in white racial attitudes at the turn of the century.

The successful enactment of the Chinese Exclusion Act compelled agribusiness interests in California to seek a replacement for the unavailable Chinese farm labor force. California growers initially turned to the Mexican population in the state as well as Japanese immigrants. Although Mexicans had slowly worked their way out of the shadows of the old rancho economy by the late nineteenth century, their population in the state was still quite small and insufficient to meet the widespread demand for a cheap, tractable agricultural work force. Consequently, California capitalist employers turned to Japan.

IN THE WAKE OF ANTI-CHINESE HYSTERIA
AND WHITE WORKING-CLASS RACISM

The Japanese government's reversal of its long-standing policy of prohibiting emigration set the stage for the immigration of Japanese nationals to California during the closing decades of the nineteenth century. Most of these first generation immigrants—the *Issei*—were indigent student-laborers and a few political exiles.[1] Like the Chinese, Japanese immigrants came to California drawn by promises of well-paying employment and the possibility of attaining the class mobility that had eluded them in their home country. Unlike the Chinese peasantry, however, most Japanese immigrants were drawn from the small farmer stratum, whose class position in Japan had been rendered precarious by the Meiji Restoration.[2] Moreover, Japanese immigrants were further distinguished from the Chinese in their generally higher rates of literacy and education. Because of Japan's system of compulsory education, the Issei were a very literate group who had attained the equivalent of an eighth-grade education.[3]

In 1890, the immigrant Issei population in California remained quite small, numbering just over 1,000 persons. By 1900 their numbers swelled to 10,151 and ten years later to 41,356.[4] The three largest concentrations of Japanese immigrants during this period were in the San Francisco and Sacramento areas and the upper San Joaquin Valley. After 1907, Japanese immigrants increasingly settled in southern California as a consequence of their growing utilization in California's burgeoning agriculture industry. By 1910, the largest concentrations of Japanese immigrants were found in Los Angeles and San Francisco, each having a population of just over 4,000.[5]

Japanese immigrants faced the same rigid racial and ethnic stratification of the labor market as did the Chinese, and their employment experience was similar. They found employment opportunities severely limited in California. Outside of agriculture, these immigrants were restricted to backbreaking jobs as laborers on the railroads, in construction trades, and in the canning and lumber industries. A few also found employment in the mining of coal and ore, smelting, meat packing, and the salt industry.[6] Facing open hostility from the white trade-union movement, only a small percentage of the Issei secured employment in urban manufacturing, primarily in the boot and shoe, clothing, and cigar-making industries. The majority of the Japanese immigrants living in urban areas made their living either as domestics (principally as house servants and gardeners) or as self-employed small entrepreneurs (restaurateurs, merchants, boarding-house keepers, and grocery store operators) catering to the Issei.[7]

Most Japanese immigrants, however, gravitated toward employment in an economic sector in which they had previous experience, agriculture. As early as 1887, Japanese farm laborers were employed in the Vaca Valley. By the early 1890s they could be found in the Newcastle fruit district, the hop-growing area of the Pajaro Valley, and the vineyards of Fresno. They also quickly secured employment in the lower Sacramento and San Joaquin River country and the Marysville and Suisun districts.[8] By 1895 the Japanese were employed in nearly every agricultural locality in California as far south as Fresno. Five years later, Japanese farm laborers had pushed into southern California and within a few years were employed in nearly every county of that section of the state. By 1909 the Japanese accounted for over 85 percent of the farm labor force in the sugar beet industry and approximately one-half of the labor in California's vineyards, nurseries, and in citrus fruit, deciduous fruit, and vegetable production.[9]

In securing a foothold in the farm labor market, the Japanese often underbid labor competitors such as the Chinese, Mexicans, and the few white workers in the industry. Once securely established in a locality, however, the Japanese startled Anglo employers by militantly demanding higher wages or the renegotiation of contract arrangements. They were willing to resort to strikes or work slowdowns to secure these demands. After initially receiving low wages in this industry, Japanese farm laborers saw their pay steadily rise in the period between 1900 and 1906.[10]

The Japanese made special use of the contract labor system not only to improve their wages and their working conditions but to attain dominance in the farm labor market and to improve their economic status in the state. Their ability to do so clearly differentiated Japanese contract workers from the Chinese before them. The Japanese tendency to organize and agitate, however, led many Anglo corporate growers to change their initially favorable opinion of them. The threat that Issei self-assertion and independence posed to white farmers in California contributed to racial hostility among European-American employers and the white population more generally.

By the early years of the twentieth century, many of the small growers in the state expressed displeasure with the Japanese, contrasting them negatively with the Chinese laborers they had formerly relied upon. At the

California Fruit Growers' Convention in 1907, for example, one horticulturalist complained that Japanese labor in the state was "not as honest and
reliable as the Chinese." Furthermore, he added,

> They are cunning—even tricky. They have no scruples about violating a
> contract or agreement when it is to their advantage to do so. They of all are far
> short of giving satisfaction as laborers in the service of Americans. This is partly
> due to their racial pride and self-consciousness of their own importance. They
> are great imitators and tireless in their efforts to acquire knowledge that will
> enable them to become contractors. . . . They are not long content to work for
> others; their ambition is to do business on their own account. While they have
> no organized unions, as we know them, they are clannish and have such a
> complete understanding among themselves that they can act promptly and in
> unison in an emergency.[11]

This racialized hostility was initially directed at Japanese farm laborers and contractors, but in later years Japanese small farmers were also
targeted. Their familiarity with agriculture production and their dominance of the farm labor force even afforded some Issei contractors and
laborers the opportunity to buy or lease small farms. The success of this
Japanese ethnic enclave in California agriculture was dramatic: by 1925
nearly 50 percent of the Japanese population was engaged in small farming.[12]

As one might expect, Anglo small-farming interests reacted with hostility to the Japanese success in an area which they believed was the exclusive
domain of free, white citizens. Opposition to Japanese farmers eventually
led to the successful enactment of the so-called Alien Land Laws of 1913
and 1920. This racially discriminatory legislation declared it unlawful for
"aliens ineligible for citizenship" to own private property in the state and
further stipulated that they were not allowed to lease land for terms longer
than three years.[13] These laws represented yet another attempt at social
closure by the white population in the state.

Japanese immigrants became the first racialized immigrant population
to challenge the precarious position of Anglo small family farmers in the
state. This challenge, however, had important antecedents. The first sign
of this emerging Issei threat to white farmers was their organization as
farm laborers in the early twentieth century.

Nowhere was the success of Japanese immigrants more apparent than
in the first unionization of Japanese and Mexican farm laborers in southern California in 1903. In February of that year over twelve hundred
Mexican and Japanese farm workers organized the Japanese-Mexican
Labor Association (JMLA) in the southern California community of Ox-

nard. The JMLA was the first major agricultural workers' union in California composed of the newly racialized ethnic populations and the first to strike successfully against white capitalist interests in the state.[14]

In addition to its significance to labor history, the Oxnard strike highlights the way class forces and racial lines were being mobilized in California at this historical juncture. Moreover, the strike provides a vehicle for comparing European-American attitudes toward Mexican and Japanese laborers at the turn of the century and throws into broad relief the way capitalist agriculture was increasingly organized along racial lines.

AGRIBUSINESS INTERESTS AND THE SOUTHERN CALIFORNIA COMMUNITY OF OXNARD

Emerging as one of the many "boom towns" in California at the turn of the century, Oxnard owed its existence to the passage of the 1897 Dingley Tariff Bill, which imposed a heavy duty on imported sugar, and the introduction of the sugar beet industry to Ventura County. The construction of an immense sugar beet factory in Ventura County by Henry, James, and Robert Oxnard, prominent sugar refiners from New York, drew hundreds into the area and led to the founding of the new community. The sugar beet factory quickly became a major processing center for the emerging U.S. sugar beet industry, refining nearly 200,000 tons of beets and employing 700 people by 1903.[15]

The new community's dependence on the developing Ventura County sugar beet industry and the tremendous influx of agricultural workers led to the division of Oxnard into clearly discernible white and nonwhite social worlds, with segregated nonwhite enclaves on the east side of town. The Mexican section of Oxnard, referred to as "Sonoratown," was initially settled by displaced Mexican workers who in the early 1900s migrated into the area seeking employment.[16] This working-class Mexican population was viewed by the European-American population with utter disdain. The local newspaper, for example, disparaged the Mexican community's odd "feasting," "game playing," and "peculiar customs." Mexicans were typically seen as a "queer" people who could be tolerated only so long as they kept to themselves.[17]

Also segregated on the east side of town, adjacent to the Mexican colonia, was the "Chinatown" section of Oxnard. Local Anglos despised the Chinese enclave even more than they did "Sonoratown." Chinatown was described in the *Oxnard Courier* as consisting of numerous "measly, low, stinking and dirty huts with all kinds of pitfalls and dark alleys where murder can be committed in broad daylight without detection."[18] Despite widespread anti-Asian sentiment in the local community, the Asian population grew to an estimated 1,000 to 1,500 people less than a decade after the founding of Oxnard.

Residents of the rest of Ventura County greatly disapproved of the impact that the nonwhite population of Oxnard was thought to have on the social character of the county. Popular opinion blamed racialized ethnic groups for all the detested vices (such as gambling, liquor, drugs, and prostitution) to be found in the town. One prominent Anglo pioneer described Oxnard at the time as a "very disreputable town," primarily inhabited by "riff raff" and "Mexicans," and a visitor in 1901 described the community as a "characteristic Boom town," with "many saloons" and numerous "Mexicans and others loitering around."[19]

Thus, two very different social worlds emerged in Oxnard during its early years. On the east side of town were the Mexican and Chinese communities, whose presence contributed to Oxnard reputedly having a "damning influence on her neighbors." The European-American residents on the west side of town, in contrast, comprised "upstanding" German and Irish farmers and several Jewish families.[20] "While the east side of town was a rip-roaring slum," according to one local historian, "the west side was listening to lecture courses, hearing WCTU [Woman's Christian Temperance Union] speakers, having gay times at the skating rink in the opera house, putting on minstrel shows . . ."[21]

The social division of Oxnard reflected the organization of the community along clearly discernible racial and class lines. Along the class axis there existed a small class of large-scale entrepreneurs (such as the Oxnard brothers and the major growers); an intermediate stratum of farmers and independent merchants operating small-scale concerns; and a large working class composed of skilled and unskilled wage workers tied to the local agricultural economy.

The local class structure was also organized along the lines being forged at the time by the racialization process. The most obvious feature of this hierarchy was the residential segregation of the community and the organization of the local labor market in racial terms. Not only did European Americans dominate the uppermost stratum, the 1900 federal manuscript census for Ventura County documents that nearly 95 percent of all farmers in the county were white men. European Americans also held the best jobs in the lower tier of white-collar, skilled, and unskilled labor.[22] At the Oxnard sugar beet factory, for example, only European-

American men were employed as permanent staff. All of the major department heads, foremen, supervisors, office, and maintenance staff were also white men. The only exception to this were the few white women employed as secretaries and stenographers.[23] Oxnard's nonwhite population, on the other hand, were overwhelmingly employed as unskilled laborers and were the primary source of contracted farm labor in the area. In 1900 nearly 50 percent of the Mexican and Japanese population and over 65 percent of the Chinese in the county were farm laborers, and another 18 to 33 percent of these groups were unskilled laborers.[24]

Only a small segment of the racialized ethnic population in the county occupied the middle rung of the local occupational structure. The most important group in this position were the local contractors who served as middlemen securing laborers for white farmers and large growers. The county's racial and class hierarchies placed these contractors in a unique position. On one hand, their class location placed them at odds with their working-class compatriots as these contractors received a sizable portion of the wages earned by the laborers working under them. On the other hand, although they benefited directly from the contract labor system, they were also in a position to protect their workers from unscrupulous local farmers. In return for securing employment and receiving a portion of their workers' wages, these contractors often fought to insure fair working conditions for those under their supervision.

PRELUDE TO THE STRIKE OF 1903

The development of the sugar beet industry in Ventura County led to a precipitous increase in the demand for seasonal farm laborers in Oxnard. Initially, sugar beet farmers in Oxnard relied upon Mexican and Chinese contract laborers. The decline in the local Chinese population after the passage of the Chinese Exclusion Act and the increasing utilization of Mexicans in other sectors of agriculture, however, led to the aggressive recruitment of Japanese farm workers to fill this labor shortage. Japanese farm laborers were first employed in the Oxnard sugar beet industry in 1899, and by 1902 there were nine Japanese labor contractors meeting nearly all seasonal need for farm laborers in the area.[25]

In the spring of 1902, however, a number of prominent Jewish businessmen and bankers in Oxnard organized a new contracting company, the Western Agricultural Contracting Company (WACC). Among the first directors and principal organizers of the company were the presidents of the Bank of Oxnard and the Bank of A. Levy, two of the most important merchants in Oxnard. The major sugar refiner in the county, the American Beet Sugar Company, also played an instrumental role in supporting the formation of the WACC.[26]

The initial purpose in forming the WACC was to provide local farmers with an alternative to the Japanese labor contractors. Local European-American farmers and individuals with interests in the American Beet Sugar Company feared that these contractors would use their control of the local labor market to press for wage increases and improvements in working conditions. Elsewhere in the state, under the leadership of Japanese contractors, Japanese farm laborers had already engaged in work slowdowns and strikes to secure concessions from white farmers.[27] The European-American businessman who formed the WACC already enjoyed a close relationship with local beet farmers; they easily negotiated new labor contracts and by February 1903 had gained control of approximately 90 percent of the contracting business.

The WACC forced all nonwhite labor contractors to subcontract through their company or go out of business, forcing Japanese contractors and their employees to work on their terms.[28] These contractors saw their commissions reduced by this subcontracting arrangement, and they were no longer able to negotiate wages directly with local farmers. The farm laborers employed on this new basis also were affected negatively. In addition to paying a percentage of their wages to the contractor who directly supervised them, they also paid a fee to the WACC for its role in arranging employment. Furthermore, the WACC routinely required its contracted workers to accept store orders from its company-owned stores instead of cash wages. Overcharging for merchandise at these stores was common.

To facilitate its operation, the WACC established—along racial lines—two different divisions to supervise not only contracted laborers but the labor contractors as well. The so-called "Jap department," located in the Chinatown section of Oxnard, was under the supervision of Inosuke Inose. Inose had formerly been one of the Japanese labor contractors and had also worked for the American Beet Sugar Company (ABSC), an association that led to his selection as the head of the Japanese department. In addition to serving as department supervisor, Inose also managed the WACC's Japanese-American Mercantile Store. Supervising the WACC's Mexican department was Albert Espinosa. Little is known about Espinosa other than his being an experienced beet worker who had won the confidence of the WACC's directors.[29]

THE ORGANIZATION OF THE JAPANESE-MEXICAN LABOR ASSOCIATION

Most of the Japanese farm laborers and labor contractors working in Oxnard became extremely dissatisfied with having to subcontract through the WACC. Mexican farm laborers in the area and the other nonwhite laborers recruited from other parts of the state also expressed displeasure with the new system. To air their grievances, a large group of disgruntled Japanese laborers and contractors organized a meeting in Oxnard during the first week of February 1903. At this meeting a group of sixty Japanese contract laborers recruited from San Francisco by Inosuke Inose complained bitterly about the operation of the WACC's Japanese department, claiming that working conditions and wages promised by the WACC and Inose had not been met. Instead of paying each worker a ten-hour-day's wage of $1.50, Inose gave them a piecework rate returning considerably less. The workers thinned beets at $3.75 per acre instead of the prevailing piecework rate of $5.00 to $6.00 per acre.[30]

The grievances of these disgruntled workers provided the key impetus for forming a union comprised of Japanese and Mexican farm workers and contractors in Oxnard. At a subsequent meeting held on February 11, 1903, approximately 800 Japanese and Mexican workers organized the Japanese-Mexican Labor Association, electing as officers a president and secretaries for Japanese and Mexican branches. Among the charter members of JMLA were approximately 500 Japanese and 200 Mexican workers.[31] The decision to form this union and challenge the WACC marked the first time that newly racialized ethnic groups successfully joined forces to organize an agricultural workers' union in the state. This was no minor achievement, as the JMLA's membership had to overcome formidable cultural and linguistic barriers. At their meetings, for example, all discussions were carried out in both Spanish and Japanese, with English serving as a common medium of communication.

Although the JMLA was primarily a farm workers' union, it actually comprised three distinct groups: labor contractors, contracted laborers, and boarding students who were only temporary workers. The Japanese contractors and, to a lesser extent, the students provided the leadership for the new union. Baba Kozaburo, the union's president, was one of the labor contractors displaced by the WACC, and it is likely that the secretary of the Mexican branch, J. M. Lizarras, was also a labor contractor. The Japanese secretary of the union, Y. Yamaguchi, is identified in one Japanese-language source as a boarding student recruited from San Francisco.[32]

Although it is not certain, it is likely that some of the Japanese leaders of the union, particularly the boarding students, were influenced by the Japanese Socialist Movement, which flourished in Japan after the Sino-Japanese War of 1894–95 and had a following among some of the Issei who immigrated to California after that date. It is a matter of record, for example, that by 1904 there existed two Socialist groups among the Issei in California, one based in San Francisco and the other in Oakland. Originally organized as "discussion-study societies," these groups were led by prominent socialists such as Katayama Sen, who helped organize the short-lived San Francisco Socialist Party in February 1904.[33]

The major purpose of the Japanese-Mexican Labor Association was to end the WACC's monopoly of the contract labor system in Oxnard in order to negotiate directly with local farmers and to secure better wages. Since the formation of the WACC, the prevailing rate of $5.00 to $6.00 per acre of beets thinned had been reduced to as low as $2.50 per acre. The new union wanted to return to the "old prices" paid for seasonal labor. The JMLA further sought to end the policy of enforced patronage. One of the WACC's company stores—the Japanese-American Mercantile Store—routinely overcharged for items by more than 60 percent, for example charging Japanese laborers $1.20 for a $0.75 pair of work overalls.

To secure their demands the JMLA membership agreed to cease working through the WACC and their subcontractors, a decision that was tantamount to calling for a strike.[34] In striking, the JMLA seriously threatened the success of the local sugar beet crop because its profitability rested on the immediate completion of the thinning operation. This labor-intensive process required that workers carefully space beet seedlings and allow only the strongest beet plants to remain. Unlike the harvest, where timeliness was not as crucial, beet thinning required immediate, continuous attention in order to ensure a high yield.

Although the JMLA was largely concerned with wages and the policy of enforced patronage, there is evidence that the leadership of the union defined their struggle in terms of class as well as race. The reforms demanded by the union struck at the heart of the existing relationship between major capitalist interests in the county. Chief among these was that between the businessmen and bankers who owned the WACC, the American Beet Sugar Company, and the major sugar beet farmers in the area. All these special interests were benefiting from the exploitative use of the contracted farm laborers working through the WACC. Although European Americans were principally faulted with exploiting Japanese and Mexican laborers, individuals such as Inosuke Inose and those contractors still subcontracting through the WACC were also seen as adversaries. The JMLA, therefore, did not simply define their struggle in racial terms.

The JMLA's position is eloquently expressed by the Japanese and Mexican secretaries of the union, Y. Yamaguchi and J. M. Lizarras, in a news release: "Many of us have families, were born in the country, and are lawfully seeking to protect the only property that we have—our labor. It is just as necessary for the welfare of the valley that we get a decent living wage, as it is that the machines in the great sugar factory be properly oiled—if the machine stops, the wealth of the valley stops, and likewise if the laborers are not given a decent wage, they too, must stop work and the whole people of this country suffer with them."[35]

Reacting to the JMLA with hostility and mistrust, the *Oxnard Courier* posed the issue of the union's demands as "simply a question of whether it will be managed by conservative businessmen." There was no particular reason for local farmers to prefer dealing with the JMLA, the *Courier*'s editor asserted, when there existed "reliable American contractors" who could provide labor at lower costs. Furthermore, the editor continued, "if an organization of the ignorant, and for the most part alien, contract labor is allowed to overpower an American company, the farmers will find themselves in a state of dependence on irresponsible contractors." To support this claim, the editor noted that it was primarily a small number of Japanese and Mexican contractors who were "the real inspiration of the union."[36]

In another editorial, the *Courier* contended that only a union "in the hands of intelligent white men" could provide the "enlightened management" needed to run such an organization and to provide the "mental and moral uplifting and material advancement" of the Japanese and Mexican laborers in Oxnard. The JMLA would not succeed, therefore, because it was essentially a fledgling union "in the hands of people whose experience has been only to obey a master rather than think and manage for themselves. . . . "[37]

For its part, the American Beet Sugar Company made clear that it would do everything in its power to insure that the new union did not disrupt the smooth operation of the sugar beet industry in Oxnard. It immediately informed the union that the company was fully in support of the WACC. In outlining the company's position, the manager of ABSC, Colonel Driffil, told the union, "I have heard that you have a scale of prices which is detrimental to the interests of the farmers, and the interests of the farmers are our interests, because if you raise the price of labor to the farmers and they see that they cannot raise beets at a profit, we will have to take steps to drive you out of the country and secure help from the outside—even if we have to spend $100,000 in doing so."[38]

The only segment of the local European-American population express-ing any support for the JMLA were a few white merchants in Oxnard. Their support of the minority union, however, was not unambiguously based on humanitarian concerns, as they were anxious to see the WACC's enforced patronage policy ended so contracted workers could freely pa-tronize their businesses.[39]

THE CALAMITOUS SUGAR BEET WORKERS' STRIKE

By the first week in March, the JMLA had successfully recruited a member-ship exceeding 1,200 workers, or over 90 percent of the total beet work-force in the county. The JMLA's recruitment drive resulted in the WACC losing nearly all of the laborers it had formerly contracted. The growing strength of the JMLA greatly alarmed beet farmers in the area, for nothing like the new union had been organized in Ventura County or, for that matter, anywhere else in southern California.

One of the first public displays of the JMLA's strength was exhibited at a mass demonstration and parade held in Oxnard on March 6, 1903. Describing the event, the *Oxnard Courier* reported that "dusky skinned Japanese and Mexicans marched through the streets headed by one or two contractors and beet laborers four abreast and several hundred strong." Although impressed by their numbers, the *Courier* described the JMLA's membership as "a silent grim band of fellows, most of them young and belonging to the lower class of Japanese and Mexicans."[40]

Unwilling to let this show of strength go unchallenged, the WACC helped form an alternative minority-led union during the second and third weeks of March, the "Independent Agricultural Labor Union" (IALU). In attempting to undercut the organizational successes of the JMLA and regain its former dominance, the WACC believed it wiser to support a nonthreatening, conservative union than face complete ruination at the hands of the JMLA. On the intial board of directors of the IALU were Inosuke Inose of the WACC and, as the *Oxnard Daily Democrat* put it, "some of the most influential and best-educated of the Japanese residents of Oxnard." The IALU described itself as a union striving "to secure and maintain harmonious relations between employers and employees of agri-cultural labor" and to defend its members from "any person or organiza-tion" preventing them to work "for wages and for such persons as shall be mutually satisfactory."[41] Thus, the IALU's purpose was not to eliminate the abusive treatment of contracted laborers but to help the sugar beet industry regain its stability in the area.

Immediately after its formation, the IALU began working in conjunction with the WACC to meet the pressing labor needs of local farmers. These efforts were, of course, seen by the JMLA as a strikebreaking tactic. Describing the ensuing tension, one county newspaper reported that "Oxnard is up against labor turmoil, and bloodspots are gathering on the face of the moon as it hovers over the sugar town. The Japanese-Mexican labor union has inspired an enmity and opposition that threatens to terminate in riot and bloodshed."[42]

This proved to be prophetic, as an outburst of violence took place a few days after the IALU was organized. Occurring on March 23, 1903 in the Chinatown section of Oxnard, the violent confrontation was triggered when members of the JMLA attempted to place their union banner on a wagon loaded with IALU strikebreakers being taken to the ranch of a local farmer. (The union's insignia consisted of a white banner with a red rising sun and a pair of clasped hands. Superimposed over this insignia were the letters "J.M.L.A.") According to one newspaper, "a fusillade of shots was fired from all directions. They seemed to come from every window and door in Chinatown. The streets were filled with people, and the wonder is that only five persons were shot." When the shooting stopped, two Mexican and two Japanese members of the JMLA had been shot. Manuel Ramirez was shot in the leg and two Japanese workers were struck, one in the arm and the other in the face. Another Mexican, Luis Vasquez, was dead, shot in the back.[43]

Responsibility for the violent confrontation was placed on the JMLA. There was scarcely a newspaper account of the Oxnard "riot" that did not blame the union for igniting the outburst. The *Los Angeles Times*, for example, reported that "agitation-crazed striking Mexicans and Japanese" had attacked "independent workmen" and precipitated a "pitched battle" in which dozens had been wounded and "thousands gone wild." The *Times* charged that "loud-mouthed and lawless union agitators" had directly triggered the violence. More specifically, it claimed that the "troublemaking" Mexican leadership of the JMLA had inflamed the "ignorant peons" into action and that "most of the firing was done by Mexicans." Even the Japanese laborers, seen as being "inclined to be peaceable," were "excited by their leaders" and fell victim to their exhortations "a good deal like sheep."[44] Although more restrained than the *Times*, the *Oxnard Cou-*

rier also blamed the union for precipitating the confrontation. "Naturally the riot and its causes have been a topic of general conversation on the streets [of Oxnard]. In most cases the union adherents are blamed for resorting to illegal and forceful methods to prevent men who are willing from working for the Western Agricultural Contracting Company. It is this that is primarily responsible for the riot. The attempt to place a union label where it was not wanted is at the root of the disturbance, and in reality the union has only itself to blame for the riot. . . ."[45]

The only weekly that did not directly blame the JMLA was the *Ventura Independent*, whose editor, S. Goodman, argued that

> The root of the evil lies in the fact that ten men for every single job were shipped into the sugar beet territory [of Ventura County], bringing together a restless irresponsible element, only lacking in leadership to make all kinds of trouble. . . .
>
> In the riot of Monday last, the Contracting Company is a measure at fault. Had someone of authority in the employment of the company, possessing a cool head, superintended the sending out of laborers, the restless element could have been subdued and all trouble averted.[46]

Outraged over the biased coverage, the JMLA issued its own public statement:

> Owing to the many false statements printed in the *Los Angeles Times* about our organization, and the murderous assaults made upon the union men last Monday afternoon, we ask that the following statement of facts be printed, in justice to the thirteen hundred men whom the Japanese-Mexican Labor Association represents.
>
> In the first place, we assert, and are ready to prove, that Monday afternoon and at all times during the shooting, the Union men were unarmed, while the nonunion men sent out by the Western Agricultural Contracting Company were prepared for a bloody fight with arms purchased, in many cases, recently from hardware stores in this town. As proof of the fact that the union men were not guilty of violence, we point to the fact that the authorities have not arrested a single union man—the only man actually put under bonds, or arrested, being deputy Constable Charles Arnold. Our union has always been law abiding and has in its ranks at least nine-tenths of all the beet thinners in this section, who have not asked for a raise in wages, but only that the wages be not lowered, as was demanded by the beet growers. . . .
>
> We assert that if the police authorities had done their duty, many arrests would have been made among the occupants of the company's house, from which the fatal volleys of bullets came. In view of the fact that many disorderly men have recently been induced to come to Oxnard by the Western Agricultural Contracting Company, and that they took part in the assaults of Monday afternoon, we demand that the police no longer neglect their duty, but arrest those persons who plainly participated in the fatal shooting.[47]

The statement was published in only two newspapers, the *Los Angeles Herald* and the *Oxnard Courier*. The principal target of the statement, the *Los Angeles Times*, refused to print it.

Shortly after the shooting, Charles Arnold was arrested for the murder of Vasquez, and a coroner's inquest held to determine his guilt or innocence. The conflicting testimony of fifty eyewitnesses was heard by an all-male Anglo jury. A number of witnesses testified that Arnold did not shoot Vasquez and, in fact, that they had not even seen him raise a gun. One witness testified that an examination of Arnold's weapons after the shooting showed that they were fully loaded and had not been fired. Testifying against Arnold were a number of Mexican witnesses claiming to have seen Arnold fire at JMLA members. Among these witnesses was Manuel Rameriz, a victim of the shooting, who testified that it was a Japanese strikebreaker in the WACC wagon who had shot him in the leg.

Despite the evidence of Arnold's guilt, it soon became apparent to JMLA members that Arnold would be cleared. At the close of the second day of hearings, for example, the county coroner notified the jury that another round of testimony was needed so that more Japanese witnesses could be heard. Angered by this request, the jury protested further continuation and stated that they were "prepared to render a verdict without further evidence." After a brief adjournment, the inquest reconvened and Arnold was cleared of any complicity in the death of Luis Vasquez.[48]

Outraged at what they believed to be a gross miscarriage of justice, members of the JMLA stepped up their efforts to win the strike. Following the March 23 confrontation, the union took the offensive and escalated its militancy. In one incident, the *Oxnard Courier* reported that "a gang of 50 Mexicans, many of them masked, visited a contracting company camp on Chas. Donlon's, cut the guy ropes of the tent and made the crew of some 18 men desert and come to town." A similar incident occurred at a labor camp on another local farmer's property.[49] Soon thereafter, Andres Garcia, the foreman on Charles Arnold's ranch, was fired upon and nearly killed by an unknown assailant. One county newspaper speculated that the assailant mistook Garcia for Arnold, the man originally charged with Luis Vasquez's murder. Since being cleared of the charge, Arnold had openly expressed opposition to the JMLA and hired non-union laborers to work on his ranch.[50]

Furthermore, the JMLA approached laborers being brought to Oxnard as strikebreakers and succeeded in winning them over to the union's side. The union stationed men at the nearby Montalvo railroad depot and met the new recruits as they arrived in the county. In one incident reported by the *Ventura Free Press*, a local rancher attempted to circumvent JMLA organizers by personally meeting incoming laborers and scurrying them off to his ranch. Before arriving at his ranch, however, the farmer was intercepted by a group of JMLA members who unloaded the strikebreakers and convinced them to join the union.[51] Discussing the success of the JMLA, one county newspaper concluded that "by the time these men reached Oxnard they were on the side of the union and against the Western Agricultural Contracting Company."[52]

The success of the JMLA in maintaining their strike led to a clear-cut union victory. In the aftermath of the violence in Chinatown, representatives of local farmers, the WACC, and the JMLA met at the latter's headquarters in Oxnard to negotiate a strike settlement. Representing the farmers were Colonel Driffill (manager of ABSC's Oxnard factory), T. H. Rice, P. S. Carr, Charles Donlon, and L. S. Rose. The WACC representative was the company's president, George E. Herz. The JMLA negotiating team was led by J. M. Lizarras, Baba Kozaburo, Y. Yamaguchi, J. Espinosa, and their counsel, W. E. Shepherd.[53] Also representing the union were Fred C. Wheeler and John Murray, socialist union organizers affiliated with the Los Angeles County Council of Labor, the California State Federation of Labor, and the AFL.

At this first meeting, J. M. Lizarras forcefully presented the JMLA's demands. Insisting that the union be able to bargain directly with local farmers, Lizarras threatened that the union would take all their members out of the county, thereby ensuring the loss of the entire beet crop, if their demands were not met.[54] John Murray chastised the farmers for not quickly coming to terms with the JMLA. He impressed upon them that they should be thankful that the union was not striking for more than it was demanding.[55] Fred Wheeler also addressed the assembly, restating the JMLA's demands and pointing out to the farmers that "you have the beets and we have the labor and want to work directly with you. We are members of the American Federation of Labor and are here to stay. It is bread and butter to us and we will deal directly with farmers."[56] (As will be seen, Wheeler's statement, giving farmers the impression that the JMLA was affiliated with the AFL, was premature.)

On this opening day of negotiations, the first sign of the JMLA winning their strike occurred when the WACC partially acceded to its demand to negotiate contracts directly with local farmers. The WACC offered the JMLA the right to provide labor on 2,000 of the 7,000 acres of farmland it had under contract; in return, it requested that the JMLA order its men back to work and agree not to unionize men working for the WACC on the remaining farm land. This offer was flatly rejected by JMLA negotiators, who insisted that they would not end their strike until the WACC's monopoly was broken and all farmers agreed to contract directly with them. At one point in the negotiations the JMLA mockingly offered a proposal whereby each party would receive the right to provide labor to local farmers in proportion to the number of men they represented, noting that the JMLA represented thirteen hundred men while the WACC had only sixty men under contract.[57] The union's strong showing at this initial session led one local county newspaper to report that the JMLA "showed a strong front, clearly demonstrating to the ranchers that they controlled the labor necessary to do their work, and without their services beet crops must perish."[58]

On the second day, Lizarras and Yamaguchi met with representatives of local farmers and the WACC at the American Beet Sugar Company factory in Oxnard. During this session the union continued to stand firm and gained the first important concession in the negotiations, an agreement from the farmers' committee to establish a minimum wage scale of $5.00, and a high of $6.00, per acre for the thinning of beets by union laborers. This was nearly double what the WACC was paying laborers before the strike.[59]

On March 30, 1903, the tumultuous Oxnard sugar beet worker's strike ended with the JMLA winning a major victory. The agreement reached included a provision forcing the WACC to cancel all existing contracts with local sugar beet growers. The only exception to this was the 1,800-acre Patterson ranch, which was owned by the same family that operated the American Beet Sugar Company. This ranch remained the only farm for which WACC would continue to provide labor. Thus, the final settlement meant that the WACC relinquished the right to provide labor to farmers owning over 5,000 acres of county farm land.[60]

IMPLICATIONS OF THE OXNARD STRIKE FOR ORGANIZED WHITE LABOR

The success of the Oxnard Strike of 1903 raised a number of important issues for the labor movement. For years, trade unions were opposed to organizing nonwhite labor in industry and were even less interested in organizing agricultural workers. The JMLA's victory, however, forced the union movement to confront the issue of including agricultural workers in their ranks. It also forced white unions to clearly articulate their position on the organization of Japanese and Mexican workers.[61]

The question of whether to admit Mexican and Japanese workers to the trade union movement became an important issue in both northern and southern California after the JMLA victory. In reporting local union discussion on whether or not to organize Asian workers in Oakland, the *Oakland Tribune*, for example, noted that the "recent strike of about 1,000 Japs and Mexicans at Oxnard against starvation wages and hard-treatment has brought the matter to the front."[62]

The official attitude of organized labor toward the JMLA was, from the very beginning, mixed and often contradictory. Certain local councils, for example, supported the JMLA and the further organizing of Japanese and Mexican workers. This tendency, led by prominent union socialists, also supported organizing all agricultural workers and including farm labor unions in the AFL. Most union councils and high-ranking AFL officials, on the other hand, opposed any formal affiliation with the JMLA. This position was based, in part, on organized labor's anti-Asian sentiment and its general opposition to organizing agricultural laborers.

Despite union opposition to minority labor and agricultural workers' unions, Fred C. Wheeler and John Murray convinced the Los Angeles County Council of Labor (LACCL) to adopt a resolution favoring the unionization of all unskilled laborers regardless of race or nationality. Shortly after the March 23rd confrontation in Oxnard, the LACCL unanimously adopted a resolution supporting the JMLA. This resolution, the *San Francisco Examiner* noted, represented "the first time that a labor council had put itself on record as in any way favoring Asiatic labor."[63]

Although the LACCL's resolution supported organizing minority workers already in the United States, it reaffirmed the local's staunch opposition to further Asian immigration. The LACCL's decision to support the JMLA thus contained an important element of self-interest and expressed the contradictory views of the radical elements of the trade union movement concerning the organization of Japanese workers.[64] Behind its public support of the JMLA, the LACCL acknowledged that Japanese and Mexican workers could successfully organize on their own and that it was therefore in the interest of the trade union movement to include them in their ranks. Additionally, if left unorganized, these workers could become strikebreakers and pose a serious threat to the white labor movement in southern California.

The key role of union self-interest in the passage of this resolution was later acknowledged by P. B. Preble, a secretary of the Oakland Federal Trades Council and a high-ranking member of the AFL. In a candid interview with the *Oakland Tribune*, Preble said of the LACCL resolution,

This is one of the most important resolutions ever brought to the attention of the [AFL] Executive Council. It virtually breaks the ice on the question of forming Orientals into unions so keeping them from 'scabbing' on the white people. . . .

Down there [southern California] the white workingmen have been plumb up against it from Japs and Mexicans who were being imported wholesale. . . . Down there, the Union has succeeded in putting this important company out of business, and the men are now selling their labor at the Union scale, without any cutting by middle men being done.[65]

The message was clear. The success of the JMLA forced the white trade-union movement to either include or specifically exclude Mexican and Japanese workers from their ranks. In Preble's works, it became an issue only "when the forces of circumstances demands it."[66]

While left elements in the trade-union movement supported the JMLA, labor's principal organization—the AFL—was essentially hostile. Although the AFL convention of 1894 formally declared that "working people must unite to organize irrespective of creed, color, sex, nationality or politics," the reaction of the Federation leadership to the JMLA belied this stated purpose.[67] Following the JMLA victory in March 1903, J. M. Lizarras—secretary of the Mexican branch of the union—petitioned the AFL Executive Council for a charter making the JMLA the first agricultural laborers' union to be admitted into the AFL. Upon receiving the JMLA's petition, which was submitted under the name of Sugar Beet and Farm Laborers' Union of Oxnard, Samuel Gompers granted the union a charter but stipulated a prohibition on Asian membership. In his letter notifying Lizarras of his decision, Gompers emphasized that "it is . . . understood that in issuing this charter to your union, it will under no circumstance accept membership of any Chinese or Japanese. The laws of our country prohibit Chinese workmen or laborers from entering the United States, and propositions for the extension of the exclusion laws to the Japanese have been made on several occasions."[68] Evidence suggests that the San Francisco Council of Labor contacted Gompers and expressed its vehement opposition to the JMLA's request for a charter. Although the LACCL publicly supported the JMLA, the prevailing union movement's opposition to Asian labor, which Gompers shared, undoubtedly influenced this decision.[69]

Left elements in the AFL reacted bitterly to Gompers's decision. In discussing the AFL's refusal to grant the requested charter, the *American Labor Union Journal* from Chicago charged that Gompers had "violated the express principles of the A.F. of L." and that it would "be impossible, so long as this ruling is sustained, to organize wage workers of California . . . for there are between forty and fifty thousand Japanese in this state, and nothing can be effectively done without their cooperation."[70] Despite the objections of a few locals and councils, there is little evidence to suggest that most unions expressed anything but tacit approval of Gompers's decision.

Gompers's refusal to grant an AFL charter allowing Japanese membership was vehemently denounced by the Mexican branch of the JMLA. Outraged at Gompers's action, the Mexican membership of the union directed Lizarras to write Gompers what is undoubtedly the strongest testimony of the solidarity reached between the Mexican and Japanese farm workers of Oxnard. On June 8, 1903, Lizarras returned the issued charter to Samuel Gompers with the following letter:

> Your letter . . . in which you say the admission with us of the Japanese Sugar Beet and Farm Laborers into the American Federation of Labor can not be considered, is received. We beg to say in reply that our Japanese brothers here were the first to recognize the importance of cooperating and uniting in demanding a fair wage scale . . .
> They were not only just with us, but they were generous when one of our men was murdered by hired assassins of the oppressor of labor, they gave expression to their sympathy in a very substantial form. In the past we have counselled, fought and lived on very short rations with our Japanese brothers, and toiled with us in the fields, and they have been uniformly kind and considerate. We would be false to them and to ourselves and to the cause of unionism if we accepted privileges for ourselves which are not accorded to them. We are going to stand by men who stood by us in the long, hard fight which ended in a victory over the enemy. We therefore respectfully petition the A.F. of L. to grant us a charter under which we can unite all the sugar beet and field laborers in Oxnard, without regard to their color or race. We will refuse any other kind of charter, except one which will wipe out race prejudices and recognize our fellow workers as being as good as ourselves. I am ordered by the Mexican union to write this letter to you and they fully approve its words.[71]

In refusing to join the AFL without the Japanese branch of the union, the JMLA ultimately closed the door to any hopes of continuing its union activities in Oxnard. The AFL decision not to admit all members of the JMLA undoubtedly contributed to the union eventually passing out of existence. A systematic review of newspaper accounts of labor activities in Ventura County through 1910 failed to uncover further mention of the JMLA after its success in April 1903. No other evidence could be found concerning further JMLA activities or the exact date that the union ceased to exist. It appears that the union continued operating for a few years and eventually disbanded. By 1906 there existed further discontent on the part of sugar beet workers in Oxnard, but no mention is made of the JMLA.[72]

For years after the Oxnard strike, AFL hostility toward organizing Japanese workers and farm laborers persisted. Not until 1910 did the AFL Executive Council attempt to organize farm workers as an element of the Federation. These efforts, however, accomplished very little. According to one authority, the AFL's activities after 1910 were explicitly "designed to favor white workers at the expense of Orientals."[73] Finally, during the war years, the Federation's efforts to organize farm laborers were abandoned altogether.[74]

DIFFERENTIAL RACIALIZATION AND THE SOCIOLOGICAL IMPLICATIONS OF THE OXNARD STRIKE

Beyond its significance for labor history, the Oxnard sugar beet workers' strike also provides insight into the differential racialization process that placed Japanese and Mexican farm workers in different "group positions" within the state. It also provides important clues to the way race and class lines were being structured in California at the turn of the century. As in other parts of the state, Oxnard developed a local class structure in which racial lines closely paralleled class divisions. The overrepresentation in Oxnard of Mexican and Japanese as contracted farm laborers and un-skilled workers and of European Americans as farmers and businessmen reveals the important convergence of these stratification lines during this period.

The local class structure in Oxnard was not, however, completely sym-metrical, nor was it a static one that approximated a caste system. Instead, a modicum of fluidity existed. The various labor contractors who served an intermediary function in procurement of farm labor were among the most important members of an intermediate, fluid stratum in Oxnard. Labor contractors functioned as both the benefactors and exploiters of the men working under their direction, and their ambiguous class position in the community undoubtedly contributed to their playing a leadership role in the formation of the JMLA.

In the final analysis, it was the displacement of these contractors by local agribusiness elites that led nonwhite contractors and farm laborers to forms bonds of solidarity in a common cause. Whether the JMLA's mem-bership wanted to merely return to the days when their compatriots pro-vided contract labor for local farmers, or truly sought to function as a strong union, cannot be determined with certainty. The paucity of infor-mation about the JMLA after the strike makes it impossible to know the extent to which the JMLA primarily defined itself as an independent union.

What evidence does exist points to the possibility that it essentially served as a way for displaced minority contractors to regain their dominance over the local market. Regardless of the motives of the various elements in the JMLA, it appears that local agribusiness elites ultimately made it impossible for the JMLA to continue to function. Whether internal divisions between farm workers and labor contractors within the JMLA played a role in its demise is not known. What is known is that the unique class alliance and bonds of ethnic solidarity that underlined the JMLA proved short-lived.

The experience of the JMLA with organized labor also clearly reveals differences in the racial attitudes of European Americans at the time. Mexicans and Japanese workers were not perceived as posing identical threats to the white working class. Differences between these two groups in racial status, citizenship, religion, language, and earlier competition with white labor undoubtedly shaped the AFL's reactions to the JMLA's petition for a Federation charter. Gompers's attitude toward the Japanese branch of the JMLA clearly illustrated that white working-class racism was not a monolithic structure impervious to differences among California's racialized ethnic groups. To the contrary, important differences existed in the way white Californians at different class locations viewed and structured their relationships with the racialized ethnic populations in the state.

European-American attitudes toward the Japanese were largely an extension of their earlier view of the Chinese. The Japanese were also seen as posing a formidable threat to the jobs, wages, working conditions, and the overall status of free white labor in the state.[75] On the other hand, Mexican workers, for the various reasons discussed earlier, were not perceived at the time as posing the same peril to the class aspirations and racial entitlements of white labor.

In sum, the Oxnard strike vividly captures how differences in the racialization of ethnic groups in California had important consequences for their life chances in the state. Public reaction to Mexican and Japanese farm laborers in Oxnard and the white labor movement's response to the JMLA provide clear evidence of this. In both cases, reaction to the Japanese was vehement and hostile, while that directed at Mexicans was moderated and attenuated by a variety of cultural, political, and economic factors. It was the unique interplay of these factors in white-supremacist California at the turn of the century that ultimately shaped and accounted for the different reaction of European Americans to the Japanese and Mexican membership of the JMLA.

Epilogue

These historical-sociological essays have interrogated the ways in which "race" served as the central organizing principle of group life in California during the last half of the nineteenth century. At this historical moment the new state's diverse ethnic populations were subjected to a racialization process that largely structured their access to material means and social status. In analyzing the racialized histories of Mexican, Native American, and Asian immigrant populations in California, I have explored both the material and ideological basis of their subordination to European Americans at every level of the new class structure. In so doing, I have made use of concepts such as "racial formation," "racialization," and "social closure" to order and give meaning to the structuring of hierarchical systems of group inequality and the class-specific contestations explored in this study.

Although this study is historical in focus and comparative in approach, it is also fundamentally sociological in its analytical assessment of this period in California history. In tracing the major confrontations between European Americans and the racialized Indian, Mexican, and Asian populations, I have avoided relying on sociological "race relations" models to illuminate and frame the relationships assessed in this study. Many of the prevailing theories in this field are based primarily on the black/white experience that scholars have generally explored at the national level. As this study has attempted to illustrate, however, race relations are historically contingent and regionally specific, varying in meaning over time as well as within different regions of the country. The historical materials documenting the racialized patterns of group inequality and conflict that unfolded in nineteenth century California do not support an analytical framing based on the black/white binary relationship forged elsewhere in the United States.

This is not to deny that elements of black/white racial formation had direct consequences for the racialization process in California. It is clear that the black experience had tremendous importance for the racializing discourses that European Americans brought with them to California. This is evident in the way that racialized images of blacks carried by white settlers into California were routinely displaced onto Native Americans. They too were subjected to racializing discourses that inscribed racial difference through invidious assessments of both the character and the bodies of non-Europeans. Like blacks in other regions of the country, Indians were repeatedly stigmatized as dark, dirty, ugly, irrational, and libidinous. The eurocentric cultural arrogance that underlay these racial representations also tainted the initial assessment European Americans made of Asians in the state; they too were subject to a unique form of "negroization." Nineteenth-century "free labor" sentiments were also clearly a product of the way European Americans had defined their racialized class interests in relation to blacks. The symbolic association of Chinese laborers with blacks gives ample evidence to the displacement of antiblack attitudes onto racialized groups that posed a direct threat to the privileged status of white workers in the state.

This influence notwithstanding, the class-specific conflicts between white Californians and the Mexican, Indian, and Asian populations were unique and merit analysis on their own terms. This is clearly illustrated in the fact that the Chinese were formally racialized as "Indian," not "black." This racial status would later be redefined in the case of Japanese immigrants who were subsequently racialized as "Mongolian." As a consequence, I have avoided the impulse to give this comparative historical study an overarching theoretical framework that might obscure important differences in the experiences of these cultural groups and their specific racialization. The primary and secondary historical materials collected here cannot be made to conform to some analytical edifices drawn from the black/white experience in other regions of the country.

Moreover, sociological "race relations" models typically give undue importance to one key variable (such as class or culture) and often fail to develop an integrated approach that is attentive to the way structural and ideological factors mutually shape racial and ethnic relations in this country. It makes little sense, for example, to argue that the nineteenth-century experiences of Asian, Mexican, and Native Americans in California were indicative of an assimilation process structurally integrating these groups into the dominant European-American culture. This study has implicitly shown that sociological paradigms which focus on "stages of assimilation" or groups having—or not having—certain cultural values facilitating their incorporation into the dominant society do not meaningfully illuminate the historical processes outlined herein.[1] While these concepts may have some utility in explaining the structural integration and cultural assimilation of white European immigrant groups in the nineteenth-century United States, they are of little utility for understanding the experiences of non-European, racialized ethnic groups in nineteenth-century California. To assign to Mexican, Asian, or Native Americans the roles and experiences of European immigrants elsewhere in the country defies both logic and an appreciation of the historicity of racial and ethnic relations in the Far West.

In a different way, this problem of reductionism also plagues those race-relations theories that foreground class as the key variable shaping or propelling the trajectory of racial and ethnic relations. Although I have assigned great importance to the role of capitalism and class divisions in these histories, I have avoided the reductionist tendencies inherent in most Marxist approaches to racial matters. Marxist scholars generally have viewed race as merely an ideological construct and racial antagonism as a manifestation of class inequality engineered at the behest of the capitalist class. At best it functions as a "secondary" stratification line that functionally responds to the exigencies of capitalist development.[2] Because they insist on viewing class as the primary basis of group stratification, Marxists typically assume that white and nonwhite workers share overriding class interests and that expressions of white working class racism represent misguided manifestations of "false consciousness." They also fail to recognize that race and class systems are mutually constitutive yet autonomous stratification systems that both have material and discursive dimensions simultaneously structuring the articulation between these hierarchical systems of group inequality.

This study has shown that the Marxist perspective on race is just as shortsighted as consensus-based explanations like assimilation theory; both fail to illuminate and meaningfully assess the historical experiences of the groups examined in this study. Certainly a straightforwardly Marxist perspective is of marginal utility in comparing the experiences of Chinese and Japanese immigrants to that of the white working class in California. While some capitalists took advantage of racial divisions within the working class, the racial antagonisms between Chinese and white workers is best understood in terms of the racially based interests and privileges that segments of the white working class sought to retain for themselves. Anti-Chinese agitation, for instance, was not merely an expression of "false consciousness" but instead was fundamentally grounded in the real material interests that motivated white working class organization along narrowly circumscribed racial lines that were politically contested. This history was part and parcel of the way that European Americans in California fought to retain their privileged access to valued resources (in this case labor-market position) and class mobility and to reaffirm their superordinate racial status.

In similar ways, a strict racial analysis of the conflict between European Americans and the racialized ethnic populations in the state also has important limitations. Chief among these is the tendency for race-centered explanations to slight the significance of class and culture as key factors mediating the experiences of both dominant and subordinate racial groups. A strict racial analysis, for example, would lead one to highlight uncritically the similarities in the historical experiences of Mexicans, Indians, and Asians in California.

As we have seen, the Mexican ranchero class did not share the same interests or fate as the Mexican working class during the late nineteenth century. Nor can overriding parallels be found across group lines in the class-specific experiences of Mexicans, Native Americans, and Asian immigrants. Although these groups shared a common racial subordination to European Americans in the state and were subjected to white supremacist ideologies and practices, the comparative differences in each group's encounter with European Americans are crucial to our understanding of the complexities and nuances in racial and ethnic patterns in this region.

While I have argued that race was the principal stratifying variable structuring ethnic group patterns and conflict in nineteenth-century California, racial status was not absolutely determinate in predicting group outcomes. Not every cultural group that entered into competition with European Americans was perceived in the same ways nor were they subjected to identical institutional closures or racializing discourses. Each group's collective attributes (such as their internal class stratification, gender composition, population demographics, occupational skills, employment background, somatic differences from the white population, and explicit cultural factors such as language, values, religion, and ethnic traditions) were critically important in shaping their respective histories.

RACE, CLASS, AND GENDER IN CALIFORNIA HISTORY

The racial contest over differential access to social rewards and privileges by different groups was mediated by a complex of other factors. Differences among the racialized populations in class, gender, and ethnicity, for example, functioned as intervening variables that had important consequences in each group's collective history with the European Americans in the state. This makes it impossible to speak of a single racial history, class antagonism, or woman's experience at this historical moment.

Although it has become fashionable from our late-twentieth-century vantage point to speak of race, class, and gender as "interrelated" or "interlocking" systems, such an analytical move conspicuously avoids the issue of primacy or determinacy. While this stance may ring true in this postmodern period, the same cannot be said for the period under investigation in this study. What resonates out most clearly in the racial histories that I have sociologically assessed is the primacy of race as the central organizing principle of hierarchical group relations in California. Race, class, and gender systems of dominance and power were not equal to one another in social significance or structural importance in defining one's "subject position" at this historical moment. White supremacist, capitalist, and patriarchal structures unfolded in a complex, historically contingent manner in which racialization fundamentally shaped the class- and gender-specific experiences of both the white and nonwhite populations.

In exploring this racial formation process I have endeavored to delineate the ways in which these racial fault lines were intimately bound up with the introduction of a new class structure and had meaningful gendered dimensions. Far from being articulated in a straightforward symmetrical form in which class and race were merely parallel structures, racialization was bound to class formation in complex ways that gave racial conflict its decidedly class- and gender-specific form. Certainly the experience of Mexican upper-class women was not identical, or remotely similar, to the experiences of Native American and Chinese women in the nineteenth century. The elite Mexican woman's class position, European cultural background, and "white" racial status privileged her over other women of color and opened an avenue for some to eventually assimilate into the dominant culture through intermarriage with European-American immigrants.

The "nonwhite" racial status and debasing cultural assessment of Native Americans and the Chinese, on the other hand, resulted in the enactment of laws forbidding their intermarriage with European Americans, and facilitated the relegation of many of these women into prostitution and sexual slavery. Next to the extreme barbarity of genocide, this degradation was clearly one of the most heinous expressions of white supremacy. It graphically demonstrates the different ways that white men defined their relationships with the female population in the state. Patriarchal dominance meant quite a different thing if one were a white, Mexican, Asian, or Native American woman. Surely one of the most chilling expressions of white male entitlement was the unbridled access that white men had to the bodies of women of color.

What stands out most clearly from this comparative history is that European Americans at every class level sought to create, maintain, or extend their privileged access to racial entitlements in California. California was, in the final analysis, initially envisioned as a white masculinist preserve. It bears recalling that the European American editors of one of the territory's first English-language newspapers, the *Californian*, proclaimed in 1848, "We desire only a white population in California." The ominous consequences of this bald proclamation are painfully captured in the essays that document the treatment of the Mexican, Chinese, Japanese, African, and Native American population in white supremacist California.

European Americans railed against racialized groups in an attempt to arrogate for themselves a set of material interests that they ultimately defined as being their due as a "white population." The crystallization of this racial identity does not belie the important ethnic and religious differences that existed among European Americans. Being English, Irish, Italian, or German had great social significance for these nationalities in their relationships with one another. So too did religious differences among European-American Protestants, Catholics, and Jews in the state. This, however, does not diminish the fact that the racial line in California was drawn along European and non-European lines. As Michael Omi and Howard Winant have reminded us, this racialization project drew a racial line around Europe rather than within it.

In the final analysis, group access to jobs, land, legal rights, housing, and other basic structures of opportunity was initially institutionalized in the nineteenth century as an enactment of group interests, to retain privileged access to social rewards for European Americans. It was one that was socially crafted and reproduced along often ambiguously delineated but socially conferred racial lines. As such, it reflects a process of privileged access to valued social resources and rewards that must continually be challenged at the level of the state and subjected to transformation on a more equitable economic and social basis.[3] While this study has explored these issues in historical terms, only the most politically naive would deny that we continue to live this history in very fundamental ways. Inequalities in the hiring, promotion, and retention of racialized groups in employment and the eurocentric cultural arrogance that continues to stigmatize and racialize California's diverse ethnic populations on the basis of national origin, language, religion, or other cultural markers has its direct origins in the historical period chronicled here. These contemporary expressions of the struggle for "group position" are accompanied by the evolving racializing discourses that the white population has historically mobilized in order to perpetuate their access to valued social resources and rewards. Although the most odious expressions of white supremacist ideologies and practices have been vigilantly contested in this century, California remains a contested racial frontier and the site of continued political struggle over the extension of this society's most cherished civil rights and equal opportunities to all cultural groups.

AUTOBIOGRAPHY AND THE HISTORICITY OF "RACE"

It would be disingenuous of me not to acknowledge that researching and writing these essays have been important to me at a very profound personal level. My work has helped me better understand the exclusively white and Mexican social worlds that I grew up with in the rural backwaters of the now (after the Rodney King trial there) notorious "Simi Valley." My family settled in this area of Ventura County as part of the great migration from Mexico arriving in this century to meet the burgeoning labor needs of California's agribusiness. It also helps make sense of the origins of the Japanese farmers, Chinese businessmen, and Asian working-class communities in and around the Oxnard area of Ventura County. Moreover, I am reminded of the absolute absence of any memory of the original Indian populations in the area. They had been completely erased from the state history I learned as a child. I grew up in a racialized world in which there were no Indians and, for that matter, no blacks; they were groups that I never meaningfully encountered until I left home to attend college.

In this way, then, my own family and personal history is intimately bound up with the larger histories chronicled in these essays. What stands out most clearly as I conclude this historical investigation is the way these essays speak to the historical experience I grew up with as I was socialized into the dominant culture in the 1950s and came of age in the 1960s. This was a social world fundamentally structured along "white" and "Mexican" lines, determining where one lived and worked as well as one's social status. In a very profound way, my own experience underscores the unique features of the nineteenth-century Mexican experience I have recounted. The old displaced ranchero elite held no importance in the starkly racialized, working-class experience I knew as a child. No one lamented the regrettable fate of Don Juan Camarillo or Don Ignacio del Valle; neither did they, for that matter, celebrate the heroic efforts of the Mexican members of the Japanese Mexican Labor Association.

While I have argued that the nineteenth-century Mexican experience was one uniquely shaped by the power and influence of the ranchero elite, this class had long been rendered only a subject of romantic fantasy at the time that I was growing up in California. The social world that I knew was one in which everyone was either white or Mexican. While one was aware of ethnic and religious differences among the local white population, these differentiations paled in the face of the distinction one made between "white people," on the one hand, and the dark-complexioned Mexican peasantry who migrated into the area during the early decades of this century. It was, I must admit, something of a surprise to discover that Mexicans in California had ever been seriously defined or viewed as "white," for to be Mexican in the southern California agricultural world that I grew up in meant that one was unambiguously *not* white.[4]

In this way the social character of "race" and the racialization of Mexicans in California are among the most important personal realizations that these essays have held for me. They speak to ways in which race is fundamentally a sociohistorical category that is historically contingent. Although I have argued that nineteenth-century Mexicans occupied an "intermediate" group position in the racial hierarchy that white supremacy structured at that historical moment, this century has witnessed the reconfiguration of these racial fault lines. What is perhaps most obvious to me today is the reassignment of Mexicans—especially the undocumented, non-English-speaking population—to the bottom end of the new racial and ethnic hierarchy. They are part of the contemporary subaltern class of non-citizen Latino and Asian workers still bound by exploitative labor relations which harken back to the nineteenth century.

It is only now, as a middle-class academic, that I am able to fully appreciate the distinctive nineteenth-century Mexican experience in California and realize that my family history was part of the second act of this historical drama, one shaped by widespread Mexican immigration in this century and the subordination of Mexicans at the bottom end of the evolving class structure. While it may appear at first glance to be a rather far-fetched analogy, I liken my own social location at this historical juncture as analogous to that of other racialized ethnic groups who initially entered into labor markets where they encountered the animosity, even wrath, of a more privileged European-American population. The often hostile reaction and consternation of European Americans to the entry of Mexican Americans such as myself into the privileged world of the academy is but a modern-day expression of the same historical patterns of social closures that I have documented in this study. Hiring, promotion, and policy issues—especially the controversy over affirmative action and multiculturalism—in this labor market sector are subject to this same intense competition for "group position" that I have explored in these historical essays. This is not to deny that much has changed and that the most enduring forms of racial discrimination have undergone profound redefinition since the Second World War. Yet, I would argue that we continue to live the history of white supremacy that I have documented in this book. While much has indeed changed, so too has little been fundamentally recast on more egalitarian terms. Race continues to loom just as large in the late twentieth century as it did in its nineteenth-century configuration. While my profound appreciation of the historical process cautions me against generalizing from one historical moment to another, I cannot ignore the clearly discernible patterns of racialized inequalities that are apparent to me in this reflexive moment. The complexities of twentieth-century immigration patterns and reconfigurings of the class structure make any easy parallels difficult to substantiate in unqualified terms. Yet the profundities of these changes do not obscure the enduring significance of race as a central organizing principle of group inequality and major determinant of one's life chances in this country.

Notes

1. See the classic reframing of U.S. race and ethnic relations as a contention for group position within the social structure in Herbert Blumer, "Race Prejudice as a Sense of Group Position," *Pacific Sociological Review* 1, no. 1 (Spring 1958): 3–7.

2. In his *The Declining Significance of Race* (Chicago: University of Chicago Press, 1980), sociologist William J. Wilson argues that racial and ethnic relations during the period from the late nineteenth to early twentieth centuries were principally structured by both the economy and the polity. It was a period of industrial expansion, class conflict, and racial oppression; an era in which the two major actors in the political economy (capital and labor) vigorously asserted their narrowly defined class interests with respect to racialized labor. According to Wilson, the explosive capitalist development of the era was marked by "the overt efforts of whites to solidify economic racial domination (ranging from the manipulation of black labor to the neutralization or elimination of black economic competition) through various forms of juridical, political, and social discrimination" (p. 4).

3. Alonso Aguilar, *Pan-Americanism: From Monroe to the Present* (New York: Monthly Review Press, 1968), pp. 31–35.

4. The absence of an explicitly sociological analysis of race relations in the American Southwest is a curious phenomenon. European-American sociologists generally have been unconcerned with the complexities of racial and ethnic patterns in this region. Instead, they have been preoccupied with black/white relations at the national level or with their experience in the Northeast, Midwest, or South. Others, of course, have explored the particular experiences of European ethnic groups in these same geographic terms.

There is still no classic work of comparative analysis in the sociological literature of race relations specifically for this region. It appears that most sociologists share the general public sentiment that race relations in the United States are primarily a black/white phenomenon and that other racial/ethnic patterns are either of secondary importance (because of their narrow regional nature) or merely reflect extensions of black/white patterns.

Fortunately, the limited scope of the sociological literature has been compensated for by the wealth of recent research by scholars in ethnic studies. This growing body of work has greatly advanced our understanding of the complexities of the experience of African, Asian, Mexican, and Native Amerians in California and the Southwest more generally. These works were indispensable to my own comparative study as key sources of historical data.

Among the most important books that have influenced my thinking on the nineteenth-century Mexican experience in California and the Southwest are the following historical studies: Mario Barrera, *Race and Class in the Southwest: A Theory of Racial Inequality* (Notre Dame: University of Notre Dame Press, 1979); Albert Camarillo, *Chicanos in a Changing Society: From Mexican Pueblos to American Barrios in Santa Barbara and Southern California, 1848–1900* (Cambridge: Harvard University Press, 1979); David Montejano, *Anglos and Mexicans in the Making of Texas, 1836–1986* (Austin: University of Texas Press, 1987); Ricardo Romo, *East Los Angeles: History of a Barrio* (Austin: University of Texas Press, 1983); Richard Griswold del Castillo, *The Los Angeles Barrio, 1850–1890: A Social History* (Berkeley and Los Angeles: University of California Press, 1979); Richard Griswold del Castillo, *La Familia: Chicano Families in the Urban Southwest, 1848 to the Present* (Notre Dame: University of Notre Dame Press, 1984); Arnoldo De León, *The Tejano Community, 1836–1900* (Albuquerque: University of New Mexico Press, 1985); Arnoldo De León, *They Called Them Greasers: Anglo Attitudes toward Mexicans in Texas, 1821–1900* (Austin: University of Texas Press, 1983); Manuel Peña, *The Texas-Mexican Conjunto: History of a Working Class Music* (Austin: University of Texas Press, 1985); Rodolfo Acuña, *Occupied America: A History of Chicanos*, 2d ed. (New York: Harper & Row, 1981); Alfredo Mirande, *The Chicano Experience: An Alternative Perspective* (Notre Dame: University of Notre Dame Press, 1985); and Mario Garcia, *Desert Immigrants: The Mexicans of El Paso, 1880–1920* (New Haven: Yale University Press, 1981).

Four recent historiographic essays that evaluate the development of Chicano historical research include Alex Saragoza, "The Significance of Recent Chicano-Related Historical Writings: An Assessment," *Ethnic Affairs* 1 (Fall 1987): 24–63; David G. Gutiérrez, "The Third Generation: Reflections on Recent Chicano Historiography," *Mexican Studies/Estudios Mexicanos* 5, no. 2 (Summer 1989): 281–96; Tomás Almaguer, "Ideological Distortions and Recent Chicano Historiography: The Internal Colonial Model and Chicano Historical Interpretation," *Aztlán: A Journal of Chicano Research* 18, no. 1 (Spring 1987): 7–28; and Vicki L. Ruiz, "Texture, Text, and Context: New Approaches to Chicano Historiography," *Mexican Studies/Estudios Mexicanos* 2, no. 1 (Winter 1986): 145–52.

Among the most influential historical studies of the Chinese and Japanese immigrant experiences in California during the period under examination are Sucheng Chan, *This Bitter-Sweet Soil: The Chinese in California Agriculture, 1860–1910* (Berkeley and Los Angeles: University of California Press, 1986); Ronald Takaki, *Strangers from a Different Shore: A History of Asian Americans*

(Boston: Little, Brown, 1989); Ping Chiu, *Chinese Labor in California, 1850–1880: An Economic Study* (Madison: The State Historical Society of Wisconsin, 1963); Alexander Saxton, *The Indispensable Enemy: Labor and the Anti-Chinese Movement in California* (Berkeley and Los Angeles: University of California Press, 1971); Victor Nee and Brett de Bary Nee, *Longtime Californ': A Documentary Study of an American Chinatown* (New York: Pantheon Books, 1973); Yuji Ichioka, *The Issei: The World of the First Generation Japanese Immigrants, 1885–1924* (New York: The Free Press, 1988); Roger Daniels, *The Politics of Prejudice: The Anti-Japanese Movement in California and the Struggle for Japanese Exclusion*, 2d ed. (Berkeley and Los Angeles: University of California Press, 1978); Roger Daniels, *Chinese and Japanese in the United States since 1850* (Seattle: University of Washington Press, 1988); Lucie Cheng and Edna Bonacich, eds., *Labor Immigration under Capitalism* (Berkeley and Los Angeles: University of California Press, 1983); Edna Bonacich and John Modell, *The Economic Basis of Ethnic Solidarity: Small Business in the Japanese-American Community* (Berkeley and Los Angeles: University of California Press, 1980); and Evelyn Nakano Glenn, *Issei, Nisei, War Bride: Three Generations of Japanese-American Women in Domestic Service* (Philadelphia: Temple University Press, 1986).

Also important were the seminal articles on the nineteenth-century Chinese immigrant experience by Lucie Cheng Hirata and Paul M. Ong. See Lucie Cheng Hirata, "Free, Indentured, Enslaved: Chinese Prostitutes in Nineteenth-Century America," *Signs: Journal of Women in Culture and Society* 5, no. 11 (Autumn 1979): 3–29; Lucie Cheng Hirata, "Chinese Immigrant Women in Nineteenth-Century California," in Carol Ruth Berkin and Mary Beth Norton, eds., *Women of America: A History* (Boston: Houghton Mifflin, 1979), pp. 224–44; Paul M. Ong, "Chinese Labor in Early San Francisco: Racial Segmentation and Industrial Expansion," *Amerasia Journal* 8, no. 1 (1981): 69–92; and Paul M. Ong, "Chinese Laundries as an Urban Occupation," in Douglas W. Lee, ed., *The Annals of the Chinese Historical Society of the Pacific Northwest* (Seattle, 1983), pp. 68–85.

Works on the California Indians that were particularly useful to this study include James J. Rawls, *The Indians of California: The Changing Image* (Norman: University of Oklahoma Press, 1984); Robert Heizer, *The Destruction of the California Indians* (Salt Lake City: Peregrine Publications, 1974); Jack D. Forbes, *Native Americans of California and Nevada* (Healdsburg, Calif.: Naturegraph Publishers, 1969); Sherburne F. Cook, *The Conflict between the California Indian and White Civilization* (Berkeley and Los Angeles: University of California Press, 1976); Sherburne F. Cook, *The Population of the California Indian* (Berkeley and Los Angeles: University of California Press, 1976); George Harwood Phillips, *Chiefs and Challengers: Indian Resistance and Cooperation in Southern California* (Berkeley and Los Angeles: University of California Press, 1975); and Albert L. Hurtado, *Indian Survival on the California Frontier* (New Haven: Yale University Press, 1988).

Other studies that helped situate the nineteenth-century experiences of racial minorities in California or the Southwest include Robert Heizer and Alan Almquist, *The Other Californians: Prejudice and Discrimination under Spain, Mexico, and the United States to 1920* (Berkeley and Los Angeles: University of California Press, 1971); Rudolph M. Lapp, *Blacks in Gold Rush California* (New Haven: Yale

University Press, 1977); Kenneth G. Goode, *California's Black Pioneers: A Brief Historical Survey* (Santa Barbara: McNally and Loftin, 1974); David J. Weber, *The Mexican Frontier, 1821–1846: The American Southwest under Mexico* (Albuquerque: University of New Mexico Press, 1982); Reginald Horsman, *Race and Manifest Destiny: The Origins of American Racial Anglo-Saxonism* (Cambridge: Harvard University Press, 1981); Edward Spicer, *Cycles of Conquest: The Impact of Spain, Mexico, and the United States on the Indians of the Southwest, 1533–1960* (Tucson: University of Arizona Press, 1962); Patricia Nelson Limerick, *Legacy of Conquest: The Unbroken Past of the American West* (New York: W.W. Norton, 1987); and Ramón A. Gutiérrez, *When Jesus Came, The Corn Mothers Went Away: Marriage, Conquest, and Love in New Mexico, 1500–1848* (Stanford: Stanford University Press, 1991).

5. This particular formulation is especially evident in the work of some Marxist scholars who have attempted a class analysis of racial matters. For example, the highly regarded sociologist Erik Olin Wright in *Class and Income Determination* (New York: Academic Press, 1979) confidently asserts in his chapter on "Race and Class" the following dubious Marxist assumptions about the relationship between these two statification systems: First, "one of the basic dynamics of capitalist development stressed by Marx as well as many non-Marxist theorists is the tendency for capitalism to transform all labor into the commodity labor power, and to obliterate all qualitative distinctions between different categories of labor. . . . In terms of the logic of accumulation developed by Marx in *Capital*, there will, therefore, be systemic tendencies in capitalism to reduce racial discrimination in the labor market and to treat black labor power as identical with any other labor power" (p. 201). Second, "in spite of the divisive character of racism and the material differences between black and white workers that racism generates, workers of all races share a fundamental class situation and thus share fundamental class interests" (p. 205). Finally, "to the extent that the working class is divided along racial and ethnic lines, the collective power of the working class is reduced, and the capacity of workers to win demands from capital will decrease. The result will be an increase in the rate of exploitation of *both* white and black workers, although the effects may well be more intense for blacks and other minorities than for whites. . . . The analysis of racism as a divide-and-conquer strategy has perhaps been the central theme in Marxist treatments of the subject" (p. 202).

While Wright makes an interesting empirical case for the importance of class position in explaining contemporary differences in black/white income, his operating assumptions provide a questionable point of departure for examining the relationship between class and race historically. His contentions are readily contradicted by the historical experiences of the racialized groups examined in this study. In fairness to Wright, he does acknowledge that it "would be a mistake" to assume that "all racial discrimination is really disguised class oppression" or that "race is an insignificant dimension of inequality in American life" (p. 197). He acknowledges correctly that the "extent to which racial or ethnic divisions within the working class are being deepened or eroded in a given capitalist society cannot, however, be derived directly from the abstract theory of capitalist economic development. It is only when such abstract theory is linked to specific political and economic developments that it becomes possible to assess the real dynamics of racism in a given society" (p. 203). Consequently, "the most obvious way in which racism intersects with class relations is in the social processes which distribute people into class positions in the first place. . . . To my knowledge, there have been no studies which systematically explore the role of racism in the distribution of individuals into different positions within the social relations of production" (p. 197). This study attempts to do just that. My conclusions, however, contradict the basic assumptions that Wright accepts as the point of departure for his structural Marxist analysis of race and class.

These same basic assumptions inform most of the important historical and contemporary studies of black/white relations by other Marxist scholars. See, for example, Barbara Jeanne Fields, "Slavery, Race, and Ideology in the United States of America," *New Left Review* 181 (May-June 1990): 95–116; Michael Reich, *Racial Inequality: A Political-Economic Analysis* (Princeton: Princeton University Press, 1981); David M. Gordon, Richard Edwards, and Michael Reich, *Segmented Work, Divided Labor: The Historical Transformation of Labor in the United States* (New York: Cambridge University Press, 1982); Albert Szymanski, "Racial Discrimination and White Gain," *American Sociological Review* 41, no. 3 (1976): 403–14; Harold M. Baron, "The Demand For Black Labor: Historical Notes on the Political Economy of Racism," *Radical America* 5 (1972): 1–46; and the classic treatment of this issue in Oliver C. Cox, *Caste, Class, and Race* (New York: Monthly Review Press, 1970 [1948]).

Although largely working within the same tradition, the important work of sociologist Edna Bonacich is particularly noteworthy in that she acknowledges the key role of white labor in historically structuring racial inequality. See Edna Bonacich, "A Theory of Ethnic Antagonism: The Split Labor Market," *American Sociological Review* 37 (1972): 547–59; "Advanced Capitalism and Black/White Relations in the United States: A Split Labor Market Interpretation," *American Sociological Review* 41 (1976): 34–51; and "The Past, Present, and Future of Split Labor Market Theory," in Cora B. Marrett and C. Leggon, eds., *Research in Race and Ethnic Relations* (Greenwich, Conn.: JAI Press, 1979), pp. 17–64.

See the perceptive assessment of the various class-based theories in the sociology of race relations in Michael Omi and Howard Winant, *Racial Formation in the United States: From the 1960s to the 1980s* (New York: Routledge and Kegan Paul, 1987), chap. 2.

Although the present study utilizes certain analytical categories drawn from Marxist theory, I also draw extensively upon the Weberian tradition within sociological literature. The outstanding work of neo-Weberian sociologist Frank Parkin and historian George Fredrickson has greatly influenced my understanding and theoretical framing of the relationship between class and racial stratification systems. I specifically discuss their contributions to this study below.

6. Omi and Winant, *Racial Formation in the United States,* pp. 61–62.

7. Ibid., p. 64.

8. Stuart Hall, "New Ethnicities," in James Donald and Ali Rattansi, eds., *"Race," Culture, and Difference* (London: Sage Publications, 1992), pp. 253–54.

9. This study is fundamentally historical in focus, sociological in approach, and comparative in nature. My primary interest is to give cohesion and sociological meaning to historical facts. My task is to write "history mediated by concepts," as

one historical sociologist has characterized this method. (See the valuable overview of various approaches to historical-sociological research in Victoria E. Bonnell, "The Uses of Theory, Concepts and Comparison in Historical Sociology," *Comparative Studies in Society and History* 22, no. 2 [April 1980]: 156–73.)

This study utilizes concepts such as "racial formation," "racialization," and "social closure" to select, organize, and interpret its historical materials. These concepts are the heuristic devices used to give new meaning and resonance to the historical patterns I explore. In attempting to trestle the often irreconcilable breach between history and sociology, I have especially appreciated George M. Fredrickson's assessment of such an enterprise. In noting the important differences between historical and social-scientific approaches to comparative race relations, Fredrickson has perceptively observed that

> one reason why so few historians have actually produced thoroughly comparative works is that the typical aim or inclination of historians tends to differ from that of most social scientists. The latter is quite properly concerned with discovering and testing general hypotheses about human behavior and social organization. The former are more likely to be fascinated by variety and concerned with the special features of individual societies. Hence social scientists usually look at a range of cases to test or demonstrate a general theory or "model" of human action or organization; while historians, if they employ a comparative perspective at all, normally do it to illuminate some special feature of the single society or civilization with which they are primarily concerned. Historians are therefore likely to find that the comparative generalizations of sociologists and political scientists are often too abstract or "macrocosmic" to do justice to the messy, complex, and ambiguous reality they confront in their own research and that, to some extent, they positively relish. If they invoke social theories and models, historians are likely to use them as heuristic devises for illuminating the particular rather than as instances illustrating the universal.
>
> George M. Fredrickson, *White Supremacy: A Comparative Study in American and South African History* (New York: Oxford University Press, 1981), p. xiv

Also see Fredrickson's discussion of these issues in chapters 10 and 15 of his *The Arrogance of Race: Historical Perspectives on Slavery, Racism, and Social Inequality* (Middletown, Conn.: Wesleyan University Press, 1988). A more general introduction to some of the nettlesome issues in historical sociology can been found in Seymour Martin Lipset, "History and Sociology: Some Methodological Considerations," in S. M. Lipset and Richard Hofstadter, *Sociology and History: Methods* (New York: Basic Books, 1968), 20–58; Neil J. Smelser, *Comparative Methods in the Social Sciences* (Englewood Cliffs, N.J.: Prentice-Hall, 1976); E. P. Thompson, *The Poverty of Theory and Other Essays* (London: Merlin Press, 1978); Arthur L. Stinchcombe, *Theoretical Methods in Social History* (New York: Academic Press, 1978); Charles Tilly, *As Sociology Meets History* (New York: Academic Press, 1981); Philip Abrams, *Historical Sociology* (Ithaca, N.Y.: Cornell University Press, 1982); and Theda Skocpol, ed., *Vision and Method in Historical Sociology* (Cambridge: Cambridge University Press, 1984).

10. For interesting examinations of various facets of the black experience in California during the period from 1848 to 1900 see Lapp, *Blacks in Gold Rush California*; Delilah L. Beasley, *The Negro Trail Blazers of California* (Los Angeles: Times Mirror Printing and Binding House, 1919); Goode, *California's Black Pioneers*; Jack D. Forbes, *Afro-Americans in the Far West: A Handbook for Educators*

(Berkeley: Far West Laboratory for Educational Research and Development, 1966); Sherman W. Savage, *Blacks in the West* (Westport, Conn.: Greenwood Press, 1976); and Heizer and Almquist, *The Other Californians*.

11. See Fredrickson's *White Supremacy*.

12. Ibid., p. xi.

13. Roy Malcom, "American Citizenship and the Japanese," *Annals of the American Academy of Political and Social Science* 92 (January 1921), p. 78; Roy Malcom, "The Japanese Problem in California," *World Affairs Interpreter* 13 (April 1942), p. 32; and Roger Daniels, "American Labor and Chinese Immigration," *Past & Present* 27 (April 1984), pp. 113–14.

14. Yuji Ichioka, "Early Japanese Quest for Citizenship: The Background to the 1922 Ozawa Case," *Amerasia Journal* 4 (1977), p. 21; Malcom, "American Citizenship," p. 79; Daniels, "American Labor and Chinese Immigration," p. 114; and Milton R. Konvitz, *The Alien and the Asiatic* (Ithaca, N.Y.: Cornell University Press, 1946), pp. 77ff.

15. Takaki, *Strangers From a Different Shore*, p. 15.

16. Ibid., pp. 298–300.

17. Omi and Winant, *Racial Formation*, p. 65.

18. Ibid.

19. Eric Foner, *Free Soil, Free Labor, Free Men: The Ideology of the Republican Party before the Civil War* (New York: Oxford University Press, 1970), p. 20.

20. This summary discussion of the "free labor ideology" is primarily drawn from Foner's *Free Soil, Free Labor, Free Men*. His argument is explicated more fully in chap. 2 below.

1. "WE DESIRE ONLY A WHITE POPULATION IN CALIFORNIA"

1. George M. Fredrickson, *White Supremacy: A Comparative Study in American and South African History* (Oxford: Oxford University Press, 1981), p. xvii.

2. Herbert Blumer, "Race Prejudice as a Sense of Group Position," *Pacific Sociological Review* 1, no. 1 (Spring 1958), p. 3.

3. Ibid., p. 5.

4. Ibid., p. 4.

5. Ibid., p. 4.

6. Frank Parkin, *Marxism and Class Theory: A Bourgeois Critique* (New York: Columbia University Press, 1979), p. 44.

7. Ibid., pp. 45–47.

8. Fredrickson, *White Supremacy*, p. xi.

9. Fredrickson argues that the term "white supremacy" is preferable to others, such as racism, because the latter primarily refers to

a mode of thought that offers a particular explanation for the fact that population groups that can be distinguished by ancestry are likely to differ in culture, status, and power. Racists make the claim that such differences are due mainly to immutable genetic factors and not to environmental or historical circumstances. Used in this way, the concept of racism is extremely useful for describing a trend in Western thought between the late eighteenth century and the twentieth that has provided *one* kind of rationale for racially repressive social systems. But nonwhites have at times been subjugated or treated as inferiors in both the United States and South Africa without the aid of an explicit racism of this sort. In recent years, racism has commonly been used in a broader sense, as a blanket term for all discriminatory actions or policies directed at groups thought to be physically distinct from a dominant or "majority" element. But this usage leaves us without a separate word for the overt doctrine of biologically inequality and inhibits a sense of the role that this ideology has played in specific historical situations.

p. ix

10. Ibid., p. 4.

11. Ibid., p. 5.

12. Ibid., pp. 7–13.

13. Ibid., p. 8.

14. Ibid., pp. 9–10.

15. I am grateful to historian Ramón Gutiérrez for pointing out the importance that these constructions played as markers of civility during this period. See his brilliant exposition of this point in *When Jesus Came the Corn Mothers Went Away* (Stanford: Stanford University Press, 1991).

16. Fredrickson, *White Supremacy*, p. 10.

17. Ibid., p. 9.

18. Ibid., p. 7.

19. Winthrop Jordan, *White over Black* (Chapel Hill, University of North Carolina Press, 1968, reprint, Baltimore: Penguin Books, 1969), p. 95.

20. Ronald T. Takaki, *Iron Cages: Race and Culture in Nineteenth-Century America* (New York: Alfred A. Knopf, 1979).

21. See Max Weber, *The Protestant Ethic and the Spirit of Capitalism* (New York: Charles Scribner's Sons, 1958).

22. Stephen Steinberg, *The Ethnic Myth: Race, Ethnicity, and Class in America* (Boston: Beacon Press, 1981), p. 10.

23. Jordan, *White Over Black*, pp. 89–90; Robert L. Allen, *Reluctant Reformers: Racism and Social Reform Movements in the United States* (New York: Anchor Books, 1975), p. 271. Also see Gary B. Nash's discussion of early white-Indian contact in *Red, White, and Black: The Peoples of Early America* (Englewood Cliffs, N.J.: Prentice-Hall, 1974).

24. Steinberg, *The Ethnic Myth*, pp. 7–8.

25. Reginald Horsman, *Race and Manifest Destiny: The Origins of American Racial Anglo-Saxonism* (Cambridge: Harvard University Press, 1981), p. 301.

26. Steinberg, *The Ethnic Myth*, p. 13.

27. Ronald Takaki, "Reflections on Racial Pattern in America," in Ronald Takaki, ed., *From Different Shores: Perspectives on Race and Ethnicity in America* (New York: Oxford University Press, 1987), p. 28.

28. Robert Blauner, *Racial Oppression in America* (New York: Harper and Row, 1972), p. 57.

29. Blauner has succinctly outlined the basic features of this process in *Racial Oppression in America* as follows:

"Like European overseas colonialism, America has used African, Mexican, and to a lesser degree, Indian workers for the cheapest labor, concentrating people of color in the most unskilled jobs, the least advanced sectors of the economy, and the most industrially backward regions of the nation. In an historical sense, people of color provided much of the hard labor (and the technical skills) that built up the agricultural base and the mineral-transport-communication infrastructure necessary for industrialization and modernization, whereas the European worked primarily within the industrialized, modern sectors. The initial position of European ethnics, while low, was therefore strategic for movement up the economic and social pyramid. The placement of nonwhite groups, however, imposed barrier upon barrier on such mobility, freezing them for long periods of time in least favorable segments of the economy.

p. 62

30. Herbert Blumer was among the first to appreciate that capitalist industrialization was not necessarily a corrosive force eliminating the importance of status distinction in industrial societies. Blumer argued that industrializing nations often utilize racial and ethnic markers as the basis for structuring their labor markets. See his important article, "Industrialization and Race Relations," in *Industrialization and Race Relations: A Symposium*, ed. Guy Hunter (London: Oxford University Press, 1965), pp. 220–53.

31. Doris Marion Wright, "The Making of Cosmopolitan California: An Analysis of Immigration, 1848–70," part 1, *California Historical Society Quarterly* 19, no. 4 (December 1940), p. 323.

32. See chapter 4 for an extended discussion of the decline in the California Indian population and issues pertaining to their population demographics.

33. Wright, "The Making of Cosmopolitan California," part 1, p. 323.

34. Doris Marion Wright, "The Making of Cosmopolitan California: An Analysis of Immigration, 1848–70," part 2, *California Historical Society Quarterly* 20, no. 1 (March 1941), p. 75.

35. Ibid., p. 74.

36. Wright, "The Making of Cosmopolitan California," part 1, p. 340.

37. Wright, "The Making of Cosmopolitan California," part 2, p. 65.

38. Ibid., p. 69.

39. Ibid.

40. Ibid., p. 72.

41. Pringle Shaw, *Rambling in California; Containing a Description of the Country, Life at the Mines, State of Society, & c.* (Toronto: publisher unknown, [1857]), p. 16, as cited by Wright, "The Making of Cosmopolitan California," part 2, p. 72.

42. Wright, "The Making of Cosmopolitan California," part 1, pp. 332–33, 338.

43. Wright, "The Making of Cosmopoitan California," part 2, p. 74. I do not mean to imply here that all European American immigrants from the northern and western United States were "free labor" advocates who favored California's entry into the Union as a free state. Differences in political sentiments, as well as racial attitudes, clearly existed among the diverse population. So too did they exist among Southerners; not every immigrant from the South favored the introduction of slavery (or other unfree labor systems) into California. Furthermore, the capitalist transformation of the state that is discussed below in sweeping historical terms was actually wracked by opposition from Mexican rancheros, Southern pro-slavery elements, and other contending class forces. More nuanced detail is presented in the chapters that follow.

44. Heizer and Almquist, *The Other Californians*, p. 203.

45. Ibid.

46. Rudolph Lapp, *Afro-Americans in California* (San Francisco: Boyd and Fraser, 1979), pp. 18, 25.

47. Patricia Nelson Limerick, *Legacy of Conquest: The Unbroken Past of the American West* (New York: W. W. Norton, 1987), p. 27.

48. Robert Glass Cleland and Osgood Hardy, *March of Industry* (Los Angeles: Powell Publishing Company, 1929), pp. 51–52; Ping Chiu, *Chinese Labor in California, 1850–1880: An Economic Study* (Madison: State Historical Society of Wisconsin, 1963), pp. 1–6.

49. Cleland and Hardy, *March of Industry*, p. 51.

50. Cleland and Hardy, *March of Industry*, p. 57; Chiu, *Chinese Labor*, pp. 40, 52.

51. Osgood Hardy, "Agricultural Change in California, 1860–1890," *Proceedings of the Pacific Coast Branch of the American Historical Association* (1929), pp. 222–23; Varden Fuller, *The Supply of Agricultural Labor as a Factor in the Evolution of Farm Labor Organization in California Agriculture*, in U.S. Senate, Committee on Education and Labor, *Hearings: Pursuant to Senate Resolution 266. Part 54, Agricultural Labor in California*, 76th Cong., 2d sess. (Washington, D.C.: Government Printing Office, 1940); Glenn Dumke, *The Boom of the Eighties in Southern California* (San Marino, Calif.: The Huntington Library, 1944), p. 63; Robert Glass Cleland, *The Cattle on a Thousand Hills*, 2nd ed. (San Marino: The Huntington Library, 1951), pp. 163–65, 183; Gerald D. Nash, *State Government and Economic Development in California, 1848–1933* (Berkeley: Institute of Governmental Studies, University of California, 1964), p. 140; Cleland and Hardy, *March of Industry*, pp. 92–93; Chiu, *Chinese Labor*, pp. 70–71.

52. Paul S. Taylor and Tom Vasey, "Historical Background of California Farm Labor," *Rural Sociology* 1 (September 1936), p. 288; Cleland and Hardy, *March of Industry*, p. 50.

53. Hardy, "Agricultural Change," pp. 219–21; Chiu, *Chinese Labor*, p. 67; "Progress of Agriculture in California," *Overland Monthly* (April 1873), reprinted in Ventura *Signal*, Apr. 26, 1873.

54. Taylor and Vasey, "Historical Background," p. 286.

55. Studies which document the disproportionate concentration of whites at the upper levels of the occupational structure during the late nineteenth century include Albert Camarillo, *Chicanos in a Changing Society: From Mexican Pueblos to American Barrios in Santa Barbara and Southern California, 1848–1930* (Cambridge: Harvard University Press, 1979), and Richard Griswold Del Castillo, *The Los Angeles Barrio, 1850–1890: A Social History* (Berkeley and Los Angeles: University of California Press, 1979).

56. Horsman, *Race and Manifest Destiny*, p. 298.

57. This discussion of the "free labor ideology" is drawn from Eric Foner's *Free Soil, Free Labor, Free Men: The Ideology of the Republican Party before the Civil War* (New York: Oxford University Press, 1970).

58. See Alexander Saxton's discussion of the impact that the Jacksonian "Producer Ethic" had on the anti-Chinese movement in California in his *The Indispensable Enemy: Labor and the Anti-Chinese Movement in California* (Berkeley and

Los Angeles: University of California Press, 1971), pp. 21–22, 40–42, 51–52, 94, 96–101, 265–69, 274.

59. Foner, *Free Soil*, p. 11.

60. Ibid., p. 20.

61. *The Californian* (San Francisco), Mar. 15, 1848, cited in Lucille Eaves, *A History of California Labor Legislation* (Berkeley: The University Press, 1910), p. 82.

62. *The California Star* (San Francisco), Mar. 25, 1848, cited in Eaves, *California Labor*, pp. 82–83.

63. J. Ross Browne, *Report of the Debates in the Convention of California on the Formation of the State Constitution in September and October, 1849* (Washington, D.C.: John T. Towers, 1850), p. 44.

64. Ibid., p. 49.

65. Ibid.

66. Ibid., pp. 139, 143–45, 147.

67. Ibid., p. 61.

68. Ibid., p. 74.

69. Lapp, *Afro-Americans in California*, p. 6.

70. *California Statutes*, 1851, p. 230; *California Statues*, 1863–64, p. 213; *California Statutes*, 1869–70, p. 838. Delilah L. Beasley, *The Negro Trail Blazers of California* (Los Angeles: Times Mirror Printing and Binding House, 1919), p. 60; Kenneth G. Goode, *California's Black Pioneers: A Brief Historical Survey* (Santa Barbara: McNally and Loftin, 1974), pp. 77–78, 83–84; Jack D. Forbes, *Afro-Americans in the Far West: A Handbook for Educators* (Berkeley: Far West Laboratory for Educational Research and Development, 1966), p. 29; Heizer and Almquist, *Other Californians*, pp. 47–48, 128, 133–34.

71. Browne, *Report of the Debates*, pp. 338–40. Also see Eugene H. Berwanger, *The Frontier Against Slavery: Western Anti-Negro Prejudice and the Slavery Extension Controversy* (Urbana: University of Illinois Press, 1967), p. 69; Taylor and Vasey, "Historical Background," p. 198; Heizer and Almquist, *Other Californians*, pp. 117–19; Cardinal Goodwin, *The Establishment of State Government in California, 1846–1850* (New York: Macmillan, 1914), pp. 120–27.

72. Goode, *Black Pioneers*, pp. 48–49; Berwanger, *The Frontier Against Slavery*, pp. 70–76; Rudolph M. Lapp, *Blacks in Gold Rush California* (New Haven: Yale University Press, 1977), p. 239; Heizer and Almquist, *Other Californians*, pp. 123–34.

73. See Lapp, *Blacks in Gold Rush California*, chap. 10.

74. Lapp, *Afro-Americans in California*, p. 4.

75. U.S. Department of the Interior, Census Office, *The Seventh Census of the United States: 1850* (Washington, D.C.: Robert Armstrong, Public Printer, 1853), p. 969; Beasley, *Negro Trail Blazers*, p. 42; Goode, *California's Black Pioneers*, pp. 71, 106–7.

76. Lapp, *Blacks in Gold Rush California*, pp. 132–33.

77. Ibid., pp. 12–48, 116–17, 271.

78. For discussions of the impact that California's Fugitive Slave Law of 1852 had on blacks in the state, see Eaves *California Labor*, pp. 94–104; Beasley, *Negro Trail Blazers*, p. 72; Lapp, *Blacks in Gold Rush California*, pp. 120–21, 126–57;

Lapp, *Afro-Americans in California*, p. 9; Goode, *Black Pioneers*, pp. 59–60; Berwanger, *The Frontier Against Slavery*, p. 70; Deliliah L. Beasley, "Slavery in California," *The Journal of Negro History* 3 (January 1918): 33–44; C. A. Duniway, "Slavery in California after 1848," American Historical Association *Annual Report* 1 (1905): 243–48; Sherman W. Savage, *Blacks in the West* (Westport, Conn.: Greenwood Press, 1976), pp. 31–32, 38–39; Forbes, *Afro-Americans in the Far West*, p. 30; Owen C. Coy, "Evidence of Slavery in California," *The Grizzly Bear* 19 (October 1916): 1–2.

—→79. Lapp, *Blacks in Gold Rush California*, p. 268.

80. Ibid., pp. 258–69.

81. Ibid., pp. 72, 95–100.

82. Lapp, *Afro-Americans in California*, p. 24.

83. Ibid., p. 26.

84. Ibid., p. 27.

85. Ibid., pp. 26, 28.

2. "THE TRUE SIGNIFICANCE OF THE WORD 'WHITE'"

1. David J. Weber, *The Mexican Frontier, 1821–1846: The American Southwest under Mexico* (Albuquerque: University of New Mexico Press, 1982), p. 196.

2. Leonard Pitt, *The Decline of the Californios: A Social History of the Spanish-Speaking Californians, 1846–1890* (Berkeley: University of California Press, 1970), p. 86.

3. Ibid., p. 10.

4. Paul W. Gates, ed., *California Ranchos and Farms, 1846–1862* (Madison: The State Historical Society of Wisconsin, 1967), pp. 5–9; Paul W. Gates, "Adjudication of Spanish-Mexican Land Claims in California," *Huntington Library Quarterly* 21 (1958): 217.

5. James J. Rawls, *Indians of California: The Changing Image* (Norman: University of Oklahoma Press, 1984), pp. 20–21.

6. Hubert Howe Bancroft, *California Pastoral* (San Francisco: The History Company, 1888), p. 278.

7. Ibid., pp. 437–38; Theodore Hittel, *History of California* (San Francisco: N. J. Stone, 1897), 3:884–85; Robert F. Heizer and Alan F. Almquist, *The Other Californians: Prejudice and Discrimination under Spain, Mexico, and the United States to 1920* (Berkeley: University of California Press, 1971), pp. 19–20; Sherburne F. Cook, *The Conflict between the California Indians and White Civilization* (Berkeley: University of California Press, 1976), pp. 302–3, 457; Fr. Zephyrin Engelhardt, *The Missions and Missionaries of California* (San Francisco: The James H. Barry Company, 1908), 4:136–37; Jesse Davis Francis, "An Economic and Social History of Mexican California, 1822–1846" (Ph.D diss., University of California, Berkeley, 1935), pp. 502, 506–8.

8. Cook, *Conflict between the California Indians*, pp. 302–3; Robert Glass Cleland, *The Cattle on a Thousand Hills: Southern California, 1850–1880*, 2d ed. (San Marino, Calif.: The Huntington Library, 1951), p. 56; Pitt, *Decline of the Californios*, pp. 15–16; Heizer and Almquist, *The Other Californians*, p.18; Bancroft, *California Pastoral*, pp 437–38.

9. Cook, *Conflict between the California Indians*, pp. 304, 457f.; Gates, *California Ranchos*, pp. 7–8; Heizer and Almquist, *The Other Californians*, p. 20.

10. Hittel, *History of California*, 3:886–87; Gates, *California Ranchos*, p. 19.

11. Miguel Torres, "Peripecias," pp. 52–53, Bancroft Collection, Bancroft Library, University of California, as cited by Engelhardt, *The Missions*, 4:737–38.

12. Cf. Eugene D. Genovese, *Roll, Jordon, Roll: The World the Slaves Made* (New York: Random House, 1974).

13. Salvador Vallejo, "Notas historicas sobre California," Ms., 1874, Bancroft Library, University of California, Berkeley, as cited by Cook, *Conflict between the California Indians*, p. 305.

14. Edward D. Castillo, "The Impact of Euro-American Exploration and Settlement," in Robert F. Heizer, ed., *California*, vol. 8 of *Handbook of North American Indians*, William C. Sturtevant., gen. ed. (Washington: Smithsonian Institution, 1978), p. 105.

15. George Simpson, *An Overland Journey round the World, during the Years 1841 and 1842* (Philadelphia: Lea and Blanchard, 1847), as cited by Heizer and Almquist, *The Other Californians*, p. 19.

16. James Clyman, "James Clyman, American Frontiersman, 1792–1881: The Adventures of a Trapper and Covered Wagon Emigrant as Told in His Own Reminiscences and Diaries," C. L. Camp, ed., *California Historical Society*, 1928, as cited by Heizer and Almquist, *The Other Californians*, p. 19.

17. John Marsh, "Letter of Dr. John Marsh to Hon. Lewis Cass," *California Historical Society Quarterly* 22 (December 1943): 321, as cited by Rawls, *Indians of California*, p. 77.

18. George Simpson, *Narrative of a Voyage to California Ports in 1841–42* (San Francisco: Thomas C. Russell, 1930), p. 29, as cited by Pitt, *Decline of the Californios*, p. 16.

19. David Montejano has perceptively noted that Anglo perceptions of the Mexican working class in Texas were also primarily shaped by class-specific considerations. According to Montejano, "As a class metaphor, the caricature of 'dirty Mexican' belonged to the lexicon of inferiority—'white trash,' 'filthy niggers'— that farmers and land holders used to describe the laboring classes. As a reference to hygiene, however, the caricature also suggested a situation where the symbolic basis for separation and control rested on the specter of contamination: the laboring class was seen not only as inferior but also as untouchable." David Montejano, *Anglos and Mexicans in the Making of Texas, 1836–1986* (Austin: University of Texas Press, 1987), p. 229.

20. This point has eluded the numerous discussions of Anglo perceptions of Mexicans during the period. Historical debate on this issue has been primarily couched in terms of European-American ethnocentrism and the cultural stereotyping of Mexicans. For an interesting discussion and debate on Anglo-American images of Mexicans during this period see Cecil Robinson, *With the Ears of Strangers: The Mexican in American Literature* (Tucson: University of Arizona Press, 1963); James D. Hart, *American Images of Spanish California* (Berkeley: The Friends of the Bancroft Library, University of California, 1960); David J. Langum, "Californios and the Image of Indolence," *Western Historical Quarterly* 9 (April 1978): 181–96; David J. Langum, "A Brief Reply," *Western Historical Quarterly* 10 (January 1979): 69; David J. Weber, "Stereotyping of Mexico's Far

Northern Frontier," in Manuel P. Servin, ed., *An Awakened Minority: The Mex-ican American*, 2d ed. (Beverly Hills, Calif.: Glencoe Press, 1974), pp. 18–24; David J. Weber, "Here Rests Juan Espinosa: Toward a Clearer Look at the Image of the 'Indolent' Californios," *Western Historical Quarterly* 1 (January 1979): 61–68; Raymund A. Paredes, "The Mexican Image in American Travel Literature, 1813–1869," *New Mexico Historical Review* 52 (January 1977): 5–29; Raymund A. Paredes, "The Origin of Anti-Mexican Sentiment in the United States," *New Scholar* 6 (1977): 130–65; and Pitt, *Decline of the Californios*, passim.

21. Richard Henry Dana, *Two Years before the Mast: A Personal Narrative of Life at Sea* (New York: Harper and Brothers, 1840), p. 214.

22. Ibid., pp. 94–95.

23. Alfred Robinson, *Life in California: During a Residence of Several Years in that Territory, Comprising a Description of the Country and the Missionary Establishments, With Incidents, Observations, etc., etc. by an American* (New York: Wiley and Putnam, 1846), p 73.

24. Pitt, *The Decline of the Californios*, pp. 12–13.

25. Dana, *Two Years before the Mast*, p. 96.

26. Ibid., pp. 96–97.

27. J. Ross Browne, *Report on the Debates in the Convention of California on the Formation of the State Constitution in September and October, 1849* (Washing-ton: John T. Towers, 1850), pp. 65, 67, 72.

28. Ibid., pp. 72–73.

29. Ibid., p. 53.

30. Ibid., p. 53.

31. *Constitution of State of California, 1849.*

32. Albert Camarillo, *Chicanos in a Changing Society: From Mexican Pueblos to American Barrios in Santa Barbara and Southern California, 1848–1930* (Cam-bridge: Harvard University Press, 1979), pp. 110–12.

33. Ibid., pp. 112–13. Also see Mario T. Garcia, "Merchants and Dons: San Diego's Attempt at Modernization, 1850–1860," *The Journal of San Diego History* 21 (Winter 1975): 52–80; Mario T. Garcia, "The Californios of San Diego and the Politics of Accommodation," *Aztlán: International Journal of Chicano Studies Research* 6 (Spring 1975): 69–85; Charles Hughes, "The Decline of the Californios: The Case of San Diego, 1846–1856," *The Journal of San Diego History* 21 (Sum-mer 1975): 1–31.

34. Pitt, *Decline of the Californios*, pp. 139, 270; David J. Weber, ed., *Foreign-ers in their Native Land: Historical Roots of the Mexican Americans* (Al-buquerque: University of New Mexico Press, 1973), p. 149.

35. Pitt, *Decline of the Californios*, p. 140.

36. Heizer and Almquist, *Other Californians*, p. 151; Weber, *Foreigners in their Native Land*, p. 149; Pitt, *Decline of the Californios*, p. 198; Camarillo, *Chicanos in a Changing Society*, pp. 19, 108.

37. Heizer and Almquist, *Other Californians*, p. 131; Weber, *Foreigners in their Native Land*, p. 152; Pitt, *Decline of the Californios*, p. 202.

38. Historians John D'Emilio and Estelle B. Friedman have cogently expressed this point as follows :

Ever since the seventeenth century, European immigrants to America had merged racial and sexual ideology in order to differentiate themselves from Indians and blacks, to strengthen the mechanisms of social control over slaves, and justify the appropriation of Indian and Mexican lands through the destruction of native peoples and their cultures. In the nineteenth century, sexuality continued to serve as a powerful means by which white Americans maintained dominance over people of other races. Both scientific and popular thought supported the view that whites were civilized and rational, while members of other races were savages, irrational, and sensual. These animalistic elements posed a particular threat to middle-class Americans, who sought to maintain social stability during rapid economic change and to insure that a virtuous citizenry would fulfill the dream of republicanism. At a time when middle-class morality rested heavily upon a belief in the purity of women in the home, stereotypes of immoral women of other races contributed to the belief in white superiority. . . . The belief in white moral superiority surfaced in relations to all racial and ethnic groups—whether the Chinese in California, who were considered a "depraved class," or the Irish in eastern cities, who were portrayed as an animalistic race with a "love for vicious excitement." Indians, Mexicans, and blacks elicited the most extensive commentaries, in part because of the nature of their contact with whites. Patterns differed, but in each region the belief that white sexual customs were more civilized, along with the assumption that Indian, Mexican, and black women were sexually available to white men, supported white supremacist attitudes and justified social control of other races.

Intimate Matters: A History of Sexuality in America (New York: Harper & Row, 1988), pp. 86–87

39. Historian Ramón Gutiérrez has insightfully captured this point when noting that

the way in which societies organize marriage provides us an important window into how economic and political arrangements are construed. When people marry, they forge affinal alliances, change residence, establish rights to sexual service, and exchange property. Besides being about the reproduction of class and power, however, marriage is about gender. The marital exchange of women gives men rights over women that women never gain over men. This feature of marriage provides a key to the political economy of sex, by which cultures organize "maleness" and "femaleness," sexual desire, fantasy, and concepts of childhood and adulthood.

Ramón Gutiérrez, "Honor, Ideology, and Class-Gender Domination in New Mexico, 1690–1846," *Latin American Perspectives* 12, no. 1 (Winter 1985): 81

See also his *When Jesus Came, the Corn Mothers Went Away* for an extended discussion of this process in colonial New Mexico.

40. Richard Griswold del Castillo, *La Familia: Chicano Families in the Urban Southwest, 1848 to the Present* (Notre Dame: University of Notre Dame Press, 1984), p. 69.

41. Richard Woolsey, "Rites of Passage: Anglo and Mexican-American Contrasts in a Time of Change: Los Angeles, 1860–1870," *Southern California Quarterly* 69, no. 2 (Summer 1987): 101.

42. In this regard, see the important essay by Gayle Rubin, "The Traffic in Women: Notes Toward a Political Economy of Sex," in Rayna Reiter, ed., *Toward an Anthropology of Women* (New York: Monthly Review Press, 1975), pp. 157–210.

43. Pitt, *Decline of the Californios*, p. 124.

44. Ibid., pp. 124–25.

45. Ibid., pp. 72–73, 268; Griswold del Castillo, *La Familia*, pp. 66–67.

46. Pitt, *Decline of the Californios*, p. 275.

47. Robinson, *Life in California*, p. 73; also see pp. 20, 43, 59.

48. Dana, *Two Years before the Mast*, p. 214. Also see Weber, "Stereotyping," p. 19; Robinson, *With the Ears of Strangers*, pp. 20–21, 26, 40–41, 84–85.

49. Cited in Pitt, *Decline of the Californios*, p. 23.

50. Cited in Reginald Horsman, *Race and Manifest Destiny: The Origins of American Racial Anglo-Saxonism* (Cambridge: Harvard University Press, 1981), p. 231.

51. *Stockton Times,* Apr. 6, 1850 (emphasis in original), as cited by Richard H. Peterson, "Anti-Mexican Nativism in California, 1848–1853: A Study in Cultural Conflict," *Southern California Quarterly* 62, no. 4 (Winter 1980): 319–20.

52. See, for example, Pitt, *Decline of the Californios*, pp. 71–75, 264–65; Robinson, *With the Ears of Strangers*, pp. 77–84; Griswold del Castillo, *La Familia*, p. 67.

53. Pitt, *Decline of the Californios*, pp. 37, 126, 228.

54. Ibid., p. 224.

55. Ibid., pp. 46, 198, 241.

56. David J. Leon and Daniel McNeil, "The Fifth Class—A 19th Century Forerunner of Affirmative Action," *California History* 64, no. 1 (Winter 1985): 52–57; Pitt, *Decline of the Californios*, pp. 267–68, 272–73; Wallace E. Smith, *This Land Was Ours: The Del Valles and Camulos* (Ventura, Calif.; Ventura County Historical Society, 1978), pp. 144, 152, 158, 160, 175.

57. Pitt, *Decline of the Californios*, pp. 270–73.

58. Ibid., pp. 268–69.

59. Ibid., pp. 256–62.

60. R. H. Allen, "The Influence of the Spanish and Mexican Land Grants on California Agriculture," *Journal of Farm Economics* 14 (October 1932): 679; Pitt, *The Decline of the Californios*, p. 118.

61. W. W. Robinson, *Land in California: The Story of Mission Lands, Ranchos, Squatters, Mining Camps, Railroad Grants, Land Scripts, Homesteads* (Berkeley and Los Angeles: University of California Press, 1948), p. 106; Pitt, *Decline of the Californios*, p. 95.

62. William A. Streeter, "Recollections of Historical Events in California, 1843–1878 by William A. Streeter of Santa Barbara," Ms., 1878, Bancroft Library, University of California, Berkeley.

63. For discussions of this divestment see Pitt, *Decline of the Californios*, chaps. 5 and 6; Robinson, *Land in California*; Cleland, *The Cattle on a Thousand Hills*; Gates, *California Ranchos and Farms*; Gates, "Adjudication of Spanish-Mexican Land Claims"; Paul W. Gates, "California's Embattled Settlers," *California Historical Society Quarterly* 13 (June 1962): 99–130; J. S. Hittel, "Mexican Land Claims in California," *Hutching's Illustrated California Magazine* 2 (April 1858): 442–48.

64. Pitt, *Decline of the Californios*, p. 278.

65. Robinson, *Life in California*, p. 254, as cited by Pitt, *Decline of the Californios*, p. 277.

66. Pitt, *Decline of the Californios*, p. 251.

67. Ibid., p. 252.

68. Ibid., p. 115.

69. Ibid., pp. 50–51.

70. Ibid., pp. 54–55.

71. Ibid., pp. 57–58.

72. Ibid., p. 57.

73. Ibid., pp. 60–63.

74. Camarillo, *Chicanos in a Changing Society*, pp. 116–17.

75. U.S. Department of the Interior, Census Office, *The Seventh Census of the United States: 1850* (Washington, D.C.: Robert Armstrong, Public Printer, 1853), p. 969; U.S. Department of the Interior, Census Office, *Population of the United States in 1860 . . . The Eighth Census* (Washington, D.C.: Government Printing Office, 1864), p. 18; U.S. Department of the Interior, Census Office, *Twelfth Census of the United States Taken in the Year 1900 . . . Population* (Washington, D.C.: United States Census Office, 1901), pp. 531, 565, 571. The percentage figures are based on a constant Mexican population of ten thousand for the period from 1850 to 1900. See Oscar Martinez, "On the Size of the Chicano Population: New Estimates, 1850–1900," *Aztlán: International Journal of Chicano Studies Research* 6 (Spring 1975): 43–67.

76. Camarillo, *Chicanos in a Changing Society*, pp. 135–36.

77. Ibid., pp. 126–39.

78. Richard Alan Griswold del Castillo, "La Raza Hispano Americano: The Experience of an Urban Culture and the Spanish Speaking of Los Angeles, 1850–1880" (Ph.D. diss., University of California, Los Angeles, 1974), p. 89.

79. California Bureau of Labor Statistics, *Fourteenth Biennial Report of the Bureau of Labor Statistics of the State of California, 1909–1910* (Sacramento: State Printing Office, 1910), p. 268; Fuller, *Agricultural Labor*, p. 19831.

80. See, for example, the following studies of the early twentieth-century conflict between the white working class and Mexican workers: Camarillo, *Chicanos in a Changing Society*, chaps. 7 and 9; Ricardo Romo, *East Los Angeles: A History of a Barrio* (Austin: University of Texas Press, 1983), chaps. 5 and 6; Juan Gomez-Quinones, "The First Steps: Chicano Labor Conflict and Organizing, 1900–1930," *Aztlán: Chicano Journal of the Social Sciences and Arts* 3 (Spring 1972): 13–49; and Pedro Castillo, "Mexicans in Los Angeles, 1890–1920" (Ph.D diss., University of California, Santa Barbara, 1977).

81. In this regard, Richard Griswold del Castillo argues that this immigration had a direct impact on the level of Anglo-Mexican intermarriages and popular Anglo perception of Mexicans in the Southwest. According to Griswold del Castillo, "One could argue the increased Mexican immigration inhibited the tendency toward exogamy. As the pool of eligible marriage partners grew, so too did the cultural and socioeconomic distances between Mexican heritage and Anglo-American populations. This in fact was a pattern in the southwestern cities. Los Angeles and San Antonio had growing numbers of Mexican immigrants and falling rates of intermarriage." Mexicans were now seen as constituting an obstacle to the white working class and became the source of their intense hostility during the 1920s and 1930s. As a consequence, the early twentieth-century experience of the Mexican

working class differed dramatically from that in the nineteenth century. See Griswold del Castillo, *La Familia*, p. 71.

3. "THE RAVAGES OF TIME"

1. Albert Camarillo, *Chicanos in a Changing Society: From Mexican Pueblos to American Barrios in Santa Barbara and Southern California, 1848–1900* (Cambridge: Harvard University Press, 1979); Richard Griswold del Castillo, *The Los Angeles Barrio, 1850–1890: A Social History* (Berkeley and Los Angeles: University of California Press, 1979); Leonard Pitt, *The Decline of the Californios: A Social History of the Spanish-Speaking Californians, 1846–1890* (Berkeley and Los Angeles: University of California Press, 1970); Mario T. Garcia, "Merchants and Dons: San Diego's Attempt at Modernization, 1850–1860," *The Journal of San Diego History* 21 (Winter 1975): 52–80; Mario T. Garcia, "The Californios of San Diego and the Politics of Accommodation," *Aztlán: International Journal of Chicano Studies Research* 6 (Spring 1975): 69–85. Also see Charles Hughes, "The Decline of the Californios: The Case of San Diego, 1846–1856," *The Journal of San Diego History* 21 (Summer 1975): 1–31; Richard Woolsey, "Rites of Passage? Anglo and Mexican-American Contrasts in a Time of Change: Los Angeles, 1860–1870," *Southern California Quarterly* 69, no. 2 (Summer 1987): 81–101; and Robert Glass Cleland, *The Cattle on a Thousand Hills: Southern California, 1850–1880*, 2d ed. (San Marino, Calif.: Huntington Library, 1951).

2. See the following sources on the granting of these estates during this period: R. H. Allen, "The Influence of Spanish and Mexican Land Grants in the Agricultural History of California," typescript, no pag., 1932, College of Agriculture, University of California, Berkeley; W. W. Robinson, *The Story of Ventura County* (Los Angeles: Title Insurance and Trust Company, 1955), p. 45; John N. Bowman, "Index of the Spanish-Mexican Land Grant Records and Cases of California," typescript, 2 vols., no pag., 1958, Bancroft Library, University of California, Berkeley.

The actual land cases that were adjudicated by U.S. courts are currently housed in the Bancroft Library at U.C. Berkeley. Those cases which involved land grants made in Ventura County include the following: U.S. District Court, California (Southern District) Land Case No. 103, "Simi"; Land Case No. 107; Land Cases Nos. 32, 117, 59, and 177; Land Cases Nos. 168, 97, 90, 60, 231, 227, 231, 303, 81, and 65; Land Cases Nos. 97, 239, 57, 318, and 53.

3. *Ventura Signal*, June 22, 1872.

4. U.S. Department of Interior, Census Office, *Federal Manuscript Agriculture Schedule of the Eighth Census, 1860: San Buenaventura Township, County of Santa Barbara, State of California*, microfilm.

5. Col. W. W. Hollister, "Statement of a Few Facts on California from 1852–1860," Ms., 1878, Bancroft Library, University of California, Berkeley.

6. *Ventura Signal*, June 22, 1872.

7. T. R. Bard to Mrs. R. Bard, Apr. 28, 1865, Thomas R. Bard Collection, Huntington Library, San Marino, California.

8. Thomas R. Bard, "Some Pioneer Letters," portfolio in *Reminiscences Col-*

lected for the Ventura County Eisteddfod, typescript, Bancroft Library, University of California, Berkeley; W. H. Hutchinson, *Oil, Land and Politics: The California Career of Thomas Robert Bard* (Norman: University of Oklahoma Press, 1965), 1:82, 84. For similar perceptions of the Mexican population of Ventura County, see W. J. Sanborn, "Memoirs of a Santa Paula Sheepherder, 1873–1875: From the Letters of Colonel W. J. Sanborn," *Ventura County Historical Society Quarterly* 1 (November 1959): 2–16; José Arnaz, "Memoirs of a Merchant: Being the Recollections of Life and Customs in Pastoral California by José Arnaz, Trader and Ranchero," translated by Nellie Van de Grift Sanchez, part 1, *Touring Topics* 20 (October 1928): 18.

9. Arnaz, "Memoirs of a Merchant," part 2, p. 47.

10. Robinson, *Ventura County*, p. 45; Bowman, *Index*.

11. A. P. Chittenden to Y. del Valle, Jan. 5, 1855, document no. 805, Del Valle Collection, Los Angeles County Museums, microfilm; Wallace E. Smith, *This Land Was Ours: The Del Valles and Camulos* (Ventura County Historical Society, 1978), pp. 92–93, 96.

12. Smith, *This Land Was Ours*, p. 98.

13. Wallace E. Smith, "The Camulos Story," *Ventura County Historical Society Quarterly* 3 (February 1958): 9.

14. Ibid. Also see R. F. del Valle to Ysabel del Valle, October 1, 1888, document no. 43935, R. F. del Valle Collection, Huntington Library, San Marino, California.

15. Richard B. Haydock, "Reminiscent It Will Be," *Ventura County Historical Society Quarterly* 10 (February 1961): 36–37.

16. Ibid.; Allen, "Influence of Spanish and Mexican Land Grants in Agricultural History"; Newton H. Chittendon, *Homes, Health, and Pleasure in Southern California* (a promotional pamphlet; San Buenaventura, Calif.: April 1883), p. 31.

17. William A. Streeter, "Recollections of Historical Events in California, 1843–1878 by William A. Streeter of Santa Barbara," Ms., 1878, Bancroft Library, University of California, Berkeley.

18. Ibid.

19. J. P. Green to T. R. Bard, June 24, 1874, Thomas R. Bard Collection, Huntington Library, San Marino, California.

20. Hutchinson, *Oil, Land and Politics*, 1:71.

21. Charles B. Huse to Levi Parsons, December 20, 1864, Thomas R. Bard Collection, Huntington Library.

22. Ibid.

23. Resentment of the eastern capitalists who began purchasing huge portions of county land grew very rapidly among the Californio elite. By the late 1860s even the most embattled Mexican landholder made every attempt to avoid selling portions of their estates to these developers and speculators. In a letter to Thomas Scott on November 9, 1867, Thomas R. Bard, his principal agent in Ventura County, testified to their resistance. "The prejudice entertained by the old residents of this county against Eastern corporations and capitalists is so great that they will do everything to prevent you from acquiring more property here, except at high prices." T. R. Bard to T. A. Scott, November 9, 1867, Thomas R. Bard Collection, Huntington Library.

24. Levi Parsons to John Wyeth, n.d., as cited by Hutchinson, *Oil, Land and*

Politics, 1:92. Also see Charles E. Huse to T. R. Bard, September 9, 1867, Thomas R. Bard Collection, Huntington Library.

25. Robert Glass Cleland, *The Place Called Sespe: The History of a California Rancho* (Chicago: R. R. Donnelley, 1963), p. 84.

26. Ibid., p. 87.

27. *Los Angeles Star*, Feb. 1, 1862 as cited by Cleland, *Cattle on a Thousand Hills*, p. 130. Also see Pitt, *Decline of the Californios*, pp. 244–45.

28. Cleland, *Cattle on a Thousand Hills*, p. 135; Pitt, *Decline of the Californios*, pp. 244–45.

29. Smith, *This Land Was Ours*, p. 127.

30. "Sketch of a California Land Title," typescript, ca. 1890, Charles Fernald Collection, Huntington Library, San Marino, California.

31. Chittendon, *Homes, Health and Pleasure*, p. 29; Carmelita Fitzgerald Nicholson, "The Last of the Dons," Ventura County Historical Society *Quarterly* 12 (October 1966): 7.

32. Pitt, *Decline of the Californios*, p. 247; Smith, *This Land Was Ours*, p. 127.

33. *Ventura Signal*, June 22, 1872. Also see T. R. Bard to J. P. Green, Aug. 4, 1867, Thomas R. Bard Collection, Huntington Library.

34. Jesse D. Mason, *Reproduction of Thompson and West's History of Santa Barbara and Ventura Counties, California* (Berkeley: Howell-North, 1961), pp. 361–62.

35. U.S. Department of the Interior, Census Office, *Federal Manuscript Population Schedule of the Eighth Census, 1860: San Buenaventura Township, County of Santa Barbara, State of California* (microfilm).

36. W. D. Hobson, "History of Ventura County," Ventura County Historical Society *Quarterly* 13 (May 1968): 9; Mrs. Yda Addis Storke, *A Memorial and Biographical History of the Counties of Santa Barbara, San Luis Obispo, and Ventura, California* (Chicago: The Lew Publishing Company, 1891), p. 183.

37. U.S. Department of the Interior, Census Office, *Federal Manuscript Population Schedule of the Ninth Census, 1870: San Buenaventura township, County of Santa Barbara, State of California* (microfilm); Santa Barbara County, California, *Great Register of the County of Santa Barbara for the Year 1867* (San Francisco: John G. Hodge & Co., 1868); Santa Barbara County, California, *Supplemental List of Registered Names upon the Great Register of the County of Santa Barbara: From October 19, 1868 to October 31, 1868* (Santa Barbara, California: Santa Barbara Post, 1868); Santa Barbara County, California, *Supplement of the Registered Names Appearing on Great Register of the County of Santa Barbara: From July 30, 1867 to October 19, 1868* (Santa Barbara Post, 1868).

38. Ventura County, California, *Great Register of the County of Ventura, From June 1, 1873 to August 20, 1873* (San Buenaventura, California: Ventura Signal Office, 1873); Ventura County, California, *Great Register of Ventura County: Supplement, 1875* (San Buenaventura, California: Ventura Signal Office, 1875); Ventura County, California, *Great Register of the County of Ventura, 1879* (San Buenaventura, California: Sheridan Brothers, Printers, 1879); Ventura County, California, *Great Register of the County of Ventura, 1882* (San Buenaventura, California: Ventura Signal Printers, 1882); Ventura County, California, *Great Register: Ventura County, California, 1892* (Ventura, California: Free Press Printers, 1892).

39. Edward Larence Walsh, "A Political History of the Formation and Establishment of Ventura County" (M.A. thesis, Loyola University of Los Angeles, 1965), p. 25; J. H. Morrison, "The Formation of Ventura County," *Ventura County Historical Society Quarterly* 4 (August 1962): 3.

40. Walsh, "A Political History," p. 26; Morrison, "The Formation of Ventura County," p. 3.

41. Hutchinson, *Oil, Land, and Politics*, 1:138.

42. T. R. Bard to T. A. Scott, September 6, 1867, as quoted by Waldemar Westergaard, "Thomas R. Bard and the Beginning of the Oil Industry in Southern California," Historical Society of Southern California, *Annual Publications* 10 (1917): 59.

43. Mason, *History of Santa Barbara and Ventura Counties*, p. 358; Hutchinson, *Oil, Land, and Politics*, 1:68.

44. Mason, *History of Santa Barbara and Ventura Counties*, p. 362; Hutchinson, *Oil, Land, and Politics*, 1:30, 68.

45. T. R. Bard to J. P. Green, Aug. 1873, as cited by Hutchinson, *Oil, Land and Politics*, 1:227.

46. J. Lopez to T. R. Bard, Aug. 28, 1879, Thomas R. Bard Collection, Huntington Library.

47. J. Lopez to T. R. Bard, November 2, 1892; J. Lopez to T. R. Bard, November 8, 1896; T. R. Bard to J. Lopez, November 20, 1896, all in Thomas R. Bard Collection, Huntington Library.

48. *Ventura Signal*, November 9, 1878.

49. *Ventura Signal*, October 4, 1873.

50. Mason, *Reproduction of Thompson and West's History*, p. 352; Allen, "Influence of Spanish and Mexican Land Grants in Agricultural History"; *Ventura Signal*, Apr. 4, 1874.

51. Thomas R. Bard to Thomas A. Scott, Aug. 14, 1867, Thomas R. Bard Collection, Huntington Library.

52. T. R. Bard to J. P. Green, Aug. 4, 1867, Thomas R. Bard Collection, Huntington Library.

53. Allen, "Influence of Spanish and Mexican Land Grants in Agricultural History."

54. T. R. Bard to Charles A. Dume, November 25, 1875; T. R. Bard to B. Burnham, July 11, 1879, Thomas R. Bard Collection, Huntington Library.

55. T. R. Bard to A. Albrecht, October 15, 1877; T. R. Bard to J. L. Delano, December 15, 1875; T. R. Bard to B. Donalechi, July 30, 1882; T. R. Bard to Camille Garmier, July 32, 1884, Thomas R. Bard Collection, Huntington Library.

56. Allen, "Influence of Spanish and Mexican Land Grants in Agricultural History."

57. Hollister, "Statement of a Few Facts on California."

58. A. Gerberding to C. Fernald, June 30, 1876; A. Gerberding to C. Fernald, May 27, 1876; A. Gerberding to C. Fernald, May 1, 1876; T. R. Bard to J. P. Green, November 25, 1872, Thomas R. Bard Collection, Huntington Library.

59. "[Squatter] Petition Sent to Congress in Support of H.R. Bill #3232," May 11, 1878, Thomas R. Bard Collection, Huntington Library.

60. U.S. Senate, Senate Report No. 413, June 12, 1876, 44th Cong., 1st sess.;

H.R. Bill #3232, "A Bill for the Relief of Settlers on Certain Lands in the State of California," 45th Cong., 2d sess., 1878.

61. T. R. Bard to J. P. Green, November 25, 1872, as cited by Hutchinson, *Oil, Land and Politics*, 1:176.

62. Fr. Zephyrin Engelhardt, *San Buenaventura: Mission by the Sea* (Santa Barbara, California; Mission Santa Barbara, 1930), pp. 112–13.

63. U.S. Department of the Interior, Census Office, *Federal Manuscript Agriculture Schedule of the Eight Census, 1860: San Buenaventura Township, County of Santa Barbara, State of California* (microfilm).

64. *Ventura Signal*, June 22, 1872.

65. Ibid.

66. *Ventura Signal*, May 29, 1875; *Ventura Free Press*, December 27, 1895; R. H. Allen, "The Spanish Land Grant System as an Influence in the Agricultural Development of California," *Agricultural History* 9 (October 1935): 94–95.

67. 1860 Census, *Agriculture Schedule*; *Ventura Signal*, September 6, 1873; Gertrude M. Reith, "Ventura: Life Story of a City" (Ph.D. diss., Clark University, 1963), pp. 94–95.

68. Bard, Erringer, and Kennedy Partnership, Private Ledger, 1875; C. P. Elliott, "Count of Sheep on Rancho Las Posas," Mar. 1, 1879; T. R. Bard to J. R. Erringer, October 28, 1879, Thomas R. Bard Collection, Huntington Library; Waldemar Westergaard, "Thomas R. Bard and Ventura County's Sheep Industry, 1870–1884," Historical Society of Southern California, *Annual Publications* 11 (1920): 8.

69. Bard, Erringer, and Kennedy Partnership, "Notice of Dissolution," December 31, 1880, Thomas R. Bard Collection, Huntington Library.

70. Ibid.

71. Ibid.

72. Michael R. Belknap, "The Era of the Lemon: A History of Santa Paula, California," *California Historical Society Quarterly* 2 (June 1968): 120; Charles Collin Teague, *Fifty Years a Rancher: A Recollection of Half a Century Devoted to the Citrus and Walnut Industries of California and to Furthering the Cooperative Movement in Agriculture* (Los Angeles: Ward Richie Press, 1944), p. 59; Sol N. Sheridan, *Ventura County, California* (San Francisco: Sunset Magazine Homeseeker's Bureau, 1909), p. 48.

73. Belknap, "The Era of the Lemon," p. 126.

74. Ibid., pp. 126–27.

75. Ibid.; Teague, *Fifty Years a Rancher*, pp. 44–45.

76. Belknap, "The Era of the Lemon," p. 126; Teague, *Fifty Years a Rancher*, p. 79.

77. Teague, *Fifty Years a Rancher*, pp. 74–79, 144.

78. Ibid., passim.

79. Torsten Magnusen, "History of the Beet Sugar Industry in California," Historical Society of Southern California, *Annual Publication* 11, part 1 (1918): 76; Dan Gutleben, "The Oxnard Beet Sugar Factory, Oxnard, California," unpublished manuscript in Ventura County Historical Museum Library, p. 4; Elizabeth Ritter, *History of Ventura County, California* (Los Angeles: H. M. Meier, 1940), p. 141; Thomas J. Osborne, "Claus Spreckels and the Oxnard Brothers: Pioneer Developers of California's Beet Sugar Industry, 1890–1900," *Southern*

California Historical Quarterly 54 (Summer 1972): 119; *Oxnard Courier*, Jan. 4, 1902.

80. *Oxnard Courier*, December 4, 1901.

81. *Oxnard Courier*, October 4, 1902.

82. *Oxnard Courier*, July 12, 1901; *Oxnard Courier*, November 9, 1901; *Oxnard Courier*, Feb. 21, 1903; Sheridan, *Ventura County*, p. 48.

83. *Oxnard Courier*, December 4, 1908; Hutchinson, *Oil, Land and Politics*, 2:94–95; Transcript of interview with Judge Charles F. Blackstone, Oxnard, California, Aug. 20, 1960, Thomas R. Bard Collection, Huntington Library; Madeline Mieda, "Hueneme as a Grain Port," *Ventura County Historical Society Quarterly* 3, part 2 (February 1958): 20.

84. Clifford M. Zierer, "The Ventura Area of Southern California," *Bulletin of the Geographical Society of Philadelphia* 30 (January 1932): 36.

85. U.S. Department of the Interior, Census Office, *Federal Manuscript Population Schedule of the Ninth Census, 1870: San Buenaventura Township, County of Santa Barbara, State of California* (microfilm).

86. U.S. Department of the Interior, Census Office, *Statistics of the Population of the United States at the Tenth Census, 1880* (Washington, D.C.: Government Printing Office, 1883), p. 382; U.S. Department of the Interior, Census Office, *Twelfth Census of the United States Taken in the Year 1900 . . . Population* (Washington, D.C.: United States Census Office, 1901), pp. 531, 656, 571.

87. *Ventura County, California: Its Resources etc.* (San Buenaventura: Bowers and Sons, 1885), pp. 3–4; *Ventura County, California* (San Francisco: The Bancroft Company, 1888), pp. 33–41; *Ventura Free Press*, December 27, 1895; Robinson, *Ventura County*, p. 45.

88. U.S. Department of the Interior, Census Office, *Federal Manuscript Manufactures Schedule of the Tenth Census, 1880: Ventura County, State of California*, microfilm. Also see *Ventura Signal*, May 22, 1875; *Ventura Signal*, Apr. 22, 1876.

89. 1880 Census, *Population Schedule*; U.S. Department of the Interior, Census Office, *Federal Manuscript Population Schedule of the Twelfth Census, 1900: Ventura County, State of California*, microfilm.

90. Collaborative historical evidence of the use of Mexican laborers in these occupations can be found in the following documents: C. P. Elliot to T. R. Bard, Mar. 11, 1878; C. P. Elliot to T. R. Bard, May 2, 1878; J. R. Erringer to T. R. Bard, November 15, 1879; Financial Statement, Rancho Las Posas, November 17, 1879; T. R. Bard to J. R. Erringer, October 28, 1879; Financial Statement, Rancho Simi, Mar. 1, 1879; T. R. Bard to José Ramon Ayala, October 15, 1880; Shearing Account Ledger, Rancho Las Posas, March 1876–March 1879; Rancho Simi Ledger 1880; C. P. Elliot to T. R. Bard, Apr. 28, 1878; C. P. Elliot to T. R. Bard, September 24, 1879, all in Bard Collection, Huntington Library.

91. 1880 Census, *Agriculture Schedule*.

92. Thomas W. More, "Day Book," in Charles Storke Papers, Bancroft Library, University of California, Berkeley.

93. *Ventura Signal*, May 17, 1872. Also see Sarah Elliott Blanchard, *Memories of a Child's Early California Days* (Los Angeles: privately printed, 1961), pp. 31–39.

94. *Ventura Signal*, Mar. 28, 1874; *Ventura Signal*, Apr. 4, 1874; *Ventura*

Signal, Aug. 12, 1876; *Ventura Semi-Weekly Free Press*, Aug. 22, 1877; *Ventura Signal*, September 22, 1877.

95. W. W. Brown, "Journal of W. W. Brown: 1901–1902," *Ventura County Historical Society Quarterly* 15 (1969): 24; William Stein, "Recollections of a Pioneer Oil Driller," *Ventura County Historical Society Quarterly* 5 (1960): 18; J. H. Russell, *Cattle on the Conejo* (Los Angeles: The Ward Ritchie Press, 1957), pp. 12–13.

96. *Ventura Signal*, Aug. 11, 1877; C. P. Elliot to T. R. Bard, July 22, 1878, Bard Collection, Huntington Library; California Bureau of Labor Statistics, *Second Biennial Report of the Bureau of Labor Statistics, The State of California for the Years 1885 and 1886* (Sacramento: State Printing Office, 1887), p. 744.

97. *Ventura Democrat*, September 17, 1885; *Ventura Democrat*, July 4, 1891; *Ventura Democrat*, Aug. 7, 1891.

98. *Ventura Signal*, May 20, 1876; *Ventura Signal*, May 19, 1877.

99. See the excellent discussion of this movement by Alexander Saxton in his *The Indispensible Enemy: Labor and the Anti-Chinese Movement in California* (Berkeley and Los Angeles: University of California Press, 1971).

100. *Ventura Free Press*, October 30, 1903.

4. "BEFORE THE MARCH OF CIVILIZATION"

1. *California State Constitution, 1849.*

2. The phrase "devils of the forest" is taken from a disparaging newspaper article about the California Indians published in the *Oroville Union* on July 25, 1863.

3. Edward D. Castillo, "The Impact of Euro-American Exploration and Settlement," in Robert F. Heizer, ed., *California*, vol. 8 of *Handbook of North American Indians*, William C. Sturtevant, gen. ed. (Washington: Smithsonian Institution, 1978), p. 99.

4. George Harwood Phillips, *Chiefs and Challengers: Indian Resistance and Cooperation in Southern California* (Berkeley: University of California Press, 1975), p. 7.

According to Phillips, "In all of southern California inter-lineage conflicts may have been frequent, but they were not prolonged affairs and the loss of life was usually insignificant. They developed mainly over territorial infractions and usually took place when food was scarce. For those whose territory was penetrated, there was reason for enmity. But retaliation rather than a desire for plunder or a need to achieve distinction was the goal when a lineage took up arms. Since many of the lineage peoples of southern California were linked by reciprocity arrangements, however, there was much peaceful interaction" (p. 17).

5. Ibid., p. 7.

6. Ibid., p. 160.

7. Tom King, "New Views of California Indian Society," *The Indian Historian* 5, no. 4 (Winter 1972): 15.

8. Malcolm Margolin, *The Ohlone Way: Indian Life in the San Francisco-Monterey Bay Area* (Berkeley, Calif.: Heyday Books, 1978), p. 1.

This discussion of the Ohlone draws heavily upon Malcolm Margolin's sensitive analysis of this Indian group. Although there were important differences among the California Indians, the Ohlone provide a good example of the hunting and gathering way of life that flourished before the arrival of Europeans. Other interesting ethnographic discussions of Indian culture and society in California can be found in the excellent collection of articles in Lowell John Bean and Thomas C. Blackburn, eds., *Native Californians: A Theoretical Perspective* (Ramona, Calif.: Ballena Press, 1976); R. F. Heizer and M. A. Whipple, eds., *The California Indians: A Source Book*, 2d. ed. (Berkeley: University of California Press, 1971); and James F. Downs, *The Two Worlds of the Washo: An Indian Tribe of California and Nevada* (New York: Holt, Rinehart and Winston, 1966).

9. Margolin, *The Ohlone Way*, p. 29.

10. Ibid.

11. Ibid., pp. 44–45.

12. Ibid., p. 24.

13. Ibid., p. 52.

14. Ibid.

15. Ibid., p. 54.

16. Ibid., pp. 16, 84–85.

There remains some controversy over the social acceptability of homosexuality among the Indians of North America. Some scholars argue that these same-sex couples were accepted by Indian society and that the individual assuming the female gender role (the berdache) was often revered and had spiritual importance in Indian society. Other scholars question the degree to which institutionalized homosexual behavior among the Indians of North America reflected fluid, "separate but equal" gender relations and social acceptance of homosexuality. Examples of the first view can be seen in Walter Williams, *The Spirit and the Flesh: Sexual Diversity in American Indian Culture* (Boston: Beacon Press, 1988); and Will Roscoe, "The Zuni Man-Woman," *OUT/LOOK* 1, no. 2 (Summer 1988): 56–67. A provocative example of the second perspective can be found in Ramón A. Gutiérrez, "Must We Deracinate Indians to Find Gay Roots?" *OUT/LOOK* 1, no. 4 (Winter 1989): 61–67.

17. James J. Rawls, *The Indians of California: The Changing Image* (Norman: University of Oklahoma Press, 1984), p. 195.

18. Robert Heizer, ed., *They Were Only Diggers: A Collection of Articles from California Newspapers, 1851–1866, on Indian and White Relations* (Ramona, Calif.: Ballena Press, 1974), p. xiv.

19. Ibid., pp. xi, xiv–xv.

20. Hinton Rowan Helper, *The Land of Gold: Reality Versus Fiction* (1855), p. 152, as cited by Rawls, *Indians of California*, pp. 194–95.

21. George Payson, *Golden Dreams and Leaden Realities* (New York: G. P. Putnam, 1853), p. 256, as cited in Rawls, *Indians of California*, p. 196.

22. Ibid.

23. Ibid., pp. 196–97.

24. Ibid., p. 197.

25. Ibid., pp. 198–99.

26. Ibid., p. 200.

27. Maurice S. Sullivan, ed., *The Travels of Jedediah Smith: A Documentary Outline including the Journal of the Great American Pathfinder* (Santa Ana, Calif.: Fine Arts Press, 1934), pp. 72–73, as cited by Rawls, *Indians of California*, p. 50.

28. John Walton Caughey, ed., *The Indians of Southern California in 1852: The B. D. Wilson Report and a Selection of Contemporary Comments* (San Marino, Calif.: Huntington Library, 1952), p. 35.

29. Margolin, *The Ohlone Way*, p. 56.

30. Ibid., p. 54.

31. *San Francisco Weekly National*, Jan. 13, 1859.

32. Special Agent G. Bailey to T. J. Henley, Superintendent of Indian Affairs in California, November 4, 1858, U.S. Department of the Interior, Office of Indian Affairs, *Report of the Commissioner of Indian Affairs, accompanying the Annual Report of the Secretary of the Interior for the Year 1858: California Superintendency* (Washington: Wm. A. Harris, Printer, 1858), p. 302.

33. Vincent Geiger to T. J. Henley, Superintendent of Indian Affairs in California, July, 1858, ibid., p. 288.

34. J. B. Vosburg to E. P. Smith, September 4, 1875, U.S. Department of the Interior, Office of Indian Affairs, *Annual Report of the Commissioner of Indian Affairs to the Secretary of the Interior for the Year 1875: California Reports* (Washington: Government Printing Office, 1875), p. 228. Indian Agent J. D. Broaddus's report to the Commission of Indian Affairs in September 1875 vividly echoes these culturally chauvinistic sentiments:

> Some few of the Indians are inclined to be industrious, but the great majority of them are idle, listless, careless, and improvident. They seem to take no thought about provision for the future, and many of them would not work at all if they were not compelled to do so. They would rather live upon the roots and acorns gathered by their women than to work for flour and beef. A rigid discipline has to be exercised and obedience required, otherwise the tendency would be to demoralize those who are inclined to work.
>
> J. L. Broaddus to E. P. Smith, September 1, 1875, ibid., p. 221

35. Charles Porter to Commissioner of Indian Affairs (H. Price), Aug. 1, 1883, U.S. Department of the Interior, Office of Indian Affairs, *Annual Report of the Commissioner of Indian Affairs to the Secretary of the Interior for the Year 1883: California Reports* (Washington: Government Printing Office, 1883), p. 10.

36. Rawls, *Indians of California*, p 201.

37. Ibid.

38. McKee, Barbour, and Wozencraft to Hon. Luke Lea, May 1, 1853, U.S. Interior Department, Office of Indian Affairs, *Report of the Commissioner of Indian Affairs, accompanying the Annual Report of the Secretary of the Interior for the Year 1853: California Superintendency* (Washington: A. O. P. Nicholson, Printer, 1853), p. 76.

39. Charles Maltby to D. A. Cooley, September 15, 1866, U.S. Interior Department, Office of Indian Affairs, *Report of the Commissioner of Indian Affairs for the Year 1866: California Superintendency* (Washington: Government Printing Office, 1866), p. 94.

40. J. Ross Browne to Charles E. Mix, September 29, 1858, Office of Indian Affairs, document no. B615, Records Group 75, National Archives, Washington, D.C., as cited in Robert F. Heizer, *The Destruction of the California Indians* (Salt Lake City: Peregrine Publications, 1974), p. 114.

41. Adam Johnston to Hon. Orlando Brown, September 16, 1850, U.S. Interior Department, Office of Indian Affairs, *Report of the Commissioner of Indian Affairs, accompanying the Annual Report of the Secretary of the Interior for the Year 1850: California Superintendency* (Washington: A. O. P. Nicholson, Printer, 1850).

42. *Sacramento Union*, September 12, 1856, as reprinted in Heizer, *They Were Only Diggers*, p. 73.

43. Rawls, *Indians of California*, pp. 171–72, 180, 182.

The situation that the California Indians confronted shortly after United States annexation was eloquently conveyed in Indian Agent Adam Johnston's 1850 report to the Commissioner of Indian Affairs, where he sympathetically describes the rapidly deteriorating condition of the Ohlone Indians (who were also known as the *Costano* or coastal Indians) in the San Francisco–Monterey bay area. Perceptively detailing the evolving cycle of violence that eventually led to the total decimation of the Ohlone in central California, Johnston noted:

> Their means of subsistence, which have heretofore been limited, are now greatly diminished on account of the immigration overrunning their state. The miners have destroyed their fish-dams on the streams, and the majority of the tribes are kept in constant fear on account of the indiscriminate and inhuman massacre of their people in many places, for real or supposed injuries. They have not any particular boundaries or fixed homes for any great length of time together, but change their locations as taste or their necessities may require. Yet they all have an indistinct and undefined idea of their right to the soil, the trees, and the streams. From these they have heretofore obtained their subsistence, which consisted of grass-seeds and roots from the earth; acorns, pine-seeds and berries from the trees and bushes; and fish from the streams. They became alarmed at the immense flood of immigration which spread over their country; it was quite incomprehensible. I have been told of several acts of depredation which were instigated by the chiefs of certain tribes, through the apprehension that their people must die of starvation, in consequence of the strangers overrunning their country, feeding their grass, burning their timber, and destroying their dams on the streams. For these innovations they claim some compensation; not in money, for they know nothing of its value, but clothing, blankets, and something to sustain life.
>
> Adam Johnston to Hon. Orlando Brown, May 23, 1850, U.S. Interior Department, Office of Indian Affairs, *1853 Report of the Commissioner of Indian Affairs: California Superintendency*

44. In this regard, see the interesting discussion of Indian women in forced concubinage and as victims of white sexual violence in Albert L. Hurtado, *Indian Survival on the California Frontier* (New Haven: Yale University Press, 1988), pp. 169–92.

45. Isaac Cox, *The Annuals of Trinity County* (Eugene, Oreg.: John Henry Nash of the University of Oregon, 1940), pp. 112, 114, as cited by Rawls, *Indians of California*, p. 99.

46. George Hanson to Commissioner of Indian Affairs, U.S. Interior Department, Office of Indian Affairs, *Report of the Commissioner of Indian Affairs, accompanying the Annual Report of the Secretary of the Interior for the Year 1861: California Superintendency* (Washington: Government Printing Office, 1861), p. 148.

47. H. P. Heintzleman to Thomas J. Henley, July 1, 1858, U.S. Interior Department, Office of Indian Affairs, *Report of the Commissioner of Indian Affairs, accompanying the Annual Report of the Secretary of the Interior for the Year 1858; California Superintendency* (Washington: William A. Harris, Printer, 1858), p. 287.

48. *California Farmer*, October 26, 1860, as reprinted in Heizer, *They Were Only Diggers*, p. 122.

49. *Sacramento Union*, June 13, 1862, as reprinted in Heizer, *They Were Only Diggers*, p. 88.

50. As cited by Heizer and Almquist, *Other Californians*, p. 26.

51. Horace Bell, *Reminiscences of a Ranger* (Los Angeles: Yarnell, Caystile, and Mathis, Printers, 1881), p. 116.

52. Castillo, "The Impact of Euro-American Exploration and Settlement," p. 108.

53. Cook, *The Conflict between the California Indians*, p. 259.

54. *San Francisco Alta California*, May 28, 1850, as reprinted in Robert F. Heizer, ed., *Collected Documents on the Causes and Events in the Bloody Island Massacre of 1850* (Berkeley: Archaeological Research Facility, Department of Anthropology, University of California, 1973), p. 18.

55. See the reconstruction of these events leading to the massacre in Albert Hurtado's *Indian Survival*, pp. 104–6.

56. See the recollection of Chief Augustine (pp. 38–41) and another unidentified Pomo informant (pp. 42–45) in Robert F. Heizer, *Collected Documents on the Bloody Island Massacre*.

57. William Ralganal Benson, "The Stone and Kelsey 'Massacre' on the Shores of Clear Lake in 1849—The Indian View," *California Historical Society Quarterly* 11, no. 3 (Sept. 1932): 268–69.

58. Ibid., pp. 271–72.

59. Ibid., pp. 272–73.

60. H. Day to Assistant Adjunct General, May 16, 1850, document no. 334, Records Group 98, RWD, National Archives, as cited by Heizer, *Destruction of the California Indians*, pp. 42–44.

61. Jack Norton, *Genocide in Northwest California: When Our Worlds Cried* (San Francisco: The Indian Historian Press, 1979), pp. 54, 56.

62. California Legislature, *Majority and Minority Reports of the Special Joint Committee on the Mendocino War* (Sacramento: State Printing Office, 1860), p. 3.

63. Ibid., p. 4.

64. Ibid.

65. Ibid., p. 24.

66. Ibid., p. 19.

67. Ibid., p. 14.

68. Ibid.

69. Ibid., pp. 14–15.

70. Ibid., p. 22.

71. Lynwood Carranco and Estle Beard, *Genocide and Vendetta: The Round Valley Wars in Northern California* (Norman: University of Oklahoma Press, 1981), p. 82.

72. Ibid., pp. 95–96.

73. *Marysville Daily Appeal*, Feb. 15, 1860, reprinted in Heizer, *They Were Only Diggers*, pp. 76–77.

74. *Harper's Monthly Magazine*, 1861, as cited by Engelhardt, *Missions and Missionaries of California*, 4:652.

75. John Walton Caughey, ed., *The Indians of Southern California in 1852: The B. D. Wilson Report and a Selection of Contemporary Comments* (San Marino, Calif.: Huntington Library, 1952), pp. xxii–xxiii.

76. Norton, *Genocide in Northwestern California*, p. 91.

77. O. M. Wozencraft, "Oration," Twenty-fifth Anniversary of the Corporate Society of California Pioneers, San Francisco, 1875. Ms., Bancroft Library, pp. 8–9.

78. Rawls, *Indians of California*, p. 205.

79. Ibid., pp. 171, 175. Slightly different figures are offered by demographer Russell Thornton in his study of the American Indian's population decline: "Primarily because of the killings, the California Indian population—which some scholars say once had been at least 310,000, perhaps over 700,000—decreased by two-thirds in little more than a single decade: from 100,000 in 1849 to 35,000 in 1860." Russell Thornton, *American Indian Holocaust and Survival: A Population History since 1492* (Norman: University of Oklahoma Press, 1987), p. 109.

80. Sherburne Cook has estimated that more than 4,000 Indians were killed as a result of physical assaults in the period from 1848 to 1865. See his *The Conflict between the California Indians*, pp. 259–300, 346–61. Also see Bean, *California: An Interpretive History*, pp. 169–70.

81. Thornton, *Indian Holocaust and Survival*, pp. 201ff. Thornton concludes that "the largest, most blatant, deliberate killing of North American Indians by non-Indians surely occurred in California, particularly in northern California during the mid 1800s. . . . Remarkable in the history is that, although many California tribes became extinct, or nearly so, others managed to survive, demographically and tribally. Many more or less viable California tribes continue today on present or former reservation and rancheria lands, separate from both the larger non-Indian California population and other Indian populations" (p. 201).

5. "UNFIT AND INCAPABLE"

1. *Constitution of the State of California, 1849*. Also see Chauncey S. Goodrich, "The Legal Status of the California Indians," parts 1 and 2, *California Law Review* 14, no. 2 (January 1926): 83–100, and 14, no. 3 (March 1926): 157–87.

2. J. Ross Browne, *Report of the Debates in the Convention of California on the Formation of the State Constitution in September and October, 1849* (Washington, D.C.: John T. Towers, 1850), pp. 61, 63, 64.

3. Ibid., p. 306. Also see Delegate McCarver's statement in support of this contention, p. 70.

4. Ibid., pp. 67–70.

5. *California Statutes*, 1851, p. 230; *California Statutes*, 1863, p. 69; *California Statutes*, 1863–64, p. 213; *California Statutes*, 1869–70, p. 838; Robert F. Heizer and Alan F. Almquist, *The Other Californians: Prejudice and Discrimination under Spain, Mexico, and the United States to 1920* (Berkeley and Los Angeles: University of California Press, 1971), pp. 46–48, 133–34; Ferdinand F. Fernandez, "Except a California Indian: A Study in Legal Discrimination," *Southern California Quarterly* 5, no. 2 (June 1968): 166, 170.

6. Heizer and Almquist, *Other Californians*, pp. 134–36.

7. Fernandez, "Except a California Indian," pp. 169–70; Heizer and Almquist, *Other Californians*, pp. 47–48, 61; Jack D. Forbes, *Native Americans of California and Nevada* (Healdsburg, Calif.: Naturegraph Publishers, 1969), p. 95.

8. Sherburne F. Cook, *The Conflict between the California Indians and White Civilization* (Berkeley and Los Angeles: University of California Press, 1976), p. 309; Fr. Zephyrin Engelhardt, *The Missions and Missionaries of California* (San Francisco: James H. Barry, 1908), 4:650; Heizer and Almquist, *Other Californians*, pp. 48–50; Varden Fuller, *The Supply of Agricultural Labor as a Factor in the Evolution of Farm Labor Organization in California Agriculture*, in U.S. Congress, Senate, Committee on Education and Labor, *Hearings: Pursuant to Senate Resolution 266, Part 54, Agricultural Labor in California*. 76th Cong., 3d sess. (Washington, D.C.: Government Printing Office, 1940), p. 19793; Forbes, *Native Americans*, p. 60.

9. W. W. Robinson, *The Indians of Los Angeles: Story of the Liquidation of a People* (Los Angeles: Glen Davidson, 1952), pp. 2–3. Also see George H. Phillips, *Chiefs and Challengers: Indian Resistance and Cooperation in Southern California* (Berkeley and Los Angeles: University of California Press, 1975), pp. 57–58.

10. *California Star*, Jan. 15, 1848.

11. Ibid.

12. *Marysville Herald*, Nov. ——, 1856 (undated), as cited in Robert F. Heizer, ed., *They Were Only Diggers: A Collection of Articles from California Newspapers, 1851–1866, on Indian and White Relations* (Ramona, Calif.: Ballena Press, 1974), p. 72.

13. California Legislature, *Majority and Minority Reports of the Special Joint Committee on the Mendocino Wars* (Sacramento: State Printing Office, 1860), p. 11.

14. James J. Rawls, *Indians of California: The Changing Image* (Norman: University of Oklahoma Press, 1984), p. 86.

15. Cook, *Conflict between the California Indians*, p. 309; Heizer and Almquist, *Other Californians*, pp. 46, 50–58.

16. *Sacramento Standard*, as reprinted in the *San Francisco Alta California*, Mar. 17, 1860.

17. Rawls, *Indians of California*, p. 91.

18. Ibid., p. 93.

19. Ibid., p. 91.

20. *San Francisco Bulletin*, Mar. 2, 1861.

21. Heizer and Almquist, *Other Californians*, p. 57.

22. Rawls, *Indians of California*, p. 86.

23. Ibid., pp. 87–88.

24. See, in this regard, Marion Lydia Lothrop, "The Indian Campaigns of General M. G. Vallejo, Defender of the Northern Frontier of California," *Society of California Pioneers Quarterly* 9, no. 1 (March 1932): 161–205.

25. Fernandez, "Except a California Indian," pp. 163–64.

26. Ibid., p. 164.

27. Rawls, *Indians of California*, p. 89.

28. Ibid., p. 106.

29. Heizer and Almquist, *Other Californians*, pp. 41, 43–45.

30. Cook, *Conflict between the California Indians*, pp. 314–15. Also see Engelhardt, *Missions and Missionaries of California*, 4:654; Heizer and Almquist, *Other Californians*, pp. 40–44.

31. *Alta California*, Oct. 2, 1854, as cited by Cook, *Conflict between the California Indians*, p. 311.

32. *Marysville Appeal*, Dec. 6, 1861, as cited by Cook, *Conflict between the California Indians*, p. 312.

33. See, for example, the collection of newspaper accounts of this Indian kidnapping and enslavement in section 1 of Heizer, *They Were Only Diggers*.

34. W. H. Brewer, *Up and Down California* (New Haven: Yale University Press, 1930), p. 493, as cited by Cook, *Conflict between the California Indians*, p. 312.

35. U.S. Interior Department, Office of Indian Affairs, *Report of the Commissioner of Indian Affairs, accompanying the Annual Report of the Secretary of the Interior for the Year 1861: California Superintendency* (Washington: Government Printing Office, 1861), p. 149.

36. Thomas J. Henley to George Moneypenney, Apr. 14, 1856, Office of Indian Affairs, document no. H109, Records Group 75, National Archives, Washington, D.C., as reprinted in Robert F. Heizer, *The Destruction of the California Indians* (Salt Lake City: Peregrine Publications, 1974), p. 233. Also see Lothrop, "The Indian Campaigns of General M. G. Vallejo," pp. 181–83.

37. Lynwood Carranco and Estle Beard, *Genocide and Vendetta: The Round Valley Wars in Northern California* (Norman: University of Oklahoma Press, 1981), p. 44, 46–47.

38. Wm. McDaniel to Thos. J. Henley, Oct. 4, 1854, Office of Indian Affairs, document no. H703, RG 75, National Archives, as reprinted in Heizer, *Destruction of the California Indians*, pp. 19–20.

39. Delfina Cuero, *Autobiography of Delfina Cuero, a Diegueno Indian, as told to Florence C. Shipek*, interpreted by Rosalie Pinto (Los Angeles: Dawson Books, 1968), pp. 60–61.

40. Ibid., p. 61.

41. Fernandez, "Except a California Indian," pp. 164–65.

42. Rawls, *Indians of California*, pp. 101–3.

43. Fuller, *Agricultural Labor*, p. 19790.

44. Cook, *Conflict between the California Indians*, p. 315.

45. Ibid., p. 315.

46. Ibid., pp. 316–23.

47. Phillips, *Chiefs and Challengers*, p. 57.

48. Cook, *Conflict between the California Indians*, p. 317; Fuller, *Agricultural Labor*, p. 19790.

49. John Caughey, *The Indians of Southern California in 1852: The B. D. Wilson Report and a Selection of Contemporary Comments* (San Marino, Calif.: Huntington Library, 1952), p. xxiv.

50. *Daily California News*, Jan. 15, 1851, as cited by Chad L. Hoopes, *Domesticate or Exterminate: California Indian Treaties Unratified and Made Secret in 1852* (Loleta, Calif.: Redwood Coast Publications, 1975), pp. 30–31.

51. Richard E. Crouter and Andrew F. Rolle, "Edward Fitzgerald Beale and the

Indian Peace Commissioners in California, 1851–1854," *Historical Society Quarterly of Southern California* 42, no. 2 (June 1960): 115.

52. Hoopes, *Domesticate or Exterminate*, p. 40.

53. Ibid., pp. 39–40.

54. Caughey, *Indians of Southern California*, p. xxiv; Rawls, *Indians of California*, p. 141.

55. Caughey, *Indians of Southern California*, p. xxv.

56. Crouter and Rolle, "Edward Fitzgerald Beale," p. 115.

57. Caughey, *Indians of Southern California*, p. xxv.

58. *Senate Journal*, 1852, pp. 600, 197–98, as cited in Goodrich, "The Legal Status of the California Indian," part 1, p. 96.

59. *Los Angeles Star*, Mar. 13, 1852.

60. *Senate Journal*, 1852, pp. 600, 197–98, as cited in Goodrich, "The Legal Status of the California Indian," part 1, p. 96.

61. *Daily Alta California*, Dec. 4, 1851, as cited by Phillips, *Chiefs and Challengers*, p. 117.

62. William E. Evans, "The Garra Uprising: Conflicts between San Diego Indians and Settlers in 1851," *California Historical Society Quarterly* 45, no. 4 (December 1966): 341–43.

63. Heizer and Almquist, *Other Californians*, p. 101.

64. Albert L. Hurtado, *Indian Survival on the California Frontier* (New Haven: Yale University Press, 1988), p. 126.

65. Walton Bean, *California: An Interpretive History*, 2d ed. (New York: McGraw-Hill, 1973), pp. 166–68; Forbes, *Native Americans*, p. 64; Andrew F. Rolle, *California: A History* (New York: Thomas Y. Crowell, 1963), pp. 393–94; Heizer and Almquist, *Other Californians*, pp. 81–82; Caughey, *Indians of Southern California*, p. 327.

66. Special Agent G. Bailey to T. J. Henley, Superintendent of Indian Affairs in California, November, 1858, U.S. Interior Department, Office of Indian Affairs, *Report of the Commissioner of Indian Affairs, accompanying the Annual Report of the Secretary of the Interior for the Year 1858: California Superintendency* (Washington: Wm. A. Harris, Printer, 1858), pp. 304–5.

67. Ibid., p. 305.

68. Ibid.

69. Forbes, *Native Americans*, p. 64.

70. Lt. M. R. Morgan to Maj. W. W. MacFall, Sept. 1, 1857, box no. 6, documents nos. M54, M61, Records Group 78, RWD, National Archives, as reprinted in Heizer, *Destruction of the California Indians*, pp. 106–7.

71. *Harper's Magazine* (1861), as cited by Caughey, *Indians of Southern California*, pp. xxxii–xxxiii.

72. Statement of C. L. Capp, 1858, Office of Indian Affairs, documents nos. B637, B638, RG 75, National Archives, as reprinted in Heizer, *Destruction of the California Indians*, p. 122.

73. Petition, Tehama County Citizens to Secretary of the Interior, 1859, Office of Indian Affairs, document no. V25, and J. Y. McDuffie to Hon. A. B. Greenwood, 1859, document no. M90, RG 75, National Archives, as reprinted in Heizer, *Destruction of the California Indians*, p. 141.

74. *Report of the Commissioner of Indian Affairs for 1862*, pp. 39–40, as cited by Heizer and Almquist, *Other Californians*, pp. 89–90.

75. Forbes, *Native Americans*, pp. 64–65.

76. Rawls, *Indians of California*, pp. 152, 158.

77. B. C. Whiting to F. A. Walker, Oct. 17, 1872, U.S. Interior Department, Office of Indian Affairs, *Annual Report of the Commissioner of Indian Affairs to the Secretary of the Interior for the Year 1872: California Superintendency* (Washington: Government Printing Office, 1872), p. 375.

6. "THEY CAN BE HIRED IN MASSES"

1. Stuart Creighton Miller, *Unwelcome Immigrant: The American Image of the Chinese, 1785–1885* (Berkeley and Los Angeles: University of California Press, 1969), p. 146.

2. For discussions of factors which led to Chinese immigration see: U.S. Congress, Joint Special Committee to Investigate Chinese Immigration, *Report of the Joint Special Committee to Investigate Chinese Immigration*, Report No. 689, 44th Cong., 2d sess., 1876 (Washington: Government Printing Office, 1877); Mary Roberts Coolidge, *Chinese Immigration* (New York: Henry Holt and Company, 1909).

3. For discussions of this "credit-ticket" system, see Gunther Barth, *Bitter Strength: A History of the Chinese in the United States, 1850–1870* (Cambridge: Harvard University Press, 1964), pp. 51, 67–68, 77–80; Coolidge, *Chinese Immigration*, pp. 48–49; Thomas Chinn, ed., *A History of the Chinese in California* (San Francisco: Chinese Historical Society of America, 1969), p. 15; Stanford M. Lyman, "Strangers in the City: The Chinese on the Urban Frontier," in Stanford M. Lyman, *The Asian in the West* (Reno: University of Nevada System, Western Studies Center, Desert Research Institute, 1970), p. 12; Stanford M. Lyman, "Contrasts in the Community Organization of Chinese and Japanese in North America," in Lyman, *The Asian in the West*, p. 60.

4. Alexander Saxton, "Race and the House of Labor," in Gary B. Nash and Richard Weiss, eds., *The Great Fear: Race in the Minds of White America* (New York: Holt, Rinehart and Winston, 1970), p. 108.

5. Roger Daniels, *Asian America: Chinese and Japanese in the United States since 1850* (Seattle: University of Washington Press, 1988), pp. 14–15.

6. Stanford Lyman, *Chinese Americans* (New York: Random House, 1974), pp. 29–30.

7. Sucheng Chan, *This Bitter-Sweet Soil: The Chinese in California Agriculture, 1860–1910* (Berkeley and Los Angeles: University of California Press, 1986), p. 404.

8. Ibid.

9. Ronald Takaki, *Strangers from a Different Shore: A History of Asian Americans* (Boston: Little, Brown, 1989), p. 79.

10. Ibid.

11. Daniels, *Asian America*, p. 69.

12. Takaki, *Strangers from a Different Shore*, p. 119.

13. Ibid. See also the extended discussion of the Chinese immigrants' social organizations in the United States in Lyman, *Chinese Americans*, chap. 3; and

Stanford M. Lyman, *Chinatown and Little Tokyo: Power, Conflict, and Community among Chinese and Japanese Immigrants in America* (Millwood, N.Y.: Associated Faculty Press, 1986), chap. 3; Daniels, *Asian America*, passim.

14. Takaki, *Strangers from a Different Shore*, p. 119.

15. Daniels, *Asian America*, p. 4.

16. Lyman, *Chinese Americans*, p. 29.

17. Chan, *Bitter-Sweet Soil*, p. 369.

18. For examples of the use of these social-cultural differences as a basis of anti-Chinese sentiment see California State Senate, Special Committee on Chinese Immigration, *Chinese Immigration: Its Social, Moral, and Political Effect: Report to the California State Senate of its Special Committee on Chinese Immigration* (Sacramento: State Printing Office, 1878); Samuel Gompers and Herman Gutstadt, *Meat vs. Rice: American Manhood against Asiatic Coolieism, Which Shall Survive?* (Reprint, San Francisco: Asiatic Exclusion League, 1908).

19. Erasmus Doolittle, *Sketches, by a Traveller* (Boston, 1830), pp. 259–60, as cited by Miller, *Unwelcome Immigrant*, p. 29.

20. Miller, *Unwelcome Immigrant*, p. 36.

21. Ibid., p. 27.

22. Ibid., pp. 27–28.

23. Takaki, *Strangers from a Different Shore*, p. 107.

24. Alexander Saxton, *The Indispensable Enemy: Labor and the Anti-Chinese Movement in California* (Berkeley and Los Angeles: University of California Press, 1971), pp. 19, 20ff; Saxton, "Race," p. 115. Stuart Creighton Miller has convincingly argued that anti-Chinese sentiment actually preceded the arrival of the Chinese immigrant to California. He notes that this animosity was propagated by American traders, travelers, missionaries, and newspapermen who traveled to China prior to 1849. See his *Unwelcome Immigrant*, chaps. 1–6.

25. Takaki, *Strangers from a Different Shore*, pp. 80–81.

26. Ibid., p. 101.

27. Dan Cauldwell, "The Negroization of the Chinese Stereotype in California," *Southern California Historical Quarterly* 1 (June 1971): 126–27.

28. Diane Mei Lin Mark and Ginger Chin, *A Place Called Chinese America* (Dubuque, Iowa: Kendall/Hunt Publishing Company, 1982), p. 51.

29. *New York Tribune*, September 29, 1854, as cited by Miller, *Unwelcome Immigrant*, p. 70.

30. S. V. Blakeslee, "Address of Rev. S. V. Blakeslee: Delivered before the General Association of Congregational Churches of California, held in Sacramento from the 9th to the 13th of October, 1887," appended to California State Senate, Special Committee on Chinese Immigration, *Chinese Immigration*, pp. 246–47. Also see Blakeslee's testimony in U.S. Senate, *Report to Investigate Chinese Immigration*, pp. 1028–43.

31. Chester H. Rowell, "Chinese and Japanese Immigrants—A Comparison," *Annals of the American Academy of Political and Social Science* 2 (September 1909): 7.

32. San Francisco Board of Supervisors, Ordinance No. 939, July 29, 1870, as reprinted in Wu, *"Chink!": A Documentary History of Anti-Chinese Prejudice in America* (New York: World Publishing, 1972), pp. 65–66; Daniels, *Asian America*, p. 39.

33. James D. Richardson, comp., *Messages and Papers of the Presidents*, 7:288, as cited by Daniels, *Asian America*, p. 44.

34. *New York Tribune,* Sept. 29, 1854, as cited by Miller, *Unwelcome Immigrant*, p. 169.

35. Miller, *Unwelcome Immigrant*, pp. 184–85.

36. Ibid., pp. 242ff.

37. Megumi Dick Osumi, "Asians and California's Anti-Miscegenation Laws," in Nobuya Tsuchida, ed., *Asian and Pacific American Experiences: Women's Perspectives* (Minneapolis: Asian/Pacific American Learning and Resource Center, 1982), p. 2.

38. Chan, *Bitter-Sweet Soil*, p. 395; Lucie Cheng Hirata, "Free, Indentured, Enslaved: Chinese Prostitutes in Nineteenth-Century America," *Signs: Journal of Women in Culture and Society 5*, no. 1 (1979): 19.

39. See, for example, Coolidge, *Chinese Immigration*.

40. U.S. Congress, Senate, Misc. Document 20, 45th Cong., 2nd sess., 1879, p. 4, as cited by Daniels, *Asian America*, pp. 53–54.

41. *People v. Hall*, 4 Cal. 399 (1854), as reprinted in Heizer and Almquist, *Other Californians*, pp. 231–32.

42. Takaki, *Strangers from a Different Shore*, p. 102.

43. *People v. Hall*, in Heizer and Almquist, *Other Californians*, p. 231.

44. Ibid.

45. Ibid., p. 233.

46. Lucille Eaves, *A History of California Labor Legislation* (Berkeley: The University Press, 1910), p. 121; Stanford Lyman, "The Significance of Asians in American Society," in Lyman, *The Asian in the West*, p. 7; Heizer and Almquist, *Other Californians*, p. 176; Wu, *"Chink!"* p. 12.

47. Coolidge, *Chinese Immigration*, p. 76; Walton Bean, *California: An Interpretive History*, 2d ed. (New York: McGraw-Hill, 1973), p. 165.

48. See Coolidge, Saxton, Ringer, Barth, etc.

49. In *This Bitter-sweet Soil*, historian Sucheng Chan argues convincingly that the development of Chinese occupational stratification in nineteenth-century California unfolded in four stages: "the initial period from 1850 to 1865, when the Chinese worked mainly as miners and traders; a period of growth and development from 1865 to the late 1870s, when they branched into agriculture, light manufacturing, and common labor; a period of consolidation from the late 1870s to the late 1880s, when they competed successfully with others in a wide variety of occupations; and a period of decline from the late 1880s to the turn of the century, when they were forced to abandon many occupations" (p. 52).

50. Takaki, *Strangers from a Different Shore*, p. 82.

51. Chan, *Bitter-Sweet Soil*, p. 56.

52. Ibid., pp. 52, 56.

53. Ibid., p. 72.

54. Leonard Pitt, "The Beginnings of Nativism in California," *Pacific Historical Review* 1 (February 1961): 36; Rodman W. Paul, "The Origin of the Chinese Issue in California," *Mississippi Valley Historical Review* 2 (September 1938): 181–96; Eaves, *California Labor*, pp. 110–13.

55. Pitt, "Nativism," p. 38; Ping Chiu, *Chinese Labor in California, 1850–1880: An Economic Study* (Madison: State Historical Society of Wisconsin, 1963), pp.

54–55; Barth, *Bitter Strength*, p. 133; Victor G. Nee and Brett de Bary Nee, *Longtime Californ': A Documentary Study of an American Chinatown* (New York: Pantheon, 1973), p. 34.

56. Takaki, *Strangers from a Different Shore*, p. 82.

57. Daniels, *Asian America*, p. 33; Takaki, *Strangers from a Different Shore*, p. 82.

58. Roger Daniels, *Asian America*, p. 34.

59. U.S. Senate, *Report to Investigate Chinese Immigration*, pp. 669, 671; Chiu, *Chinese Labor in California*, pp. 9, 46; Saxton, *Indispensable Enemy*, p. 4.

60. Saxton, *Indispensable Enemy*, p. 63; Alexander Saxton, "Race and the House of Labor," p. 108; Chiu, *Chinese Labor in California*, pp. 46–47; Daniels, *Asian America*, p. 19.

61. U.S. Senate, *Report to Investigate Chinese Immigration*, p. 666–67.

62. Ibid. p. 667; G. H. Hecke, "The Pacific Coast Labor Question, From the Standpoint of a Horticulturalist," *Proceedings of the Thirty-Third Fruit Growers' Convention of the State of California . . . 1907* (Sacramento: W. W. Shannon, Superintendent State Printing, 1908), p. 68; John P. Irish, "Labor in the Rural Industries of California," ibid., pp. 55, 65.

63. Chiu, *Chinese Labor in California*, pp. 71–73; Paul S. Taylor and Tom Vasey, "Historical Background of California Farm Labor," *Rural Sociology* 1 (September 1936): 292; Saxton, *Indispensable Enemy*, p. 4; Varden Fuller, *The Supply of Agricultural Labor as a Factor in the Evolution of Farm Labor Organization in California Agriculture*, in U.S. Senate, Committee on Education and Labor, *Hearings: Pursuant to Senate Resolution 266, Part 54: Agricultural Labor in California*. 76th Cong., 3d sess. (Washington: Government Printing Office, 1940), p. 4.

64. Chan, *Bitter-Sweet Soil*, p. 107.

65. Ibid., pp. 400–401.

66. Ibid., p. 405.

67. Ibid., p. 406.

68. Ibid., p. 388.

69. Ibid., p. 381.

70. Ibid.

71. Ibid., p. 370–71.

72. *San Francisco Daily Morning Call*, Aug. 20, 1877, as cited by Chan, *Bitter-Sweet Soil*, p. 373.

73. Chan, *Bitter-Sweet Soil*, p. 374.

74. Ibid., p. 328.

75. *Pacific Rural Press*, Apr. 10, 1886, as cited by Chan, *Bitter-Sweet Soil*, p. 378.

76. Takaki, *Strangers from a Different Shore*, p. 87.

77. Paul M. Ong, "Chinese Labor in Early San Francisco: Racial Segmentation and Industrial Expansion," *Amerasia Journal* 8, no. 1 (1981): 74–75.

78. Ibid., p. 75.

79. Ibid., pp. 75–77.

80. Takaki, *Strangers from a Different Shore*, p. 88.

81. Chan, *Bitter-Sweet Soil*, p. 59.

82. Coolidge, *Chinese Immigration*, pp. 126–27; Nee and Nee, *Longtime Cali-*

forn', pp. 33, 44–45; Chiu, *Chinese Labor in California*, p. 9; Saxton, *Indispensable Enemy*, pp. 4–5, 71–79; Takaki, *Strangers from a Different Shore*, p. 87.

83. Chan, *Bitter-Sweet Soil*, p. 65.

84. Ong, "Chinese Labor in Early San Francisco," p. 80.

85. Ibid.

86. Ibid., pp. 80–81.

87. Ibid., p. 81.

88. Barth, *Bitter Strength*, pp. 197–211; Coolidge, *Chinese Immigration*, pp. 498–501; Eaves, *California Labor*, pp. 138–39; Miller, *Unwelcome Immigrant*, pp. 173–76; Takaki, *Strangers from a Different Shore*, pp. 95–99; Daniels, *Asian America*, p. 41–42.

89. Nee and Nee, *Longtime Californ'*, p. 44.

90. California State Senate, Special Committee on Chinese Immigration, *Chinese Immigration*, p. 47; also see pp. 48–49, 61, 116, 132, 190–92, 197–99, 209.

91. Ibid., p. 146.

92. Chan, *Bitter-Sweet Soil*, p. 59.

93. Mark and Chin, *A Place Called Chinese America*, pp. 61–62. Also see Chan, *Bitter-Sweet Soil*, p. 386, and the important work on Chinese women by Judy Yung, "Unbinding the Feet, Unbinding Their Lives: Social Change for Chinese Women in San Francisco, 1902–1945" (Ph.D. diss., University of California, Berkeley, 1990). According to Joyce Mende Wong, the "long, sorry episode of Chinese prostitution in America can be traced, in part, to the economic situation in China and the status women held there. In mid-nineteenth-century China, women generally held no important positions, received little or no education, and a vast majority were poor. They were expected to bear male children and tend to domestic affairs." Joyce Mende Wong, "Prostitution: San Francisco Chinatown, Mid- and Late-Nineteenth Century," *Bridge: An Asian American Perspective*, Winter 1978, pp. 25–26.

94. Wong has argued that in austere times (such as during war and natural disasters) Chinese families often resorted to infanticide or the abandonment, mortgaging, or selling of children, particularly female children who could not carry on the ancestral line in patrilineal Chinese society. "Prostitution," pp. 23–26. According to Sucheng Chan, "Among unmarried women, only those who could bring economic returns—such as prostitutes, laundresses, or seamstresses—were considered valuable enough to ship overseas." *Bitter-Sweet Soil*, p. 387.

95. Hirata, "Free, Indentured, Enslaved," pp. 4–5.

96. Ibid., p. 6.

97. Lucy Cheng Hirata, "Chinese Immigrant Women in Nineteenth-Century California," in Carol Ruth Berkin and Mary Beth Norton, eds., *Women of America: A History* (Boston: Houghton Mifflin, 1979), pp. 225–26.

98. Hirata, "Free, Indentured, Enslaved," p. 10; Wong, "Prostitution," p. 24.

99. Hirata, "Free, Indentured, Enslaved," p. 9.

100. Hirata, "Chinese Immigrant Women," p. 226.

101. Hirata, "Free, Indentured, Enslaved," pp. 24–25.

102. Paul Jacobs and Saul Landau, *To Serve the Devil* (New York: Vintage Books, 1971), 2:151, 152, as cited by Wong, "Prostitution," p. 24.

103. Hirata, "Free, Indentured, Enslaved," p. 15.

104. G. B. Densmore, *The Chinese in California: Description of Chinese Life in San Francisco: Their Habits, Morals, and Manners* (San Francisco: Pettit and Russ, 1880), p. 84, as cited by Wong, "Prostitution," pp. 23–24.

105. Hirata, "Free, Indentured, Enslaved," p. 19; Takaki, *Strangers from a Different Shore*, pp. 121–23.

106. Hirata, "Free, Indentured, Enslaved," p. 21.

107. Ibid., p. 27.

108. *California Statutes*, 1869–70, pp. 330–31. Also see California State Senate, *Chinese Immigration*, passim.; E. C. Sandmeyer, *The Anti-Chinese Movement in California* (Urbana: University of Illinois Press, 1939), p. 52.

109. Hirata, "Chinese Immigrant Women," p. 234.

110. Ibid., pp. 234–35.

111. In this regard see Peggy Pascoe, *Relations of Rescue: The Search for Female Moral Authority in the American West, 1874–1939* (New York: Oxford University Press, 1990).

112. Roger Daniels, "American Historians and East Asian Immigrants," in Norris Hundley, ed., *The Asian American: The Historical Experience* (Santa Barbara, Calif.: Clio Press, 1976), p. 6; Miller, *The Unwelcome Immigrant*, p. 193; Nee and Nee, *Longtime Californ'*, p. 49; Fuller, *Agricultural Labor*, 19814–15.

113. See Alexander Saxton's important historical analysis of this process in *The Indispensable Enemy*.

114. Saxton, *Indispensable Enemy*, pp. 263–65; Saxton, "Race," p. 117; Herbert Hill, "Anti-Oriental Agitation and the Rise of Working-Class Racism," *Society* 10 (January/February 1973): 46.

115. Paul, "Origin of the Chinese Issue," pp. 185–88; Sandmeyer, *Anti-Chinese Movement*, pp. 27, 42; Lyman, *Chinese Americans*, p. 59; Nee and Nee, *Longtime Californ'*, p. 39.

116. *California Statues*, 1860, p. 307; *California Statutes*, 1862, pp. 462–63; Wu, *"Chink!"* p. 14; California Constitution of 1879, Article XIX, secs. 2, 3; Daniels, *Asian America*, p. 39.

117. For a discussion of these exclusion measures, see Sandmeyer, *Anti-Chinese Movement*, chaps. 5 and 6; Walter MacArthur, "Review of Exclusion History," *Annals of the American Academy of Political and Social Science* 182 (January 1909): 19–26.

118. Ong, "Chinese Labor," p. 86–87.

7. "IN THE HANDS OF PEOPLE"

1. Yuji Ichioka, *The Issei: The World of the First Generation Japanese Immigrants, 1885–1924* (New York: Free Press, 1988), pp. 7–19.

2. U.S. Senate, Committee on Immigration, *Abstract of the Report on Japanese and Other Races in the Pacific and Rocky Mountain States* (Washington: Government Printing Office, 1911), pp. 46–48; Yamato Ichihashi, *Japanese Immigration: Its Status in California* (San Francisco: Marshall Press, 1915), pp. 3–11; Yamato Ichihashi, *Japanese in the United States: A Critical Study of the Problems of the Japanese Immigrants and Their Children* (Stanford: Stanford University Press,

1932), pp. 1–5, 66–67, 80–81, 87–90. Also see: Ira B. Cross, *A History of the Labor Movement in California* (Berkeley and Los Angeles: University of California Press, 1935), pp. 262–63; H. A. Millis, *The Japanese Problem in the United States: An Investigation for the Commission of Relations with Japan, Appointed by the Federal Council of the Churches of Christ in America* (New York: Macmillan, 1915), pp. 4–5; Harry H. L. Kitano, *Japanese Americans: The Evolution of a Subculture* (Englewood Cliffs, N.J.: Prentice-Hall, 1969), pp. 13–14; Roger Daniels, *The Politics of Prejudice: The Anti-Japanese Movement in California and the Struggle for Japanese Exclusion* (New York: Atheneum, 1968), pp. 1–7; Ronald Takaki, *Strangers from a Different Shore: A History of Asian Americans* (Boston: Little, Brown, 1989), p. 43 and Ichioka, *The Issei*, p. 8.

3. Takaki, *Strangers from A Different Shore*, p. 45.

4. U.S. Department of the Interior, Census Office, *Report on Population of the United States at the Eleventh Census: 1890* (Washington: Government Printing Office, 1895); U.S. Department of the Interior, Census Office, *Twelfth Census of the United States Taken in the Year 1900 . . . Population* (Washington: United States Census Office, 1901), pp. 531, 565, 571.

5. Ichihashi, *Japanese in the U.S.*, p. 100; Daniels, *Politics of Prejudice*, pp. 12–13.

6. U.S. Senate, *Abstract*, p. 49; Masakazu Iwata, "The Japanese Immigrant in California Agriculture," *Agricultural History* 1 (January 1962): 27; Kitano, *Japanese Americans*, p. 15.

7. U.S. Senate. *Abstract*, p. 49; Daniels, *Politics of Prejudice*, p. 15.

8. Iwata, "Japanese Immigrants," p. 27; Millis, *Japanese Problem*, pp. 109–10.

9. U.S. Senate, *Abstract*, pp. 53–54; Iwata, "Japanese Immigrants," p. 27; Varden Fuller, *The Supply of Agricultural Labor as a Factor in the Evolution of Farm Labor Organization in California Agriculture*, in U.S. Senate, Committee on Education and Labor, *Hearings: Pursuant to Senate Resolution 266. Part 54, Agricultural Labor in California*. 76th Cong., 3d sess. (Washington: Government Printing Office, 1940), p. 19831; Ichihashi, *Japanese in the U.S.*, pp. 176–77.

10. U.S. Senate., *Abstract*, pp. 54–55; Daniels, *Politics of Prejudice*, pp. 8–9; Millis, *Japanese Problem*, pp. 111–12.

11. G. H. Hecke, "The Pacific Coast Labor Question, From the Standpoint of a Horticulturalist," *Proceedings of the Thirty-Third Fruit-Growers' Convention of the State of California . . . 1907* (Sacramento: W. W. Shannon, Superintendent State Printing, 1908), pp. 69–70. Also see Chester H. Rowell, "Chinese and Japanese Immigrants—A Comparison," *Annals of the American Academy of Political and Social Science* 2 (September 1909): 5.

12. Takaki, *Strangers from a Different Shore*, p. 193.

13. Spencer C. Olin, "European Immigrant and Oriental Alien: Acceptance and Rejection by the California Legislature of 1913," *Pacific Historical Review* 25, no. 3 (August 1966): 311–13; Daniels, *Politics of Prejudice*, p. 63; Kitano, *Japanese Americans*, p. 17; Takaki, *Strangers from a Different Shore*, p. 203.

14. Despite the significance to labor history of the Oxnard sugar beet workers' strike of 1903, only one work treating it has ever been published, John Murray's first-hand account, "A Foretaste of the Orient," *International Socialist Review* 4 (August 1903): 72–79. For brief references to the Oxnard strike and its significance,

see the following Federal Writers' Project reports: *Oriental Labor Unions and Strikes—California Agriculture* (Oakland, 1938), typescript, 11–13; *Unionization of Migratory Labor*, 1903–1930 (Oakland, 1938), typescript, 3–4, both in Bancroft Library, University of California, Berkeley. For discussion of the Oxnard strike within the context of minority labor history, see Juan Gomez-Quiñonez, "The First Steps: Chicano Labor Conflict and Organizing, 1900–1920," *Aztlán: Chicano Journal of the Social Sciences and Arts* 3 (1972): 13–49; Karl Yoneda, "100 Years of Japanese Labor History in the USA," in Amy Tachiki, Eddie Wong, and Franklin Odo, eds., *Roots: An Asian American Reader* (Los Angeles: UCLA Asian-American Studies Center, 1971), 150–58.

15. Torsten Magnusen, "History of the Beet Sugar Industry in California," Historical Society of Southern California, *Annual Publication* 11, part 1 (1918): 76; Dan Gutleben, "The Oxnard Beet Sugar Factory, Oxnard, California," unpublished manuscript in Ventura County Historical Museum Library, Ventura, California; Elizabeth Ritter, *History of Ventura County, California* (Los Angeles: H. M. Meier, 1940), p. 141; Thomas J. Osborne, "Claus Spreckels and the Oxnard Brothers: Pioneer Developers of California's Beet Sugar Industry, 1890–1900," *Southern California Historical Quarterly* 54 (Summer 1972): 119; Sol N. Sheridan, *Ventura County, California* (San Francisco: Sunset Magazine Homeseeker's Bureau, 1909), p. 48; *Oxnard Courier*, Jan. 4, 1902, Feb. 21, 1903.

16. *Oxnard Courier*, Sept. 11, 1903; William T. Dagodag, "A Social Geography of La Colonial: A Mexican-American Settlement in the City of Oxnard, California" (unpublished M.A. essay, San Fernando Valley State College, 1967), p. 5.

17. *Oxnard Courier*, Mar. 22, 1902, Apr. 4, 1902.

18. *Oxnard Courier*, Mar. 23, 1906.

19. Transcript of interview with Mrs. Reginald Shand, Moorpark, California, Aug. 25, 1960, in Thomas R. Bard Collection, Huntington Library, San Marino, California; W. W. Brown, "The Journal of W. W. Brown: 1901–1902," *Ventura County Historical Society Quarterly* 15 (Oct. 1969): 15.

20. *Oxnard Courier*, Feb. 11, 1910; W. H. Hutchinson, *Oil, Land, and Politics: The California Career of Thomas Robert Bard* (Norman: University of Oklahoma Press, 1956), 2:96; Vera Bloom, "Oxnard: A Social History of the Early Years," *Ventura Country Historical Society Quarterly* 4 (February 1956): 19.

21. Bloom, "Oxnard," p. 19.

22. See chapter 3 above. For a more detailed quantitative study of this racial and class stratification, based on data drawn from the federal manuscript census schedules, see Tomás Almaguer, "Class, Race, and Capitalist Development: The Social Transformation of a Southern California County, 1848–1903" (Ph.D. diss., Univ. of California, Berkeley, 1979).

23. *Oxnard Courier*, Oct. 11,1902.

24. See chapter 3 above.

25. Nanka Nikeijin Shogyo Kaigisho, *Nan Kashu Nihonjinshi* [hereafter referred to as *History of the Japanese in Southern California*] (Los Angeles, 1956), pp. 54–55; Kashiwamura Kazusuke, *Hoku-Bei Tosa Taidan* [hereafter referred to as *A Broad Survey of North America*] (Tokyo, 1911), pp. 223–24; *Oxnard Courier*, Oct. 11, 1903.

26. *Oxnard Courier*, Feb. 28, 1903; Kashiwamura, *A Broad Survey of North America*, p. 223; Nanka, *History of the Japanese in Southern California*, pp. 54–55.

27. See for example U.S. Senate, *Abstract*, p. 53; Fuller, *The Supply of Agricultural Labor*, p. 831; Iwata, "Japanese Immigrants," p. 27; Yamato Ichihasi, *Japanese in the United States: A Critical Study of the Problems of the Japanese Immigrants and Their Children* (Stanford: Stanford University Press, 1932), pp. 176–77; Daniels, *Politics of Prejudice*, pp. 8–9; Millis, *The Japanese Problem in the United States*, pp. 111–12.

28. Kashiwamura, *A Broad Survey of North America*, p. 224; *Oxnard Courier*, Feb. 28, 1903.

29. *Oxnard Courier*, Mar. 27, 1902, Feb. 28, 1903.

30. Ibid., Feb, 7, 14, 1903; *San Francisco Examiner*, Mar. 27, 1903.

31. Nanka, *History of the Japanese in Southern California*, p. 53; Kashiwamura, *A Broad Survey of North America*, p. 225; *Oxnard Courier*, Mar. 27, 1903; *Ventura Free Press*, Mar. 6, 1903; *Ventura Weekly Democrat*, Feb. 27, 1903.

32. Kashiwamura, *A Broad Survey of North America*, pp. 223–25. Also see Nanka, *History of the Japanese in Southern California*, p. 53.

33. Yuji Ichioka, "A Buried Past: Early Issei Socialists and the Japanese Community," *Amerasia Journal* 1 (July 1971): 3.

34. *Oxnard Courier*, Mar. 7, 14, 1903; *Ventura Independent*, Mar, 5, 1903; *Ventura Free Press*, Mar. 7, 27, 1903.

35. *Los Angeles Herald*, Mar. 29, 1903; *Oxnard Courier*, Mar. 28, 1903.

36. *Oxnard Courier*, Mar. 7, 28, 1903.

37. Ibid., Mar. 28, 1903.

38. Murray, "A Foretaste of the Orient," pp. 73–74.

39. *Ventura Weekly Democrat*, Feb. 27, 1903; *Ventura Free Press*, Mar. 6, 1903.

40. *Oxnard Courier*, Mar. 7, 1903.

41. *Ventura Daily Democrat*, Mar. 27, 1903; *Ventura Free Press*, Mar. 27, 1903; *Los Angeles Herald*, Mar. 27, 1903.

42. *Ventura Daily Democrat*, Mar. 1, 1903.

43. Ibid., Mar. 24, 26, 27, 1903; *Los Angeles Herald*, Mar. 24, 1903; *Oxnard Courier*, Mar. 28, 1903; *Ventura Free Press*, Mar. 27, 1903; *Santa Barbara Morning Press*, Mar. 24, 1903; *San Francisco Call*, Mar. 24, 25, 1903; *San Francisco Examiner*, Mar. 26, 1903.

44. *Los Angeles Times*, Mar. 24, 25, 1903.

45. *Oxnard Courier*, Mar. 28, 1903.

46. *Ventura Independent*, Mar. 26, 1903.

47. *Los Angeles Herald*, Mar. 29, 1903; *Oxnard Courier*, Mar. 28, 1903. Also see Murray, "A Foretaste of the Orient," pp. 76–77.

48. *Oxnard Courier*, Apr. 4, 1903; *Ventura Daily Democrat*, Mar. 31, 1903.

49. *Oxnard Courier*, Mar. 28, 1903. Also see *Los Angeles Times*, Mar. 24, 1903.

50. *Ventura Daily Democrat*, Mar. 31, 1903; *Los Angeles Times*, Apr. 1, 1903; *Los Angeles Times and California Mirror*, Apr. 4, 1903; *Ventura Independent*, Apr. 2, 1903.

51. *Ventura Free Press*, Mar. 27, 1903.

52. Ibid.

53. *Ventura Daily Democrat*, Mar. 27, 1903; *Los Angeles Times*, Mar. 26, 1903.

54. *Los Angeles Times*, Mar 26, 1903.

55. Ibid., Mar. 27, 1903.

56. *Oxnard Courier*, Mar. 28, 1903.

57. Ibid., Apr. 4, 1903.

58. *Ventura Daily Democrat*, Mar. 26, 1903.

59. *Los Angeles Times*, Mar. 27, 1903.

60. *Ventura Free Press*, Apr. 3, 1903; *Oxnard Courier*, Apr. 4, 1903; *Ventura Weekly Free Democrat*, Apr. 3, 1903; *Oakland Tribune*, Apr. 11, 1903.

61. Stuart Jamieson, *Labor Unionism in American Agriculture*, U.S. Department of Labor, Bureau of Labor Statistics Bulletin No. 836 (Washington: Government Printing Office, 1945), p. 5.

62. *Oakland Tribune*, Apr. 1, 1903.

63. *San Francisco Examiner*, Mar. 26, 1903.

64. *Oakland Tribune*, Apr. 21, 1903.

65. Ibid.

66. Ibid.

67. *Proceedings, AFL Convention, 1894*, 25.

68. Samuel Gompers to J. M. Lizarras, May 15, 1903, as cited by Murray, "A Foretaste of the Orient," pp. 77–78.

69. *Los Angeles Citizen*, Feb. 7, 1930.

70. *American Labor Union Journal*, June 25, 1903, as cited by Phillip S. Foner, *History of the Labor Movement in the United States* (New York: International Publishers, 1947–65), 4:277.

71. J. M. Lizarras to Samuel Gompers, June 8, 1903, as cited by Murray, "A Foretaste of the Orient," p. 78. Also see Foner, *History of the Labor Movement*, 3:277.

72. On February 2, 1906, a new organization called the "Cooperative Contracting Company" placed an advertisement in the *Oxnard Courier* identifying itself as an alternative to existing contracting companies in Oxnard. While it was not a union, the new company did claim to represent the interests of "Japanese laborers" in Oxnard. Their advertisement read as follows: "We Japanese laborers who have been in Oxnard for years, wish to make contracts for the harvesting of sugar beets direct with the growers. Don't make your agreement with other contractors, because for years we laborers have been depressed by them. Contractors' ill-treatment of laborers is the growers' loss directly. We trust them no more. We can and will do better work than has ever been done here."

73. Jamieson, *Labor Unionism*, pp. 57–58. Also see Lewis L. Lorwin and Joan A. Flexner, *The American Federation of Labor: History, Policies and Prospects* (Washington, D.C.: Brookings Institution, 1933), p. ii; Federal Writers' Project, *Oriental Labor Unions and Strikes—California Agriculture*; Federal Writers' Project, *Unionization of Migratory Labor*; Federal Writers' Project, *The Migratory Agricultural Worker and the American Federation of Labor to 1938 Inclusive* (Oakland, 1938), typescript, Bancroft Library, University of California, Berkeley.

74. Jamieson, *Labor Unionism*, p. 58.

75. For two excellent discussions of the role of white labor in the anti-Chinese and anti-Japanese movements see Alexander Saxton, *The Indispensable Enemy:*

Labor and the Anti-Chinese Movement in California (Berkeley and Los Angeles: University of California Press, 1971) and Daniels, *Politics of Prejudice.*

EPILOGUE

1. Assimilation theory has a long and time-honored tradition in the sociology of race relations. It is beyond the purview of this study to critically assess the theoretical shortcomings of this consensus-based literature or its inapplicability to historical research such as the one undertaken in this book. For useful assessments of this voluminous and diverse literature see Michael Omi and Howard Winant, *Racial Formation in the United States: From the 1960s to the 1980s* (New York: Routledge and Kegan Paul, 1987); Robert Blauner, *Racial Oppression in America* (New York: Harper and Row, 1972); Mario Barrera, *Race and Class in the Southwest: A Theory of Racial Inequality* (Notre Dame: University of Notre Dame Press, 1979); and Thomas F. Pettigrew, ed., *The Sociology of Race Relations: Reflections and Reform* (New York: The Free Press, 1980).

2. The most recent restatement of this contention can be found in David R. Roediger, *The Wages of Whiteness: Race and the Making of the American Working Class* (London and New York: Verso, 1991). Although he acknowledges both the material and discursive dimensions of white racial formation, Roediger ultimately identifies two "needs" of capitalism as the key determinants of the racialization process. In outlining his main thesis, Roediger contends that "whiteness was a way in which white workers responded to a fear of dependency on wage labor and to the necessities of capitalist work discipline" (p. 13). This class reductionism and functionalist logic obscures the ways in which racialization is a defining feature of the imposition of white supremacy, not merely the consequence of proletarianization and the structuring of the labor process under capitalism. As I have argued here, the very positioning of ethnic groups and placement of individuals within the social relations of production was predicated on who had—and who did not have—privileged access to the class structure. This opportunity for class mobility was fundamentally a racial issue, not the imperative of capitalist class relations, in nineteenth-century California.

See also the Marxist article of faith that race is merely an illusory ideological construct in historian Barbara Jeanne Fields's "Slavery, Race, and Ideology in the United States of America," *New Left Review* 181 (May–June 1990): 95–118.

3. Frank Parkin has named these struggles "usurpationary actions." According to Parkin, "Usurpation is that type of social closure mounted by a group in response to its outsider status and the collective experiences of exclusion. What usurpationary actions have in common is the aim of biting into the resources and benefits accruing to dominant groups in society—a range of possibilities extending from marginal redistribution to complete expropriation. But whatever the intended scale of usurpation it is a form of action that generally draws upon alternative standards of distributive justice to those solemnized by the rules of exclusion." Frank Parkin, *Marxism and Class Theory: A Bourgeois Critique* (New York: Columbia University Press, 1979), p. 74.

4. The ambiguous nature of the Mexican's racial status has also been clearly

evident throughout this century. From their original nineteenth-century designation as "white," ethnic Mexicans were reclassified in 1930 into a separate status
based on their nationality as "Mexican." This racial reassignment may have reflected the mounting anti-Mexican labor hostility directed at the largely mestizo
immigrant population that immigrated into the United States during this century.
During the period from 1940 to 1990, ethnic Mexicans were once again enumerated
on the decennial census as "white" but distinguished clearly by 1980 as being of
"Spanish/Hispanic origin or descent." In 1990 many ethnic Mexicans apparently
chose to check the box marked "Other" as their racial status rather than unambiguously designating themselves as white. See U.S. Department of Commerce, Bureau
of the Census, *200 Hundred Years of U.S. Census Taking: Population and Housing
Questions, 1790–1990* (November 1989). For a fascinating discussion of twentieth-
century Mexican immigration into the United States and the ensuing controversy
among native-born Mexicans over immigration policy see David G. Gutiérrez,
*Walls and Mirrors: Mexican Americans, Mexican Immigrants, and the Politics of
Ethnicity* (Berkeley and Los Angeles: University of California Press, forthcoming).

Bibliography

Abrams, Philip. *Historical Sociology*. Ithaca, N.Y.: Cornell University Press, 1982.

Acuña, Rodolfo. *Occupied America: A History of Chicanos*. 2d ed. New York: Harper and Row, 1981.

Aguilar, Alonso. *Pan-Americanism: From Monroe to the Present*. New York: Monthly Review Press, 1968.

Allen, R. H. "The Influence of Spanish and Mexican Land Grants in the Agricultural History of California [1932]." Typescript, n. pag. Berkeley: University of California, College of Agriculture.

———. "The Influence of the Spanish and Mexican Land Grants on California Agriculture." *Journal of Farm Economics* 14 (October 1932): 679–90.

———. "The Spanish Land Grant System as an Influence in the Agricultural Development of California." *Agricultural History* 9 (October 1935): 127–42.

Allen, Robert L. *Reluctant Reformers: Racism and Social Reform Movements in the United States*. New York: Anchor Books, 1975.

Almaguer, Tomás. "Class, Race, and Capitalist Development: The Social Transformation of a Southern California County, 1848–1903." Ph.D. diss., University of California, Berkeley, 1979.

———. "Ideological Distortions and Recent Chicano Historiography: The Internal Colonial Model and Chicano Historical Interpretation." *Aztlán: A Journal of Chicano Research* 18, no. 1 (Spring 1987): 7–28.

Arnaz, José. "Memoirs of a Merchant: Being the Recollections of Life and Customs in Pastoral California by José Arnaz, Trader and Ranchero." Translated by Nellie Van de Grift Sanchez. Parts 1 and 2. *Touring Topics* 20 (October 1928): 36–41, 46–47.

Bancroft, Hubert Howe. *California Pastoral*. San Francisco: The History Company, 1888.

Bard, Thomas R. "Some Pioneer Letters." Portfolio in *Reminiscences Collected for*

259

the Ventura County Eisteddfod. Typescript. Bancroft Library, University of California, Berkeley.

Baron, Harold M. "The Demand For Black Labor: Historical Notes on the Political Economy of Racism." *Radical America* 5 (1972): 1–46.

Barrera, Mario. *Race and Class in the Southwest: A Theory of Racial Inequality*. Notre Dame: University of Notre Dame Press, 1979.

Barth, Gunther. *Bitter Strength: A History of the Chinese in the United States, 1850–1870*. Cambridge: Harvard University Press, 1964.

Bean, Lowell John, and Thomas C. Blackburn, eds. *Native Californians: A Theoretical Perspective*. Ramona, Calif.: Ballena Press, 1976.

Bean, Walton. *California: An Interpretive History*. 2d ed. New York: McGraw-Hill, 1973.

Beasley, Deliliah L. "Slavery in California." *Journal of Negro History* 3 (January 1918): 33–44.

———. *The Negro Trail Blazers of California*. Los Angeles: Times Mirror Printing and Binding House, 1919.

Belknap, Michael R. "The Era of the Lemon: A History of Santa Paula, California." *California Historical Society Quarterly* 48, no. 2 (June 1968): 113–40.

Bell, Horace. *Reminiscences of a Ranger*. Los Angeles: Yarnell, Caystile, and Mathis, Printers, 1881.

Benson, William Ralganal. "The Stone and Kelsey 'Massacre' on the Shores of Clear Lake in 1849—The Indian Viewpoint." *California Historical Society Quarterly* 11, no. 3 (Sept. 1932): 266–73.

Berwanger, Eugene H. *The Frontier against Slavery: Western Anti-Negro Prejudice and the Slavery Extension Controversy*. Urbana: University of Illinois Press, 1967.

Blakeslee, S. V. "Address of Rev. S. V. Blakeslee: Delivered before the General Association of Congregational Churches of California, held in Sacramento from the 9th to the 13th of October, 1887." Appended to California Legislature, Senate, Special Committee on Chinese Immigration, *Chinese Immigration: Its Social, Moral, and Political Effect. Report to the California State Senate of its Special Committee on Chinese Immigration*. Sacramento: State Printing Office, 1878.

Blanchard, Sarah Elliott. *Memories of a Child's Early California Days*. Los Angeles, 1961.

Blauner, Robert. *Racial Oppression in America*. New York: Harper and Row, 1972.

Bloom, Vera. "Oxnard: A Social History of the Early Years." *Ventura County Historical Society Quarterly* 4 (February 1959): 13–20.

Blumer, Herbert. "Race Prejudice as a Sense of Group Position." *Pacific Sociological Review* 1, no. 1 (Spring 1958): 3–7.

———. "Industrialization and Race Relations." In *Industrialization and Race Relations: A Symposium*, edited by Guy Hunter, 220–53. London: Oxford University Press, 1965.

Bonacich, Edna. "A Theory of Ethnic Antagonism: The Split Labor Market." *American Sociological Review* 37 (1972): 547–59.

———. "Advanced Capitalism and Black/White Relations in the United States: A

Split Labor Market Interpretation." *American Sociological Review* 41 (1976): 34–51.

———. "The Past, Present, and Future of Split Labor Market Theory." In *Research in Race and Ethnic Relations*, edited by Cora B. Marrett and C. Leggon, 17–64. Greenwich, Conn.: JAI Press, 1979.

———, and John Modell. *The Economic Basis of Ethnic Solidarity: Small Business in the Japanese American Community*. Berkeley and Los Angeles: University of California Press, 1980.

Bonnell, Victoria E. "The Uses of Theory, Concepts and Comparison in Historical Sociology." *Comparative Studies in Society and History* 22, no. 2 (April 1980): 156–73.

Bowman, John N. "Index of the Spanish-Mexican Land Grant Records and Cases of California [1958]." 2 vols. Typescript, no. pag. Bancroft Library, University of California, Berkeley.

Brown, W. W. "The Journal of W. W. Brown: 1901–1902." *Ventura County Historical Society Quarterly* 15 (October 1969): 8–56.

Browne, J. Ross. *Report of the Debates in the Convention of California on the Formation of the States Constitution in September and October, 1849*. Washington, D.C.: John T. Towers, 1850.

Burawoy, Michael. *Manufacturing Consent: Changes in the Labor Process under Monopoly Capitalism*. Chicago: University of Chicago Press, 1979.

California Bureau of Labor Statistics. *Second Biennial Report of the Bureau of Labor Statistics, The State of California for the Years 1885 and 1886*. Sacramento: State Printing Office, 1887.

———. *Fourteenth Biennial Report of the Bureau of Labor Statistics of the State of California, 1909–1910*. Sacramento: State Printing Office, 1910.

California Legislature. *Majority and Minority Reports of the Special Joint Committee on the Mendocino Wars*. Sacramento: State Printing Office, 1860.

California Legislature. Senate. Special Committee on Chinese Immigration. *Chinese Immigration: Its Social, Moral, and Political Effect: Report to the California State Senate of its Special Committee on Chinese Immigration*. Sacramento: State Printing Office, 1878.

Camarillo, Albert. *Chicanos in a Changing Society: From Mexican Pueblos to American Barrios in Santa Barbara and Southern California, 1848–1930*. Cambridge: Harvard University Press, 1979.

Carranco, Lynwood, and Estle Beard. *Genocide and Vendetta: The Round Valley Wars in Northern California*. Norman: University of Oklahoma Press, 1981.

Castillo, Edward D. "The Impact of Euro-American Exploration and Settlement." In *California*, edited by Robert F. Heizer, 98–127. Vol. 8 of *Handbook of North American Indians*, William C. Sturtevant, General Editor. Washington, D.C.: Smithsonian Institution, 1978.

Castillo, Pedro. "Mexicans in Los Angeles, 1890–1920." Ph.D. diss., University of California, Santa Barbara, 1977.

Caughey, John Walton, ed. *The Indians of Southern California in 1852: The B. D. Wilson Report and a Selection of Contemporary Comments*. San Marino, Calif.: Huntington Library, 1952.

Cauldwell, Dan. "The Negroization of the Chinese Stereotype in California." *Southern California Historical Quarterly* 1 (June 1971): 123–30.

Chan, Sucheng. *This Bitter-Sweet Soil: The Chinese in California Agriculture, 1860–1910.* Berkeley and Los Angeles: University of California Press, 1986.

Cheng, Lucie, and Edna Bonacich, eds. *Labor Immigration under Capitalism.* Berkeley and Los Angeles: University of California Press, 1983.

Chinn, Thomas, ed. *A History of the Chinese in California.* San Francisco: Chinese Historical Society of America, 1969.

Chittendon, Newton H. *Homes, Health, and Pleasure in Southern California.* San Buenaventura, Calif.: April 1883.

Chiu, Ping. *Chinese Labor in California, 1850–1880: An Economic Study.* Madison: State Historical Society of Wisconsin, 1963.

Cleland, Robert Glass. *The Cattle on a Thousand Hills.* 2d ed. San Marino, Calif.: The Huntington Library, 1951.

———. *The Place Called Sespe: The History of a California Rancho.* Chicago: R. R. Donnelley & Sons, 1963.

Cleland, Robert Glass, and Osgood Hardy. *March of Industry.* Los Angeles: Powell Publishing Company, 1929.

Cook, Sherburne F. *The Conflict between the California Indians and White Civilization.* Berkeley and Los Angeles: University of California Press, 1976.

———. *The Population of the California Indian.* Berkeley and Los Angeles: University of California Press, 1976.

Coolidge, Mary Roberts. *Chinese Immigration.* New York: Henry Holt and Company, 1909.

Cox, Oliver C. *Caste, Class, and Race.* New York: Monthly Review Press, 1970 [1948].

Coy, Owen C. "Evidence of Slavery in California." *The Grizzly Bear* 19 (October 1916): 1–2.

Cross, Ira B. *A History of the Labor Movement in California.* Berkeley and Los Angeles: University of California Press, 1935.

Crouter, Richard E., and Andrew F. Rolle. "Edward Fitzgerald Beale and the Indian Peace Commissioners in California, 1851–1854." *Historical Society Quarterly of Southern California* 42, no. 2 (June 1960): 107–32.

Cuero, Delfina. *Autobiography of Delfina Cuero, a Diegueno Indian, as told to Florence C. Shipek.* Interpreted by Rosalie Pinto. Los Angeles: Dawson Books, 1968.

D'Emilio, John, and Estelle B. Friedman. *Intimate Matters: A History of Sexuality in America.* New York: Harper and Row, 1988.

Dagodag, William T. "A Social Geography of La Colonial: A Mexican-American Settlement in the City of Oxnard, California." M.A. essay, San Fernando Valley State College, 1967.

Dana, Richard Henry. *Two Years Before the Mast: A Personal Narrative of Life at Sea.* New York: Harper and Brothers, 1840.

Daniels, Roger. "American Historians and East Asian Immigrants." In *The Asian American: The Historical Experience,* edited by Norris Hundley, 1–25. Santa Barbara, Calif.: Clio Press, 1976.

Daniels, Roger. *The Politics of Prejudice: The Anti-Japanese Movement in California and the Struggle for Japanese Exclusion.* New York: Atheneum, 1968.

———. "American Labor and Chinese Immigration." *Past & Present* 27 (April 1964): 113–14.

———. *Asian America: Chinese and Japanese in the United States since 1850.* Seattle: University of Washington Press, 1988.

Davis, Angela. *Women, Race, and Class.* New York: Random House, 1981.

De León, Arnoldo. *They Called Them Greasers: Anglo Attitudes toward Mexicans in Texas, 1821–1900.* Austin: University of Texas Press, 1983.

———. *The Tejano Community, 1836–1900.* Albuquerque: University of New Mexico Press, 1985.

Downs, James F. *The Two Worlds of the Washo: An Indian Tribe of California and Nevada.* New York: Holt, Rinehart and Winston, 1966.

Dumke, Glenn. *The Boom of the Eighties in Southern California.* San Marino, Calif.: The Huntington Library, 1944.

Duniway, C. A. "Slavery in California after 1848." American Historical Association *Annual Report* 1 (1905): 243–48.

Eaves, Lucille. *A History of California Labor Legislation.* Berkeley: The University Press, 1910.

Engelhardt, Fr. Zephyrin. *The Missions and Missionaries of California.* 4 vols. San Francisco: James H. Barry, 1908.

Evans, William E. "The Garra Uprising: Conflicts Between San Diego Indians and Settlers in 1851." *California Historical Society Quarterly* 45, no. 4 (December 1966): 339–49.

Fernandez, Ferdinand F. "Except a California Indian: A Study in Legal Discrimination." *Southern California Quarterly* 5, no. 2 (June 1968): 161–75.

Fields, Barbara Jeanne. "Slavery, Race, and Ideology in the United States of America." *New Left Review* 181 (May–June 1990): 95–118.

Foner, Eric. *Free Soil, Free Labor, Free Men: The Ideology of the Republican Party before the Civil War.* New York: Oxford University Press, 1970.

Foner, Phillip S. *History of the Labor Movement in the United States.* 4 vols. New York: International Publishers, 1947–65.

Forbes, Jack D. *Afro-Americans in the Far West: A Handbook for Educators.* Berkeley: Far West Laboratory for Educational Research and Development, 1966.

———. *Native Americans of California and Nevada.* Healdsburg, Calif.: Naturegraph Publishers, 1969.

Francis, Jesse Davis. "An Economic and Social History of Mexican California, 1822–1846." Ph.D diss., University of California, Berkeley, 1935.

Fredrickson, George M. *White Supremacy: A Comparative Study in American and South African History.* Oxford: Oxford University Press, 1981.

———. *The Arrogance of Race: Historical Perspectives on Slavery, Racism, and Social Inequality.* Middletown, Conn.: Wesleyan University Press, 1988.

Fuller, Varden. *The Supply of Agricultural Labor as a Factor in the Evolution of Farm Labor Organization in California Agriculture.* In U.S. Congress. Senate. Committee on Education and Labor. *Hearings: Pursuant to Senate Resolution*

266. *Part 54, Agricultural Labor in California*. 76th Cong., 2d sess. Washington, D.C.: Government Printing Office, 1940.

Garcia, Mario T. "Merchants and Dons: San Diego's Attempt at Modernization, 1850–1860." *The Journal of San Diego History* 21 (Winter 1975): 52–80.

———. "The Californios of San Diego and the Politics of Accommodation." *Aztlán: International Journal of Chicano Studies Research* 6 (Spring 1975): 69–85.

———. *Desert Immigrants: The Mexicans of El Paso, 1880–1920*. New Haven: Yale University Press, 1981.

Gates, Paul W. "Adjudication of Spanish-Mexican Land Claims in California." *Huntington Library Quarterly* 21 (May 1958): 213–36.

———. "California's Embattled Settlers." *California Historical Society Quarterly* 13 (June 1962): 99–130.

———, ed. *California Ranchos and Farms, 1846–1862*. Madison: The State Historical Society of Wisconsin, 1967.

Genovese, Eugene D. *Roll, Jordon, Roll: The World the Slaves Made*. New York: Random House, 1974.

Glenn, Evelyn Nakano. *Issei, Nisei, War Bride: Three Generations of Japanese-American Women in Domestic Service*. Philadelphia: Temple University Press, 1986.

Gomez-Quiñones, Juan. "The First Steps: Chicano Labor Conflict and Organizing, 1900–1930." *Aztlán: Chicano Journal of the Social Sciences and Arts* 3 (Spring 1972): 13–49.

Gompers, Samuel, and Herman Gutstadt. *Meat vs. Rice: American Manhood against Asiatic Coolieism: Which Shall Survive?* Reprint, with introduction and appendices. San Francisco: Asiatic Exclusion League, 1908.

Goode, Kenneth G. *California's Black Pioneers: A Brief Historical Survey*. Santa Barbara: McNally and Loftin, 1974.

Goodrich, Chauncey S. "The Legal Status of the California Indians." Parts 1, 2. *California Law Review* 14, no. 2 (January 1926): 83–100, and 14, no. 3 (March 1926): 157–87.

Goodwin, Cardinal. *The Establishment of State Government in California, 1846–1850*. New York: Macmillan, 1914.

Gordon, David M., Richard Edwards, and Michael Reich. *Segmented Work, Divided Labor: The Historical Transformation of Labor in the United States*. New York: Cambridge University Press, 1982.

Griswold del Castillo, Richard Alan. "La Raza Hispano Americano: The Experience of an Urban Culture and the Spanish Speaking of Los Angeles, 1850–1880." Ph.D. diss., University of California, Los Angeles, 1974.

———. *The Los Angeles Barrio, 1850–1890: A Social History*. Berkeley and Los Angeles: University of California Press, 1979.

———. *La Familia: Chicano Families in the Urban Southwest, 1848 to the Present*. Notre Dame: University of Notre Dame Press, 1984.

Gutiérrez, David G. "The Third Generation: Reflections on Recent Chicano Historiography." *Mexican Studies/Estudios Mexicanos* 5, no. 2 (Summer 1989): 281–96.

———. *Walls and Mirrors: Mexican Americans, Mexican Immigrants, and the*

Politics of Ethnicity. Berkeley and Los Angeles: University of California Press, forthcoming.

Gutiérrez, Ramón A. "Honor, Ideology, and Class-Gender Domination in New Mexico, 1690–1846." *Latin American Perspectives* 12, no. 1 (Winter 1985): 81–104.

———. "Must We Deracinate Indians to Find Gay Roots?" *OUT/LOOK* 1, no. 4 (Winter 1989): 61–67.

———. *When Jesus Came, the Corn Mothers Went Away: Marriage, Conquest, and Love in New Mexico, 1500–1848*. Stanford: Stanford University Press, 1991.

Gutleben, Dan. "The Oxnard Beet Sugar Factory, Oxnard, California." Ms. Ventura County Historical Museum Library, Ventura, California.

Hall, Stuart. "New Ethnicities." In *"Race," Culture, and Difference*, edited by James Donald and Ali Rattansi, 252–59. London: Sage Publications, 1992.

Hardy, Osgood. "Agricultural Change in California, 1860–1890." *Proceedings of the Pacific Coast Branch of the American Historical Association* (1929): 216–30.

Hart, James D. *American Images of Spanish California*. Berkeley: The Friends of the Bancroft Library, University of California, 1960.

Haydock, Richard B. "Reminiscent It Will Be." *Ventura County Historical Society Quarterly* 10 (February 1965): 18–40.

Hecke, G. H. "The Pacific Coast Labor Question, From the Standpoint of a Horticulturalist." *Proceedings of the Thirty-Third Fruit-Growers' Convention of the State of California . . . 1907*. Sacramento: W. W. Shannon, Superintendent State Printing, 1908.

Heizer, Robert F. *The Destruction of the California Indians*. Salt Lake City: Peregrine Publications, 1974.

———, ed. *Collected Documents on the Causes and Events in the Bloody Island Massacre of 1850*. Berkeley: Archaeological Research Facility, Department of Anthropology, 1973.

———, ed. *They Were Only Diggers: A Collection of Articles from California Newspapers, 1851–1866, on Indian and White Relations*. Ramona, Calif.: Ballena Press, 1974.

———, and Alan F. Almquist. *The Other Californians: Prejudice and Discrimination under Spain, Mexico, and the United States to 1920*. Berkeley and Los Angeles: University of California Press, 1971.

———, and M. A. Whipple, eds. *The California Indians: A Source Book*. 2d. edition. Berkeley and Los Angeles: University of California Press, 1971.

Hill, Herbert. "Anti-Oriental Agitation and the Rise of Working Class Racism." *Society* 10 (January/February 1973): 43–54.

Hirata, Lucie Cheng. "Chinese Immigrant Women in Nineteenth-Century California." In *Women of America: A History*, edited by Carol Ruth Berkin and Mary Beth Norton, 224–44. Boston: Houghton Mifflin, 1979.

———. "Free, Indentured, Enslaved: Chinese Prostitutes in Nineteenth-Century America." *Signs: Journal of Women in Culture and Society* 5, no. 11 (Autumn 1979): 3–29.

Hittel, J. S. "Mexican Land Claims in California." *Hutching's Illustrated California Magazine* 2 (April 1858): 442–48.

Hittel, Theodore. *History of California.* 4 vols. San Francisco: N. J. Stone, 1897.

Hobson, W. D. "History of Ventura County." *Ventura County Historical Society Quarterly* 13 (May 1968): 2–24.

Hollister, Col. W. W. "Statement of a Few Facts on California from 1852–1860 [1878]." Ms. Bancroft Library, University of California, Berkeley.

Hoopes, Chad L. *Domesticate or Exterminate: California Indian Treaties Unratified and Made Secret in 1852.* Loleta, Calif.: Redwood Coast Publications, 1975.

Horsman, Reginald. *Race and Manifest Destiny: The Origins of American Racial Anglo-Saxonism.* Cambridge: Harvard University Press, 1981.

Hughes, Charles. "The Decline of the Californios: The Case of San Diego, 1846–1856." *The Journal of San Diego History* 21 (Summer 1975): 1–31.

Hurtado, Albert L. *Indian Survival on the California Frontier.* New Haven: Yale University Press, 1988.

Hutchinson, W. H. *Oil, Land and Politics: The California Career of Thomas Robert Bard.* 2 vols. Norman: University of Oklahoma Press, 1965.

Ichihashi, Yamato. *Japanese Immigration: Its Status in California.* San Francisco: The Marshall Press, 1915.

———. *Japanese in the United States: A Critical Study of the Problems of the Japanese Immigrants and Their Children.* Stanford: Stanford University Press, 1932.

Ichioka, Yuji. "A Buried Past: Early Issei Socialists and the Japanese Community." *Amerasia Journal* 1 (1971): 1–25.

———. "Early Japanese Quest for Citizenship: The Background to the 1922 Ozawa Case." *Amerasia Journal* 4 (1977): 1–22.

———. *The Issei: The World of the First Generation Japanese Immigrants, 1885–1924.* New York: The Free Press, 1988.

Irish, John P. "Labor in the Rural Industries of California." *Proceedings of the Thirty-Third Fruit Growers Convention of the State of California . . . 1907.* Sacramento: W. W. Shannon, Superintendent State Printing, 1908.

Iwata, Masakazu. "The Japanese Immigrants in California Agriculture." *Agricultural History* 1 (January 1962): 25–37.

Jamieson, Stuart. *Labor Unionism in American Agriculture.* United States Department of Labor, Bureau of Labor Statistics, Bulletin No. 836. Washington, D.C., 1945.

Jordan, Winthrop. *White Over Black.* Baltimore: Penguin Books, 1969.

Kashiwamura Kazusuke. *Hoku-Bei Tosa Taidan [A Broad Survey of North America].* Tokyo, 1911.

King, Tom. "New Views of California Indian Society." *The Indian Historian* 5, no. 4 (Winter 1972): 12–17.

Kitano, Harry H. L. *Japanese Americans: The Evolution of a Subculture.* Englewood Cliffs, N.J.: Prentice-Hall, 1969.

Konvitz, Milton R. *The Alien and the Asiatic.* Ithaca, N.Y.: Cornell University Press, 1946.

Lamphere, Louise, Patricia Zavella, Felipe Gonzales, with Peter B. Evans. *Sunbelt Working Mothers: Reconciling Family and Factory.* Ithaca: Cornell University Press, 1993.

Langum, David J. "Californios and the Image of Indolence." *Western Historical Quarterly* 9 (April 1978): 181–96.

———. "A Brief Reply." *Western Historical Quarterly* 10 (January 1979): 69.

Lapp, Rudolph M. *Blacks in Gold Rush California*. New Haven: Yale University Press, 1977.

———. *Afro-Americans in California*. San Francisco: Boyd and Fraser, 1979.

Leon, David J., and Daniel McNeil. "The Fifth Class—A 19th Century Forerunner of Affirmative Action." *California History* 64, no. 1 (Winter 1985): 52–57.

Limerick, Patricia Nelson. *Legacy of Conquest: The Unbroken Past of the American West*. New York: W. W. Norton, 1987.

Lipset, Seymour Martin. "History and Sociology: Some Methodological Considerations." In *Sociology and History: Methods*, edited by S. M. Lipset and Richard Hofstadter. New York: Basic Books, 1968.

Lorwin, Lewis L., and Joan A. Flexner. *The American Federation of Labor: History, Policies and Prospects*. Washington, D.C.: Brookings Institution, 1933.

Lothrop, Marion Lydia. "The Indian Campaigns of General M. G. Vallejo, Defender of the Northern Frontier of California." *Society of California Pioneers Quarterly* 9, no. 1 (March 1932): 161–205.

Lyman, Stanford M. *The Asian in the West*. Reno: Western Studies Center, Desert Research Institute, University of Nevada System, 1970.

———. *Chinese Americans*. New York: Random House, 1974.

———. *Chinatown and Little Tokyo: Power, Conflict, and Community Among Chinese and Japanese Immigrants in America*. Millwood, N.Y.: Associated Faculty Press, 1986.

MacArthur, Walter. "Review of Exclusion History." *Annals of the American Academy of Political and Social Science* 182 (January 1909): 19–26.

Magnusen, Torsten. "History of the Beet Sugar Industry in California," Historical Society of Southern California, *Annual Publication* 11, part 1 (1918): 68–79.

Malcom, Roy. "American Citizenship and the Japanese." *Annals of the American Academy of Political and Social Science* 92 (January 1921): 77–81.

———. "The Japanese Problem in California." *World Affairs Interpreter* 13 (April 1942): 28–38.

Margolin, Malcolm. *The Ohlone Way: Indian Life in the San Francisco-Monterey Bay Area*. Berkeley: Heyday Books, 1978.

Mark, Diane Mei Lin, and Ginger Chin. *A Place Called Chinese America*. Dubuque, Iowa: Kendall/Hunt Publishing Company, 1982.

Martinez, Oscar. "On the Size of the Chicano Population: New Estimates, 1850–1900." *Aztlán: International Journal of Chicano Studies Research* 6 (Spring 1975): 43–67.

Mason, Jesse D. *Reproduction of Thompson and West's History of Santa Barbara and Ventura Counties, California*. Berkeley: Howell-North, 1961.

Mieda, Madeline. "Hueneme as a Grain Port." *Ventura County Historical Society Quarterly* 3, part 2 (February 1958): 14–20.

Miller, Stuart Creighton. *Unwelcome Immigrant: The American Image of the Chinese, 1785–1885*. Berkeley and Los Angeles: University of California Press, 1969.

Millis, H. A. *The Japanese Problem in the United States: An Investigation for the Commission of Relations with Japan, Appointed by the Federal Council of the Churches of Christ in America.* New York: The MacMillan Company, 1915.

Mirande, Alfredo. *The Chicano Experience: An Alternative Perspective.* Notre Dame: University of Notre Dame Press, 1985.

Montejano, David. *Anglos and Mexicans in the Making of Texas, 1836–1986.* Austin: University of Texas Press, 1987.

Morrison, J. H. "The Formation of Ventura County." *Ventura County Historical Society Quarterly* 4 (August 1962): 13–16.

Murray, John. "A Foretaste of the Orient." *International Socialist Review* 4 (August 1903): 72–79.

Nanka Nikeijin Shogyo Kaigisho. *Nan Kashu Nihonjinshi [History of the Japanese in Southern California].* Los Angeles, 1956.

Nash, Gary B. *Red, White, and Black: The Peoples of Early America.* Englewood Cliffs, N.J.: Prentice-Hall, 1974.

Nash, Gerald D. *State Government and Economic Development in California, 1848–1933.* Berkeley: Institute of Governmental Studies, University of California, 1964.

Nee, Victor G., and Brett de Bary Nee. *Longtime Californ': A Documentary Study of an American Chinatown.* New York: Pantheon Books, 1973.

Nicholson, Carmelita Fitzgerald. "The Last of the Dons." *Ventura County Historical Society Quarterly* 12 (October 1966): 2–21.

Norton, Jack. *Genocide in Northwestern California: When Our Worlds Cried.* San Francisco: The Indian Historian Press, 1979.

Olin, Spencer C. "European Immigrant and Oriental Alien: Acceptance and Rejection by the California Legislature of 1913." *Pacific Historical Review* 25, no. 3 (August 1966): 303–15.

Omi, Michael, and Howard Winant. *Racial Formation in the United States: From the 1960s to the 1980s.* New York: Routledge and Kegan Paul, 1987.

Ong, Paul M. "Chinese Labor in Early San Francisco: Racial Segmentation and Industrial Expansion." *Amerasia Journal* 8, no. 1 (1981): 69–92.

———. "Chinese Laundries as an Urban Occupation." In *The Annals of the Chinese Historical Society of the Pacific Northwest,* edited by Douglas W. Lee, 68–85. Seattle, 1983.

Osborne, Thomas J. "Claus Spreckels and the Oxnard Brothers: Pioneer Developers of California's Beet Sugar Industry, 1890–1900." *Southern California Quarterly* 54 (Summer 1972): 117–25.

Osumi, Megumi Dick. "Asians and California's Anti-Miscegenation Laws." In *Asian and Pacific American Experiences: Women's Perspectives,* edited by Nobuya Tsuchida, 1–37. Minneapolis: Asian/Pacific American Learning and Resource Center, 1982.

Paredes, Raymund A. "The Mexican Image in American Travel Literature, 1813–1869." *New Mexico Historical Review* 52 (January 1977): 5–29.

———. "The Origin of Anti-Mexican Sentiment in the United States." *New Scholar* 6 (1977): 130–65.

Parkin, Frank. *Marxism and Class Theory: A Bourgeois Critique.* New York: Columbia University Press, 1979.

Pascoe, Peggy. *Relations of Rescue: The Search for Female Moral Authority in the American West, 1874–1939.* Oxford University Press, 1990.

Paul, Rodman W. "The Origin of the Chinese Issue in California." *Mississippi Valley Historical Review* 2 (September 1938): 181–96.

Peña, Manuel. *The Texas-Mexican Conjunto: History of a Working Class Music.* Austin: University of Texas Press, 1985.

Peterson, Richard H. "Anti-Mexican Nativism in California, 1848–1853: A Study in Cultural Conflict." *Southern California Quarterly* 62, no. 4 (Winter 1980): 309–27.

Pettigrew, Thomas F., ed. *The Sociology of Race Relations: Reflections and Reform.* New York: The Free Press, 1980.

Phillips, George Harwood. *Chiefs and Challengers: Indian Resistance and Cooperation in Southern California.* Berkeley and Los Angeles: University of California Press, 1975.

Pitt, Leonard. "The Beginnings of Nativism in California." *Pacific Historical Review* 1 (February 1961): 23–38.

———. *The Decline of the Californios: A Social History of the Spanish-Speaking Californians, 1846–1890.* Berkeley and Los Angeles: University of California Press, 1970.

Rawls, James J. *Indians of California: The Changing Image.* Norman: University of Oklahoma Press, 1984.

Reich, Michael. *Racial Inequality: A Political-Economic Analysis.* Princeton: Princeton University Press, 1981.

Reith, Gertrude M. "Ventura: Life Story of a City." Ph.D. diss., Clark University, 1963.

Ritter, Elizabeth. *History of Ventura County, California.* Los Angeles: H. M. Meier, 1940.

Robinson, Alfred. *Life in California: During a Residence of Several Years in that Territory, Comprising a Description of the Country and the Missionary Establishments, With Incidents, Observations, etc., etc. by an American.* New York: Wiley and Putnam, 1846.

Robinson, Cecil. *With the Ears of Strangers: The Mexican in American Literature.* Tucson: University of Arizona Press, 1963.

Robinson, W. W. *Land in California: The Story of Mission Lands, Ranchos, Squatters, Mining Camps, Railroad Grants, Land Scripts, Homesteads.* Berkeley and Los Angeles: University of California Press, 1948.

———. *The Indians of Los Angeles: Story of the Liquidation of a People.* Los Angeles: Glen Davidson, 1952.

———. *The Story of Ventura County.* Los Angeles: Title Insurance and Trust Company, 1955.

Roediger, David R. *The Wages of Whiteness: Race and the Making of the American Working Class.* London and New York: Verso, 1991.

Rolle, Andrew F. *California: A History.* New York: Thomas Y. Crowell, 1963.

Romo, Ricardo. *East Los Angeles: A History of a Barrio.* Austin: University of Texas Press, 1983.

Roscoe, Will. "The Zuni Man-Woman." *OUT/LOOK* 1, no. 2 (Summer 1988): 56–67.

Rowell, Chester H. "Chinese and Japanese Immigrants—A Comparison." *Annals of the American Academy of Political and Social Science* 24 (September 1909): 3–10.

Rubin, Gayle. "The Traffic in Women: Notes Toward a Political Economy of Sex." In *Toward an Anthropology of Women*, edited by Rayna Reiter, 157–210. New York: Monthly Review Press, 1975.

Ruiz, Vicki L. "Texture, Text, and Context: New Approaches to Chicano Historiography." *Mexican Studies/Estudios Mexicanos* 2, no. 1 (Winter 1986): 145–52.

———. *Cannery Women/Cannery Lives: Mexican Women, Unionization, and the California Food Processing Industry, 1930–1950*. Albuquerque: University of New Mexico Press, 1987.

Russell, J. H. *Cattle on the Conejo*. Los Angeles: The Ward Ritchie Press, 1957.

Sanborn, W. J. "Memoirs of a Santa Paula Sheepherder, 1873–1875: From the Letters of Colonel W. J. Sanborn." *Ventura County Historical Society Quarterly* 1 (November 1959): 2–20.

Sandmeyer, E. C. *The Anti-Chinese Movement in California*. Urbana: University of Illinois Press, 1939.

Santa Barbara County, California. *Great Register of the County of Santa Barbara for the Year 1867*. San Francisco: John G. Hodge and Co., 1868.

———. *Supplement of the Registered Names appearing on Great Register of the County of Santa Barbara: From July 30, 1867, to October 19, 1868*. Santa Barbara: Santa Barbara Post, 1868.

———. *Supplemental List of Registered Names upon the Great Register of the County of Santa Barbara: From October 19, 1868, to October 31, 1868*. Santa Barbara: Santa Barbara Post, 1868.

Saragoza, Alex. "The Significance of Recent Chicano-Related Historical Writings: An Assessment." *Ethnic Affairs* 1 (Fall 1987): 24–63.

Savage, Sherman W. *Blacks in the West*. Westport, Conn.: Greenwood Press, 1976.

Saxton, Alexander. "Race and the House of Labor." In *The Great Fear: Race in the Minds of White America*, edited by Gary B. Nash and Richard Weiss, 98–120. New York: Holt, Rinehart and Winston, 1970.

———. *The Indispensable Enemy: Labor and the Anti-Chinese Movement in California*. Berkeley and Los Angeles: University of California Press, 1971.

Sheridan, Sol N. *Ventura County, California*. San Francisco: Sunset Magazine Homeseeker's Bureau, 1909.

Skocpol, Theda, ed. *Vision and Method in Historical Sociology*. Cambridge: Cambridge University Press, 1984.

Smelser, Neil J. *Comparative Methods in the Social Sciences*. Englewood Cliffs, N.J.: Prentice-Hall, 1976.

Smith, Wallace E. "The Camulos Story." *Ventura County Historical Society Quarterly* 3 (February 1958): 2–11.

———. *This Land Was Ours: The Del Valles and Camulos*. Ventura, Calif.: Ventura County Historical Society, 1978.

Spicer, Edward. *Cycles of Conquest: The Impact of Spain, Mexico, and the United States on the Indians of the Southwest, 1533–1960*. Tucson: University of Arizona Press, 1962.

Stein, William. "Recollections of a Pioneer Oil Driller." *Ventura County Historical Society Quarterly* 5 (May 1960): 2–20.

Steinberg, Stephen. *The Ethnic Myth: Race, Ethnicity, and Class in America.* Boston: Beacon Press, 1981.

Stinchcombe, Arthur L. *Theoretical Methods in Social History.* New York: Academic Press, 1978.

Storke, Mrs. Yda Addis. *A Memorial and Biographical History of the Counties of Santa Barbara, San Luis Obispo, and Ventura, California.* Chicago: The Lew Publishing Company, 1891.

Streeter, William A. "Recollections of Historical Events in California, 1843–1878 by William A. Streeter of Santa Barbara [1878]." Ms. Bancroft Library, University of California, Berkeley.

Szymanski, Albert. "Racial Discrimination and White Gain." *American Sociological Review* 41, no. 3 (1976): 403–14.

Takaki, Ronald T. *Iron Cages: Race and Culture in Nineteenth-Century America.* New York: Alfred A. Knopf, 1979.

———. "Reflections on Racial Pattern in America." In *From Different Shores: Perspectives on Race and Ethnicity in America*, edited by Ronald T. Takaki, 26–37. New York: Oxford University Press, 1987.

———. *Strangers from a Different Shore: A History of Asian Americans.* Boston: Little, Brown, 1989.

Taylor, Paul S., and Tom Vasey. "Historical Background of California Farm Labor." *Rural Sociology* 1 (September 1936): 281–95.

Teague, Charles Collin. *Fifty Years a Rancher: A Recollection of Half a Century Devoted to the Citrus and Walnut Industries of California and to Furthering the Cooperative Movement in Agriculture.* Los Angeles: Ward Richie Press, 1944.

Thompson, E. P. *The Poverty of Theory and Other Essays.* London: Merlin Press, 1978.

Tilly, Charles. *As Sociology Meets History.* New York: Academic Press, 1981.

U.S. Congress. House. H.R. Bill 3232. "A Bill for the Relief of Settlers on Certain Lands in the State of California." 45th Cong., 2d sess. 1878.

U.S. Congress. Senate, 44th Congress, 1st Session, 1876, Senate Report No. 413, June 12, 1876.

U.S. Congress. Senate. Committee on Immigration. *Abstract of the Report on Japanese and Other Races in the Pacific and Rocky Mountain States.* Washington, D.C.: Government Printing Office, 1911.

U.S. Congress. Senate. Joint Special Committee to Investigate Chinese Immigration. *Report of the Joint Special Committee to Investigate Chinese Immigration.* 44th Cong., 2d sess., 1876. Report No. 689.

U.S. Department of Commerce. Bureau of the Census. *200 Hundred Years of U.S. Census Taking: Population and Housing Questions, 1790–1990.* November 1989.

U.S. Department of the Interior. Census Office. *The Seventh Census of the United States: 1850.* Washington, D.C.: Robert Armstrong, Public Printer, 1853.

———. *Population of the United States in 1860 . . . The Eighth Census.* Washington, D.C.: Government Printing Office, 1864.

———. *Federal Manuscript Agriculture Schedule of the Eighth Census, 1860: San*

Buenaventura Township, County of Santa Barbara, State of California. Microfilm.

———. *Federal Manuscript Population Schedule of the Eighth Census, 1860: San Buenaventura Township, County of Santa Barbara, State of California.* Microfilm.

———. *Federal Manuscript Population Schedule of the Ninth Census, 1870: San Buenaventura Township, County of Santa Barbara, State of California.* Microfilm.

———. *Federal Manuscript Manufactures Schedule of the Tenth Census, 1880: Ventura County, State of California.* Microfilm.

———. *Statistics of the Population of the United States at the Tenth Census, 1880.* Washington, D.C.: Government Printing Office, 1883.

———. *Report on Population of the United States at the Eleventh Census: 1890.* Washington, D.C.: Government Printing Office, 1895.

———. *Twelfth Census of the United States Taken in the Year 1900 . . . Population.* Washington, D.C.: United States Census Office, 1901.

———. *Federal Manuscript Population Schedule of the Twelfth Census, 1900: Ventura County, State of California.* Microfilm.

U.S. Department of the Interior. Office of Indian Affairs. *Report of the Commissioner of Indian Affairs, accompanying the Annual Report of the Secretary of the Interior for the Year 1850: California Superintendency.* Washington, D.C.: A. O. P. Nicholson, Printer, 1850.

———. *Report of the Commissioner of Indian Affairs, accompanying the Annual Report of the Secretary of the Interior for the Year 1858: California Superintendency.* Washington, D.C.: Wm. A. Harris, Printer, 1858.

———. *Report of the Commissioner of Indian Affairs, Accompanying the Annual Report of the Secretary of the Interior for the Year 1861. California Superintendency.* Washington, D.C.: Government Printing Office, 1861.

———. *Report of the Commissioner of Indian Affairs for the Year 1866: California Superintendency.* Washington, D.C.: Government Printing Office, 1866.

———. *Annual Report of the Commissioner of Indian Affairs to the Secretary of the Interior for the Year 1872: California Superintendency.* Washington, D.C.: Government Printing Office, 1872.

———. *Annual Report of the Commissioner of Indian Affairs to the Secretary of the Interior for the Year 1875: California Reports.* Washington, D.C.: Government Printing Office, 1875.

———. *Annual Report of the Commissioner of Indian Affairs to the Secretary of the Interior for the Year 1883: California Reports.* Washington, D.C.: Government Printing Office, 1883.

U.S. Department of Labor. Works Projects Agency. Federal Writers' Project. *Oriental Labor Unions and Strikes—California Agriculture.* Typescript. 1938. Bancroft Library, University of California, Berkeley.

———. *Unionization of Migratory Labor, 1903–1930.* Typescript. 1938. Bancroft Library, University of California, Berkeley.

———. *The Migratory Agricultural Worker and the American Federation of Labor to 1938 Inclusive.* Typescript. 1938. Bancroft Library, University of California, Berkeley.

Ventura County, California. *Great Register of the County of Ventura, from June 1, 1873 to August 20, 1873*. San Buenaventura, Calif.: Ventura Signal Office, 1873.

———. *Great Register of Ventura County: Supplement, 1875*. San Buenaventura, California: Ventura Signal Office, 1875.

———. *Great Register of the County of Ventura, 1879*. San Buenaventura, Calif.: Sheridan Brothers, Printers, 1879.

———. *Great Register of the County of Ventura, 1882*. San Buenaventura, Calif.: Ventura Signal Printers, 1882.

———. *Great Register: Ventura County, California, 1892*. Ventura, Calif.: Free Press Printers, 1892.

Ventura County, California. San Francisco: The Bancroft Company, 1888.

Ventura County, California: Its Resources etc. San Buenaventura, Calif.: Bowers and Sons, 1885.

Walsh, Edward Larence. "A Political History of the Formation and Establishment of Ventura County." M.A. thesis, Loyola University of Los Angeles, 1965.

Weber, David J. "Stereotyping of Mexico's Far Northern Frontier." In *An Awakened Minority: The Mexican American*, edited by Manuel P. Servin, 18–24. 2d ed. Beverly Hills, Calif.: Glencoe Press, 1974.

———. "Here Rests Juan Espinosa: Toward a Clearer Look at the Image of the 'Indolent' Californios." *Western Historical Quarterly* 1 (January 1979): 61–68.

———. *The Mexican Frontier, 1821–1846: The American Southwest Under Mexico*. Albuquerque: University of New Mexico Press, 1982.

———, ed. *Foreigners in Their Native Land: Historical Roots of the Mexican Americans*. Albuquerque: University of New Mexico Press, 1973.

Weber, Max. *The Protestant Ethic and the Spirit of Capitalism*. New York: Charles Scribner's Sons, 1958.

Westergaard, Waldemar. "Thomas R. Bard and the Beginning of the Oil Industry in Southern California." Historical Society of Southern California, *Annual Publications* 10 (1917): 57–69.

———. "Thomas R. Bard and Ventura County's Sheep Industry, 1870–1884." Historical Society of Southern California, *Annual Publications* 11 (1920): 5–11.

Williams, Walter. *The Spirit and the Flesh: Sexual Diversity in American Indian Culture*. Boston: Beacon Press, 1988.

Wilson, William J. *The Declining Significance of Race*. Chicago: University of Chicago Press, 1980.

Wong, Joyce Mende. "Prostitution: San Francisco Chinatown, Mid- and Late-Nineteenth Century." *Bridge: An Asian American Perspective*, Winter 1978, pp. 23–28.

Woolsey, Richard. "Rites of Passage? Anglo and Mexican-American Contrasts in a Time of Change: Los Angeles, 1860–1870." *Southern California Quarterly* 69, no. 2 (Summer 1987): 81–101.

Wozencraft, O. M. "Oration." 25th Anniversary of the Corporate Society of California Pioneers. San Francisco, 1875. MS. Bancroft Library, University of California, Berkeley.

Wright, Doris Marion. "The Making of Cosmopolitan California: An Analysis of

Immigration, 1848–70." Parts 1, 2. *California Historical Society Quarterly* 19, no. 4 (December 1940): 323–43, and 20, no. 1 (March 1941): 65–79.

Wright, Erik Olin. *Class and Income Determination*. New York: Academic Press, 1979.

Wu, Cheng-Tsu, ed. *"Chink!"*: *A Documentary History of Anti-Chinese Prejudice in America*. New York: World Publishing, 1972.

Yoneda, Karl. "100 Years of Japanese Labor History in the USA." In *Roots: An Asian American Reader*, edited by Amy Tachiki, Eddie Wong, and Franklin Odo, 150–58. Los Angeles: UCLA Asian-American Studies Center, 1971.

Yung, Judith. "Unbinding the Feet, Unbinding Their Lives: Social Change for Chinese Women in San Francisco, 1902–1945." Ph.D. diss., University of California, Berkeley, 1990.

Zavella, Patricia. *Women's Work and Chicano Families: Cannery Workers of the Santa Clara Valley*. Ithaca: Cornell University Press, 1987.

———. "Reflections on Diversity among Chicanas." *Frontiers* 12, no. 2 (1991): 763–85.

Zierer, Clifford M. "The Ventura Area of Southern California." *The Bulletin of the Geographical Society of Philadelphia* 30 (January 1932): 26–58.

Index

Compositor:	ComCom, Inc.
Text:	Sabon
Display:	Sabon
Printer:	Haddon Craftsmen, Inc.
Binder:	Haddon Craftsmen, Inc.